MARK HOLLINGSWORTH writes regularly for the *Sunday Times*, the *Mail on Sunday* and the *Financial Times*, and is the author of an acclaimed study of MI5.

STEWART LANSLEY is an award-winning television and radio producer and the author of *Top Man*, a biography of Sir Philip Green.

Also by Mark Hollingsworth and Stewart Lansley:

MARK HOLLINGSWORTH
The Press and Political Dissent: A Question of Censorship
Blacklist: The Inside Story of Political Vetting
(with Richard Norton-Taylor)
The Economic League: The Silent McCarthyism
MPs for Hire: The Secret World of Political Lobbying
A Bit on the Side: Politicians and Who Pays Them
(with Paul Halloran)
The Ultimate Spin Doctor: The Life and Fast Times of Tim Bell
Defending the Realm: Inside MI5 and the War on Terrorism
(with Nick Fielding)
*Saudi Babylon: Torture, Corruption and Cover-up Inside the
House of Saud*
Thatcher's Fortunes: The Life and Times of Mark Thatcher
(with Paul Halloran)

STEWART LANSLEY
Poverty and Progress in Britain
Housing and Public Policy
Poor Britain (with Joanna Mack)
Beyond our Ken (with Andy Forrester and Robin Pauley)
Councils in Conflict (with Sue Goss and Christian Wolmar)
After the Gold Rush
Top Man: How Philip Green Built his High Street Empire
(with Andy Forrester)
Rich Britain: The Rise and Rise of the New Super-Wealthy

MARK HOLLINGSWORTH AND STEWART LANSLEY

LONDON GRAD

FROM RUSSIA WITH CASH

THE INSIDE STORY OF THE OLIGARCHS

FOURTH ESTATE · *London*

Fourth Estate
An imprint of HarperCollins*Publishers*
77–85 Fulham Palace Road
Hammersmith
London W6 8JB

Visit our authors' blog at www.fifthestate.co.uk
Love this book? www.bookarmy.com

This Fourth Estate paperback edition published 2010
1

First published in Great Britain by Fourth Estate in 2009

A catalogue record for this book is
available from the British Library

ISBN 978-0-00-735637-9

Typeset in Minion by G&M Designs Limited,
Raunds, Northamptonshire

Printed and bound in Great Britain by
Clays Ltd, St Ives plc

'There are no barriers to a rich man'
– Russian proverb

CONTENTS

LIST OF ILLUSTRATIONS

Roman Abramovich and Daria Zhukova © Big Pictures
Chelsea win the Premier League © Reuters
Mikhail Khodorkovsky © Camera Press
Vladimir Putin and Oleg Deripaska © PA
Boris Yeltsin and Boris Berezovsky © PA
Boris Berezovsky in Surrey © Camera Press
Alexander Lebedev, Mikhail Gorbachev and Bono
   © Getty Images
Evgeny Lebedev, Mikhail Gorbachev and Geordie Greig
   © Getty Images
Naomi Campbell and Vladimir Doronin © Big Pictures
Pelorus in St Petersburg © PA
Helicopter in Sardinia © Big Pictures
Roman Abramovich's Boeing 767 © Rex Features
Natalia Vodianova and Justin Portman © PA
Damien Hirst and Daria Zhukova © Getty Images
Christian Candy and Nick Candy © Getty Images
Prince Michael of Kent © Camera Press
Lord Bell © Camera Press
Nat Rothschild © Getty Images
George Osborne © PA
Queen K © Getty Images
Lord Mandelson © Camera Press
Stephen Curtis © PA

ACKNOWLEDGEMENTS

The authors would like to thank the scores of people who have agreed to be interviewed during the writing of this book. Some have done so openly while, because of the controversies surrounding the arrival of the Russian super-rich in London, many only agreed to cooperate on the condition of strict anonymity.

Our sources have been diverse. Some are rich Russians who now live in London while others are visitors from Moscow. Many know or have worked closely with the small group of businessmen who have risen up the world's wealth leagues as a result of the sell-off of lucrative Russian state assets in the 1990s.

We have also been fortunate to draw on the work of lawyers, academics, business intelligence investigators, political risk analysts, and those who introduced newly affluent Russians to London as private security consultants, estate agents, art, antique, and wine dealers, and private-jet, yacht, and luxury-car brokers.

While this book is the first in-depth account of the new, wealthy Russians in London, we stand on the shoulders of other journalists and authors whose work precedes us. First and foremost among them is Keith Dovkants of the London *Evening Standard*. We also wish to acknowledge the reporting of Andrew Jack, former Moscow correspondent of the *Financial Times* and author of *Inside Putin's Russia*, Dominic Midgley and Chris Hutchins, authors of *Abramovich: The Billionaire from Nowhere*, Misha Glenny, the author of *McMafia: Crime Without Frontiers*, Dominic Kennedy of *The Times*, David Leppard of the *Sunday Times*, Terry Macalister of the *Guardian*, Glen Owen of the *Mail on Sunday*, Thomas Catan, Adrian Gatton and the screenwriter and novelist Jill Wickersham.

The editors of the London *Evening Standard* magazine, *ES*, and the paper's former editor Veronica Wadley deserve credit for understanding the importance of the oligarchs and the Londongrad phenomenon. The Frontline Club in London, which champions independent journalism throughout the world, has promoted a greater understanding of all things Russian.

In the United States we are grateful to Will Ferraggiaro in Washington, DC, who, as always, conducted excellent interviews with former US diplomats and officials. And we appreciate the insights of Richard Behar, the award-winning former *Fortune* reporter, Andrew Meier, former *Time* magazine correspondent in Moscow and author of *The Lost Spy: An American in Stalin's Secret Service*, and Glenn Simpson, the former investigative journalist for the *Wall Street Journal*.

In Moscow few journalists are as well informed as Will Stewart, and we are also grateful to officials from the Russian General Prosecutor's Office, as well as Vincent Petrillo, a British businessman who knows more than most about the oil and gas sector in Russia.

We also appreciate the expert guidance of Alex Yearsley, former head of Special Projects at Global Witness, the influential non-governmental organization. He gave us access to his formidable international network of contacts, which enriched every aspect of this book. He seems to know everyone in this murky world. And this book could not have been written without our researcher, Tom Mills, who proved to be tireless, resourceful, diligent, and skilful. He did a superb job in disseminating complex corporate information and tracking down sources.

We are especially indebted to M. A. Nicholas for her many insights, both on Russia and the Russians, from her numerous visits there and her earlier graduate work at the Harriman Institute of Columbia University in New York, as well as for her contribution to the research, structure, and cover design of the book. We would also like to thank Lucy Cottrell and Anne Rannie for their helpful comments on early drafts, while Stewart would like to thank Andrew Lownie, his literary agent, for support throughout.

Finally, we are most grateful to Richard Collins for his diligent copy-editing, to Rachel Rayner for a superb job in compiling the photographs, and most of all to John Elliott, our commissioning editor at Fourth Estate, for his astute, incisive, and meticulous editing and advice.

MARK HOLLINGSWORTH AND STEWART LANSLEY
London, July 2009

CHAPTER 1

The Man Who Knew Too Much

'I have dug myself into a hole and I am in too deep. I am not
sure that I can dig myself out'
– STEPHEN CURTIS, *January 2004*

6.56 P.M., WEDNESDAY, 3 MARCH 2004. A brand-new white
six-seater £1.5-million Agusta A109E helicopter lands under an
overcast sky at Battersea heliport in south-west London.
Waiting impatiently on the tarmac and clutching his two unregistered mobile phones is a broad-shouldered 45-year-old
British lawyer named Stephen Curtis. He is not in the best of
moods. Three minutes earlier he had called Nigel Brown,
Managing Director of ISC Global Ltd, which provided security
for him, regarding disputed invoices sent to a Russian client.
'This is causing problems!' he shouted and then paused. 'Look,
I have to go now. The helicopter is here.'

Curtis climbs aboard the helicopter and manoeuvres his
bulky frame into the passenger cabin's left rear seat. A member
of the ground staff places his three pieces of hand luggage on
the seat in front of him and the pilot is given departure clear-
ance. At 6.59 p.m. the chopper lifts off into the gloomy
London sky. It is cold and misty with broken cloud at 3,800
feet, but conditions are reasonable for flying with visibility of
7 kilometres.

1

The lawyer turns off his mobile phones and sits back. After a day of endless and stressful phone calls from his £4 million luxury penthouse apartment at Waterside Point in nearby Battersea, he is looking forward to a relaxing evening at home at Pennsylvania Castle, his eighteenth-century retreat on the island of Portland off the Dorset coast.

By the time the helicopter approaches Bournemouth Airport, after a flight of less than one hour, it is raining lightly and the runway is obscured by cloud. The Agusta is cleared to land and descends via Stoney Cross to the north-east where, despite the gloom, the lights of the cars on the A27 are now visible in the early evening darkness. The pilot, Captain Max Radford, an experienced 34-year-old local man who regularly flies Curtis to and from London, radios air traffic control for permission to land on runway twenty-six.

'Echo Romeo,' replies Kirsty Holtan, the air traffic controller. 'Just check that you are visual with the field.'

'Er, negative. Not this time. Echo Romeo.'

The air traffic controller can only see the helicopter on her remote radar monitor. Concerned, she increases the runway lighting to maximum intensity. This has the required effect and a mile from the airport the pilot radios: 'Just becoming visual this time.'

'Golf Echo Romeo. Do you require radar?' asks Holtan.

'Yes, yes,' replies Radford, his voice now strained; he repeats the word no less than eleven times in quick succession.

Suddenly, the chopper descends sharply to the left. It then swings around almost out of control. Within seconds it has fallen 400 feet. 'Golf Echo Romeo. Is everything O.K.?' asks a concerned Holtan.

'Negative, negative,' replies Radford.

They are just 1.5 kilometres east of the threshold of runway twenty-six when the height readout is lost on the radar. For the next fifty-six seconds the pilot confirms that he has power but then suddenly, frantically, radios: 'We have a problem, we have a problem.' As the chopper loses power, at 7.41 p.m. Radford shouts down the open mike: 'O.K., I need a climb, I need a climb.'

Radford hears a low horn, warning that the speed of the main rotor blades has dropped. He keeps his finger on the radio button and can be heard struggling to turn out of a dive, but he has lost control. 'No. No!' he shouts in a panic. They are his last words.

The helicopter, now in free fall, nose dives into a field at high speed and explodes on impact, sending a fireball 30 feet into the air. The aircraft is engulfed in flames, with the debris of the wreckage strewn across a quarter of a mile. 'I heard a massive bang and rushed up to the window and just saw this big firewall in front of me,' recalled Sarah Price, who lives beneath the flight path. 'The whole field appeared to be on fire. It was horrific.'

Some thirty-five firefighters rush to the scene, but the two men aboard – Stephen Curtis and Max Radford – die instantly. Later that night their charred bodies are taken to the mortuary at Boscombe, Dorset, where an autopsy is performed the following day. Their corpses are so badly burnt that they can only be identified using DNA samples taken by Wing Commander Maidment at the RAF Centre of Aviation Medicine at Henlow in Bedfordshire.

The news of Curtis's dramatic death was not only deeply traumatic to his wife and daughter, it also sent shock waves through the sinister world of the Russian oligarchs, the Kremlin, and a group of bankers and accountants working in the murky offshore world where billions of pounds are regularly moved and hidden across multiple continents. That was not all. Alarm bells were also ringing in the offices of Britain's intelligence and law enforcement agencies, for Stephen Curtis was no ordinary lawyer. Since the 1990s he had been the covert custodian of some of the vast personal fortunes made from the controversial privatization of the country's giant state enterprises. Two of his billionaire clients – Mikhail Khodorkovsky and Boris Berezovsky – had entrusted Curtis to protect and firewall their wealth from scrutiny by the Russian authorities.

The Russians liked and trusted the highly intelligent, gregarious Curtis. Generous, a heavy drinker, loyal, amusing, and extravagant, he slipped naturally into their world. Also impatient, ruthless, and aggressive when required, he restructured their companies, moved their funds between a bewildering series of bank accounts lodged in obscure island tax havens, established complex trusts, and set up an elaborate offshore ownership of their assets. On their arrival in London he found them properties, introduced them to the most powerful bankers, entertained them late into the night, and recommended private schools for their children and even Savile Row tailors for their suits.

By early 2004, Curtis had not only introduced his wealthy new Russian clients to many aspects of British life, but he was also the guardian of many of their secrets. He was the only person who could identify and unravel the opaque ownership of their assets – property, yachts, art, cars, jewellery, and private jets as well as their bank accounts, shareholdings, companies, and trusts. 'Stephen knew everything because he set up their whole infrastructure,' said a close friend. He salted away billions of pounds in an intricate, sophisticated financial maze, which the Russian government later tried, mostly unsuccessfully, to unravel.

Operating from his office in a narrow, four-storey Mayfair house at 94 Park Lane, Curtis found that working for oligarchs was also lucrative. The product of a relatively modest upbringing himself, Curtis amassed a sizeable personal fortune from his new clients, enough to enable him to acquire his own helicopter, a private aircraft, and a penthouse apartment in London, as well as Pennsylvania Castle. He donated substantial sums to charity, entertained his friends at the castle, and hosted expensive holidays in the Caribbean.

But Stephen Curtis was a lawyer who knew too much. Although he loved flirting with risk and thrived on the pressure and excitement of working with the Russians, he also became increasingly nervous about his own vulnerability and the safety of his family. At the time of his death he was caught in the middle of an epic power struggle, one of the highest-stakes contests between state and business ascendancy in the world – between the most powerful man in Russia, President Vladimir Putin, and its wealthiest businessman, Mikhail Khodorkovsky.

By October 2003, Curtis had been working for Khodorkovsky for six years when his billionaire client was arrested at gunpoint in central Siberia for alleged massive tax evasion and fraud. A month later the Mayfair lawyer found himself further embroiled in the conflict when he was appointed chairman of the Gibraltar-based Menatep, the bank that controlled Yukos, Khodorkovsky's $15 billion oil company. Russian newspapers suddenly began referring to a 'mystery man' in Gibraltar who controlled Russia's second-biggest oil producer. Billions of pounds were at stake, the political survival of Putin was in the balance, and Curtis was billed to play a pivotal role in the forthcoming court drama.

In March 2004 the trial of Khodorkovsky was imminent and the pressure on Curtis was intense. On the morning after his death on 3 March, the offices of two Swiss companies connected to Yukos were raided by Swiss police at the request of the Russian prosecutors. Documents were seized, suspects were interviewed in Geneva, Zurich, and Freiberg, and Swiss bank accounts containing $5 billion were frozen.

Moreover, just a few weeks earlier Curtis had taken another critical and high-risk decision: to cooperate covertly with British police officials. Until only recently a back-room lawyer (secretive, low profile, discreet), he found himself suddenly thrust into the spotlight as chairman of a highly controversial Russian company. Sensitive and highly strung at the best of times, he felt increasingly exposed in this new role. Sooner or later he feared the Russian authorities would come knocking on his door asking questions about his own role in alleged tax avoidance and the filtering of cash out of the country.

As he was legally obliged, Curtis had been scrupulous in reporting 'suspicious transactions', or the merest hint of criminal activity, to the National Criminal Intelligence Service (NCIS) at Scotland Yard, which investigates money laundering and organized crime. In May 2003, for example, he had filed a suspicious transaction report about one of his Russian clients. Now he needed protection for another reason: he feared that he might become the target of commercial enemies – rival oil companies and minority investors of Yukos who claimed that they were being defrauded. He also knew that contract killings in Russia were commonplace. 'I have dug myself into a hole and I am in too deep,' he told a colleague. 'I am not sure that I can dig myself out.'

In the last few weeks of his life Curtis was under constant surveillance by commercial and Russian state investigators and was considering moving offices. His telephones were tapped and in early 2004 his security consultants discovered a small magnet used to secure a listening device at his country home in Dorset. According to Eric Jenkins, an uncle who often visited him in Gibraltar, where his nephew lived for most of the year, Curtis received numerous anonymous threats and intimidating phone calls. He took them seriously enough to hire a bodyguard. 'There certainly were death threats against Stephen,' confirmed Nigel Brown, whose company also provided security for Curtis's clients Berezovsky and Khodorkovsky. 'The timing of his death was very suspicious and there were people out there who had a motive to kill him. He just knew too much.'

At first Curtis dismissed the threats, but when one phone call mentioned his wife and 13-year-old daughter, he decided to act. In mid-February 2004, deeply worried, he approached the Foreign Office and NCIS and offered full but covert cooperation. He would provide information about Russian commercial activities in Britain and the oligarchs' assets, in return for protection for himself and his family. Up to that point his relationship with NCIS had been a limited, almost standard form of cooperation, a role many solicitors play. For NCIS Curtis was a potentially prized informant with insider knowledge of controversial Russian business activity in London. He was immediately assigned a controller, but after only two meetings the NCIS officer was transferred to another operation. Curtis asked to be assigned another controller but before this was done, he was dead.

A week before the fatal crash Curtis had told a close friend at his apartment at Waterside Point, 'If anything happens to me in the next few weeks, it will not be an accident.' He had laughed nervously but he was not joking. He had played the messages left on his mobile phone to colleagues at his law firm. 'Curtis, where are you?' asked a voice with a Russian accent. 'We are here. We are behind you. We follow you.' At the inquest his uncle, Eric Jenkins, testified that his nephew had repeated the same words of warning to him.

The frequent threats convinced some of Curtis's colleagues and relations that he was murdered. 'Definitely', one former employee of his law firm claimed. 'It was done by remote control. They knew about his flight plans in advance because they were tapping his phones.' Dennis Radford, the father of the pilot, told the subsequent inquest that he did not think that the Air Accidents Investigation Branch (AAIB) had properly investigated the possibility of foul play. 'The lack of security at Bournemouth Airport is such that, had anybody wished to sabotage the aircraft, they would have unchallenged and unrestricted access for that purpose,' he said.

Witnesses say that they heard an unexplained and incredibly loud bang just before the crash. 'I heard a kind of thump noise and the dog started barking, so I came outside and I heard another couple of bangs. It made a particularly harsh noise, as if the engine was malfunctioning,' Jack Malt, who lives near the crash site, testified at the inquest. 'There was a period of silence in the moments before the explosion so I guess the engines must have cut out,' said Sarah Price, who lives 300 yards from the site of the crash. She also heard a massive bang just before the explosion. And Gavin Foxwell, another local resident, told the inquest that the helicopter made 'a stuttering, unusual sound, as if it was struggling to stay aloft'.

The death of Stephen Curtis remains a mystery to this day. However, no credible evidence of sabotage or murder has ever been discovered. The investigation by the AAIB concluded:

> The possibilities of unauthorised interference were considered. An improvised explosive device could have been positioned in the cabin or the baggage hold. All cabin doors at the undamaged skin of the baggage door were, however, recovered from the accident site. No evidence of damage other than consistent with ground impact was found on any of them. In particular no high velocity particle impacts were noted in any of these door components.

At the inquest Paul Hannant, the Senior Inspector of the AAIB, said, 'If you are going to bring an aircraft like this down, you have either got to destroy the main rotor system or interfere with the main gearbox. The only other real way is to interfere with the controls. If you disconnect the controls, that would be immediately apparent to the pilot … Any attempt to use a corrosive device or a remote control device would also have been apparent to Captain Radford.'

Ultimately, deteriorating weather conditions and pilot inexperience were blamed for the crash. According to the AAIB inspector, 'The most likely cause of the accident was that Captain Radford became disorientated during the final stages of the approach to Bournemouth Airport.' Yet, while the weather on the fateful night of 3 March 2004 was poor – light drizzle, broken cloud, and overcast sky – flying conditions were not especially hazardous. As his father Dennis later claimed, 'Max had flown many, many times in considerably worse conditions than that. And if he became disorientated, why was he on the radio describing the runway and talking to the control tower twenty-nine seconds before the crash?'

At the inquest assessments of Radford's experience and competence were mixed. He had been a pilot since 1993, had recorded 3,500 flying hours, and had been flying Curtis regularly. During his operational training for flying the new, upgraded Agusta A109E, Radford consulted two flight instructors. 'I felt his confidence exceeded his competence,' testified Alan Davis, but Richard Poppy concluded that Radford was 'competent' to fly the Agusta A109E. While the AAIB found that he had not used instrument flying since 2000, they accepted that he was very familiar with the route and had 'already achieved seventy-eight hours' over the previous two months.

The inquest jury at Bournemouth Town Hall took just over one hour to reach a verdict of 'accidental death'. Despite the verdict, however, some close relations remain sceptical to this day. They point out that Radford was a responsible, cautious pilot who had refused to fly Curtis in the past when the weather was poor, notably for a New Year's Eve party at Pennsylvania Castle.

Curtis's former security advisers remain suspicious, too. Nigel Brown is adamant that it was an assassination and is highly critical of the police. 'What I cannot understand is why there has never been a proper murder investigation', he has said.

'There was a just cause of suspicion because Stephen had received death threats, there was a motive because of what he knew, and there were suspicious circumstances. But the police did not interview me or my colleagues or Stephen's clients or his employees. Usually, the police would interview the last person to speak to him and I was that person. We may not know for sure what happened to Stephen but I think there could have been a more thorough inquiry.'

While Curtis's wife Sarah has never believed that her husband was murdered, she has reflected on why it was a Russian businessman who first informed her about the death of her husband. 'I am sorry that Stephen is dead,' he told her. The police did not telephone until an hour later to say that 'there has been an accident'.

It is a measure of the accuracy of the premonitions Curtis had about a premature death that he left detailed instructions for his funeral. This was partly influenced by his superstitious, almost fatalistic nature. He believed in ghosts and in the after-life and always thought that he would die young. 'I will never make old bones', he once said, well before he met the Russians.

But Curtis had also been diagnosed with leukemia and a rare blood disease. This manifested itself in bizarre ways. During a sailing trip he once hit his head heavily on the boom of the boat and a friend was stunned to see his bloody flesh wound apparently heal before his very eyes. Curtis needed regular blood transfusions to stabilize him and took Warfarin to thin his blood and prevent clotting. He also wore surgical stockings to inhibit deep-vein thrombosis. After two operations at a private clinic, he was told that he could no longer travel by airplane because this would worsen his condition. But he *could* fly by helicopter, which was why, just three months before his death, he upgraded to the Agusta A109E.

Typical of his flamboyant and irreverent personality, he requested that his funeral should not be a mournful event but a 'celebration of his life' and that mourners were 'not obliged to wear traditional black'. On Wednesday, 7 April 2004 some 350 relations, friends, and business associates gathered inside All Saints Church in Easton on the Isle of Portland near the Curtis family home at Pennsylvania Castle. Such was the lawyer's popularity that a further 100 stood outside and loudspeakers were installed to broadcast the proceedings. At 1.50 p.m. a glass carriage bearing Curtis's coffin arrived, drawn by two black-plumed horses and adorned with flowers that spelt the word 'Daddy'. The carriage was followed by a Rolls-Royce Phantom, carrying his widow Sarah and his daughter Louise, and two Bentleys and a Ferrari, ferrying other relations and close friends.

Preceded by a Scottish piper who played the 'Skye Boat Song', the coffin was carried by six bearers into the church, followed by a tearful Sarah and Louise, both wearing pink coats and dresses. As they slowly walked down the aisle, Sarah noticed the intense, brooding figure of Boris Berezovsky, dressed in black, in the congregation with his girlfriend, two bodyguards, and a Russian entourage. Most of Curtis's clients attended. Notable absentees were representatives of his clients IKEA, which did not want to be associated with his controversial Russian clients, as well as most Yukos executives. Indeed, the only Yukos executive to attend was Vasily Alexanyan, a close friend of Curtis and the oil company's former legal director. Alexanyan was furious that his colleagues had boycotted the funeral despite the risky operations Curtis had conducted for their company.

At 2.00 p.m. the service began with traditional hymns, followed by a piano solo by Louise. It was evident that Curtis was well loved. One speaker described him as epitomizing a line from Rudyard Kipling's poem *If*, which reads: 'If you can talk with crowds and keep your virtue/or walk with kings – nor lose the common touch'. His closest friend, Rod Davidson, told the congregation, 'In business he was in a league of his own. He would start off with an earthquake, build it up to a crescendo and [was] always setting his sights beyond the stars … He was the most generous of men and I think of him now at the pearly gates giving St Peter a red Ferrari and providing Playstations for the cherubs.'

But there was also palpable tension in the air because of the conspicuous and, to some, menacing presence of the Russian contingent, who attracted frequent nervous glances. When Berezovsky and his colleagues left their seats at the end of the service, the remainder of the congregation moved out of the way to let them pass first.

The local mourners and Sarah's friends were mostly conventional, middle-class English people who lived quiet, rural lives in the pristine Dorset village of Easton. They were hardly used to the hard Russian faces or the battery of television cameras, photographers, and police that greeted them as they left the church that bright spring afternoon. To the local villagers it must have looked like the cast of *The Godfather* or *The Sopranos* had arrived.

Sarah was devastated by her husband's death, but she was also confused by and concerned about the media attention. 'Why are there so many cameras here?' she asked outside the church. 'I don't understand.' A former secretary, Sarah's life was family, music, friends, the castle, and the English countryside. Stephen had told her nothing about his secret life in London, Gibraltar, and Russia. A lover of James Bond films, Curtis revelled in this covert existence. He compartmentalized his life, mainly to protect Sarah. 'I don't want to know,' she once remarked and would have recoiled from the dark, cut-throat world of the Russian super-rich.

Sarah recognized none of the Russian mourners. 'Who's this? Who's that?' she asked one of Stephen's colleagues in a state of increasing bewilderment. 'What on earth was my husband doing with those Russians?' she asked another friend. Not wanting to worry her, they declined to answer.

After the service the procession escorting Curtis's body was accompanied by the song 'You'll Never Walk Alone', with Sarah's soprano voice ringing out the final words as she followed her husband's coffin. The burial took place in the gardens of Pennsylvania Castle, attended only by family and close friends. Curtis was laid to rest to the strains of the bagpipe melody 'Highland Cathedral'.

As the guests mingled in the marquee after the burial the atmosphere was tense and apprehensive. Many former clients were anxious to know the identities of the other guests and whom they worked for. 'It was a weird situation for a wake,' said a former employee of Curtis's law firm. 'People were looking over their shoulders to see who was talking to who. The strange thing was that I knew some of our clients knew each other, but they would not acknowledge each other at the funeral in case they were photographed or associated with other clients. It was very bizarre, almost comical.' At 9.45 p.m. a spectacular fireworks display erupted over the English Channel.

The funeral of Stephen Langford Curtis brought together an uneasy, unsettling gathering of two cultures: the conventional, light-hearted, understated English middle class and the dark, intense, stern-faced, focused Russian business elite.

Little more than a decade earlier the Russian presence in Britain had been barely noticeable. It would have been rare to hear a Russian accent in a Knightsbridge boutique, a Mayfair restaurant, or even on the London underground, let alone at the funeral of a mysterious, even obscure, British lawyer. There was no sign then of what was to come: the arrival in Britain of a wave of first affluent, then super-rich, Russians. The influx that followed the collapse of communism in 1991 started slowly but by the end of that decade the Russian desire to move to London had reached what one insider has described as 'fever pitch'.

Although there are no official figures for the size of the London-based Russian and former-Soviet community, it is widely accepted that by 2008 it numbered well in excess of 300,000. This was large enough to spawn four Russian-language newspapers, the glossy magazine *New Style*, a plethora of Russian networking clubs and internet sites, and a host of Russian social events.

Although by then the Russian community was diverse, most of its members were ordinary professionals who had chosen to live, work, and settle in London. Many had British husbands or wives. It is this group, rather than the oligarchs, who jokingly referred to London as 'Moscow-on-Thames'. Some worked for international organizations or Russian companies based in London while others had set up their own businesses. Some found jobs as estate agents, in the City, and in retail to target or cater for Russian clients. They mostly came to Britain to escape the crime, political uncertainty, and economic turbulence and were a very select middle-class group compared with the wider Russian population.

Some still commuted back and forth from Moscow, by commercial rather than by private jet. Flight SU247 from Moscow touched down at Heathrow on Friday evenings, carrying what its Aeroflot crew called '*voskresnuy muzh*', which translates as 'Sunday husbands'. These were transcontinental commuters, a mix of oil executives, bankers, and importers and exporters who had homes and families in London but who worked in Moscow. For them it was a weekly ritual: Friday and Sunday nights on a four-hour flight, weekends in London, and the week in their Moscow office.

Dominating this steady stream of migrants was a tiny but much more high-profile group – the oligarchs, a cadre of privileged insiders who had acquired Russia's state-owned natural resources and, by the end of the 1990s, had come from nowhere to join the ranks of the world's super-rich. While some of Russia's nouveaux riches – billionaires and multi-million-aires – have remained in Russia, most have moved or built a base abroad, shifting their mountain of assets with them. While a few have selected Israel, New York, or Switzerland, most have chosen London. From the millennium, this group scattered its new-found wealth like confetti, helping to transform London into the world's leading playground of the super-rich, contributing to runaway property prices, soaring profits for luxury goods retailers, and bringing displays of opulence not seen since the 1920s.

Some of the Russian ultra-rich were, through fear of arrest, driven out of Russia and took up residence in London. Others became international super-nomads, living partly in London, partly in Russia, while travelling the globe in their private jets and luxury yachts. Many kept a discreet foot in both camps. Along with the next tier of the Russian rich, the oligarchs were lured by London's accommodating tax laws, compliant banking system, relaxed lifestyle, unobtrusive City regulations, elite schools, and independent judicial system.

This book tells the story of four Russian oligarchs: Boris Berezovsky, the intense, extrovert fugitive who has plotted against Putin's Russia from his gilded London base; Roman Abramovich, the wily, reserved owner of Chelsea Football Club whose multi-billion-pound oil fortune came from outmanoeuvring his former friend and now bitter enemy Berezovsky; Mikhail Khodorkovsky, the intellectual who naively believed that he was more powerful than the state and ended up in a Siberian jail; and Oleg Deripaska, the ruthless young pretender and aluminium magnate who rose to become the richest of all of them, helped along by his cosy relationship with Vladimir Putin.

During the course of the 1990s these four men built huge fortunes at electric speed by exploiting the flawed post-Soviet scramble to build a Western-style market economy. Though it was Russia itself that was the source of their personal wealth, it was London that provided the backdrop to the next phase in their meteoric climb up the global rich lists.

For Abramovich, London has helped to satisfy his apparently insatiable appetite for conspicuous consumption. For Deripaska, banned from entering the United States, the capital has been a crucial base for building his diverse and colossal global business empire. Before his incarceration, Khodorkovsky used London to woo the British political and business establishment in his international campaign to transform his tarnished global reputation. For Berezovsky, who has been fighting extradition since 2001, London has provided a refuge from Russian prosecutors who have accused him of alleged tax evasion and fraud, charges that he has strenuously denied.

In contrast to the corrupt, politicized judiciary in Russia, London has also offered legal sanctuary and a fair due process of law. While indicted Russian businessmen have been arrested and detained in Spain, France, Italy, and the United States, Britain has refused to accept any of the dozens of extradition attempts by the Russian authorities, souring diplomatic relations in the process. 'I think they [Russians] feel that this is a country of law,' said Berezovsky. 'They feel that they are well protected here.'[1]

London has long attracted the extravagantly rich, but the post-millennium wave of foreign wealth was unprecedented. In the decade up to 2008, trillions of pounds of foreign capital settled in the UK. For those who make money out of money, it was a golden decade for tax lawyers, accountants, and bankers. 'The British have found a new vocation,' said William Cash, the well-connected publisher who founded *Spear's Wealth Management Survey*, the glossy quarterly that chronicles the activities of the super-rich. 'That is being the financial bag-carriers of the world. Britain's ruling classes used to own the wealth. Now they've become the fee-earning servants, servicing the global financial elite.'[2]

By 2007, before the devastating impact of the global economic meltdown of the following year, London had displaced New York as the financial capital of the world. It did so by providing an unrivalled tax avoidance industry and a much lighter regulatory touch. After 9/11 and a series of high-profile financial scandals on Wall Street, the US Government passed a new law – the Sarbanes-Oxley Act – which imposed much tougher corporate requirements on the disclosure of information, accountancy procedures, and the process of listing on the New York Stock Exchange. This made New York less attractive to the world's business rich and London seized its chance. The United States also introduced much tighter visa restrictions for foreign businessmen, which did not compare favourably with the more open UK border controls.

For moneyed Russians London also provides logistical advantages: the flight from Moscow is just four hours, while south-east England enjoys a ring of airports with facilities for private jets. According to James Harding, editor of *The Times*, 'From London it is possible to work a normal day and talk to Tokyo in the morning and Los Angeles in the afternoon. A businessman can get on a plane from Moscow and be in central London in five hours, from Bombay in seven, even from Beijing in nine. This is one of the reasons why over the past twenty-five years London has turned itself into an international market-place while New York has remained essentially a domestic financial capital.'[3]

However, tax remains the primary factor. 'New York is obviously very stable, but most of the other big centres of wealth management would have questions over them', said David Harvey of the Society of Trust and Estate Practitioners whose members unashamedly help wealthy families pay as little tax as is legally possible. 'Tokyo's gone through a period of depression,

Singapore is relatively new, and Germany was until recently a tax-heavy jurisdiction. If you're looking to avoid tax legally, you're as well going to London as anywhere else.'[4]

The UK boasts an unrivalled tax-avoidance industry – and an abundance of highly paid accountants able to devise complex ways of hiding an individual's wealth. In 2007 the International Monetary Fund ranked London alongside Switzerland, Bermuda, and the Cayman Islands as 'an offshore financial centre'.

Most countries have required their residents – including wealthy foreigners – to pay domestic taxes on their worldwide income and capital gains. In the UK foreigners can claim they are 'domiciled' abroad even though they may have lived in Britain for years and have British passports. Under this rule, 'non-domiciles' would only pay tax on their UK income and not on overseas income, usually the bulk of their earnings. Furthermore, by purchasing property through offshore trusts, foreign buyers could avoid both capital gains tax when they sell and most of the stamp duty usually paid at the initial purchase.

For a Russian billionaire living in London, his earnings from his homeland have been tax-free in the UK. 'There is one reason above all why these people are coming to London and that is the tax law,' said Natasha Chouvaeva, a London-based Russian journalist. Although this advantage was partially reduced in 2008 when, following a mounting media and public outcry, the government introduced a £30,000 annual levy on non-domiciled residents, it was an inconsequential sum for the super-rich.

The origins of the oligarchical influx lie in the privatization of Russia's vast and valuable state assets in the 1990s, an explosive process that enriched the few, opened up a huge gulf between rich and poor, and enraged the Russian people. A World Bank report in 2004 showed that, in effect, thirty individuals controlled 40 per cent of the $225 billion output of the

Russian economy in its most important sectors, notably in natural resources and automotives. The study concluded: 'Ownership concentration in modern Russia is much higher than in any country in continental Europe and higher than any country for which data is available.'[5]

Little of this unprecedented accumulation of wealth has been invested in Russia in business or charity. Rather, most of the money has been secreted abroad, with billions of dollars hidden in a labyrinth of offshore bank accounts in an array of tax havens, from Switzerland and Jersey to the British Virgin Islands and Gibraltar. Much has ended up being deposited in and managed by British banks. Stashed away, it has been almost impossible to trace. Despite attempts by Russian and British law enforcement agencies, little of it has been recovered and requisitioned back to Russia.

Russia is where the money originated, but it has not been a comfortable place to spend it – too many people pointing fingers in Moscow restaurants, too much scrutiny by the tax police, and the constant fear of assassination. The Russian rich cannot go anywhere without bodyguards and bullet- and bomb-proof cars. Even wearing bespoke suits attracts attention. But in the UK or Europe they have been able to go mostly unrecognized and can relax, spending their gains without fear of censure or of being called to account. After buying their multi-million pound town houses and country estates, they have indulged their sybaritic lifestyles, cruising in St Barts, skiing in Gstaad, and shopping in Knightsbridge.

For their wives it has been heaven. 'London is a metropolis,' said Olga Sirenko, who edits a website for Russian expatriates. 'It is fashionable. It has all the boutiques and the culture. Moscow doesn't have that kind of chic.' Aliona Muchinskaya, who has lived in Britain since 1991 and runs her own PR company, says that Russians now dismiss Paris as being 'too dowdy and villagey'. London, by contrast, is 'bustling and busy with its restaurants and nightclubs. Russians can hire Rolls-Royces and private jets more easily here.'

On arrival in London the first port of call for the affluent, socially aspiring Russian was to the estate agent, notably Savills, Knight Frank, or Aylesford. Deals were cut at high speed: no mortgages, just cash. In 2006 one-fifth of all houses sold for over £8 million went to Russians. For properties over £12 million, the figure was higher still. But Russians have been extremely selective in location, not merely restricting themselves to the golden postcodes – SW1, SW3, W1, and W8 – but only to certain streets and squares within them. Owning a British country property is also prestigious. Again, their choice of location has been very specific: St George's Hill and Wentworth Park, both in Surrey.

The next decision for the oligarch seeking to emulate the British aristocracy was which top boarding school to send their offspring to, for a British education is another motivating factor for moving to the UK. Public schools generally offer high academic standards and a secure, friendly environment. In Moscow, by contrast, kidnapping is a constant and real fear. While London's elite estate agents set up offices in Moscow and St Petersburg to woo ultra-rich buyers, British public schools, colleges, and universities have also sent their senior teaching staff to Russia on recruitment drives.

By 2008, it was no longer surprising to find Russian students at British schools and top universities, whether it was Abramovich's teenage daughter at an independent all-girls' school in London or foreign minister Sergei Lavrov's daughter at the London School of Economics. School numbers soared from 2000 and some Russian parents started to seek schools where there were no other Russians. The fees – up to £30,000 a year – may not have been a problem, but old habits died hard. A headmistress of one top girls' public school told the story of a Russian whose daughter had failed the entrance exam and who offered her a suitcase full of cash. He promised to pay for anything – a new gym, classrooms, a swimming pool. 'Things don't work like that over here,' said the bemused headmistress. At another top school a parent asked permission to land his helicopter on the cricket field when visiting his child.

While most Russian children eventually return home, an English education is regarded as a commercial benefit. 'I know that some oligarchs only hire students with a Western education,' said Boris Yarishevsky, president of the Russian Society at the London School of Economics.[6] This also extends to politicians. 'I know people whose fathers occupy really high positions in the Russian government and I know they study in London,' he added. 'I don't think that they would want me to give out their names, though.'[7] It is quite possible that one day Russia – like many African and Middle Eastern states – will elect a President who has been educated at a British private school.

The UK has long been a haven for Russian exiles and dissidents. Anti-tsarist radicals flocked to London in the early twentieth century and Revolutionary Congresses were held here every two years. At the 1907 Social Democratic Congress the *New York Times* reported that an arrest warrant had been issued for one notable attendant, Vladimir Ilyich Lenin: 'A Famous Rebel in London. Lenin Will Be Arrested if he Returns to Russia – Real Name Ulianoff' ran its headline. Lenin was not a permanent exile but visited the city six times between 1902 and 1911. At Seven Sisters Church in Holloway, north London, he met workers whom he described as 'bursting with socialism', while the area around Whitechapel and other parts of the East End swarmed with radicals. During one of his trips Lenin saw *Hamlet* at the Old Vic and visited Speaker's Corner and the National Gallery. It was at the British Museum in 1902 that he first met Leon Trotsky, who had just escaped from Siberia.

After the 1917 Revolution, relatively few affluent Russians fled to London – only 15,000 by 1919. Far more moved to the Slavic states, to Berlin, and to a lesser extent to France and China, particularly Shanghai. Those who did arrive in Britain were a mix of aristocrats and middle-class liberal intellectuals, notably the family of the philosopher Isaiah Berlin who arrived in 1919 and settled in the Surrey town of Surbiton. 'I am an Anglophile, I love England,' Berlin once reflected. 'I have been very well treated in this country, but I remain a Russian Jew.'[8] Other descendants of this first wave of Russian immigration include the actress Dame Helen Mirren (born Ileyna Vasilievna Mironov), winner of an Oscar for *The Queen*, and the Liberal Democrat leader Nick Clegg.

During the Cold War there was always a sprinkling of new Russians coming to London. Some were dissidents fleeing the gulags; others were high-level KGB defectors who ended up rubbing shoulders in London with White Russians – mostly the offspring of those who had fled Russia after 1917. The latter lived mostly quiet lives, spoke good English, and were largely Anglicized. The 1991 Census recorded 27,011 residents living in the UK while claiming the former Soviet Union as their place of birth. Most of them would have been Russian.

The collapse of the Eastern Bloc in the late 1980s had a dramatic impact on the pace of Russian arrivals, unleashing a new and unprecedented wave of migration from Russia and former Soviet and East European states. In 1991 the British Embassy in Moscow issued barely 100 visas – to a mixture of those working for Russian companies, students, and Russians who had married Britons – while only one Russian living in the UK was granted citizenship. Even by the mid-1990s, Londoners would have started to become aware of the occasional unrecognizable foreign accent in a shop or in the street – those Russians who did come congregated in a few favourite restaurants and nightclubs – but otherwise the early arrivals remained largely anonymous. Gradually that trickle turned into a flood. By 2006, the number of Russian visas issued had soared to 250,000, while the number granted citizenship in that same year had risen to 1,830. Berezovsky has likened the twenty-first-century Russian wave to the influx of nineteenth-century Russians to Paris. 'It used to be that Russian aristocrats spoke French and went to France,' he said. 'The modern Russian speaks English and feels more comfortable in England.'[9]

The early Russian migrants – mostly professional middle class but by no means wealthy – were joined within two or three years by a quite different stratum of Russian society. These were what their countrymen dubbed 'the new Russians', and they started to arrive between 1993 and 1994. This is the group that was beginning to make money, though not on the same subsequent scale, out of Boris Yeltsin's economic reforms, the easing of restrictions on private enterprise, and the first wave of privatization. They were a mix of state bureaucrats, entrepreneurial hustlers, Kremlin insiders, and former KGB officials; others were members of emerging Russian-based criminal gangs.

This group of 'new Russians', who were always outnumbered by 'ordinary' Russian migrants, were by and large not coming to London to settle down. They came on short-term tourist or business visas, to attend a conference or a business meeting, or on shopping and spending trips. As one Russian already living here who knew some of them put it, 'At this time there was no real dream to come and settle in London. It was difficult to get a permanent visa except illegally, work permits were scarce, and most of this group could make much more money in Moscow than in London. They had money and came here for a week or two at a time to burn it.'

During the 1990s, Britain gradually eased its entry regulations. Tourist and business visas became easier to acquire. Especially welcomed by the authorities were those with money.

Anxious to encourage investment from abroad, the government bent the rules to encourage the arrival of the super-rich. 'Essentially, if you are coming to the country with money to spend, you're very much welcomed with open arms,' said John Tincey, Vice-Chairman of the Immigration Service Union, in 2007.[10]

In 1996 the Conservative government of John Major introduced a new 'investor visa' for those wanting to make the UK their main home and able to invest at least £1 million in the country. Of this at least £750,000 had to be invested in either government bonds or UK-registered companies. Those investing in this way were, after five years, allowed to apply for permanent residency and eventually UK citizenship. Only one other country in the world – the United States – operated such a scheme (though with a much lower entry fee) and a number of wealthy Russians took advantage of the rule. All they needed to do was meet the investment cash criterion.

The process of seduction worked. The Russians, along with the super-rich of other nations, poured into Britain. As *Forbes* magazine described it in 2006: 'London attracts the elite of the world's rich and successful. It can lay claim unchallenged to one title: it is the magnet for the world's billionaires.'[11]

Once here, the newly enriched Russians were not shy about spending their way through the capital. They quickly became addicted to high living the British way. In London, history, culture, and the attractions of consumer spending often come together in classic British brands that seem to have a special appeal. The more traditional, the more alluring: shopping at Fortnum & Mason and Burberry, buying a £900 bottle of port at the St James's wine merchant Berry Bros & Rudd, tea at Claridge's, and dinner at Rules. The Russians also took to two other British institutions, London's leading auctioneers Sotheby's and Christie's. Here, at the height of the art boom of the mid-noughties, they could be found outbidding other collectors and leading international dealers for the works of French Impressionists and contemporary British artists.

But the staggering spending of Russians is not based just on a crude materialistic desire for luxury goods; it also stems from a fatalistic mindset and generally pessimistic approach to life. For centuries the Russian people have suffered enormous hardship, poverty, starvation, and brutal repression: an estimated 20 million died during Stalin's regime, and another 1.1 million perished during the siege of Stalingrad alone during 1942–3. Even after the collapse of the Soviet empire, millions continued to live in a state of permanent insecurity and anxiety exacerbated by a harsh winter climate, economic instability, and a corrupt rule of law. Even the new billionaires and their families believe that they could lose everything tomorrow. A favourite Russian saying goes: 'Never say never to poverty or prison. Both could happen tomorrow.' This is why they spend. And they also believe in another Russian adage: 'That which does not grow and expand will expire and will then die.'

For the Russian male the addiction to spending has manifested itself in the acquisition of yachts, jets, and cars. 'We have a positive attitude towards the English car culture,' said Alexander Pikulenko, motoring correspondent for the Moscow radio station Ekho Moskvy.[12] In 2007 an estimated 40 per cent of Mercedes-Benz sold at their central London showroom went to Russians. The Russians also brought the good times to the UK's fledgling private aviation industry and helped turn scores of Britain's own home-grown entrepreneurs, such as the young property tycoons Candy and Candy, into multi-millionaires almost overnight.

For Russian women London's luxury shops became the magnet for this 'rouble revolution', with Harrods the favourite. Many Russian wives – and probably their daughters as well – would no doubt love their husbands to buy it. There is a joke that Russian émigrés like to tell. On his deathbed a wealthy

Russian summons his wife to his side. 'Olga, when I die, will you promise that you will do something for me? Promise that you will bury me in Harrods.' Shocked, his tearful wife begs him to reconsider, telling him that he is rich enough to build his own mausoleum in Moscow. 'No, no, no,' he interrupts. 'Don't you see, if I am buried in Harrods, at least I know you will visit me at least once a week.' A close second to Harrods is Harvey Nichols, just up the road, where, at the height of the London boom, they employed six Russian-speaking assistants on its five shop floors.

For specialized jewellery the oligarchs' wives and mistresses would move closer to the West End. Almost every shop in Old Bond Street started to employ a Russian speaker, while top jewellers like Asprey and Theo Fennell attributed their increase in profits from the late 1990s to their expanding Russian client base and their taste for expensive one-off designer pieces. Russian wives would think nothing of buying a £5,000 alligator-skin bag and a £90,000 diamond ring. 'They are like children in a sweet shop,' observed one employee.

After a morning being chauffeured around their favourite fashion stores, the wives and daughters would retreat for lunch to Roka in Charlotte Street, the Russian-style tearoom and restaurant, Troika, in Primrose Hill, or Harvey Nichols' Fifth Floor Restaurant. Their husbands preferred the bars at the Dorchester and Lanesborough hotels for early evening drinks. Then it was dinner at the most expensive, exclusive restaurants, notably Le Gavroche and Cipriani in Mayfair. Even being halfway across the world was not a problem. Late one afternoon Roman Abramovich was in Baku in Azerbaijan and told his aide that he wanted sushi for dinner. The aide ordered £1,200 worth of sushi from Ubon in Canary Wharf, the sister restaurant of Nobu, the fashionable Japanese Park Lane restaurant. It was then collected by limousine, driven to Luton Airport, and flown 3,000 miles by private jet to Abramovich in Azerbaijan.[13] At an estimated total cost of £40,000, it must rank as the most expensive takeaway in history.

Behind the glitz, the glamour, and the wealth lies another side of the Russian invasion. Their arrival may have transformed London financially, but it has also turned Britain's capital into a murky outpost of Moscow. While the tycoons have been applauded by the City, luxury goods manufacturers, and property magnates, they hardly represent a harmonious community. Behind the mass spending sprees lies a much more sinister world of bitter personal feuds. Many of the Russians are at war with each other as well as with the Russian state. As a result, former friends and business partners have become sworn public enemies.

At issue is the ownership of billions of pounds' worth of assets. 'They are ruthless,' said one who has had regular business dealings with the wealthiest Russians. 'Their word means nothing. They will shaft you if they are given half a chance. It is the law of the jungle. Many of them owe huge sums of money to others.'

Their presence, then, has also introduced to Britain some of the uglier elements of the Russian state. 'As soon as the oligarchs arrived, so the politics followed them. That is why they all take such elaborate and expensive security precautions,' another businessman explained.

The cut-throat political and business battles being fought for control of the nation's vast oil, gas, and mineral resources were once confined to Russia itself. Gradually, however, those bitter corporate and personal wars spilt over into Britain. For a while they went unnoticed, at least by the press and the public, if not by the security services. It was only in December 2006, after the former Russian state security officer turned dissident, Alexander Litvinenko, died a long, painful, and public death in a London hospital as a result of polonium-210 poisoning that the implications of Britain's wooing of Russian billionaires and dissidents became fully apparent. The British government wanted their money but only if they kept their acrimonious internal battles at the border. Litvinenko's murder exposed the frailty of this strategy of benign tolerance.

As one Russian who personally knows several oligarchs put it, 'The UK government may not care how these guys made their money or what they get up to as long as they don't bring their dubious activities into Britain. But we can't have it both ways. We can't let them in and expect the seedy elements to stop short of the English Channel.'

The country's leading expert on Russian history, Professor Robert Service of St Antony's College, Oxford, agrees: 'The British government has collaborated with the City of London in offering a haven for businessmen from Russia who need to expatriate their money. More circumspect, New York and Stuttgart have failed to compete in pursuit of Russian capital. Britain asks few questions about the provenance of new Russian wealth. Hence the hitmen who keep on arriving on our shores to settle accounts by violent means.'[14]

CHAPTER 2

The Russian Billionaires' Club

'What is hard to dispute is that, while hundreds of people became seriously rich, 150 million Russians now live in a country which sold its mineral wealth for a mess of pottage'[1]
— DOMINIC MIDGLEY *and* CHRIS HUTCHINS, 2005

IN 2002 THE RUSSIAN FILM *Oligarkh* was released. Its main character, Platon Makovsky (Platon is the Russian name for Plato), was a young, idealistic academic who abandoned his studies for the shady world of post-Soviet-era business. Platon devised a series of questionable deals by which he outfoxed his opponents: the Russian secret service. First, he rapidly became the richest man in Russia with financial and political power equal to the state. Then he ended up as the government's rival and sworn enemy.

Set during the economic convulsions that followed the collapse of communism, *Oligarkh* was a graphic, if fictional, account of a small group of businessmen who acquired the nation's wealth. But the film also presented the characters as visionaries who provided the lifeblood of a country paralyzed by fear of change. As the *New Yorker* noted:

Once a freedom-loving idealist, Platon used his genius to become a monster, unhesitatingly sacrificing his ideals and his closest friends. This is the tragedy of this super-talented individual who embodies all that is most creative in the new Russia and, at the same time, all which is worst for the country that he privatised for his own profit.[2]

Based on the novel *Bolshaya Paika* (*The Lion's Share*) written by Yuli Dubov, who went on to work for Berezovsky, the film broke Russian box-office records and drew gasps from the audience at the scenes of obscene private opulence. It has been broadly compared to the early years of one of the country's most notorious oligarchs: Boris Berezovsky. Played by Russian sex symbol Vladimir Mashkov, the leading character was portrayed sympathetically as a freedom-loving patriot who proclaimed at one point that he would rather go to jail than leave Russia.

Although there were scenes of armed standoffs, the plot mostly glossed over the methods by which such a small clique made such huge fortunes so quickly. Berezovsky accepted that the film was based – if somewhat loosely – on his own early life. He invited the director to his London home for a viewing of the film and told the BBC, 'As a work of art I think it is primitive. But I appreciate the effort to understand people like me. It is the first attempt in recent Russian cinema to understand the motivations of those at the peak of power, who drive reforms and make changes rather than cope with them.'[3]

As they started to beat a path to London, and as their reputations grew, so the new breed of super-rich Russians began to intrigue the British public: 'We like to follow them because we are astonished at how people who not that long ago were queuing for bread are now able to outbid the rest of the world's super-rich for Britain's finest houses,' one Mayfair property agent told us.

In his early sixties, Berezovsky is old enough to remember the bread queues in his own country, but such a modest lifestyle did not extend into his adult years. The man once known as the 'Grey Cardinal' because of his dominating influence at the Kremlin was not shy when it came to spending his fortune. In 1995 he bought himself a palatial residence outside Moscow, complete with servants, and accumulated a fleet of sports cars. He acquired an interest in fine wine and smoked only the best cigars. His brazen lifestyle soon became the stuff of legend. Here was a man with a way of life that had once been the province only of the Russian aristocracy before the Revolution.

With an estimated fortune of £1.5 billion at the time, he epitomized the term 'Russian oligarch'. His power was such that by the autumn of 1996 he could boast that he and six other individuals controlled 50 per cent of the Russian economy.[4] Berezovsky was exaggerating, but from the early 1990s Russia was quickly transformed from a highly centralized economy to one in which some thirty or so individuals owned and controlled the commanding heights: its vast natural resources and manufacturing. Russia moved at high speed from being a political dictatorship to a society not just heavily owned by a tiny, super-wealthy elite, but one wielding, for a while, enormous political power.

The word 'oligarch' was first used in Russia on 13 October 1992, when Khodorkovsky's Bank Menatep announced plans to provide banking services for what it called 'the financial and industrial oligarchy'. This was for clients with private means of at least $10 million. By the mid-1990s, the word was common parlance across Russia.

The origins of the word lie in Classical Greek political philosophy. Both Plato's *Republic* and Aristotle's *Politics* describe rule by an elite rather than by the democratic will of the people. Historically, 'oligarch' was a word used to describe active opponents of Athenian democracy during the fifth century BC, when Greece was ruled on several occasions by brutal oligarch regimes that butchered their democratic opponents.

Like their ancient Greek counterparts, few of the modern Russian oligarchs became mega-rich by creating new wealth but rather by insider political intrigue and by exploiting the weakness of the rule of law. Driven by a lust for money and power, they secured much of the country's natural and historic wealth through the manipulation of the post-Soviet-era process of privatization.

When Boris Yeltsin succeeded Mikhail Gorbachev as President in 1991, Russia had reached another precarious stage in its complex history. It had difficulty trading its vast resources and was short of food, while its banking system suffered from a severe lack of liquidity. Its former foe the United States – in Russia referred to as *glavni vrag* (the main enemy) – was watching events eagerly. Within weeks, advisers from the International Monetary Fund (IMF) and the World Bank teamed up with powerful Russian reformist economists close to the Kremlin to persuade Yeltsin to introduce an unbridled free-market economy involving the mass privatization of state assets. It was a dramatic process of 'reverse Marxism' implemented at speed.

This was to become Russia's second full-scale revolution – though this time from communism to capitalism – in three generations. 'Russia was broke. There was grave doubt in late 1991 that they could feed their population in the coming year,' explained James Collins, former US Ambassador to Russia. 'The government had lost control over its currency because people were printing it in other republics. The policy of what became known as "shock therapy" was discussed internally [in the US government] and nobody stood up and said "no, don't do that". The whole system was falling apart and was best summed up by my predecessor Ambassador Robert Strauss who said, "It's like two pissants on a big log in a middle of a river going downstream and arguing about who was steering".'

The first wave of privatization came in the form of a mass voucher scheme launched in late 1992 – just nine months after

Yeltsin assumed the presidency. All Russians were to be offered vouchers to the value of 10,000 roubles (then worth about $30, the equivalent of the average monthly wage). These could, over time, be exchanged for shares either in companies that employed them or in any other state enterprise that was being privatized. To acquire the vouchers, citizens had to pay a mere 25 roubles per voucher, at the time the equivalent of about 7 pence.

In the four months from October 1992, a remarkable 144 million vouchers were bought, mainly in agricultural and service firms. The Kremlin presented this ambitious scheme as offering everyone a share in the nation's wealth. Yeltsin promised it would produce 'millions of owners rather than a handful of millionaires'. It may have been a great vision but it never materialized. Russia's citizens were poor, often unpaid, and many had lost their savings as inflation soared and the rouble collapsed. Moreover, after seventy years of communism, most Russians had no concept of the idea of share ownership. There wasn't even a Russian word for privatization.

There were, however, plenty of people who understood only too well what privatization meant and the value of the vouchers. They started buying them up in blocks from workers. Among those cashing in was Mikhail Khodorkovsky – who would later become the richest man in Russia. Street kiosks selling vodka and cigarettes began doing a brisk trade in vouchers. Stalls began to appear outside farms and factories offering to buy them from workers. Hustlers started going from door to door.

Even though holders were being offered far less than the vouchers were worth, most exchanged them for cash to pay for immediate necessities. Russia became a giant unregulated stock exchange as purchasers were persuaded to trade their vouchers for prices that were nearly always well below their true value. They would exchange them for a bottle of vodka, a handful of

US dollars, or a few more roubles than they had paid for them. It proved a mass bonanza for those prepared to prey on a country suffering from mass deprivation.

Hundreds of thousands also lost their vouchers in 'voucher saving funds'. Some funds were little more than covert attempts by companies to buy up their own shares for a song. Members of the old KGB power elite often laid claim to mines and enterprises in what became known as 'smash-and-grab' operations. For a nation ignorant of the concept of shares and unable to appreciate the potential value of their vouchers, people were easily encouraged to part with their stakes. For the winners it was easy and big money.

Instead of a share-owning democracy, a newspaper poll in July 1994 revealed that only 8 per cent of Russians had exchanged their vouchers for shares in enterprises in which they worked. Moreover, because the assets being sold were massively undervalued, the successful purchasers obtained the companies for well below their real value. Indeed, the 144 million vouchers issued have been estimated to have valued the assets at a mere $12 billion. In other words, much of the country's industrial and agricultural wealth was being sold for a sum equivalent to the value of a single British company such as Marks & Spencer.

In just two years, by the beginning of 1995, around half the economy, mostly in the shape of small- and medium-sized businesses, had been privatized. The next crucial issue in the 'second Russian Revolution' was how to privatize the remaining giant state-owned oil, metallurgical, and telecommunications industries. These were still operated by former Soviet managers – the 'red directors', the Soviet-era bosses renowned for their corruption and incompetence who had managed the state firms – many of whom were laundering money and stashing away revenue abroad. Russia was still mired in a severe economic crisis with plunging share prices and rampant inflation. The indecisive and capricious Yeltsin was ill, often drunk and rarely in control, while the state was running out of money to pay pensions and salaries.

Taking advantage of the growing crisis, a handful of businessmen dreamed up a clever ruse that appeared to offer a solution. This was a group that had already become rich by taking advantage of the early days of Mikhail Gorbachev's *perestroika* (restructuring), which, for the first time in the Soviet Union, allowed small private enterprises to operate. Led by a leading insider, Vladimir Potanin, the cabal offered Yeltsin a backroom deal known in the West as 'loans for shares'. This was an arrangement (coming at the end of the voucher privatization scheme) whereby they would lend the government the cash it so desperately needed in return for the right to buy shares in the remaining state enterprises. In effect, Yeltsin was auctioning off the state's most desirable assets. If the government subsequently defaulted on repaying the loans – which the scheme's architects knew was inevitable – the lenders would keep the shares by way of compensation.

For Yeltsin, the plan provided much needed cash while on paper it did not look like the mass giveaway it turned out to be. Between 1995 and 1997, more than twenty giant state-owned enterprises, accounting for a huge share of the country's national wealth, were offloaded in this way. In return, the government received a total of some 9.1 trillion roubles, about £1.2 billion at the time. One of the main beneficiaries of this deal was Boris Berezovsky.

Boris Abramovich Berezovsky was born in Moscow in January 1946 to a Jewish family. An only child, his father was a construction engineer and his mother a paediatric nurse. Berezovsky's family were not members of the Communist Party and his upbringing was modest and for a time – when his father was unemployed for two years – he experienced poverty. 'I wasn't a member of the political elite,' he later said. 'I am a Jew. There were massive limitations. I understand that perfectly well,' he told an audience of journalists at London's Frontline Club in London in June 2007.

A mathematics whizz kid, Berezovsky graduated with honours from Moscow State University. In early 1969 he joined the Institute of Control Sciences, where he gained a PhD and worked for more than twenty years. Intelligent, precocious, and energetic, he is also remembered for being intensely ambitious. 'He always raised the bar to the highest notch and went for it,' a close colleague recalled. 'He was always in motion, always racing towards the goal, never knowing or fearing obstacles ... His mind was always restless, his emotions ever changing, and he often lost interest in what he had started.' Another friend from this period said, 'He has this attitude which he has maintained all his life – never stop attacking.'

This was corroborated by a fellow student, 'He was a compressed ball of energy ... Constantly in motion, he was burning with plans and ideas and impatient to make them happen. He had an insistent charm and a fierce burning desire and he usually got what he wanted.'

As a scientist, Berezovsky wrote more than a hundred research papers on such subjects as optimization theory and decision-making. He was a director of a laboratory that researched automation and computer systems for industry. The young mathematician craved prestige and focused his energy on winning prizes to get it. He was awarded the prestigious Lenin Komsomol Prize (an annual Soviet award for the best works by young writers in science, engineering, literature, and the arts) and then tried but failed to win the even more illustrious State Prize. According to Leonid Boguslavsky, a former colleague at the Institute, his dream was to win the Nobel Prize.

In 1991 Berezovsky left academia and was appointed a member of the Russian Academy of Sciences, an achievement he remains proud of to this day. He later boasted that there were only eight hundred members of the Russian Academy of Sciences and that even Leonid Brezhnev had wanted to be among that number.

Berezovsky married Nina Vassilievna when he was twenty-three. Within three years the couple had two daughters – Elizaveta and Ekaterina, both now in their thirties. Despite his academic achievements, Berezovsky initially had to scrimp to buy winter tights and school exercise books for his children. *Perestroika* offered him escape from his straitened circumstances. His first scheme involved selling software he had developed to the State Committee on Science and Technology. 'We convinced them that it was a good product, and we sold tens of thousands of copies of this software. And those were the first millions of roubles that we earned, and a million roubles was a whole lot,' he told his audience at the Frontline Club.

In 1989 Berezovsky turned to the automobile industry. 'They stopped paying my salary, so I started a business,' he recalled. 'Every Russian had two wishes – for an apartment and a car. The women generally had the last say on the apartment; so I went into cars.'[5] Initially, this involved selling second-hand Mercedes imported from East Germany. Then, taking advantage of the new freedom to travel, he went to West Germany. There he bought a used Mercedes, drove it back through almost non-existent customs, and sold it for three times what he had paid for it.

But the real source of Berezovsky's early wealth came from exploiting his connections, gained through his academic work, with the Soviet Union's largest car manufacturer and producer of the Lada, the AvtoVaz factory based in the industrial city of Togliatti. Off the back of his friendship with the factory's Director, Vladimir Kadannikov, Berezovsky founded a company called LogoVaz, which took over responsibility for selling the

Ladas. The effect was to separate production from sales in a way that maximized the profits from the business for Berezovsky and his partners. It was perfectly legal and it was a strategy widely deployed by directors of state companies and the new entrepreneurs at the time.

Berezovsky also went on to establish the country's first chain of dealerships for Mercedes, Fiat, and Volvo, which he later referred to as 'a complete service, with workshops, showrooms, and credit facilities. Really, we created the country's car market. There was no market then; people won cars in lotteries or for being "best worker" or they applied and stayed on a waiting list for years.'[6]

In relation to that waiting list, Russians have a joke about the long delays of the period. Vladimir has been waiting for six years to buy his own car, when he is suddenly summoned to the local ministry office. 'I have good news for you,' says the clerk. 'Your car will be delivered to you in five years from today.'

'Wonderful,' says Vladimir. 'Will it come in the morning or the afternoon?'

'Why, what difference does it make?' responds the perplexed clerk.

'Well,' answers Vladimir, 'I have already arranged for a plumber to come that morning.'

The dealership chain was created at a time when the automobile industry was rife with organized crime and protection rackets. Berezovsky's Moscow dealership was targeted by Chechen gangs, which also controlled the production lines at AvtoVaz. Berezovsky, at times personally a target of the gangs, has always denied any mafia connection. In September 1993 his LogoVaz car parks were attacked three times and his showrooms bombed with grenades. When his Mercedes 600 sedan was blown up nine months later, with Berezovsky in the back and his chauffeur killed, LogoVaz issued a statement blaming 'forces in society that are actively trying, by barbarically criminal means, to keep civilian entrepreneurship from developing in this country.'

> I can tell you right here and now that not a single oligarch has bowed to the Mafia. Oligarchs themselves are stronger than any mafia, and stronger than the government, to which they have also refused to bow. If we are talking of the visible tip of the iceberg, not the part of the iceberg concealed behind the surface or in the dark, I haven't bowed to the government either.[7]

By 1993 Berezovsky had already built an extensive business empire. One of his new enterprises was the All-Russian Automobile Alliance. Owned by various companies but headed by Berezovsky, ARAA promised the production of a 'people's car', to be produced by AvtoVaz in collaboration with General Motors in the United States. On the back of a huge advertising campaign, it offered bonds in the scheme and the promise of cheaper cars, cash redemption, and a free lottery once the new production line was up and running. Wooed by the 'get-rich-quick' promise, more than 100,000 Russians bought $50 million of shares in the project. But when General Motors backed out of the scheme and it collapsed, thousands lost their money.

By now Berezovsky had acquired a younger, second wife, Galina Becharova. They lived together for several years before being married at a civil ceremony in Russia in 1991. They had a son, Artem, and a daughter, Anastasia. Although they separated three years later, they never divorced. Berezovsky sent his two daughters from his first marriage – Elizaveta and Ekaterina – to Cambridge University.

By 1995 AvtoVaz had terminated the LogoVaz contract. The ambitious oligarch turned his attention from cars to planes, lobbying to install his business associates in key managerial positions in the state-owned airline, Aeroflot. Thanks to his growing influence at the Kremlin, he ensured that two of his intermediary companies based in Switzerland – Andava and Forus – provided Aeroflot with financial services. This gave Berezovsky huge influence over the company.

Much of Berezovsky's business ascendancy was based on his Kremlin connections and personal friendship with President Yeltsin. Since coming to power as Russia's first democratically elected leader following his resistance against the hardliners' putsch of 1991 (it had toppled Gorbachev and was bent on restoring a Soviet-style dictatorship), Yeltsin seemed to relax. But gradually he became increasingly impatient, drank more, and appeared ever vulnerable to the solicitations of sycophants and businessmen, especially as he distrusted the old KGB machine.

Berezovsky's relationship with Yeltsin was cemented by his shrewd offer to finance the publication of the President's second volume of memoirs, *Notes of a President*, in 1994, arranging for royalties to be paid into a Barclays bank account in London. According to one account, before long, the President was complaining that the royalties were too low. 'They [the ghostwriter, Valentin Yumashev, and Berezovsky] understood that they had to fix their mistake,' claimed General Aleksandr Korzhakov, former KGB officer and Yeltsin's closest friend and one-time bodyguard. 'They started filling Yeltsin's personal bank account in London, explaining that this was income from the book. By the end of 1994, Yeltsin's account already had a balance of about $3 million.'[8]

A grateful Yeltsin ensured that Berezovsky became part of the Kremlin inner circle. Already a multi-millionaire, he was now well placed to benefit from the next wave of state sell-offs. In December 1994 Yeltsin signed a decree that handed over a 49 per cent stake in ORT, the main state-owned television station and broadcaster of Channel One, primarily to Berezovsky, without the auction required by law. The remaining 51 per cent remained in state hands. Berezovsky paid a mere $320,000 for the station. As most Russians get their news from the television, this also provided Berezovsky with a vital propaganda base for dealing with the Kremlin.

But perhaps Berezovsky's biggest prize was in oil. In December 1995 he acquired a claim, via the 'loans for shares' scheme, to the state-owned oil conglomerate Sibneft (Siberian Oil) – then Russia's sixth-largest oil company – for a cut price of $100 million, a tiny fraction of its true value. The deal was done with two associates. One was his closest business partner, the ruthlessly sharp Arkady 'Badri' Patarkatsishvili, the other was the then unknown Roman Abramovich, twenty years younger than Berezovsky but canny enough to find $50 million for a 50 per cent stake. It was from this moment that Abramovich, at first under his mentor's tutelage but then through his own business acumen, manipulated his way to a billion dollar fortune founded on cunning negotiating skills and political patronage. It was a relationship that Berezovsky would later bitterly regret.

If there is a key to Abramovich's relentless drive, it is the orphan in him. He was born in 1966 to Irena and Arkady, Jewish Ukrainians living in Syktyvkar, the forbidding capital of the Komi republic in northern Siberia. He lost both parents before the age of three: his mother died of blood poisoning following an abortion and his father was felled by an errant crane on a building site. Roman was adopted by his Uncle Leib and his wife Ludmilla, a former beauty queen. The family lived in the industrial city of Ukhta, where Leib was responsible for the supply of essentials to the state-owned timber business. Roman enjoyed a relatively comfortable upbringing and was, it is said, the first boy in his area to have a modern cassette player.

In 1974 Roman moved to Moscow and lived with his uncle Abram, a construction boss, who would become his surrogate father. Although they lived in a tiny two-room apartment, it lay in the heart of the capital on Tsvetnoi Boulevard, just across from the Central Market and the Moscow Circus. The young Roman did not excel at school and in 1983 was called up for national service in the Red Army and posted to an artillery unit in Kirzach, 50 miles north-east of Moscow.

On his return to the big city, Abramovich was guided and protected by his uncle in the ways of the grey market economy of *perestroika*. It was not unusual for ordinary Russians to indulge in smuggling and black marketeering and, despite his shyness, the young Abramovich did not hold back. He had honed his skill in the army. 'Roman was head and shoulders above the rest when it comes to entrepreneurship,' recalled Nikolai Panteleimonov, a former army friend. 'He could make money out of thin air.'

When Abramovich was discharged from the army, he studied highway engineering and then returned to the secondary economy: transporting luxury consumer goods like Marlboro cigarettes, Chanel perfume, and Levi and Wrangler jeans from Moscow back to Ukhta.

In 1987 the budding entrepreneur met his first wife, Olga Lysova, the daughter of a high-ranking government diplomat. The couple married that December in a Moscow registry office in the presence of fifteen family and friends. The following year Abramovich established a company that made toys – including plastic ducks – and sold them in the Moscow markets. He also bought and sold retreaded tyres. An intuitive negotiator, he was able to put customers at ease. He was soon earning three to four thousand roubles a month – more than twenty times the salary of a state worker – and could afford to buy a Lada.

In 1989 Abramovich and his first wife divorced. Olga says her husband persuaded her that they should divorce so that they could emigrate to Canada together, claiming that the immigration laws made it easier for him to go there if he was not married. Once he was a Canadian citizen, he would come back for Olga and her daughter from a previous relationship.

Instead, Abramovich left Olga and gave her enough money to live on for two years, although she later claimed that all she got was the 'crummy flat'.[9] A year later Abramovich married Irina Malandina, an air hostess with Aeroflot. They met on one of his business flights and in 1992 their first child, Anna, was born.

When the Soviet Union collapsed, Abramovich, who had attended the Gubkin Institute of Oil and Gas in Moscow, established an oil-trading firm called ABK, based in Omsk, the centre of the Siberian oil business. In post-communist Russia it was possible to make enormous profits by buying oil at controlled domestic prices and selling it on in the unregulated international market. All that was needed was an export licence, which Abramovich acquired through his connection with a customs official.

It was his friendship with Boris Berezovsky that transformed Abramovich from a hustler and mid-level oil trader into a billionaire. The two men first met at a New Year's Eve party in 1994 on board the luxury yacht belonging to Petr Aven, a wealthy banker and former state minister. The select gathering of guests had been invited on a cruise to the Caribbean island of St Barts. Berezovsky was impressed by Abramovich's technical know-how and his unassuming manner that belied a calculating intelligence. Casually dressed and often with a few days' growth of beard, his understated, gentle demeanour and apparently unthreatening manner often resulted in fellow businessmen underestimating him.

In stark contrast to his mentor, with his hyperactive, restless personality, Abramovich comes across as a chess player, thinking deeply through all the possible permutations on the board. Berezovsky later acknowledged that, of all the businessmen he had met, Abramovich was the best at 'person-to-person relations'.[10]

* * *

Spotting the young oil trader's commercial nous, Berezovsky recruited him as a key partner in the Sibneft deal. This conglomerate had been created from four state-owned enterprises: an oil and gas production plant, Noyabrskneftegas; an oil exploration arm, Noyabrskneftegas Geophysica; a marketing company called Omsknefteproduckt; and, most important of all, Russia's largest and most modern oil refinery at Omsk.

The three partners responsible for the acquisition of Sibneft all played different but key roles. Abramovich assessed Sibneft's business potential, Berezovsky smoothed the privatization with the Yeltsin administration, and Badri Patarkatsishvili organized half the financing. In late 1995, 49 per cent of the company was sold at auction to the three men through their Petroleum Financial Company, known as NFK. The majority 51 per cent stake was to be held by the state for three years while the lenders were allowed to manage the assets. Under the plan, if the loan was not repaid within three years, legal ownership would transfer to the lenders. In the event, most of the remaining 49 per cent was auctioned a short while later, in January 1996, with control going to Berezovsky and his associates.

When ownership of Sibneft was secured, Berezovsky was already consumed by Kremlin politics and Patarkatsishvili was running ORT. It was thus agreed that Abramovich would manage the new company. According to Berezovsky Abramovich was in essence holding their shares in trust for both the other partners.

October of 1998 saw the deadline for the state's repayment of the loan; as expected, it was not met. Ownership of Sibneft therefore passed to NFK. By now, Abramovich held, on paper, the lion's share of the oil giant through various companies. At thirty-two, he was well on his way to becoming one of Russia's richest men. All decisions during the process of acquisition by the three partners in the deal – Abramovich, Berezovsky, and Patarkatsishvili – were made mostly at meetings at which only the three men were present and no minutes were taken.

Nothing was ever formally put in writing and there was little or no documentation. The absence of a paper trail was deliberate – as was so often the way with many of the power-broking deals of the period – and it was partly for this reason that who actually owned what was later to become the subject of a bitter feud between Berezovsky and Abramovich. Many of the deals that forged the transfer of Russia's wealth were concluded in this way – in shady rooms with no independent witnesses, tape recorders, or documentation, all done on the basis of a hand-shake. Unsurprisingly, many of these remarkable agreements started to unravel, as the former business allies later became bitter rivals and enemies.

Meanwhile, one of Berezovsky's oligarchic rivals was an earnest, geeky former mathematician named Mikhail Khodorkovsky. As early as 1989, he was wealthy enough to found his own bank and would also become a billionaire through the privatization of state assets. Mikhail ('Misha') Borisovich Khodorkovsky, an only child, was born in Moscow in June 1963 to a lower-middle-class family with a Jewish father and a Christian mother. In his early years the family lived in cramped communal housing, though circumstances later improved when his father was promoted.

Khodorkovsky's nursery school was next door to the factory where his father worked and he remembers climbing the fence with his friends to steal pieces of metal. It was Misha's dream from an early age to become a director of a factory and the other children at his nursery school accordingly nicknamed him 'Director'. Khodorkovsky left school in 1981 and read chemistry at the Mendeleev Institute of Chemical Technology in Moscow, specializing in the study of rocket fuel. He supported his studies by working as a carpenter in a housing cooperative and it was at university that he met his first wife Elena, a fellow student.

Their first son, Pavlik, was born in 1985 and the young scientist grimly recalls going out at six o'clock every morning with ration coupons to buy baby food. Khodorkovsky graduated from the Mendeleev Institute at the top of his year in 1996. Although his earliest ambitions to work in defence were thwarted by the fact that he was a Jew, he became the Deputy Secretary of Moscow's Frunze district Komsomol – the Young Communist League. Like many Komsomol leaders, he used the organization's real-estate holdings and political connections to profit from *perestroika*.

In 1986 Khodorkovsky met his second wife Inna and set up the Centre for Scientific and Technical Youth. Purportedly a youth group, the Centre was merely a front for their commercial activities. 'He dealt in everything: blue jeans, brandy, and computers – whatever could make money,' recalled a former senior Yukos executive.[11] Khodorkovsky and his colleagues peddled new technologies to Soviet factories, imported personal computers, and sold French brandy. Leonid Nevzlin, who became his closest business associate, recalls that all this was done with the backing of the Communist Party: 'To a certain extent, Khodorkovsky was sent by the Komsomol and the party [into the private sector].'[12]

By 1987 Khodorkovsky's enterprises boasted many Soviet ministries as clients, employed 5,000 people, and enjoyed annual revenue of eighty million roubles. Later that year the Komsomol's central committee gave its organizations the authority to set up bank accounts and raise and spend their own money. Pouncing on this opportunity, the perspicacious Khodorkovsky set up Bank Menatep. The bank soon expanded and by 1990, a year before the fall of communism, it was even setting up offshore accounts, seven years before he hired the lawyer Stephen Curtis.

After Yeltsin came to power, Khodorkovsky soon came to appreciate the value of connections. He started courting senior bureaucrats and politicians, holding lavish receptions for high-level guests at top clubs in Moscow as well as at smart dachas owned by Menatep on the Rublevskoye Highway, the exclusive residential area to the west of the capital. By 1991, he was an adviser to the Russian Prime Minister Ivan Silaev. For a brief spell, he was a deputy fuel and energy minister.

One of Yeltsin's early market reforms was to end the Central Bank's monopoly of banking for government institutions. Those entrepreneurs who had already set up banks were well placed to take advantage of this relaxation of the rules. Russia then, as now, was a country where little happened unless a bribe was paid – *vzyat* or *kapusta* as it is called in Russian. In the case of the transfer of deposits, it was widely alleged that the banks that paid the biggest bribes to high-level politicians and state officials would receive the wealthiest new clients. And the payments were often deposited offshore. According to Bill Browder, an American banker who set up Hermitage Capital Management, one of the largest funds investing in Russia, 'These entrepreneurs would set up banks and in many cases would go to government ministers and say, you put the ministries on deposit in my bank and I'll put five or ten million bucks in a Swiss bank account with your name on it.'[13]

The paybacks offered entry into the highly lucrative business of handling state money. By 1994, Menatep was responsible for funds collected for the victims of the Chernobyl disaster of 1986 as well as the finances of Moscow's city government and the Ministry of Finance itself. At thirty-one and by now a multi-national tycoon, Khodorkovsky hired the accountancy firm Arthur Andersen to audit his books and spent $1 million on advertisements in the *New York Times* and the *Wall Street Journal*. His office was an imposing Victorian-style castle in central Moscow with huge bronze letters announcing its presence and surrounded by a tall wrought-iron fence with sharp spikes. The grounds swarmed with armed security guards, some in well-tailored suits, others in black uniforms and boots.

Flush with cash, Khodorkovsky was now able to target the industrial enterprises next in line to be sold off. It was the sale of the vast Siberian oil company Yukos, in what was a remarkably profitable deal that was to turn Khodorkovsky into a super-rich international tycoon. The process of transfer of vast state industries via the 'loans for shares' scheme was supposed to be handled by open auctions. In reality they were nothing of the sort. Only select bidders were invited to tender, and in many cases the auctions were actually controlled by the very people making the bids – sometimes using companies to disguise their identity.

In the case of Yukos, it was Khodorkovsky's Menatep that was in charge of processing the bids in the auction. In a hotly contested auction, higher bids were disqualified on 'technical grounds' and Khodorkovsky won the auction. In this way he and his partners acquired a 78 per cent stake in Yukos and 2 per cent of the world's oil reserves for a mere $309 million. When the shares began trading two years later in 1997, Yukos's market capitalization was worth thirty times that figure. One by one, the state's industrial conglomerates were being sold off at 'liquidation-sale prices' according to Strobe Talbott, former US Assistant Secretary of State.[14]

It was a pattern repeated in the other auctions. The Sibneft auction for example, was managed by NFK. In most cases there was ultimately only one bidder. In some instances the auction was not even won by the highest bidder.

The 'loans for shares' scheme turned many of the buyers from rouble multi-millionaires into dollar billionaires almost overnight. Initially, the lenders acquired only a proportion of the assets, but over the next couple of years the government also sold off the remaining tranches of shares in a series of lots, again without the competitive bids and auctions promised, and with the original lenders securing the remaining shares for themselves.

By now ordinary Russians had lost patience with the process of privatization. The economy was in tatters, few had benefited from the voucher fiasco, while many had ploughed their savings into schemes that had simply swallowed up their money. There was widespread disbelief that a few dozen political and business insiders were walking off with Russia's industrial and mineral wealth at cut prices. Disillusioned with the President and his policies, ordinary Russians began to exhibit a yearning for what they saw as the security and stability of communism. There was suddenly a real prospect that the shambolic, drunken Yeltsin would lose the forthcoming election in 1996 to the revitalized Communist Party candidate Gennady Zyuganov.

Opinion polls recorded Yeltsin's popularity at a derisory 6 per cent. 'It's all over,' said one American diplomat in Moscow. 'I'm getting ready for Yeltsin to go.'[15] Promising to stop the auctions for the remaining shares, Zyuganov fully intended to pursue the oligarchs. At the time the international investor and philanthropist George Soros, now one of the oligarchs' greatest critics, warned Berezovsky somewhat acidly that if the communists were to win, 'you are going to hang from a lamppost'.[16]

Berezovsky was only too aware that he had enemies among the communists. At a secret meeting in Davos in the Swiss Alps during the World Economic Forum in February 1996, he galvanized the wealthiest businessmen known in Russia as 'the Group of Seven'. They agreed to bankroll Yeltsin's election campaign in return for the offer of shares and management positions in the state industries yet to be privatized.

The seven parties privy to the 'Davos Pact' were mainly bankers – Mikhail Khodorkovsky, Vladimir Potanin, Alexander Smolensky, and Petr Aven, as well as media tycoon Vladimir Gusinsky, industrialist Mikhail Fridman, and, of course, Berezovsky himself.

Television was the key to the election campaign. The campaign was bankrolled through a secret fund known as the Black Treasury. Money was spent cultivating journalists and local political bosses. But most was used to pay for flattering documentaries of Yeltsin shown on private TV stations, billboards put up by local mayors, and even on pro-Yeltsin rock concerts. And Berezovsky brazenly used his ownership of Channel One, Russia's most powerful television network, to lionize Yeltsin and attack his communist opponent.

Central to the campaign were Western spin doctors. Tim (now Lord) Bell, the media guru who had helped Margaret Thatcher win three elections in Great Britain between 1979 and 1990, was hired. Bell had also worked closely with the campaign team responsible for California Governor Pete Wilson's remarkable comeback election victory in 1994, just two years earlier. In conditions of secrecy likened to protecting nuclear secrets, the American image consultants Dresner-Wickers moved into Suite 120 of the President Hotel in Moscow. 'Secrecy was paramount,' recalled Felix Braynin, a Yeltsin aide. 'Everyone realized that if the Communists knew about this before the election, they would attack Yeltsin as an American tool. We badly needed the team, but having them was a big risk.'[17]

Working closely with Yeltsin's influential daughter Tatyana (Tanya) Dyachenko, who was based next door in Room 119, the Americans were treated like royalty. They were paid $250,000 plus expenses and enjoyed an unlimited budget for polling, focus groups, and research. They were told that their rooms and phones were bugged and that they should leave the hotel as infrequently as possible.

The Americans suggested employing dirty tricks such as trailing Zyuganov with 'truth squads', which would heckle him and provoke him into losing his temper, but mostly they campaigned in a politically orthodox style. Photo opportunities and TV appearances were organized so as to appear spontaneous. Focus groups, direct mailing, and opinion polls were also widely employed, and the election message was hammered home repeatedly: 'Whatever it is that we are going to say and do, we have to repeat it between eight and twelve times,' said one of the American political consultants.[18]

Yeltsin proved to be an adept, populist campaigner. He smiled more and was even inspired to get on stage at a rock concert and do a few moves. From facing the political abyss, Yeltsin was re-elected with a 13 per cent lead. It was a staggering result and with it the newly enriched oligarchs had protected their fortunes and their power base. 'It was a battle for our blood interests,' acknowledged Berezovsky.[19]

The now all-powerful Berezovsky had proved a master manipulator. When asked about his influences, he rejected Machiavelli in preference to Lenin. 'Not as an ideologue,' he remarked, 'but as a tactician in political struggle. Nobody had better perception of what was possible ... Lenin understood the psychology of society.'[20]

It was now payback time and Yeltsin kept his part of the deal: some oligarchs received huge new government accounts, bought more state assets on the cheap, and paid only minimal taxes. In his memoirs, Strobe Talbott described the deal in the run-up to the presidential elections as a 'Faustian bargain in which Yeltsin sold the soul of reform'. But the Russians replied that the favour they were doing the oligarchs was nowhere near as bad as the communist victory it helped to avert. As they saw it, unlike Dr Faustus who made a pact with the Devil that guaranteed his damnation, Yeltsin had made an accommodation with what he was convinced was the lesser of two evils – a deal that would help Russia avoid the real damnation of a return to power by the communists.'[21]

Some of the oligarchs, notably Abramovich and Berezovsky, formed a coterie around Yeltsin that became known as the 'family'. The leading member of the 'family' – and the gatekeeper to the President – was Yeltsin's youngest and much loved daughter, Tatyana. Despite having no knowledge of business or political affairs, she was his most influential adviser, could secure special favours from the state, and became very rich in her own right. The friendship between the two oligarchs and the President's daughter blossomed. According to Aleksandr Korzhakov, Berezovsky lavished Tatyana with presents of jewellery and cars, notably a Niva (a Russian version of a Jeep). 'The vehicle was customized to include a special stereo system, air-conditioning and alarm system, and luxury interior. When the Niva broke down, Berezovsky immediately gave her a Chevrolet Blazer [a sports utility vehicle then worth $50,000].'[22]

According to Strobe Talbott, 'Berezovsky's close ties to Yeltsin's daughter Tatyana earned him a reputation as a modern-day Rasputin … At the height of Berezovsky's influence, when his name came up in people's offices in Moscow – including near the Kremlin – my hosts would sometimes point to the walls and start whispering or even, in a couple of cases, scribble notes to me. This was a practice I had not seen since the Brezhnev era in furtive encounters with dissident intellectuals.'[23]

If Berezovsky was the dominant uncle of the 'family', Abramovich was the quiet but precocious nephew who had a talent for charming the most important member – Tatyana. One TV executive, Igor Malashenko, was stunned by the young oil trader's access: 'I arrived one night at Tanya's dacha and here was this young guy, unshaven and in jeans, unloading French wine, very good wine, from his car, stocking the fridge, making shashlik. I thought to myself, "They've got a new cook". But when I asked Yumashev [Tanya's husband], he laughed and said, "Oh no, that's Roman". He's living with us while his dacha is being renovated.'[24]

In October 1996 Berezovsky was at the height of his power and was made Deputy Secretary of the country's National Security Council – with responsibility for resolving the Chechnya conflict. (The first Chechen war began in 1994 when Chechnya tried to break away from the Russian Federation. Yeltsin's government argued forcibly that Chechnya had never been an independent entity within the Soviet Union. The ensuing bitter struggle was disastrous for both sides.) A whirlwind of energy, Berezovsky was a frequent visitor to the cabinet offices of the Kremlin, clutching a worn leather briefcase in one hand and a new huge grey Motorola mobile phone in the other. While he waited to see Yeltsin, his phone would constantly ring. 'Cannot talk. In Kremlin', he would respond in his rapid-fire speech. Berezovsky wore officials down with his ceaseless networking and lobbying. When government ATS hotlines were installed in the guesthouse of his office at LogoVaz and his dacha at Alexandrovka, the telephone calls became even more frenzied.

In many ways such crony capitalism had much in common with the worst features of the Soviet era. For a while Berezovsky and his colleagues functioned like a politburo: conducting backroom deals behind the scenes, secretly conspiring with and against each other, just as the senior apparatchiks had done under communism. As one prime minister was replaced with another, Berezovsky would hand the incoming leader pieces of paper bearing the names of the ministers he wanted in the new government. The oligarchs now viewed the world through the prism of their personal interests. 'It is my fundamental belief that, leaving aside the abstract concept of the interests of the people, government should represent the interests of business,' he admitted.[25]

Nevertheless, Yeltsin's circle was not immune from outside pressure. At one point the independent prosecutor-general, Yuri Skuratov, started an investigation within the Kremlin itself. Yeltsin promptly sacked him, but Skuratov refused to quit and the Russian Federation Council twice refused to ratify his dismissal. Some years later, in 1999, the FSB was tasked with discrediting him. In a classic KGB-style entrapment, ORT broadcast a short, grainy video of 'a man resembling' Skuratov apparently romping with two prostitutes. It was never clear if it was Skuratov or not but, nonetheless, that was the end of him.[26]

By 1998, Russia was bankrupt. Shares nose dived, interest rates had reached 150 per cent, and bankruptcies soared. By August of that year, one analyst noted: 'Russia's credit rating is below Indonesia's. The size of its economy is smaller than Switzerland's. And its stock market is worth less than the UK water industry.'[27]

Throughout this turmoil, the genuine political influence of the business elite was forever being exaggerated, not least by themselves. They had become so rich so quickly that they were suffering from what Stalin used to call 'dizziness with success'. Their influence quickly began to wane after 1997.[28] Berezovsky was dismissed from the Security Council, although a few months later he returned as the Executive Secretary of the Confederation of Independent States, which involved coordinating the individual parts of the Russian Federation. None of this either undermined his personal fortune or prevented him from continuing to plot the future of Russia.

The oligarchs and their associates were not the only Russians making a killing out of the transition from communism to capitalism and who later started showering London with money. Among the other winners were the 'red directors'. The property agent who ran the Russian desk at the London estate agents Savills, remembers an older Russian client, aged about sixty-five, who owned a chemicals factory. One of the 'red directors', he was looking to spend several million pounds on a property in London in 2002. Despite his wealth, he was still nostalgic for the communist system that had once served people like him so well. Having been shown around an apartment, he asked, quite out of the blue, where Karl Marx was buried. A short time later he visited Highgate Cemetery. He clearly had much to thank the intellectual father of the Soviet state for.

During the 1990s, Russia was a place where shrewd business operators played fast and loose with the country's fledgling market economy. With no regulatory infrastructure to ensure a smooth, efficient – and legal – transition, it was a goldmine for clever, aggressive operators.

Nothing illustrates the forces at work more graphically than the case of aluminium. The control for this lucrative mineral became the subject of a seven-year long bitter and deadly struggle that became known as the aluminium wars. It left a trail of bloodshed that gave Siberia its reputation as the 'Wild East'.

One of those to emerge triumphant in the battle for aluminium was Oleg Deripaska, although his route to wealth differed from that of the other oligarchs. He was a 23-year-old student when the Soviet Union collapsed in 1991, but by 1994 had made big money from trading in metal. Unlike the other oligarchs, Deripaska did not acquire his fortune through the privatization auctions or via political connections. His control of the aluminium industry was largely due to the way in which he outmuscled and outwitted his competitors and his prowess with the hostile takeover. Deripaska was a post-Soviet corporate raider, borrowing from techniques pioneered by American and British tycoons, notably Sir James Goldsmith.

In person, Deripaska, tall with cropped blond hair and deep blue eyes, is deceptive, a man of few words. Negotiations were more like poker or chess than orthodox business deals. He shared many of the characteristics of his friend Roman Abramovich – externally reserved and even more boyish-looking. Despite appearances, however, Deripaska was a serious operator with nerves of steel. The editor of Russia's *Finans* business magazine once described him as 'A very harsh person. Without that quality it would have been impossible to build up so much wealth.'[29]

Like Abramovich, Deripaska also became a member of the Yeltsin 'family' – but more directly. In 2001 he married Polina Yumashev, daughter of Yeltsin's chief of staff, who was himself married to Yeltsin's daughter, Tatyana. Deripaska first met Polina at Abramovich's house. Their wedding was the social event of the year in Russia and they soon had two children. Like Abramovich, Deripaska arranged for one of the children to be born in London and employed a British nanny. It was a smart, some say strategic, marriage because, after Yeltsin left office in 2000, President Putin's first Presidential Decree granted immunity from criminal prosecution to Yeltsin and all his relatives, a move seen by many as a *quid pro quo* for his backing.

Oleg Vladimirovich Deripaska was born on 2 January 1968 in Dzerzhinsk, 400 kilometres east of Moscow and at the heart of the Russian chemicals industry (the city was named in honour of the first head of the Soviet secret police). His father died when he was only four and he was brought up by his grandparents on a traditional Cossack family farm in Krasnodar, southwestern Russia.

Although Deripaska's parents were Jewish, he was more conscious of his Cossack heritage. 'We are Cossacks of the Russian Federation,' he later said. 'We are always prepared for war. This is a question of being able to deal with problems and any situation. It is the case that difficulties are not a catastrophe.'[30] A serious and studious teenager, he was accepted, despite his humble origins, into Moscow State University to study quantum physics. However, before he started his course, he was called up to serve in the army and was stationed on a barren steppe on the border with China.

Despite his raw intelligence, times were hard for the young student. Following national service, he returned home to find the country on the brink of collapse and he worked on building sites across Russia. There seemed to be little future in quantum physics and so he abandoned his studies. His first job was in 1992 as a director of a company that sold military hardware following the withdrawal of Russian forces from East Germany. He then worked as a metals trader in Moscow, before deciding to concentrate on the aluminium industry.

At the time the industry was dominated by the brothers Mikhail and Lev Cherney. Born in Tashkent, the brothers grew up in Uzbekistan and, through exploiting the opportunities created by the introduction of a free market, had, by the early 1990s, already built up a substantial business manufacturing and exporting coal and metal. By late 1993, the businessmen held majority stakes in Russia's largest aluminium smelters, but then Mikhail Cherney's name was tarnished by allegations in the Russian press of controversial business methods, claims that he strongly denied as smears peddled by his business and political enemies. Despite a series of allegations by international law enforcement agencies, Mikhail Cherney has never been convicted of any crime. By 1994, he had settled in Israel and ran his business empire from there.

That year Mikhail Cherney – now calling himself Michael – gave the then 26-year-old Deripaska his first big break, hiring him to run one of his giant smelters – the Sayanogorsky aluminium plant, the largest in the republic of Khakassia. Dedicated and technically brilliant, Deripaska increased production and somehow persuaded the impoverished workforce not to strike. But he was also a neurotic, paranoid manager and trusted no one. He suffered from hypertension and his brain rarely switched off. He hardly slept and, when he did, would wake in the early hours and visit factories and work on some new technology or other. He loved concentrating on the tiny, often petty, technical details of the business and on commercial contracts.

In the endless political and business power struggles of the time, Deripaska soon came into conflict with the local mafia.

The Sayanogorsky plant was threatened by raids by armed gangs determined to seize control, and he received constant death threats, on more than one occasion coming within a whisker of being a victim of the bloodshed himself. Sometimes he even slept by his furnaces on the factory floor to protect them from being taken over by mobsters. He survived, and saw off the criminal syndicates at work within the industry.

During this period, Deripaska showed remarkable acumen, some say genius, in wresting control from the gangs of mercenary local officials and brutal competitors. This earned him a certain legitimacy and respect among his peers. By 1999 – in less than five years – he had risen from being one of Cherney's lowly subordinates to being his business equal. Over the next three years, Deripaska bought out all his remaining rivals, including Cherney himself, to emerge as the sole owner of Rusal, the giant aluminium corporation. In less than a decade, Deripaska, the student of quantum physics and former manager of a smelting works, had risen to control the entire aluminium industry. Even by the standards of 1990s Russia, his was a meteoric rise, but one dogged by bitter division and dispute.

Russia in the 1990s witnessed a transfer of wealth of epic proportions. What happened there could be seen as the equivalent of Margaret Thatcher deciding to sell all Britain's nationalized industries, from British Gas to British Telecom, for a fraction of their real value to a handful of her favourite tycoons who had donated money to the Conservative Party.

Some of the beneficiaries liked to defend their activities by comparing themselves to the nineteenth-century industrial and financial tycoons such as John D. Rockefeller, J. P. Morgan, and Cornelius Vanderbilt, who built massive fortunes out of oil, finance, and the railroads in the United States in the late nineteenth and early twentieth centuries. Rockefeller, Morgan, and Vanderbilt were dubbed the 'robber barons' for their ruthless and exploitative tactics. Khodorkovsky once described his hero, 'if he had one', as John D. Rockefeller, the founding father of the American oil industry and the world's first billionaire. But Rockefeller's business methods also became so unpopular that towards the end of his life he was known by his staff as the 'most hated man in America'.

Many of the oligarchs evoked similar reactions among the Russian people. Whatever their business records, the American robber barons devoted their lives to building their giant monopolies in oil, railroads, and steel from scratch. The modern Russian oligarchs have no such defence. Few of them laid the pipelines, built the factories, assembled the rigs, or even took the necessary financial and commercial risks. Few created new wealth. Few of them knew much about the industries that landed in their laps. When Khodorkovsky acquired Yukos and went to visit one of its main sites, his host was astonished to discover that he had never seen an oil field before. The oligarchs acquired their fortunes by manipulating the system with a mixture of bare-knuckle tactics and political patronage. While the robber barons reinvested their money at home, the oligarchs moved much of their acquired wealth out of the country.

Successive studies have confirmed the impact of the scale of personal enrichment on the concentration of economic owner-ship in Russia. One found that in 2001 Russia's top-twelve privatized companies had revenues that were the equivalent of the entire federal budget. Of Russia's sixty-four largest private companies, just eight oligarch groups controlled 85 per cent of their revenues.[31]

There were alternatives. It was Western leaders and financial institutions that rejected a Marshall Plan for Russia, such as the one for a social cushion advocated by George Soros. Jeffrey Sachs, the influential American economist and one of the key architects of the push for the 'big bang' approach – the privatization of the economy at speed – later admitted that when he suggested such a plan to the White House, 'there was absolutely no interest at all. None, and the IMF just stared me down like I was crazy.'[32] Instead, the Yeltsin government was pressed to move forward with 'big bang' regardless of its economic and human consequences. Those in power at the time argue that all the options for political and economic transition from communism carried high risks. But then the West's top priority was to create a malleable and compliant country offering cheap oil and no return to its past Soviet system. Other considerations were secondary.

The Western advisers knew that such a long-standing form of government based on corruption and authoritarianism could not be reformed overnight, not least in a country where the ownership of private property had been a crime for the past seventy-five years. But as Professor Michael Hudson, a Wall Street financial economist, observed: 'Was there really not a middle ground? Did Russia have no choice between "wild capitalism" at one extreme and the old Soviet bureaucracy at the other? Both systems were beginning to look suspiciously similar. Both had their black-market economies and respective dynamics of economic polarization.'[33]

Some commentators argue that the emergence of an oligarchic class was inevitable, others that the creation of an economic elite was necessary for a quick transition to capitalism. Yet others claim that in replacing the old corrupt and incompetent command and control system it was even desirable. Berezovsky later defended his own activities as the inevitable result of capitalism. 'I don't know any example where property is split in a fair way,' he said. 'It doesn't matter how property is split. Everyone will not be happy.' But he also admitted making 'billions' out of privatization and that Yeltsin 'gave us the chance to be rich'.[34]

Inevitable or desirable, the social cost to Russia was immense. The broad consensus is that the privatization process was one of the most flawed economic reforms in modern history. Industrial production declined by some 60 per cent during the 1990s, vast swathes of the economy were wiped out, and much of the population was plunged into poverty. The vast amount of money that poured out of Russia to be hidden away in offshore bank accounts accentuated the dramatic economic crisis of 1998. During the 1990s, what was known as 'capital flight' became one of the country's most debilitating economic problems. According to economists at Florida International University, 'It erodes the country's tax base, increases the public deficit, reduces domestic investment and destabilises financial markets.'[35]

The investment fund Hermitage Capital has estimated that between 1998 and 2004, £56 billion in capital flowed out of Russia, most ending up offshore. Although some of this was legitimate, with investors looking for a safer home than a Russian bank, most was not. Russia's Economic Development and Trade Ministry says that between $210 and $230 billion left Russia during the reforms, approximately half of which was 'dirty' money, linked to money laundering or organized crime. The IMF's estimate is that $170 billion escaped the country in the seven years leading up to 2001. Other sources suggest that around $300 billion of assets in the West belong to Russian citizens, almost half from 'uncertain' sources.[36]

This was money that could have been used to rebuild factories, start new businesses at home, and invest in infrastructure. In effect, Russia lost the equivalent of one-third of its gross foreign debt in this way. Although there was legislation designed to prevent such capital flight, it was largely ignored. By 2000, privatization had rendered a once mighty country, which spans eleven time zones, rotten to the core, according to the *New York Times* columnist Thomas Friedman: 'At every level, different ministries, department heads, agencies and mayoralties have gone into partnership with private businesses, local oligarchs or criminal elements, creating a kind of 21st-century Russian feudalism.' Friedman quoted the Russian political analyst Sergei Markov: 'The Russian state looks like a big Charles Atlas, full of muscles. But as you get closer you realize that this Atlas is actually dead. Inside, this huge body is full of worms who are eating the body and feeding off it.'[37]

As well as the oligarchs and the 'red directors', others were moving their money abroad during the 1990s. Though some of them were small players who simply didn't trust the banks, most were wealthy, criminal, or members of the KBG – renamed the FSB (the Federal Security Service) in 1992. Some of the proceeds of crime were laundered through purchasing buildings, bars, and restaurants in Eastern Europe, but much of it ended up swirling around London's nightclubs and casinos. Some passed through British banks.[38]

The money often arrived in the form of hard cash, and stories of recent émigrés turning up with suitcases full of banknotes in the 1990s are legion within the Russian community in London. One small-time British property agent who used to socialize in a nightclub frequented by the Russians told of how he had been introduced to a young woman who happened to be the daughter of a senior FSB official. When she discovered he dealt in property, she asked if she could come and see him the next day. When she arrived at his office, he noticed that the woman was carrying a revolver in her coat pocket. When he asked how she would be paying, she explained that it would be by cash, literally. She opened up a large case stuffed with banknotes. The agent thanked her and politely asked her to take her business elsewhere.

Whether they were buying property, jewellery, or cars, payment was often by cash. Mikhail Ignatief, who arrived in London in 1991 at the age of twenty-one with his English fiancée, set up a successful travel business and used to help and advise Russians on shopping or business trips. He remembered one client asking his help to buy a Range Rover and arranged for one of his team to take him to the nearest showrooms. The client was shown around and said he wanted three cars, all to be shipped back to Russia. He then opened up a large leather bag stuffed with banknotes. A somewhat concerned manager called the police and the matter was only settled when the man was persuaded to go to a bank, deposit the money, and then pay by cheque.

The privatization process of the 1990s that led to London being awash with Russian money had no shortage of critics in and outside of Russia. Chrystia Freeland, the former Moscow bureau chief of the *Financial Times*, described the events as 'a cynical manipulation of a weakened state … Yet as I watched them plot and profit, I couldn't help asking myself how different the Russians really were from our own hero-entrepreneurs … our society so fawningly lauds for producing an era of unprecedented prosperity … The future oligarchs did what any red-blooded businessman would do. The real problem was that the state allowed them to get away with it.'[39] In his influential book, *Failed Crusade*, Stephen F. Cohen, Professor of Russian Studies at New York University, called US policy towards Russia in the 1990s 'the worst American foreign policy disaster since Vietnam'.[40]

One of the architects of privatization, Vladimir Potanin, later accepted its flawed nature: 'Although I do not deny I was the author, I would like to point out that the concept was changed to a great extent as a result of political pressure on government from the red directors … The government allowed no access to foreign investors and other measures. This was later criticised and rightly so.'[41] In October 1993 a reflective Khodorkovsky told *Frontline*, the American news programme: 'Russian law allowed us to do things that were unthinkable in the Western business world.'

Even at the time advocates of privatization accepted that huge mistakes were made. In 1998 Boris Nemtsov, one of the young reformers who was once seen as a potential successor to Yeltsin, said, 'The country is built as a freakish, oligarchic capitalist state. Its characteristics are the concentration of property in the hands of a narrow group of financiers, the oligarchs. Many of them operate inefficiently, having a parasitic relationship to the industries they control.'[42]

By 1999, the oligarchs' priority was to protect their power and wealth and to ensure a successor to Yeltsin who would be as compliant as he had been. 'The problem was that a lot of the people who had the potential to lead Russia were themselves up to their necks in relationships with these people,' observed William Wechsler, a US National Security Council and Treasury official. 'The fear was that Russia would become like a nuclear-armed Colombia. That prospect was terrifying but to me it was real … Then along comes Putin from the KGB, which was obviously not clean. In the subsequent fight between Putin and the oligarchs, everyone was saying it was a good-guy-bad-guy situation. To me, this was a bad-guy-bad-guy situation.'

CHAPTER 3

Putin's Purge

'Boris, if you go down this road, I predict in a year's time you
will be in exile … or worse, sitting in jail'
— ALEX GOLDFARB *to Boris Berezovsky*[1]

IN 1722, IN ORDER to transform the country from a disparate
medieval society into a centralized autocratic state, Peter the
Great set about purging the corruption that was endemic in
Russian society. This included the elimination of everyone who
took bribes. One of those targeted was Aleksandr Menshikov,
his most successful general and the most powerful man after the
Tsar himself. Menshikov was horrified. 'If you do, Your Majesty,
you risk not having a single subject left', he told his monarch.[2]

When Vladimir Putin became President in 2000, he had less
latitude than Peter the Great, who simply executed his more
recalcitrant subjects. Even modern Russia's arbitrary judicial
system would not sanction summary executions of avaricious
businessmen. Putin, who knew his history, would therefore
have to come up with a different strategy to deal with a group he
viewed as a major obstacle to his ambitions for the reshaping of
Russia.

While there were whispers of a clampdown, the oligarchs
believed they would retain their power and luxurious lifestyles
and remain a protected species. After all, theirs was a cabal of

the business elite who had engineered the new President's ascendancy. Just as the oligarchs had connived and conspired to re-elect Yeltsin in 1996, so a group of them manipulated Putin into the Kremlin. In return for their backing, they expected Putin to be as malleable as his predecessor, allowing them to continue to exert influence, accumulate wealth, and be immune from prosecution. They badly misjudged him.

While Putin was Acting President and Prime Minister in 1999, there were signs of trouble to come, when the Prosecutor-General reviewed the way in which Vladimir Potanin, one of the architects of privatization, had acquired Norilsk Nickel, the giant state-owned mining group. 'They were certainly feeling uncomfortable,' said one government official. And with good reason. Within two months of becoming President, on the baking hot day of 28 July 2000, Putin summoned twenty-one oligarchs to the Kremlin. 'It was more like a gathering ordered by Don Corleone than a meeting summoned by a leader of the Western world,' noted one who was present.[3] Khodorkovsky and Deripaska were both at the gathering but Berezovsky, now himself under investigation by the prosecutors, was not invited.

Before those assembled in the cabinet room, Putin effectively read Russia's richest and most powerful business clique the riot act. He would not review the privatizations but they would no longer enjoy special privileges inside the Kremlin. During the meeting, Putin insisted that Potanin pay the $140 million he was alleged to owe on the purchase of Norilsk Nickel. At times the meeting became heated and at one stage the President pointed at a well-known tycoon and accused him of being guilty of '*oligophrenia*' (which means 'mental retardation'). The plutocrats were stunned. It was not the script they had been expecting.

The new confrontational President concluded the meeting – which lasted two hours and forty minutes – by setting up a permanent mechanism for consultations between businessmen and the state. The days of cliques and coteries were gone, he warned. Now the relationship was to be institutionalized. Access to Putin would be restricted through quarterly meetings with the Russian Union of Industrialists and Entrepreneurs – in effect, the oligarchs' trade union.

Putin's message to the shocked gathering was simple: they could keep their ill-gotten gains provided they kept out of politics and paid their taxes. The details of the meeting were promptly leaked so that in a poll a week later 57 per cent of Russians said they already knew about it. Berezovsky, omitted from the gathering, accused those present of being cowardly. 'They are as timid as rabbits,' he sniffed after the meeting.[4]

This was a watershed moment in the story of the oligarchs and an event that was to prompt the steady exodus to London of one wave of super-rich Russians after another. Those present knew only too well that the tide had turned. In case they were in any doubt, Putin used his State of the Nation address on July 8 to condemn the ambitious tycoons and especially the way they controlled the media. 'They want to influence the masses and show the political leadership that we need them, that they have us hooked, that we should be afraid of them,' he declared. 'Russia can no longer tolerate shadowy groups that divert money abroad and hire their own dubious security services.' He later added, 'We have a category of people who have become billionaires overnight. The state appointed them as billionaires. It simply gave out a huge amount of property, practically for free. They said it themselves: "I was appointed a billionaire." They get the impression that the gods themselves slept on their heads, that everything is permitted to them.'[5]

The oligarchs, blinded by their own power and influence, had greatly underestimated the sardonic but humourless Putin. In public the new President was a cold, unsmiling bureaucrat. Apart from periodic outbursts of aggression, he rarely displayed emotion. Russian journalist Elena Tregubova says that when she first interviewed Putin in May 1997, she found him a 'barely noticeable, boring little grey man ... who seemed to disappear, artfully merging with the colours of his office'.[6] As is so often the case with autocrats, people seemed to be preoccupied with his eyes, 'No one is born with a stare like Vladimir Putin's,' reported *Time* magazine. 'The Russian President's pale blue eyes are so cool, so devoid of emotion that the stare must have begun as an effect, the gesture of someone who understood that power might be achieved by the suppression of ordinary needs ...'[7]

In private his aides say that the intense and brooding Putin is intelligent, honest, intensely loyal, and patriotic. 'He smiled a lot, his body language was relaxed and informal, his eyes were soft, and his speech quiet,' reflected British author John Laughland.[8] In stark contrast to his predecessor, he drinks Diet Coke and works out regularly. He is also able to relax, notably by listening to classical composers such as Brahms, Mozart, and Tchaikovsky. His favourite Beatles song is *Yesterday*. He has never sent an e-mail in his life, and, while he grew up in an officially atheist country, he believes in God.

When Vladimir Vladimirovich Putin was born in 1952, his 41-year-old mother Maria, a devout Orthodox Christian, defied the official state atheism and had him baptized. She had little education and did menial jobs – from a night-security guard to a glass washer in a laboratory. His father Vladimir fought in the Second World War and was badly wounded in one leg. After the war, he worked as a lathe operator in a car factory and was ferociously strict with his son. Putin's only forebear of any note was his paternal grandfather, who had served as a cook to both Lenin and Stalin.

The family lived in a fifth-floor communal apartment at 15 Baskov Lane in central St Petersburg, where the young Putin had to step over the rats in the entrance to the apartment block on his way to school. Universally known as 'Volodya', he was a serious, hard-working, but often angry child. His former school friends and teachers describe him as a frail but temperamental boy who never hesitated to challenge stronger kids. He has described himself as having been a poor student and a hooligan. 'I was educated on the street,' he told a biographer. 'To live and be educated on the street is just like living in the jungle. I was disobedient and didn't follow school rules.'[9]

Putin found discipline by learning 'sambo', a Soviet-era combination of judo and wrestling, at the age of twelve. It places a premium on quick moves, a calm demeanour, and an ability to not show any emotion or make a sound. A black belt, he won several inter-city competitions. Initially, he practised the sport so as to build up his slender physique and to be able to stand up for himself in fights, but his developing obsession with the sport not only kept him out of trouble, it also made him somewhat reclusive.

Meanwhile, the teenage Putin dreamed of becoming a KGB spy like the Soviet heroes portrayed in books and films. His favourite television programme was *Seventeen Moments of Spring*, a series about a Soviet spy operating in Nazi Germany. In his ninth year at school he visited the KGB headquarters in Leningrad. Told that the best way to get into the service was to obtain a law degree, in 1970 the aspiring agent enrolled at Leningrad State University, where he studied law and German and practised judo.

In 1975, his final year at university, he was recruited by the KGB. Posted to Leningrad, he spent seven uneventful years in counter-intelligence. At the age of thirty, he married Lyudmila Aleksandrovna, then twenty-two, an outspoken, energetic air stewardess, and the couple had two daughters. He was next posted to Dresden in East Germany, where he worked closely with the Stasi, the secret police, in political intelligence and counter-espionage. It was an isolated life and not a prestigious posting. More favoured agents worked in Western capitals, or at least in East Berlin. But his perseverance brought him the nick-name '*Nachalnik*' (Russian for boss or chief).

When the Berlin Wall came down in 1989, Putin and his KGB colleagues destroyed files in the KGB's Dresden HQ. He remembers calling Moscow for orders. 'Moscow kept silent,' he said later. 'It was as if the country no longer existed.' In 1990 Lieutenant Colonel Putin retired from active KGB service and became Assistant Rector in charge of foreign relations at Leningrad State University, a significant reduction in status. 'It was even less important than working for Intourist,' said Oleg Kalugin, a former official in the Leningrad KGB. 'This was a KGB cover rather than a career move. Putin was demobilized into the KGB reserve.'[10]

By this time, his former judo tutor Anatoly Sobchak had become the first democratically elected mayor of St Petersburg and he immediately recruited Putin as Chairman of the City Council's International Relations Committee. By 1994, a year after his wife suffered a serious spinal injury in a car crash, Putin became First Deputy Mayor, gaining a reputation for probity and an ascetic lifestyle. Even his bitter enemy Berezovsky admits that his future nemesis was not corrupt: 'He was the first bureaucrat that I met who did not ask for some money and he was absolutely professional.'[11]

In June 1996 Mayor Sobchak, having failed to address the economic crisis and rising levels of crime, lost his bid for re-election. His successor offered to keep Putin on but he declined and resigned out of loyalty to his former boss. Now unemployed in St Petersberg, he moved to Moscow where he became Deputy Chief of the presidential staff, overseeing the work of the provincial governments. Tough, aloof, and relentlessly focused, he was renowned for his industriousness and severity.

In contrast to the wild, erratic Yeltsin, Putin was the solid, reliable apparatchik. Impressed by his honesty, diligence, and loyalty, by June 1998 Yeltsin was beginning to see him as a potential FSB Director. The following month the current incumbent Nikolai Kovalev was forced to resign over an internal scandal, whereupon Putin received a sudden summons to meet Prime Minister Kirienko at Moscow's Sheremetyevo Airport. After they shook hands, Kirienko offered Putin his congratulations. When Putin asked why, he replied, 'The decree is signed. You have been appointed director of the FSB.'[12]

Within days, Putin had purged the FSB of potential enemies, firing nearly a dozen senior officials and replacing them with loyal subordinates. Many of these came from the 'Chekists', the clan of agents based in St Petersburg when Putin was the director there, and named after the brutal early Soviet-era 'Cheka', or secret police. One man who welcomed his appointment was Berezovsky. At this point their interests coincided: Putin needed political allies and the oligarch was rid of at least one enemy, the spymaster Kovalev, who had been leaking damaging stories about his business methods. By 1998, Berezovsky had lost his post at the National Security Council and much of his former influence at the centre of power and saw the security apparatus – which mostly resented the rise of the oligarchs – as a real threat. To survive in the feral atmosphere of Russian politics, Berezovsky needed new, powerful allies and was delighted when Putin was appointed over more senior KGB figures. 'I support him 100 per cent,' he said.[13]

But within a few months, another cloud appeared on Berezovsky's horizon: the appointment of a new hardline Prime Minister, Yevgeny Primakov, former head of foreign intelligence. The timing was especially bad for Berezovsky. Ordinary citizens blamed the oligarchs for bankrupting the economy, Yeltsin was mentally and physically in decline, and, amid the tensions and continuing jockeying for position that dominated Yeltsin's second term, Berezovsky's power base was slipping further away. When the calculating but now vulnerable Berezovsky realized that the Yeltsin 'family' was warming to Putin, he swung his own media empire behind the new FSB boss, later leading the cabal that backed him as Prime Minister. In return, he expected Putin to be both compliant and loyal.

Berezovsky now began courting Putin, once even inviting him on a five-day skiing holiday in Switzerland. The two became friends. On one occasion Putin called Berezovsky 'the brother he never had'. On 22 February 1999 – by which point state investigations into his business empire had already been launched – Berezovsky threw a birthday party for his new partner, Yelena Gorbunova. The party was intended to be a small, private gathering, but Putin turned up uninvited with a huge bouquet of roses. This appeared to be a genuine act of solidarity towards Berezovsky because they shared a common enemy in the form of Prime Minister Primakov, a man who disliked Putin because he had been chosen to head the FSB over the Prime Minister's far more senior colleagues.

In July 1999 Berezovsky flew to France, where Putin was staying in Biarritz with his wife and daughters. By this time, Primakov himself had been dismissed by Yeltsin and replaced with an interim Prime Minister, Sergei Stepashin. The two men met for lunch and Berezovsky, now sidelined but still well informed about Kremlin politicking, told Putin that Yeltsin was about to appoint him Prime Minister. The following month, as predicted, Yeltsin dismissed Stepashin and appointed Putin. He was Yeltsin's fifth Prime Minister in seventeen months.

At first Putin was deeply unpopular, with an approval rating of only 5 per cent, mainly because of his association with the despised figures of Yeltsin and Berezovsky. What turned his fortunes was a series of devastating Moscow apartment bombings in September that led to 246 deaths. Political enemies of Putin later alleged that the bombings were deliberately engineered by the state to turn the public mood and justify the latest attacks on Chechnya. Whether or not the Chechens were indeed the perpetrators of the outrages, Putin responded aggressively, first bombing Chechnya and then initiating a land invasion. Militarism played well with the Russian people and the Prime Minister's popularity soared.

Putin's newly formed Unity Party took 23 per cent of the vote in the Duma elections in December 1999, compared with 13 per cent by Primakov's Fatherland All-Russia Party. Yeltsin, now close to the end of his presidency, capitalized on the new popularity and offered the top post to Putin. When asked to take the reins, Putin initially declined, but Yeltsin was persistent. 'Don't say no,' he pressed. Berezovsky also urged him to accept. In his New Year's Eve address in 1999 Yeltsin famously announced his resignation and Putin's appointment as interim President. This gave him the advantage of being able to campaign as an incumbent President. Three months later, in the 2000 presidential election, Putin took a remarkable 53 per cent of the vote. Kremlin watchers satirized his success, comparing it to Chauncey Gardiner's unwitting rise to power as President of the United States in Jerzy Kosinski's 1971 novel *Being There*. Berezovsky, who had continued to use the media to publicly declare his support for the way that he believed Putin would run Russia, expressed delight.

Putin's dramatic decision to take on the oligarchs within weeks of coming to power had been carefully planned. He knew he had to stem the disastrous outflow of capital and quickly encouraged the authorities to toughen up on the collection of taxes. He had come to two conclusions about the oligarchs. First, as Yeltsin had also discovered, the oligarchs had the potential to be as – if not more – powerful than the President himself. Second, because the vast majority of ordinary Russians loathed them, Putin knew there would be a beneficial political dividend in being seen to take them on.

Some oligarchs certainly had no shortage of enemies, among them the senior ranks of the security apparatus whose power had ebbed away during the Yeltsin years. They resented the way that these tycoons had sapped their own political strength and reaped a vast financial windfall. They saw them as upstarts. Few of them had served as senior officials during the Soviet era and they were viewed as outsiders. When Putin, so recently the head of the FSB, came to power, the security and intelligence apparatchiks, especially the 'Chekists', returned to favour. Of the President's first twenty-four high-level appointments, ten were drawn from the ranks of the old KGB. This group, known as the *siloviki* – individuals with backgrounds in the security and military services – now saw their chance for revenge. 'A group of FSB operatives, dispatched undercover to work in the Russian government, is successfully fulfilling its task,' said the new President. He was only half joking.[14]

Putin also had a powerful collective ally in the Russian people. While the oligarchs enriched themselves, by the end of the 1990s the government could claim that as many as 35 per cent of Russians lived below the official poverty line.[15] Many felt that the nation's resources had been sucked dry by what Karl Marx had referred to as 'Vampire Capitalism', whereby 'the vampire will not let go while there remains a single muscle, sinew, or drop of blood to be exploited'.

To show how they feel, Russians love to tell popular jokes to foreign visitors. 'A group of "new Russian" businessmen were meeting in a posh Moscow restaurant where the décor was of a very high standard. A waiter showed them to their tables and pointed out that the table was made of very expensive marble and that they should put nothing heavy on it, such as a briefcase. He went away to get vodkas and when he returned he was horrified to see a bulging briefcase lying on the table. 'I thought I told you not to put briefcases on the table,' he said. The man replied, 'That's not my briefcase. It's my wallet.'

The oligarchs were only too aware of the widespread resentment. As Anatoly Chubais, Yeltsin's Privatization Minister and chief political architect of the giant giveaways in the mid-1990s, acknowledged, 'Forty million Russians are convinced that I am a scoundrel, a thief, a criminal, or a CIA agent, who deserves to be shot, hanged, or drawn and quartered'.[16]

Putin wasted no time in waging war on the oligarchs. But human rights activists accused him of manipulating the judicial process against businessmen to suit his political interests. They claim that the President has steadily taken control of the judiciary by controlling the appointment of judges. For Putin it was a power struggle and the state needed to reinstate its supremacy. His reputation for ruthlessness was typified by another Russian joke: Stalin's ghost appears to Putin in a dream in which he asks for his help in running the country. Stalin advises, 'Round up and shoot all the democrats, and then paint the inside of the Kremlin blue. 'Why blue?' Putin asks. 'Ha,' replies Stalin. 'I knew you wouldn't ask me about the first part.'

The President's first target was Vladimir Gusinsky, who had made money in the early days of perestroika by promising extravagant rates of return on investors' money and was one of the first of the dynamic young wheeler-dealers to build a fortune off the back of the transition to capitalism. He also built a substantial media empire, including the first private national television network, NTV, a daily newspaper, *Sevodny*, and had a part stake in the fledgling liberal radio station *Ekho Moskvy* – all under the umbrella of the conglomerate Media-Most. He was the nearest the Russians had to a Rupert Murdoch.

Gusinsky was somewhat unique among the oligarchs in that he could at least claim that his empire had not been mostly acquired from the state. Nevertheless, he ruthlessly exploited the business loopholes of the time and was a master at manipulating government loans, concessions, and regulations by taking advantage of political contacts in order to gain state finance. Gusinsky denied anything untoward, but ended up with state loans of close to half a billion dollars, which he used to support a supercharged lifestyle.

By the late 1990s, his media empire had brought him considerable power as well as enormous political influence. It was not to last, however. On 11 May 2000, six weeks before Putin's dramatic ultimatum to the oligarchs gathered in the Kremlin cabinet room, masked police armed with machine guns raided the offices of Gusinsky's Media-Most. Then, in June, Gusinsky was arrested and charged with fraud and imprisoned. Gunning for his first oligarch suited Putin's wider political strategy but the thin-skinned President was also taking revenge for the way in which he believed Gusinsky had used his influence to oppose him, and for the biased way Putin felt his television channel had earlier attacked his policy on Chechnya.

The charges were dropped and Gusinsky was released after he agreed to sell Media-Most to the state gas and oil group Gazprom for $300 million. In August 2000 he fled to his sumptuous villa in Sotogrande, southern Spain. Visitors to the villa had even included Putin and his wife. Following later attempts to persuade Spain to extradite Gusinsky, he left for Greece before settling in Israel, where he has joint nationality. He was merely the first of a long line of Russian exiles under Putin's reign.

The President's next target was his former friend and the man who had helped him in his rise to power – Boris Berezovsky. Even before Putin became President, the storm clouds had been gathering over the 'boss of bosses'. He was out of favour at the Kremlin, politically isolated, and deeply unpopular. Although he had always insisted the collapse was not his fault, ordinary Russians had not forgotten the failure of the 'people's car' in which thousands had lost their savings.

Nevertheless, Berezovsky always saw himself as a buccaneering capitalist, a catalyst who had helped to transform Russia. 'We were true heroes,' he told *Frontline* in October 2003. 'Because of us, Russia was put on a new course.' He admitted that the oligarchs had made mistakes in their business practices during a 'murky time', but added, 'We didn't break any laws, but if you call giving bribes a crime, then all oligarchs were criminals.'[17]

Public animosity was the least of Berezovsky's problems. In early 1999, following months of threats, the Prosecutor-General, Yuri Skuratov, visited Prime Minister Primakov in January 1999 and said, 'I am going to start a criminal case against Boris Berezovsky.' Primakov asked him on what grounds and he replied, 'In connection with the fact that Berezovsky is hiding Aeroflot's money in Swiss banks.'[18]

Over the following weeks the police raided more than twenty offices and apartments in Moscow with connections to Berezovsky. The Moscow-based American *Forbes* journalist Paul Klebnikov, in 2004 the victim of a contract killing in Moscow, witnessed the first raid – on the headquarters of oil giant Sibneft – from his room in the Hotel Baltschug:

> 'Suddenly, three white vans screeched up to the building [Sibneft's headquarters] across the street. A dozen men in face masks, camouflage uniforms, and automatic rifles jumped out. Then, accompanied by other men in brown leather jackets, carrying briefcases and video cameras, they entered the building.'[19]

This being Russia, the investigation would not run smoothly. On the day of the first raids Skuratov resigned – officially because of 'ill health'. He had been admitted to a Kremlin hospital on the previous day with a 'bad heart'. But when his resignation was later rejected by the Duma, he stated that he was not in fact ill and was reinstated. The somewhat botched effort to oust Skuratov was typical of the manoeuvrings and internal jostling that characterized Russian politics at the time.

By now, however, the investigation had gathered momentum and continued under a special prosecutor, Nikolai Volkov. The alleged fraud was that millions had been siphoned off from Aeroflot, the airline Berezovsky had controlled since 1994, and into Swiss bank accounts in violation of Russian foreign exchange rules. Volkov claimed that his team's examination of the company's books uncovered a Byzantine network of companies by which Aeroflot's funds were rerouted. Once Volkov started to look into things, a computer printout appeared behind his desk, a jumble of arrows and boxes that at first glance resembled a map of the human genome. In fact, it was a sketch of how Aeroflot funds were allegedly routed through a complex network of Russian and foreign companies in countries including Belgium, Cyprus, Germany, Lithuania, Panama, Syria, and Switzerland.

The two companies claimed to be at the heart of the fraud were Andava and Forus, both Swiss-registered financial service companies based in Lausanne with only a handful of staff.

Forus – or 'for us' as prosecutors nicknamed it – was set up in 1992 to facilitate Western finance for Berezovsky's companies. When Aeroflot acquired its Boeings and Airbuses, for example, Forus arranged short-term loans to make the down payments. The company also handled Aeroflot's revenues from foreign airlines, which paid to operate in Russia or fly over Russian airspace. These charges amounted to almost $100 million a year.

Andava was formed in 1994, the day after a 49 per cent stake in Aeroflot was privatized, and its main role was to handle the airline's foreign ticket sales, essentially its lucrative overseas earnings.

On 6 April 1999 the Prosecutor-General issued the former Kremlin insider with an arrest warrant. It alleged that Berezovsky had siphoned off $250 million of Aeroflot money through Andava. Berezovsky, who was in France, responded conspicuously by holding a press conference at a Paris hotel. He insisted that the charges were baseless and politically motivated. 'The time when the country is run by people with naked behinds is past us', he said. Berezovsky has repeatedly denied the Aeroflot accusations, claiming that Andava and Forus performed legitimate business services for the airline and that any misappropriation was done by the KGB. He argued that when he acquired Aeroflot, he discovered that the KGB had been using the airline as a cash cow, siphoning off the airline's revenues into offshore accounts to finance international spying operations. He said that he had merely closed these accounts and channelled all foreign revenue through Andava in Switzerland.

Three days later Russian Interior Minister Sergei Stepashin announced that if Berezovsky returned to Russia and spoke to prosecutors, he would not be arrested. 'Berezovsky will arrive in Russia, present his explanations, and this, I hope, will be the end of the incident,' he said.

A week later Berezovsky returned to Moscow, visited the Prosecutor-General's office and was questioned for four hours. He was released after the interview and told his own television crews, 'The case against me was instigated by the Prime Minister in violation of the law'. On 26 April 1999 Berezovsky was formally charged and barred from leaving Moscow while prosecutors investigated the case.

On 1 July 1999 Swiss police raided the Lausanne-based offices of Andava and Forus in response to requests by Skuratov. The Swiss investigation was led by Carla Del Ponte, the Swiss prosecutor who had uncovered connections between the Italian drug trade and Swiss money launderers in the late 1980s and had, as a result, been targeted for assassination by the Italian mafia. She later became Chief Prosecutor of the International War Crimes Tribunal in The Hague.

Then, out of the blue, on 4 November 1999 the Russian Prosecutor-General's office terminated its investigation. But although things seemed to have gone quiet, the case was far from over.

The threat of prosecution still hung over Berezovsky's head and the highly public controversy would haunt him for years to come, even though he strenuously protested his innocence. In mid-July 2000, however, he received some good news: PricewaterhouseCoopers announced that it had investigated Forus's transactions with Aeroflot – on Forus's behalf – and had found no evidence that funds were being illegally transferred. But while the investigation seemed to go quiet for several years, the Russian authorities later tried to extradite Berezovsky from London to Moscow. It was all to no avail: the extradition application failed and Berezovsky did not return to Russia. Eventually, on 28 November 2007, a Russian court convicted and sentenced Berezovsky – *in absentia* – to six years in jail. From his new base in London, he dismissed the conviction as 'trumped up' and 'politically motivated'.

Berezovsky's business dealings have always been subject to controversy. One person who fell out badly with Berezovsky over his business methods was George Soros. The two had once been friends and Soros had considered financing a number of the oligarch's deals in the 1990s. But by 2000, the 'love affair had turned sour', according to Alex Goldfarb, one of Berezovsky's closest allies. Soros once told Goldfarb, 'Your friend is an evil genius. He destroyed Russia single-handedly.' Berezovsky retorted, 'Soros lost money because the "young reformers" fooled him ... And then he tried to convince the West – out of spite – that the oligarchs were evil and should not be allowed to control the beast.'

Business for Berezovsky was a vehicle for bringing in the wealth to finance his real interest: indulging in political intrigue. He was easily bored by the detail of entrepreneurship and left that to others. At a conference in Moscow in 2000 Ian Hague, manager of the emerging markets Firebird Fund, which invested heavily in Russia, asked Berezovsky directly, 'Could you explain how it is that every time you've been involved with a company, its capitalization has run down to zero?' Berezovsky countered that the value of just about all Russian companies had fallen because of political uncertainty, adding later that each of the companies with which he had been connected had actually improved its performance.

Although events were moving against him, Berezovsky retained enough powerful contacts to get himself elected to the Duma in December 1999 as a deputy for Karachayevo-Cherkessia, a small republic close to Chechnya. This carried the additional advantage of providing immunity from prosecution. Although he may still have hoped to reattach himself to Putin's coat-tails, it is also likely that, despite their apparent closeness, Berezovsky had by now started to have doubts about Putin. Years later he would admit to having second thoughts about Putin as President, but put them to one side.[20]

In the ruthless, cut-throat world of Kremlin politics alliances rarely survived for long and Berezovsky was fast losing friends. Desperate for political intelligence, in October 1999 he even asked Roman Abramovich to attend Putin's birthday celebrations in St Petersburg. Abramovich did so and reported back to his mentor, 'You sent me to spy on spies but I found no spies there. Normal crowd, his age, wearing denim, someone playing guitar. No KGB types around whatsoever.'[21]

Berezovsky had every reason to feel nervous about Putin. While both men had once been friends and Berezovsky had thrown his political weight, money, and television channel behind Putin's successful bid for the presidency, within weeks of his succession, the two alpha males were at war.

There were fierce political differences: Putin was vigorously prosecuting the Chechen war, while Berezovsky argued that a military solution was not possible and openly called for peace talks. They also had very different visions for the future of Russia: Berezovsky advocated a liberal, economic, pro-Western approach that would have kept the oligarchs and himself at the centre of power and with access to contracts. Putin preferred a central role for the state. He was more interested in moderniz-ing Russia than in democratizing it. 'The stronger the state, the freer the individual,' he wrote in an open letter to the Russian people before becoming President.

From the moment Putin became President, Berezovsky embarked on a series of politically reckless acts. Such bravado was typical of the man but it was also his undoing. When Gusinsky was arrested, Berezovsky was shocked. He had not expected Putin to go so far. Two weeks later a furious Bere-zovsky fired off an open letter attacking what he saw as Putin's authoritarianism. This was triggered, too, by Putin's intention to exert greater central control over Russia's regional authorities. Quoting Aristotle and the Russian poet Osip Mandelstam, who had died in one of Stalin's gulags, the letter was the first public declaration of their emerging differences. Berezovsky was even more outspoken in a television interview on ORT: 'All the decrees, all the laws proposed by Putin are directed at again enslaving people.'

Berezovsky was incensed by the way that Gusinsky had been forced to sell up and go into exile. Although the media baron was a former rival, and the two had become bitter opponents, Gusinsky's fate intensified Berezovsky's deepening doubts about Putin. In interviews he denounced Putin and compared his policy of centralizing state power to the human rights abuses of Chile's General Pinochet. The next month he resigned his seat in the Duma, thereby losing his immunity from prose-cution. He had been elected only six months earlier. 'I do not want to take part in this spectacle,' he said. 'I do not want to participate in Russia's collapse and the establishment of an authoritarian regime.'[22] He also declared that he intended to create a new opposition party to take on Putin directly.

A fired-up Berezovsky dismissed dire warnings from his inner circle. His old friend Alex Goldfarb told him, 'Boris, if you go down this road, I predict in a year's time you will be an exile ... or worse, sitting in jail ... For Putin, the substance does not matter – as long as he sees you as one of his gang. But if you go against him publicly, you will cast yourself out of his pack.'[23]

The feud finally reached a critical state over the way Berezovsky used his media empire. In 1994 Berezovsky, in partnership with Badri Patarkatsishvili, had been awarded a 49 per cent stake in the television station ORT, broadcaster of Channel One. Under Patarkatsishvili's leadership, ORT was instrumental in the campaign that saw Yeltsin re-elected in 1996, and the company was handsomely rewarded. By late 1998, Berezovsky and Patarkatsishvili had increased their holdings in ORT. Channel One, the nation's most popular television station, has an audience coverage of 98 per cent across Russia. As well as ORT, Berezovsky also owned the major weekly business newspaper *Kommersant* and the popular daily *Nezavisimaya Gazeta*. By 2000, he was, with Gusinsky, one of Russia's most powerful media tycoons.

Patarkatsishvili was Berezovsky's closest friend and by far his most important business partner. They were like brothers. Known as 'the Enforcer' in Berezovsky's inner circle, Patarkatsishvili implemented all his most commercial controversial schemes. A smart, strategic businessman, it was always he who found the money.

Badri Patarkatsishvili was born in October 1955 to a family of Jewish Georgians in Tbilisi. Quiet, unassuming, erudite, and an authentic Zionist, Badri, which means 'son of a little man', was different in many ways from his best friend. For Berezovsky, his Jewishness suited him and provided business and political opportunities. For Badri, it defined him and he was heavily involved in Israeli charities. Also, in contrast to his confidant, Badri always preferred living in the shadows and shunned the spotlight most of his life. He hated politics and media attention and it was out of character when he later rose to become a key figure in Georgia's own fevered politics.

Bright and ambitious, Badri's first job was in a Georgian textile factory, where he rose to become Deputy Director of the plant. After the collapse of the Soviet Union, the factory was privatized at Badri's initiative and became the private company Maudi Manufacturing, which he took over.

During the 1990s, Badri became co-owner of almost all of Berezovsky's companies and held executive positions. This is how they worked: Berezovsky generated a huge number of ideas and then Badri decided if they were feasible and profitable. 'Badri made Boris all his money,' a former associate who knows both well explained. 'Badri was his business mentor. Without him, Boris would be nothing and nowhere. He would still be a second-hand car dealer ... Boris is incapable of closing a deal and seeing things through. He does not have the patience or the concentration. He is also very bad at judging people. But Badri is the real thing. He checks out the financial details and makes it happen. They had a symbiotic relationship and complemented each other. Badri was his only true business partner. They were very, very close.'

According to Aleksander Korzhakov, former head of the Presidential Security Service: 'The official position of Badri at that time was Deputy Chairman of the board of directors of LogoVaz. In fact, his responsibility was to ensure the repayment of debts and to provide protection against gangsters.[24]

Badri's earliest collaboration with Berezovsky was in 1990 when he became Regional Director for the Caucasus of Berezovsky's car distribution company LogoVaz. In 1992 he became Deputy Chairman and was awarded a 3.5 per cent share in the company. A year later he moved from Georgia to Russia, first to the town of Lyubertsy, then to a flat in Moscow. Otari Kvantrishvili, the boss of a Georgian organized crime group in Russia (and killed by rivals in 1994), used his connections with Russian authorities to arrange Badri's residence visas in Lyubertsy and Moscow.

At ORT Badri and Berezovsky soon crossed swords with Vladislav Listyev, one of the country's most popular television presenters. A charismatic figure, he was appointed by Berezovsky as the new Managing Director, but they fell out over an attempt by Listyev to end the advertising monopoly. The broadcaster believed that the advertising companies were being run by organized crime, which was bringing them millions in revenue, but his decision to take on the mafia cost him his life. On 1 March 1995, a few weeks after taking over as manager, he was shot dead outside his home. Badri was arrested on suspicion of the murder but was later released. However, suspicions over his involvement never disappeared, though he always maintained that the FSB tried to frame him for the killing.

In the summer of 2000 Putin was growing increasingly impatient with the way that Berezovsky and Badri were using ORT and their media empire as a blunt instrument to destabilize his regime. This came to a head in August when a nuclear-powered submarine, the *Kursk*, sank, killing all 118 crew. ORT television news broadcast interviews with the wives and sisters of the submariners who attacked Putin for handling the incident ineptly. Putin, meanwhile, was on holiday in the Black Sea and was seen jet-skiing while ORT transmitted footage of perilous, icy waters and distraught families. Putin's refusal to cut his holiday short turned the tragedy into a major political and public relations disaster.

Furious, Putin blamed Channel One's owner, Berezovsky, for the negative coverage and telephoned him to complain. Berezovsky suggested a meeting, to which Putin agreed. But when Berezovsky arrived the next day, he was greeted not by Putin but by Alexander Voloshin, the shadowy, reclusive head of staff. Voloshin had once advised Berezovsky during his political cultivation of Yeltsin but now, as head of the presidential office, he issued a stark warning to his former friend, 'You have two weeks to sell back your shares in ORT or you will suffer the same fate as Gusinsky.' Berezovsky refused and demanded a meeting with Putin personally.

Three days later Berezovsky was summoned to meet the President at the Kremlin. It was a heated exchange, with the two denouncing each other face to face. A clearly tense Putin first listened to Berezovsky as he mounted a defence of ORT's coverage. According to Berezovsky, the President then coldly repeated the threats made by Voloshin and made his own position only too clear: 'You are starting a fight against me. Your channel is interviewing prostitutes who say they are wives and sisters.'

Berezovsky replied that they were genuine relations and that they had already granted interviews to the state TV company but, as these were not broadcast, they approached ORT.

The President was unimpressed: 'I want the state to control ORT.'

'How?' asked Berezovsky. 'It belongs to me.'

'We'll take control. You need to sell.'

'I don't need to sell.'

The President then got up, said goodbye, and walked out. It was the last time they spoke.[25]

A shaken Berezovsky was now faced with the full reality of his decision to back Putin for President. Shortly afterwards, he was again questioned about the alleged embezzlement of Aeroflot funds. Unperturbed, Berezovsky ensured that ORT continued its hostile coverage of the handling of the *Kursk* disaster.

After his former cheerleader refused to sell his ORT shares and ignored his threats, Putin approached Badri. At that stage the two were still on friendly terms. Badri was telephoned by the head of the FSB, Nikolai Patrushev, and summoned to his office. From there, he was escorted to the Kremlin and greeted by an impatient Putin. 'What strange game is Berezovsky playing?' he asked. 'I want both of you to clear out of television. No one has the right to take risks with television.'[26] Putin said they could sell the shares and negotiate a price with media minister Mikhail Lesin. As Badri departed, the President said that they were friends but if he stayed in television they would become enemies.

Badri subsequently met with Mikhail Lesin, who offered $300 million for the ORT shares – the maximum the state would pay. But Berezovsky still refused to sell. Instead, he announced that he would put the shares into a trust to be managed by a group of journalists and other representatives (a bluff that came to nothing).

The rift between Putin and Berezovsky was now irreparable. In October 2000 Putin was asked by a journalist about his former supporter. 'The state has a cudgel in its hands that you use to hit just once, but on the head,' he replied.[27] (He later told reporters, with a half-smile, that his favourite judo move was the '*deashibati*', a swift attack that knocks one's opponent off his feet.[28]) On 17 October the media tycoon spent two hours at the Prosecutor-General's office in Moscow, facing further questioning over the Aeroflot allegations.

A week later Berezovsky mounted the steps of his private jet, a Bombardier Global Express, to take him from Moscow to Nice, a journey he had made hundreds of times. On this occasion, however, there was to be no return flight. Life for Russia's most controversial oligarch would never be the same again.

CHAPTER 4

Hiding the Money

'It's like the Wild West out there [in Russia]. A few businessmen own everything. It's amazing'

— STEPHEN CURTIS

CLOCHER DE LA GAROUPE is a spectacular, rambling villa in Cap d'Antibes in the heart of the Côte d'Azur. Set in 50 manicured acres of fragrant gardens, olive trees, and terraces that run down to the Mediterranean, the magnificent Italianate property is protected by a well-guarded gate tower and is a full mile from its ornate entrance. There are three sizeable villas – two for guests and one for its owner, commanding an impressive view of coastline and sea – along with a gymnasium, tennis court, and large swimming pool. The surrounding gardens are styled in the grand formal English manner with sweeping lawns and hedges.

The American composer Cole Porter rented the property in 1922. Along with fellow American, the artist Gerald Murphy, Porter famously raked the beach clean of seaweed that year, and wrote many of his most famous songs in the villa, notably his hit musical *Hitchy-Koo*.

Boris Berezovsky bought the place for $13.4 million in September 1997, a typically conspicuous statement of his personal wealth and extravagant tastes. It was soon put to good use and not just as a summer retreat. The chateau, just down the coast from Cannes, was the scene of many of Berezovsky's most important business deals and much of his political scheming. It was here in 1998, during Russia's deepening financial crisis, that he conspired with other oligarchs on who to back as Yeltsin's successor when the President started to rapidly lose his faculties. The following year Vladimir Putin and his family were among those who were invited as guests.

In the autumn of 2000, when Berezovsky was facing up to the full implications of his spectacular rift with Putin and the Russian prosecutors were closing in, the chateau provided the perfect retreat. On 30 October 2000 the state seized his high-security nineteenth-century dacha in Alexandrovka, which he leased from the Kremlin. On 1 November 2000 the Russian Deputy Prosecutor, Vasily Kolmogorov, announced that he was launching criminal proceedings and summoned Berezovsky to appear in Moscow for questioning over the hundreds of millions alleged to be missing from Aeroflot's Swiss-based accounts. The prosecutor said that if he failed to attend, an international arrest warrant would be issued. Knowing he would not emerge from the process unscathed, the next day he took a momentous decision: to remain in the South of France and become a fugitive. Berezovsky has repeatedly denied the accusations, claiming that they were politically motivated.

As he reflected on his predicament in his Cap d'Antibes retreat, the oligarch decided to remain defiant. Publicly, Berezovsky said that he still planned to return to Russia, but privately the decision had already been made. Two weeks later, on 14 November, he declared that he would not return to Moscow. 'I have been compelled to choose between becoming a political prisoner or a political emigrant,' he said.[1]

For the next month Berezovsky stayed in France. With his future now in the balance, his options were bleak: return to

Moscow and face trial or lead a life of exile. The threatened international arrest warrant was then issued by the Russian Prosecutor-General. Although Interpol issued a 'red notice' that alerted other countries to this warrant, it did not oblige or mandate police to arrest him. But with the threat intensifying and his options rapidly narrowing, Berezovsky took a life-changing decision – London would be a safer refuge. He already had links to the UK – his daughters had gone to Cambridge and he owned a luxury apartment at Palace Gate in Kensington Palace Gardens – and so in early 2001 he travelled to London, a move he hoped would be temporary.

Berezovsky's immediate concern as he quit Russia was how to protect his personal fortune. He still owned – or believed he still owned – large stakes in LogoVaz, Aeroflot, Sibneft, Rusal, and ORT – all jointly with Patarkatsishvili. He also had interests in the television channel TV6 and several newspapers. One of his greatest fears was that Putin would simply seize these assets. Then, several weeks after he fled Russia, he received a telephone call from his old friend Roman Abramovich.

Berezovsky's former protégé, also a shareholder in Sibneft and Rusal, explained that he wanted to meet on 'urgent business'. It was mid-December 2000 and Berezovsky was somewhat bemused by the call. The next day Abramovich drove the ten minutes from his own magnificent villa at Château de la Croix to Berezovsky's Château de la Garoupe, where they were joined by Badri Patarkatsishvili. The meeting was not the usual informal, backslapping event the three men were used to. Instead, the atmosphere was uncharacteristically tense. There was now much at stake between the three men and Berezovsky had every reason to be wary of his old friend. While Berezovsky had turned himself into an enemy of Putin, he suspected that Abramovich had become the President's *consigliere*.

Top of the agenda was the media company ORT. Putin was still fuming about Channel One's critical coverage of the sinking of the *Kursk* and he was still demanding that the two tycoons sell their 49 per cent holding back to the state.

It was a measure of the tension and importance of this meeting that conflicting versions of what was said later emerged and have since become the subject of a hard-fought lawsuit being contested between the two oligarchs in London. According to Berezovsky, Abramovich was sent on the specific orders of Putin to exert intense pressure on them to sell up. He claims that Abramovich, in the role of the President's willing messenger, warned him that unless he sold his ORT shares, Putin would simply seize the television station without compensation. Berezovsky later maintained that this was a trick to force him and Patarkatsishvili to sell their ORT stake at a knockdown rate, thereby cheating them out of millions.

According to Berezovsky, central to the negotiations was the fate of Nikolai Glushkov, who had been arrested on 7 December 2000 on charges relating to his management of Aeroflot. He was being held at Lefortovo jail in Moscow, notorious as the place where the KGB tortured political prisoners in the Soviet era. Berezovsky believed the arrest was part of the wider campaign by the Kremlin to curb his power. He claimed that Glushkov was essentially being used by the Putin administration as a hostage to prompt him and Patarkatsishvili into relinquishing their assets. According to Berezovsky, Abramovich told the partners that, if they sold their shares in ORT, Putin would release Glushkov from prison. Frustrated and cornered, Berezovsky had no leverage and reluctantly accepted the terms. He needed substantial funds to finance his London lifestyle and knew there was a risk that his stake might otherwise be seized without compensation.

Abramovich's account of events is entirely at odds with Berezovsky's. While he accepts that he was at such a meeting, he maintains that he was present in a quite different capacity – in order to assist Berezovsky, at his request, to sell Berezovsky's

ORT shares. Abramovich has denied making any threats or acting as an agent of Putin or the Russian state, claiming that Berezovsky was anxious to sell his ORT shares and actually asked for his help. Far from making threats, the future Chelsea FC owner claims that he, in fact helped Berezovsky and made money for him – by buying his stake in ORT at a price higher than he would otherwise have got.

On any view of the matter, the deal was not going to be straightforward. Neither Abramovich nor Putin would want to be seen publicly doing business with a man being investigated by the Russian state for fraud and for whom there was an international arrest warrant. All sides knew that, in order for the transaction to work, it would need to be entirely clandestine. But how could such a deal be constructed?

The solution was provided by the lawyer Stephen Curtis. He had already been working for Khodorkovsky, knew Abramovich, and advised Berezovsky. He relished the challenge of constructing a convoluted scheme by which to sell the ORT shares.

The fast-talking Curtis found working for the Russians exciting and challenging. He loved the complex and often unorthodox structure of their business and finances, but his colleagues had been less than happy when he first started to work for them. Late one evening in 1998, sitting in the back of his Mercedes, he told a confidant, 'I need to tell you something. We've got some major new Russian clients.' The friend was dismayed. 'That's crazy,' he replied. 'Why are you getting into bed with the Russians? It will be a disaster. They play by different rules. If you fall out with them, they will come after you. You are dealing with the Devil.' Curtis laughed and brushed aside the comments, 'Well, I will jump on their backs and ride all the way down to hell.' He was mesmerized by the high rollers and high stakes. This was his chance for the big time. After one particular trip to Moscow, he told his staff breathlessly, 'It's like the Wild

West out there. A few businessmen own everything. It's amazing.'

Blessed with remarkable intellect and a prodigious memory, Stephen Langford Curtis was born in Sunderland on 7 August 1958. His father was an accountant. With a law degree from Aberystwyth University, Curtis's career took off in the early 1980s when he was a tax solicitor at the City law firm Fox and Gibbons. Most of their clients were from the Middle East and the astute, softly spoken Curtis developed an affinity with the Arabs, especially those from the Gulf States. In 1990 he set up his own law firm, Curtis & Co., specializing in commercial and property transactions.

It was in 1997 that Curtis first recruited Russian clients when he started working for Khodorkovsky's Bank Menatep. Some months later, in 1998, he advised the American defence and communications contractor Lockheed Martin when they were looking for a local (Russian-based) partner to help establish a satellite company for direct broadcasting in Russia. Menatep recommended Berezovsky and that is how the two men first met. Meetings took place in London between Lockheed directors and Berezovsky executives but the deal never materialized.

Curtis was a gifted lawyer and a generous man, but he was also chaotic, disorganized, and extravagant. Despite having wealthy clients such as Mahdi Al-Tajir, the billionaire business-man and former customs official in Dubai, he was always over-drawn and beset by cash-flow problems. Even before the appearance of the Russians, he would buy Ferraris or Bentleys for rich new clients with his own money, something he could ill afford to do. He sometimes had to borrow cash from his own employees and once a client even had to help bail him out. He liked to take expensive holidays and was a regular gambler at London casinos. And he loved to buy jewellery, most especially from W. Roberts at Hatton Garden for his wife and girlfriends.

He was also a frequent visitor to Chanel on New Bond Street, where one of his girlfriends worked.

For a Mayfair law firm, the offices of Curtis & Co. were remarkably informal and the senior partner was gregarious and inclusive. Late on a Friday afternoon he would dispense champagne, his arm around the shoulders of members of his staff. People liked Curtis. He was amusing, endearing, and engendered trust. 'He was one of those people who could remember everyone's name and make them think that he was their closest and devoted friend,' said a former colleague. 'He was phenomenally charming and made you think that you were the most important person in the room.' The Russians – by nature often sceptical, fearful, and paranoid – trusted him with hundreds of millions of their money. To the astonishment of his colleagues, he was able to buy properties, art, and jewellery on their behalf with few questions asked.

On one occasion Curtis was given a Russian doll with a diamond necklace inside the ornament. His young daughter nonchalantly played with the doll and then threw it into her toy box. Curtis did not realize its value until he saw the same doll in a store in Red Square, Moscow. He was stunned at the price of the bejewelled doll and immediately retrieved it from his daughter's playroom on his return.

However, Curtis was too shrewd to be completely mesmerized by the mysterious new Russians. He knew there were risks and so applied the old adage of 'know your client' even more stringently. In 2000, shortly after starting to work for Berezovsky, he bought a private security firm, ISC Global Ltd, which he then used to investigate his intriguing new clients and their associates.

By late 2000, Curtis was a close confidant of Berezovsky and it was to him that the oligarch turned with the problem of how to sell his ORT shares discreetly. Curtis's solution required the use of a middleman, ostensibly in order to keep the parties at arm's length from one another. With his network of high-worth clients spread around the world, many with their own financial networks through which money could be funnelled, Curtis was perfectly positioned to put the pieces in place.

Soon Curtis was coordinating the deal. He set up accounts at Clydesdale Bank in London for Berezovsky and Patarkatsishvili and the ORT shares were transferred, via an intermediary, to an Abramovich-owned company, which then sold them on to the state-owned savings bank Sberbank for the same price – $160 million. Abramovich himself made no money from the clandestine deal, which was concluded by July 2002.

After fees had been paid to the lawyers and other parties who had provided services, Berezovsky and Patarkatsishvili each received around $70 million. Curtis even suggested that Patarkatsishvili – by then based in Georgia – take residence in the United Arab Emirates to avoid paying any tax on his receipts. True to form, details of the commissions received by all the parties were never put in writing.

Although Berezovsky received $70 million for his shares, he has long protested that they were worth more, and had indeed been offered more before he fled Russia. Yet some have claimed that he was fortunate to receive even this much for his 49 per cent stake in ORT, as Putin could easily have seized ORT and nationalized it, leaving Berezovsky with nothing.

Even more infuriating for Berezovsky, Vladimir Glushkov was not released from prison. The Kremlin failed, he claimed, to keep its part of the agreement and Glushkov continued to languish in Lefortovo jail. For Putin, however, mission had been accomplished: the state had regained control of the popular television channel and Berezovsky could no longer use it as a propaganda weapon. Meanwhile, Abramovich was soon to capture another prize – the highly profitable Sibneft oil company.

It was the division of this giant conglomerate that was to become the source of the next dispute between the two oligarchs. According to Abramovich he was the 100 per cent owner of Sibneft, although he was prepared to acknowledge that Berezovsky and Patarkatsishvili had played a crucial role in providing political protection when they had initially acquired the lucrative oil company together. For their part, Berezovsky and his business partner were adamant that they owned a substantial holding in Sibneft that was 'held on trust' on their behalf by Abramovich – as part of an option arrangement – even though there was no written agreement to that effect.

Both sides accept that in May 2001 Abramovich met Patarkatsishvili at Munich Airport to discuss Sibneft, but Abramovich and Berezovsky are completely at odds as to what the precise purpose of this meeting was and what went on at it. According to Berezovsky, Abramovich offered another stark warning to his former business associates: as long as they retained a stake in Sibneft, there was a risk of confiscation by the Kremlin. Boxed in again, Patarkatsishvili raised the subject of the imprisonment of Glushkov. Abramovich assured Patarkatsishvili, according to Berezovsky, that if they sold their holding in Sibneft, this time Glushkov would definitely be released. Berezovsky alleges that, once again, on this occasion, Abramovich was acting with Putin's knowledge and approval.

Abramovich denies this. His position, by contrast, is that he did not purchase or offer to purchase Berezovsky's and Badri's stake at all, as, on his account, they had no stake to sell. Rather, according to Abramovich, by the time of the Munich Airport meeting, at an earlier meeting with Patarksishvili, he had agreed to pay Berezovsky $1.3 billion 'in recognition of the political assistance and protection Berezovksy had provided in respect of the creation of Sibneft'.

According to Berezovsky, it was after the meeting in Munich that the haggling started. Patarkatsishvili, Berezovsky says, telephoned him in private to let him know what had happened.

Again, on Berezovsky's account, they reluctantly agreed to accept Abramovich's offer, and again, a discreet way of conducting the deal needed to be found. On this occasion, Berezovsky claims, a middleman was again required.

Berezovsky alleges that at this point Sheikh Sultan bin Khalifa bin Zayed Al-Nahyan, eldest son of the ruler of Abu Dhabi, agreed to take this role. Although the precise nature of the underlying deal between Berezovsky and Abramovich is vigorously disputed and shrouded in mystery, what is not in doubt is that there was some such deal, that the Sheikh became involved in it and that the person who introduced the Sheikh to the deal was Stephen Curtis.

Curtis had come to know Sheikh Sultan through one of his clients, a flamboyant Jordanian banker called Eyhab Jumean. Born on 6 August 1964, and educated at Harrow, Jumean was a talented gymnast from a powerful military family. He took great pride in his physical appearance, but loved money even more. In 2001 he bought a 33 per cent stake in Chinawhite, the celebrity nightclub off London's Piccadilly, for a mere £33,333 in cash. It proved a lucrative investment.

Jumean was briefly married to the South African supermodel Gina Athan. With a flat in Paris and a yacht and speedboat moored on the French Riviera, when in London he hosted regular parties at Chinawhite. Jumean's gadget-filled £12 million London home on Brick Street, around the corner from both Berezovsky's and Curtis's offices in Mayfair, housed no fewer than six sports cars and a Harley-Davidson. Jumean is a car fanatic: in 2001 he bought a Porsche 911 for £97,000 and a Ferrari 360 Spider F1 for £133,000. One friend recalls seeing Jumean press a button in his house, at which the entire outer courtyard suddenly descended like a lift. He was then led down into an underground car park that was dominated by a Ferrari, a Lotus, and four Lamborghinis. 'It was incredible, like a scene out of *Thunderbirds*,' said the friend.

Jumean funded his extravagant lifestyle by managing the private finances and investments of Sheikh Sultan. From 1998, he managed the Sheikh's private wealth – based on the Gulf States' oil reserves – and invested his millions in the US and UK. During his visits to Abu Dhabi, Jumean would dress in Arab garb. Adjusting well to life in the Sheikh's court, he was handsomely rewarded.

Curtis's work for Jumean had led him to Sheikh Sultan. After advising the Sheikh on some property acquisitions in the UK and a hotel investment in Dubai, Curtis established a rapport with him. When contemplating how to structure the Sibneft deal, it dawned on Curtis that Sheikh Sultan would be the perfect intermediary. As the Sheikh had official diplomatic status and was personally beyond reproach, the banking authorities would be more likely to accept him as a source of funds. He was also low key and low profile.

For his part, the Sheikh was intrigued by the oligarchs. An amiable soul, he too loved gadgets and was fascinated that Berezovsky had his own private telephone network. While in London, Sheikh Sultan stayed at the Carlton Park Tower Hotel in Knightsbridge, owned by Sheik Mohammed, ruler of Dubai, and enjoyed discreet dinner parties at the private dining club of celebrated Swiss chef and restaurateur Anton Mosimann to discuss the investment of his oil millions.

The transaction in which the Sheikh became involved was deliberately complex, using third parties and offshore companies and trusts. Secrecy was again vital. As with the ORT deal, there was the risk of seizure by the state. 'The concern was that if Berezovsky and Abramovich dealt directly within Russia, then the proceeds would be retained in Russia,' said Curtis.

Berezovsky alleges that under the terms of the plan, agreed in the summer of 2001, Sheikh Sultan would buy the Sibneft stake from Berezovsky and Patarkatsishvili and then sell it onto Abramovich.

Abramovich, by contrast, denies that there was any deal to purchase shares in Sibneft from Berezovsky and Patarkatsishvili, whether involving the Sheikh or not. The only money he agreed to pay to Berezovsky in connection with Sibneft was the $1.3 billion in return for 'political assistance and protection'.

The verbal dealings between the oligarchs made Curtis nervous. Concerned with the solicitors' regulations relating to potential money-laundering implications, he was rigorous in disclosing the transaction to the compliance office of Clydesdale Bank (into whose accounts the proceeds of any deal that ensued between Berezovsky and Abramovich were to be deposited). The bank's executives were equally anxious to comply with the letter of the law. During one meeting attended by Curtis, Berezovsky, Abramovich and their lawyers, the bank's compliance officer told Sheikh Sultan: 'We need your passport and one of your utility bills as proof of identity.' His aide was bemused and stunned. 'But he is the son of the Crown Prince of Abu Dhabi,' he said. 'He does not carry around copies of his electricity bills.'

An amused Sheikh responded by taking out his wallet and handing over a wodge of dirhams. The bank's chairman was shocked. 'Why are you offering me cash?' he asked.

'Well, you asked me for proof of identity,' he replied. 'My face is on these bills.'

The meeting dissolved into laughter.

To receive and protect the proceeds from both the ORT and the 'Sibneft' deal, offshore trusts were set up in Gibraltar – the Itchen Trust for Berezovsky and the Test Trust for Patarkatsishvili. Each trust then opened bank accounts with Clydesdale at their Fleet Street branch in London to receive the funds. For Patarkatsishvili, a key adviser was Josef Kay who was not only a trustee but also a protector of the Test Fund. This gave Kay significant influence: a protector can remove and appoint trustees, hire auditors, and oversee its management. In terms of protecting Patarkatsishvili's assets, maintaining privacy, and avoiding unwanted attention, Kay played a key role. Patarkatsishvili was, of course, the beneficiary of the trust.

As protector, Kay was an important custodian of Patarkatsishvili's assets. Born in Georgia in 1958 as Iosif Kakiashvili, he is a half-cousin of Patarkatsishvili, whom he describes as 'like a brother'. In the 1970s he emigrated to the United States through Israel, gained citizenship, and lived in Dix Hills, New York, where his parents still reside. His route to wealth started in the 1990s when he worked for Patarkatsishvili as Commercial Director of ORT-Videos, which distributed down-market, low-quality videos – a lucrative market in Russia at the time.

A small but robust man with a muscular physique, Kay speaks with a pronounced Brooklyn accent. In May 2000 he married Sophia Boubnova, a 26-year-old impoverished Russian from Irkutsk in Siberia, and moved to London. He bought a flat on Park Street, Mayfair, and rented a third-floor office at Stanhope Gate, just off Park Lane and around the corner from the Hilton Hotel. The following month Kay's relationship with Patarkatsishvili was cemented when he set up Bili SA, a Luxembourg-registered company that managed some of the billionaire's assets, notably his private jet. Kay's newly glamorous wife Sophia loved London and frequented the nearby Harry's Bar restaurant on South Audley Street. The couple were desperate to become players in the Londongrad community, and their dream came true on 27 December 2001 when Kay was granted an investor's visa, requiring him to deposit at least £1 million in the UK, three-quarters of it in government securities. He is just one of a number of rich Russian émigrés to have taken advantage of the scheme that provides unique residential rights.

* * *

By August 2001, approximately £250 million had been paid by Sheikh Sultan to Berezovsky and Patarkatsishvili (divided equally between their respective offshore trusts). Then came a bombshell. Clydesdale Bank suddenly announced that they would accept no further deposits. Clydesdale said they had received a directive from their new parent company, the National Australia Group, which had switched their policy away from accepting large deposits from super-rich clients.

Eventually, a solution was found. In March 2003, part of the remaining balance of the Sibneft proceeds was deposited in an offshore account in the Netherlands Antilles, and the remainder in a wealth and asset management company based in Mayfair. This money was then reinvested. Eventually Sheikh Sultan paid out a total of £650 million.

In a complex commercial transaction, all of those involved in the Sibneft deal received substantial fees, including Sheikh Sultan. Curtis personally received £9 million.

While Berezovsky was now some £300 million richer, he was furious with Abramovich: he believed he had been short-changed on the Sibneft deal and manipulated by his former protégé. And, even worse, his friend Glushkov had still not been released from jail, adding to the growing animosity between the two men. It was even claimed that in April 2001 there had been an attempt, orchestrated by Berezovsky, to spring Glushkov from jail. The operation was allegedly led by Andrei Lugovoi, Berezovsky's security chief at ORT and later the chief suspect in the murder of the former FSB officer Alexander Litvinenko in London in 2006.

Mindful that the Russian prosecutors were investigating his close business relationship with Berezovsky, Patarkatsishvili fled Russia in early 2000 to his Georgian homeland. In June 2001 the Russian prosecutor issued an international arrest warrant against him through Interpol, on charges of complicity in the attempted jailbreak of Glushkov. It was not until 2004 that Glushkov was eventually acquitted of charges of fraud and money laundering relating to Aeroflot. He denied that he had attempted to escape, claiming it was stage-managed by the FSB.[2]

Forced into exile in Georgia (which refused to extradite him to Russia), Patarkatsishvili sold his shares in his major Russian businesses, but the spectre of investigation and sequestration of assets continued to dog him. In August 2002, in order to stall such a threat, Patarkatsishvili created a new family trust to protect his assets. Two months later the Prosecutor-General duly charged him with embezzlement of funds from AvtoVaz and LogoVaz, the Russian car manufacturers.

Despite their windfall, fear of appropriation of their assets and extradition haunted both Berezovsky and Patarkatsishvili throughout 2002. Their futures were far from secure. While Berezovsky had applied to the Home Office for political asylum in October 2001, there was no guarantee of success. Then, in March 2002, an extradition warrant was issued by the Russian authorities. The warrant accused Berezovsky of defrauding the region of Samara by stealing and illegally selling cars while head of LogoVaz. The extradition case would be heard before a British judge, and if extradited Berezovsky faced the grim prospect of being sent back to Russia to face a trial and possibly a long jail sentence. Berezovsky maintains the charges were unfounded and politically motivated.

It was partly to protect his vast wealth from Russian prosecutors that every time Berezovsky bought a house or shares, quite legitimately, he used a different company known as a Special Purpose Vehicle (SPV). If all his assets were lodged under the name of one company, he could lose everything, but if one SPV was being sued or prosecuted, he could fall back on another. It was all part of an elaborate barrier to ensure that assets were kept separate from each other, and the SPVs were created to avoid businesses being linked. Berezovsky rarely did anything under his own name. He never kept money in one place, always dispersing funds into multiple accounts in different locations and entities.

One of Berezovsky's most important SPVs was the Itchen Trust (into which the proceeds from the Sibneft deal had been placed), registered in Gibraltar and used to buy and protect his primary assets, notably his properties. This helped hide the identity of his assets and, importantly, ensure that if he died, was jailed, or went bankrupt, the funds would be distributed to his family and closest friends.

Berezovsky entrusted his eldest and favourite daughter Ekaterina, known as Katya, to be the protector of the Itchen Trust, to translate his wishes to the trustees and ensure his interests were secure. Katya is very much like her father: tough, intelligent, impatient, charming, and cunning. Closely involved in his business affairs, she married Yegor Shuppe, owner of the company Cityline. The couple lived in Berlin before settling in Surrey.

The initial primary trustee of Itchen was Ruslan Fomichev, a Russian banker and Berezovsky's principal financial aide. When Fomichev first moved to London in 2001, he rented a penthouse flat on Eaton Square for £5,000 a week, and then a ground floor flat at nearby Eaton Place. Although he aspired to be part of London society, when he first arrived from Moscow he hardly looked the part, dressing only in jeans and looking generally dishevelled. 'He looked like a Polish construction worker,' recalled a former colleague, 'and so Stephen [Curtis] decided to smarten him up.' The Mayfair lawyer sent Fomichev across the West End to his Savile Row tailor. The next day he walked into 94 Park Lane in hunting and shooting gear so ill-fitting that the office fell about laughing. But it did not take long for Fomichev to integrate (he even went shooting with celebrity chef Marco Pierre White) and by 2007, he was adorning the society pages of *Tatler* alongside his beautiful, talented, and highly intelligent wife Katya, a PhD from Moscow University. In 2008 they were listed as the thirteenth 'most invited couple in London'.

Fomichev became one of Berezovsky's sharpest financial operators and had soon amassed a pot of gold for himself. He bought a £3 million apartment suite in Belgrave Square, an old embassy building, and hired the upmarket interior designer Nicholas Haslam to renovate the property. He spent £1.5 on refurbishing the interior, including a glass floor in the drawing room and lime-green chairs to complement the huge Julian Schnabel painting on the wall. The library resembled a hunting lodge from the pages of *Anna Karenina*. Above the desk hung a Francesco Clemente canvas, with a bald head and staring face bearing a striking resemblance to Vladimir Putin. The apartment spread through different buildings and there was a vast underground swimming pool.

The opinionated Fomichev loved to live life on the edge: he drove a Porsche around London and in his spare time was addicted to adrenalin sports – heli-skiing in Greenland, shooting, and yacht- and cresta-racing. The family skied in St Moritz, where they also have a house.

Many feared the secretive Fomichev, and Curtis was keen to impress him. He found a private school for Fomichev's children and on one occasion telephoned a fellow solicitor every ten minutes and launched into a tirade of abuse – just to impress his Russian client who sat nearby laughing uproariously.

Remarkably, in the autumn of 2002 Berezovsky removed his daughter Katya as a beneficiary of the Itchen Trust and replaced her with Damian Kudriavev, a close confidant and political adviser, as well as the International Red Cross. At a time when he was under investigation by the Swiss and Russian prosecutors, the oligarch also removed his name from the list of beneficiaries.

This meant that between December 2002 and February 2003 Kudriavev, a 27-year-old former computer programmer, and the International Red Cross were the sole beneficiaries of around $250 million of Berezovsky's assets. But the oligarch completely trusted Kudriavev, his young protégé, media adviser, IT consultant, and virtually the only person that he could talk to in any confidence. Berezovsky seems to think more quickly than he speaks and he often talks so fast that few people, including his own Russian staff, can understand him. A gifted chess player, Kudriavev seemed to be the only person able to follow his boss's chaotic train of thought.

Probably because of the impending extradition proceedings, in March 2003 Katya was reinstated as the protector and beneficiary of the Itchen Trust. Berezovsky knew that the prosecutors would seize his assets if he were extradited to Russia. Katya, on the other hand, was protected from action against her father.

Although Kudriavev was employed to manage Berezovsky's IT systems and mobile phones, his close affinity with his boss brought him a much broader influence. An air of mystery surrounds Kudriavev. In an elaborate tale he claimed that he fled Russia and moved to Israel because he was pursued by the FSB, which had killed his dog and burnt his dacha. But he never explained why he placed under surveillance in the first place. Moreover, colleagues could never understand how such a close associate of Berezovsky was able to travel so freely to and from Moscow while his boss was the subject of an international arrest warrant. Kudriavev claimed this was because his name was spelt incorrectly in his passport. The easy-going, laid-back Kudriavev was well looked after: he bought a luxury flat in Holland Park, west London, drove around in sports cars, and travelled the world, notably to India – all at Berezovsky's expense.

For a man who has admitted that he is not an astute judge of people, Berezovsky has taken remarkable risks with the stewardship of his multi-million-pound fortune. He even lent his trustees millions of dollars on an unsecured basis with no due diligence. Stephen Curtis thought this was reckless and advised against it but Berezovsky ignored his counsel. Appointing known associates and family members as trustees was also a gamble. If the trust could be linked to its beneficiary, then the cloak of secrecy would be removed. For this reason, trusts are often administered by anonymous lawyers and nondescript company formation agents. But Berezovsky took the risk of deploying his associates as individual trustees out of fear that professional, corporate trustees would steal his money.

As Russia's Most Wanted, Berezovsky became much more vigilant about security. When he first arrived in London he moved into an apartment in Kensington Palace Gardens, which he had bought in 1995. At first he seemed surprisingly unprepared for his new life. He did not even possess any credit cards. A prestigious location was important and so he rented an office at Melrose House in Savile Row, refurbished by the young property dealers Candy and Candy. But his communications system was primitive. For example, he was using an unsecured Virgin e-mail account that could easily have been infiltrated by the FSB.

It was not until 2002, when he moved into new offices at Down Street, near Hyde Park Corner, that a brand-new, ultra-secure computer system was installed. Security became an obsession. Berezovsky even created his own e-mail and telephone network outside conventional norms. His mobile phone bills had been astronomical – thousands of pounds a month. Now, with an early version of Skype, they were substantially reduced. He used Siemens' 'Top-Sec' S35 mobile phones because their scramble signals made them almost impossible to bug. For this reason, they were often used by MI5 officers and the British Army. But they were expensive, at £2,000 apiece, and not easy to find, so they were purchased cheaper in Russia and then brought into the UK.

Berezovsky's operational base has been functional as well as security-driven. To get into his private office, you are required to be fingerprinted. Dominated by photographs of Berezovsky with VIPs and celebrities, his inner sanctum cost an estimated £1 million. The most expensive and elaborate carpet, wood panels, and security gadgets were installed. In the hallway leading to the office boardroom the wall is lined with black-and-white photographs of Russian leaders, from Tsar Nicholas onwards, among them his arch enemy Vladimir Putin. In the back of his office is a private room and bedroom where very few people have ventured. The private room has been a constant source of speculation by members of his staff. 'We all thought that that was where he kept his most secret documents or held his most important meetings,' said one former aide.

Such is the importance of security that Berezovsky insists on hiring a female or elderly security guard to operate reception downstairs so as to disguise the identity and nature of the occupants within. There are no buttons for punching in codes for entry to rooms; all are accessed by a biometric fingerprint security system. Nor did Berezovsky trust British security operatives, preferring former members of the French Foreign Legion. One review of his security by an experienced Israeli operative found that his close-protection team was loyal, tough but unsophisticated, and unlikely to offer him much protection in a firefight. His main bodyguard had been a former member of the French Special Forces and was recruited from Israel.

Surrounded by bodyguards, Berezovsky soon became obsessed with intelligence and espionage. He believed that MI5, the CIA, and the FSB had all been investigating him and kept him under surveillance, including hacking into his computers. He regularly reviewed his network, which used Linux rather than Microsoft software. He even thought there was a spy inside the church directly across from his second-floor office. He also took seriously the suggestion that Scotland Yard has planted an undercover officer inside his headquarters. 'I have information that there is a police informant inside your office, but I do not know his name,' his security consultant Keith Hunter told him. Berezovsky's friends argue that he was entitled to be vigilant, given that in 1994 a bomb blew up his Mercedes and killed his chauffeur.

Every time this wiry, intense man, always dressed in either a dark pinstripe suit or black leather jacket, left his office, an elaborate security operation swung into action. A bodyguard would check that the foyer and street were clear. Berezovsky would always travel in convoy – often altering his route and drivers – with two armoured Mercedes Maybach limousines, one bodyguard in the front seat and one in the back, a black backup Jeep, and motorcycle outriders.

On one occasion Berezovsky hired six identical limousines, travelling in pairs and heading off in different directions to throw off potential tails. At a function in April 2007 at the Royal United Services Institute, a short distance from Downing Street, his cavalcade, complete with motorcycle outriders, was almost presidential.

After the murder of Alexander Litvinenko, Berezovsky suspected that a 'traitor' had leaked sensitive information from his office. Internal security was reviewed and a new company was hired – Risc Management headed by Keith Hunter, who advised the oligarch since 2000. One director of Risc was Tim Collins, the former British Army officer who became famous during the second Iraq War, in March 2003, for his eloquent eve-of-battle speech to his troops.

For Berezovsky it was perfectly normal to spend freely in Mayfair's restaurants, clubs and bars. Alloro, on Dover Street, Sumosan, a Japanese restaurant in Albemarle Street, Harry's Bar and Annabel's were particular favourites. Something of a hypochondriac, and constantly checking his heart rate, at home he employed an Italian chef for his special diet.

Berezovsky also enjoyed the company of young women, often ending up at the Library Bar of the Lanesborough Hotel on Hyde Park Corner in the company of a statuesque Russian blonde – as well as the obligatory pair of bodyguards. Late one afternoon a hotel guest was amazed to see a nervous Russian approach Berezovsky and kneel before him. He then took the tycoon's hand and kissed his ring, shaking. 'It's O.K., it's O.K.,' whispered Berezovsky and the suppliant retreated looking relieved. 'It was astonishing,' said the eyewitness. 'It was like a scene out of *The Godfather* with Marlon Brando taking pity on a guy who owed him money.'

Since his arrival in England, Berezovsky has invested close to £50 million in country houses, including £3 million for Heath Lodge in Iver, Buckinghamshire, for his influential investment adviser Natalia Nosova; Pentlands in St George's Hill, Surrey, for £4.5 million; and Warren Mere House in Thursley, near Guildford, Surrey, bought for £4.5 million for one of his daughters and her family.

In August 2001 Berezovsky purchased Bakeham House at Wentworth Park, an estate near Virginia Water in Surrey, for £20.5 million from Scott Young, a wealthy Scottish property developer. He bought it after flying over the premises in a helicopter with Stephen Curtis and an estate agent. Typically, Berezovsky, supported by Curtis, would insist on completing such deals at speed and worry about any problems later. Contracts for Bakeham House were exchanged the next morning and the deal was completed by the following Monday. Berezovsky did not even look inside the property.

Bakeham House has became Berezovsky's main residence. He has lived there with Yelena Gorbunova and two of his children since 2002. Indeed, the stunning Yelena owns the grand house and oversees a staff of some twenty servants and gardeners. They have never married since Berezovsky has not divorced his second wife, Galina. For over a decade Galina never sought financial settlement but lived the high life in an £8 million apartment in west London. It was not until 2008 that she requested a divorce. 'His relationship with Galina is perfectly amicable,' said Lord Bell, the spokesperson for Berezovsky. 'There are no issues between them that I am aware of. They are negotiating a divorce settlement.'[3]

Berezovsky commutes to his Mayfair office but rarely stays in London overnight. He prefers his country estate, which abuts thirty acres of well-manicured lawns and four golf courses that make up the prestigious Wentworth Golf Club. The mansion is impenetrable, with imposing steel gates, and is monitored twenty-four hours a day by Berezovsky's security staff. This is where most of his meetings are held.

Once word got out that Berezovsky was prepared to splash out on expensive country houses, he was soon besieged by estate agents. 'They are like flies on shit,' he snapped to an aid. Security was paramount. During one helicopter tour of a £28 million Elizabethan mansion in Surrey, he noticed that the main gate stood virtually on the A3 and that there was a deer fence around and public footpaths through the estate. He even asked the shocked estate agent if the footpaths and chapel could be closed. But he was intrigued and uncharacteristically looked around the estate with Yelena. All in black, Berezovsky resembled Ian Fleming's Dr No as he stepped out of his cream-and-grey Agusta helicopter after it landed on the immaculately kept lawn.

Berezovsky did not buy that particular property because of security concerns, but he did buy another Surrey mansion, Hascombe Court, near Godalming, for £9 million. It had been owned by the former Radio One DJ and television presenter Chris Evans. Designed in 1908 by a pupil of Edwin Lutyens, with formal gardens laid out by Gertrude Jekyll, the eight-bedroom house set in 10 acres of parkland was bought unseen for another of his daughters.

The deal was conducted in strict secrecy and Chris Evans repeatedly asked the identity of the purchaser, but Berezovsky refused to allow his estate agent to disclose his name. Even his daughter and her husband did not see the property until after the oligarch had bought it for them as a wedding present.

In London, however, Berezovsky had more problems finding the right house for himself. He considered Toprak Mansions on The Bishops Avenue, then marketed for £50 million, making it one of the most expensive houses in the UK, but he found the atmosphere 'sterile'. In 2004 he made an offer of £37.1 million for 15 Kensington Palace Gardens, but he was outbid by fellow Russian oligarch Leonid Blavatnik, who paid £5 million more.

To facilitate his search for London properties – for himself and his family – he turned to the interior designers Candy and Candy. The brothers have become the most trumpeted, well-known, and powerful interior designers and property developers in London. At turbo-charged speed they have propelled themselves onto a multi-billion-pound property empire. In the early post-millennium years the brothers fast developed a sense of the insatiable appetites of the new Russian billionaires.

When, in April 2001, they showed Berezovsky the glossy brochure for a deluxe, glistening, hi-tech Buckingham Suite apartment in Belgrave Square, he was impressed and purchased it for his daughter Katya. The property – selling for £4.15 million – promised all the characteristics that appealed to acquisitive Russian oligarchs: bullet-proof CCTV cameras, a fingerprint entry system that can remember 100 fingerprints, remote-controlled cinema and television screens in the bathroom walls, laser-beam alarms, and smoke bombs. An electronic system recognized the resident's favourite music and TV programmes and followed him or her from one room to another.

The indulgent suite designed to suit the tastes of the new twenty-first-century super-rich was dominated by oak, black walnut, and polished granite surfaces. The furniture was bespoke and everywhere was the best marble and leather. Outside there was a Japanese garden with a fountain shooting water into a pool, which was then pumped into a moat around the edges of the garden.

By 2002, there was an aura about the brothers, and wealthy Russians wanted to buy a 'Candy and Candy' flat. In June 2002 Andrei Melnichenko, a young Russian banker, paid £2.95 million for a three-bedroom penthouse apartment in Berkeley Square, previously lived in by Christian Candy himself. This property was dominated by extravagant marble surfaces, and the oligarch installed his young Russian girlfriend into it.

The brothers even started to emulate the lifestyles of their Londongrad clients, buying their own £10 million second-hand yacht, *Candyscape*, joining the private jet set, and moving to Monte Carlo. Like many of their clients, the brothers' business is based in a complex offshore structure.

Gradually, Berezovsky integrated himself into the British way of life. He bought property in the right areas, hired some of the most powerful law firms in the country, and even, in December 2003, spoke at that most respected of London institutions, the Reform Club. While his initial arrival was barely noticed, his wealth – he was prepared to spend £1 million a month on his private jet and £40,000 for a QC's opinion on a property dispute – and dynamic political apparatus soon began to open doors.

Despite the questionable provenance of his wealth and his controversial role in Russia in the 1990s, there was no shortage of influential members of the British establishment prepared to be courted. Berezovsky and Yelena would often be seen with Lady Carla Powell, the socialite wife of Lord Powell, the former private secretary and adviser on foreign affairs to Margaret Thatcher. Lady Carla hosted the most influential political salon in London at her Bayswater home, where fellow guests included Peter Mandelson and Lord Bell, and Berezovsky and Yelena regularly attended Goodwood and Ascot, the latter on occasion as guests of the Duke of Devonshire.

Berezovsky's search for social acceptance extended to rubbing shoulders with members of the aristocracy and minor royalty. The Marquis of Reading (whose great-grandfather, the first Marquis, was Lord Chief Justice, Ambassador to the United States, and Viceroy of India) was educated at Eton and served in the 1st Queen's Dragoons. Describing himself as a 'Sino-British consultant', he first met Berezovsky in Moscow in the early 1990s when he was exploring business opportunities.

Simon Reading would often drop by at Berezovsky's office without making an appointment as a 'courtesy call'. On one occasion Reading happened to mention a charity dinner in passing and Berezovsky handed over a cheque for £25,000. Berezovsky pays for dinners and for his part, Reading invites him to VIP receptions and dinner parties. Fixated by moving with the powerful, Berezovsky would become obsessive about who attends these events, demanding to know who else was coming, who he would be sitting next to, and for his staff to confirm that certain people would attend.

The Marquis gave Berezovsky an entrée into the City and also introduced him to Prince Michael of Kent. Useful yet again for widening Berezovsky's upmarket social circle, Prince Michael offered impressive, and useful, credentials. He entered Sandhurst in 1961 and served in Germany, Hong Kong, and Cyprus before subsequently joining the Defence Intelligence Staff, retiring from the army with the rank of major in 1981. With a full beard and moustache, it is said that Prince Michael bears a striking resemblance to the murdered Tsar Nicholas II (his English grandfather, George V, was Nicholas's first cousin), so much so that when he visits parts of rural Russia on one of his trips to the country, startled locals have been known to drop to their knees in amazement, as if the Tsar had been brought back to life.

By late 2002, Berezovsky needed all the powerful friends that he could get. Earlier that year the Russian Prosecutor-General launched a new criminal investigation, alleging that Berezovsky had helped to create and finance Chechen rebel groups. 'This applies primarily to the funding of unlawful armed formations and their leaders,' said Nikolai Patrushev, then head of the FSB, adding that his agency planned to document the charges and relay the information 'to our partners abroad, and wait for a proper reaction from them'.[4]

Berezovsky admitted to the *New York Times* that he had had extensive contacts with Chechen separatist leaders, especially from 1997 to 1999, when he was a deputy national security adviser to President Yeltsin, but strenuously denied funding terrorism. He admitted giving $2 million of his own money in 1997 to a Chechen field commander, Shamil Basayev, who was also Chechnya's Prime Minister. The money was intended for the restoration of a cement factory, he said, but he admitted that it might have been used for other purposes. 'It was not my function to control how he spent the money,' Berezovsky said, adding that Russian security officials were aware of the gift at the time, though they were not happy about it.[5]

Then, in the late spring of 2003, as Berezovsky nervously awaited the outcome of his political asylum request and for the extradition case hearings to begin, there was more uncomfortable news: his former protégé Roman Abramovich was spending more time and money in London. Flush with the flow of dividends from Sibneft – now almost wholly owned by him – Abramovich had been seen attending football matches in west London, buying more expensive property – not far from Berezovsky's Down Street office – and was planning to buy a major British asset. While the future of Berezovsky continued to look precarious, there was a new oligarch in town, one unburdened by such concerns.

CHAPTER 5

The Russians Have Landed

'Before Abramovich bought Chelsea, Russians were not particularly conspicuous when it came to the wider public. Nor had the media cottoned on to their potential significance. Abramovich's move on Chelsea changed all that. It was a big public statement – it was in effect an announcement that the Russians have landed'

– ALEXANDER NEKRASSOV, *London-based journalist*

AT THE HEART OF Roman Abramovich lies a remarkable paradox. On the one hand he had outpaced and outmanoeuvred all bar one of his business colleagues and rivals to accumulate, by the middle of 2008, a multi-billion-pound fortune. Much of his wealth was spent in London building a glittering portfolio of property, jets, yachts, and, later, works of art. On the other hand his taste for the good life masked a surprising character: a slight, casually dressed, diffident, self-taught dealmaker with an instinct for survival. On the surface this nondescript-looking billionaire with a prodigious spending appetite could be mistaken for any Russian construction worker then making a living in London.

When he first made big money in the early 1990s, Abramovich quickly set out to acquire a jet-set image. 'We used to make jokes about him because, as he began to move up the ladder, he started to change, living up to his new role, wearing expensive cufflinks, only the best suits, moving from the driver's seat into the back of the car because you had to hire a chauffeur,' a friend related. 'At first his friends used to take the mickey out of him: "Why are you becoming so formal, wearing all those smart clothes?" "Why are you sitting in the back of the car?" And he would say, "Well, I have to have a chauffeur", and we would say, "Don't be ridiculous".'

While Abramovich soon shed the tailored suits, ties, and crisp white shirts, he steadily began to acquire demonstrable symbols of wealth. His main criteria seemed to be size and expense. The chauffeur-driven limousines were just the start. He developed a taste for lobster, sushi, and designer clothes. One house, one yacht, one jet, and one sports car was not enough; he needed quantities of them and the more expensive, the better. He shares this mentality with most, though not all, of the new Russian financial elite. 'If they see a piece of antique furniture and it is priced at £100,000 and I negotiate a discount that cuts the price to £75,000, they will still insist on paying £100,000,' said one property consultant.

The obsession with ostentatious displays of wealth among newly enriched Russians started in the early 1990s. 'The first thing that came out of *perestroika* was the wealth,' said Valerie Manokhina, a photographer who knew the Abramovichs at the time. 'Some people were suddenly awash with money and the first thing they did was build a beautiful dream-like lifestyle.'

That dream could not be realized in Russia itself. Instead, Russian money steadily made its way out of the homeland, much of it in London's direction. The first wave of mostly middle-class, professional Russians came to Britain to study, start businesses, or work for Russian companies such as Aeroflot and the Bank of Moscow. They were by no means wealthy and mostly kept out of the limelight.

But the most conspicuous arrivals were the second wave, beginning to arrive in 1993 to 1994 – a group dubbed the 'New Russians' by their countrymen: those making money out of Yeltsin's reforms, though not nearly on the scale of the oligarchs. London was the place they could 'burn' the money they had filtered out of Russia, sometimes in cash, sometimes via offshore companies.

It was a group that sowed the first seeds of the spending frenzy that was later to typify Londongrad's super-rich community, although to a greater extreme in the years to come. One Russian who knew some of them well was Alexander Nekrassov. He had come to London in 1989 as a reporter for Tass, the Russian news agency, and remembers being able to cash in himself by virtue of his good English and knowledge of Britain. Some of his compatriots, making their first journey to London, turned to him for help. He soon built a sizeable personal bank account by offering advice and helping to open doors. On one occasion a Russian émigré paid him £22,000 just for writing a letter on his behalf to help him get a business visa.

Steadily, London began to turn into a playground for these newly enriched Russians and they soon developed a reputation for being loud and flashy with their money. Moscow had not yet succumbed to the Westernization and commercialization that later brought the world's luxury retailers and brands to its doors, but in London they singled out the most expensive hotels, such as the Lanesborough, gathered at the most lavish restaurants, tipped extravagantly (a cultural import from Moscow where the wealthy tip wherever they go), and paid exorbitant prices for rare wines. Car showrooms started doing a roaring trade. Top-of-the-range Jaguars were soon being shipped back home.

The new migrants' favourite haunts were often casinos like the Colony Club in Mayfair's Hertford Street. Renowned for their love of partying, one popular hangout in the mid-1990s was Tramp in Jermyn Street. Another was the Number One Yacht Club on a pleasure boat on the Thames opposite Temple station. Friday evening became Russian night. As one participant remembered, 'At the Yacht, they would swill back bottles of vodka one at a time and listen to bleached blondes singing Russian pop songs. Unlike the English, there was nothing self-conscious about the Russians. Despite the views over Westminster Bridge, you could have been in Moscow.'

One waiter who used to work in a Thames-side restaurant near Pimlico also remembered the Russians from the time. 'They took a particular liking to this restaurant and money was certainly not an issue. They would get very drunk and boisterous, dance on the tables, and often do a lot of damage. They would simply leave great bundles of notes behind in compensation.'

Maxie's basement nightclub in Knightsbridge was popular from as early as 1991 and became something of a gathering point. It initially attracted a mixed crowd – intellectuals, students, and professionals – although there was also no shortage of heavy gold jewellery on display. Saturday soon turned into Russian night, with specially invited bands and singers often playing *blatnaya* – traditional songs of the Russian underworld. Groups of dark, sharp-suited businessmen would sit at their reserved tables while the younger crowd could be distinguished by their Levis, leather trousers, or leather jackets. The women rarely wore anything other than heavy make-up and expensive couture. In this pre-oligarch age hundreds rather than thousands of pounds were typically spent on one night – usually on 70 per cent proof vodka and several bottles of Dom Perignon. Eventually Maxie's was forced to close after a serious fight broke out involving Armenians and Russians.

Aliona Muchinskaya arrived in London in 1991 at the age of nineteen as a correspondent for *Moscow Komsomolets*, the organ of the Moscow Communist Party's Youth League. She married a Briton, went on to help found the London-based PR company Red Square, and remembers well the members of the second wave with their hard currency. 'They were not always the perfect ambassadors; *nyekultumy* [uncultured], as we say,' she recalls. 'They loved flaunting their wealth: gold Rolexes, gold cufflinks, shiny suits that were always too tight.'

As Russian accents became more commonplace from the mid-1990s, restaurants, hotels, and some retailers started making comparisons with the arrival of the Arabs in the 1970s. While the press began running occasional articles about Russian excesses, the new rich of this early wave had not yet arrived in sufficient numbers and with sufficiently deep pockets to make the kind of public splash that was to follow later. Indeed, it was not until after the millennium that London's top property agents and exclusive retailers began to feel the full impact of the Russian invasion.

The birth of super-rich Londongrad can really be dated to April 2000, the month Vladimir Putin was elected President, when the febrile state of Russian politics and the oligarchs' uneasy relationship with Putin launched a third wave of migration. It was the turn of Russian billionaires and multi-millionaires to shower London with money. What also distinguished most of this group was an obsession with secrecy and security. They were largely desperate for anonymity. The richest Russians, their wives, and entourages – with the rare exception of Berezovsky – preferred to be inconspicuous, and were much less likely to attract attention by splashing out in hotel bars or ostentatiously buying an entire restaurant a round of drinks. The vulgarity and flashiness of the earlier years gave way to a new era, one defined by discretion and a preference for secrecy.

The oligarch who epitomizes this curious combination of a desire for privacy and jet-fuelled lifestyle is the enigmatic Roman Abramovich. Cold and unemotional, he shuns publicity. 'He is not known for his wit and can easily give the impression of a somewhat grey nonentity, lacking a sense of humour or wider intelligence,' one friend has said. A former acquaintance who first met him when they were students remembers him as 'very shy in a good way. He was always lacking in self-confidence. But he is also very uptight. He always felt that he needs to do things the way they should be done, according to the rules.'

In contrast to many rich Russians, Abramovich now seldom drinks and is not known for wild partying. This is not just due to diffidence. 'He is very astute,' said a friend. 'He is both shy and calculating. He knows that if he goes partying, there is a risk that he might be watched and photographed and end up on the wrong end of some unwanted publicity. He's very careful.' A workaholic, he stood out as the very antithesis of the *nouveaux riches* Russians of the second wave. Obsessed with enhancing his fortune, Abramovich was more likely to be networking quietly among the international yachting fraternity at the International Yacht Club of Antibes in the South of France than frolicking until the early hours in a nightclub. The few photographs he authorized for publication show him with his ex-wife and his children. Before his divorce from second wife Irina in March 2007, he liked to be seen as a family man, a claim that now seems a little hollow.

But behind the apparent aloofness and sullenness lies a sharply contrasting character – and one with a love affair with excess. Abramovich has enjoyed a lifestyle that caps those of all his fellow oligarchs, all the British-based super-rich in the spending stakes, and is on a par with the world's mega-rich. In a study of Britain's Biggest Spenders commissioned by *Virgin Money* in 2007, he topped the list of tycoons surveyed, from the Aga Khan to Lakshmi Mittal. Such indulgence is regarded with disdain by some Russians. 'Abramovich is a tragic figure,' says former KGB agent turned oligarch Alexander Lebedev. 'There is something Shakespearean about him. He has all this money. What does he do? He buys houses. He has homes everywhere but he is unhappy. I think he has more than fifteen houses, here, France, the Caribbean – everywhere.'[1]

Abramovich's first serious foray into London was in 1997 when he rented a large apartment at 81 Cadogan Place, just off Sloane Square, with his then wife Irina and their two children. Irina was pregnant and wanted their third child to be born in Britain. 'It was massive, five bedrooms, very expensive but totally tasteless, full of expensive furniture but hardly comfortable,' said Valerie Manokhina, a former family friend who first came to London in the mid-1990s. 'There was no garden. It was totally unsuitable for children. They just wanted to be near Harrods.' It was the location that clinched it. Even then Belgravia and Knightsbridge, with its reputation for classy shopping, held a fascination for the newly emerging Russian super-rich. Valerie asked Irina why she chose the flat. '"Well, it was Roman's secretary who found it," she replied. 'It told us a lot about Russians at the time. They didn't know their way around. They simply asked their secretary to get a flat near Harrods.'

The family stayed at the flat for a few months. Their second daughter was born on 2 April 1997 at the Portland Hospital, a private maternity hospital in central London. To celebrate, the family threw a large party at their apartment, but shortly afterwards they moved to the South of France.

Apart from a small circle of Russian insiders, Abramovich was virtually unknown in the late 1990s. Despite his wealth and political connections to the Yeltsin family, he was soon dubbed the 'stealth oligarch' by this circle. In late 1998 Valerie and her husband, Viktor, were on holiday with Roman and Irina and came back with several photographs. Although he was becoming known as one of the oligarchs, he was still a shadowy figure, to the extent that no photograph of him had yet found its way into the press. Apart from his inner circle, nobody would have been able to recognize him. Valerie remembers a Moscow journalist getting excited about seeing the holiday pictures. 'We showed him the pictures and he was the first journalist to know what Abramovich actually looked like,' she recalls.

In 1999 the Abramovichs slipped quietly and more permanently into the UK. They acquired Fyning Hill, a 420-acre estate in the village of Rogate in West Sussex for £12 million from the late Australian media magnate Kerry Packer. It was a property Abramovich purchased perfectly legally through an offshore company registered in the British Virgin Islands. Such an offshore arrangement is a tax avoidance device, albeit an entirely legal one. Built in the 1920s, the mock-Tudor mansion offered the oligarch two things he most valued: a distinguished former owner (King Hussein of Jordan had lived there before selling the property after a £1 million jewellery robbery attracted press attention) and – more importantly – seclusion. The house, set in grounds the size of eighty football pitches, is invisible from the road. It boasted perimeter-wide surveillance cameras and a helipad that enabled its owners to enter and leave undetected.

The estate also came with two of the best polo grounds in the country, stables for 100 horses, a tennis court, a rifle range, a trout lake, a go-kart track, a clay pigeon shoot, an indoor pool, Jacuzzi, and a plunge pool. Abramovich once reportedly ordered in 20,000 grouse and pheasant to indulge his passion for shooting. In 2002 he applied for permission to build a ten-lane bowling alley, an indoor swimming pool, a gym, a family room, a steam room, a sauna, and a plant room.

Irina Abramovich's initial experience of Knightsbridge had struck a chord. In early 2000 the couple bought two luxury flats at Lowndes Square for £1.2 million. Sparsely furnished, they were rarely used, since by then Abramovich was spending most of his time in Moscow and Siberia. But as if aping Britain's landed aristocracy, the couple now had a country pile and two

London pads – and not just any old pads, either. One of London's smartest and most colourful addresses, Lowndes Square offers not just grand listed buildings but, crucially, location: it lies close to Sloane Street and is, conveniently, a few minutes' walk from Harrods. More infamously, in the early 1960s John Profumo, Secretary of State for War in Harold Macmillan's Cabinet, used an apartment in Lowndes Square to entertain Christine Keeler. (Intriguingly, Keeler had also had a relationship with Yevgeny Ivanov, senior military attaché at the Soviet Embassy, a liaison in those Cold War days that has been partially blamed for the fall of Macmillan's government.) In the 1970s Lowndes Square was the backdrop to Nicholas Roeg's film *Performance*, starring Mick Jagger and James Fox.

At the time Abramovich's acquisitions sparked not a flicker of national press interest. What catapulted the oligarch from a cipher into an international name overnight was his purchase of Chelsea Football Club in July 2003. Although the deal – worth £140 million – took the football world by surprise, the man brought up as an orphan close to the Arctic Circle and captivated by the excitement of English football had been plotting the move for a while.

Abramovich's purchase of Chelsea – promptly nicknamed 'Chelski' by excited tabloids – meant that he would never again be able to escape the limelight. It was also a defining moment in the history of Londongrad. 'Before that the Russians were not particularly conspicuous when it came to the wider public,' said Alexander Nekrassov. 'Nor had the media cottoned on to their potential significance. Abramovich's move on Chelsea changed all that. It was a big public statement – it was in effect an announcement that the Russians have landed.'

The Abramovichs' decision to put down such firm roots in London stemmed from both personal and business motives. Although Abramovich had taken Putin's warnings to the oligarchs seriously, the purchase of Chelsea is likely to have been inspired by another motive: insurance. Despite playing the political game, he could never be sure of what Putin was thinking. The high-profile acquisition of Chelsea provided a form of protection while London offered him a base, and an escape route should he need to take it.

By this point Abramovich was a very rich man, rich enough to buy the club, pay off its debts, and go on a spending spree for the world's best football players. Much of his increasing wealth had come from mass dividends as a result of soaring oil prices. In 2000 Sibneft paid £28 million in dividends. Those rose to nearly £600 million in 2001 and even higher figures in 2002 and 2003. The lion's share of this dividend flow went to Abramovich, with a minority going to his fellow core shareholders, among them Evgeny Shvidler.

In 2004, at the age of thirty-seven, Abramovich entered the *Sunday Times Rich List* – which includes foreign domiciles living and working in Britain as well as British citizens. He shot from nowhere to first place as Britain's wealthiest man. The newspaper estimated his fortune at £7.5 billion. Most of this – £5.3 billion – came from his 60 per cent personal stake in Sibneft.

Abramovich may have taken Chelsea fans by storm, but he was not universally popular. The purchase caused disquiet among some key advisers in the Kremlin. It hardly went down well with his former partner Boris Berezovsky, either. More seriously, in early 2004 Abramovich's past returned to haunt him when the London-based European Bank for Reconstruction and Development (EBRD) started legal action against him. Set up in 1991, the EBRD – funded by taxpayers in Britain, Europe, the United States, and Japan – invested in emerging markets in the former Soviet Union. In 1997 the bank made a substantial loan to a Moscow-based bank called SBS-Agro, and, as part of its collateral, it insisted on first call on a loan that SBS-Agro had made to Runicom SA, Abramovich's old Swiss-based trading company.

During the 1998 economic crisis SBS-Agro collapsed – large numbers of records also went missing – and the debt was duly reassigned to Runicom SA. But when challenged by EBRD, Runicom SA claimed that the debt – which, through interest and penalties, had now risen sharply – had already been repaid to SBS-Agro. This was vehemently denied by EBRD.

Although EBRD privately acknowledged that it was unlikely to recover the full amount, it sued for the money in a Russian court but lost the case. Runicom SA produced documents claiming to prove it had repaid the debt in 1998. EBRD alleged they were forged and took the case to a Russian appeal court. This time, in January 2002, it won a judgement in its favour for £9 million.

Four months later Runicom SA declared itself bankrupt, failing to honour the ruling. EBRD then hired London-based private investigators to identify the assets of Abramovich. Because Runicom SA had been run by nominees – designated representatives – it proved difficult to demonstrate that Abramovich was directly liable for any of the debt. But later the EBRD alleged that Runicom SA had funded hundreds of thousands of pounds of personal expenses. The most notable allegation was that a payment of 27,800 Swiss francs had been made for a stay at a beauty farm for Irina Abramovich. In 1999 Runicom SA allegedly paid £4,700 towards a hotel bill for Roman Abramovich and a business associate, while the company also purchased two yachts – *Stream* and *Sophie's Choice*.

Legal writs were eventually served on Abramovich personally at Stamford Bridge, Chelsea's Football Club's home, in February 2005, following a Champions' League match. Asked why it had taken so long to serve the papers, Richard Wallis, spokesman for the EBRD, said, 'If you are asking me whether it would be extremely difficult to serve on Mr Abramovich because he is surrounded by millions of bodyguards, then my answer is I don't want to comment. I'll leave it to your own imagination.' It was not the last time the Chelsea owner was to be served with a legal writ in London. By the autumn of 2008 the case still remained unresolved, though EBRD claimed they remained determined to pursue it.

None of this interrupted Abramovich's inexorable rise in the wealth stakes. Although in 2003 his two daughters were still being educated at the prestigious Moscow Economic School, the couple started a search for a large London property suitable for their five children and live-in staff. They looked at Old Swan House on Chelsea Embankment, one of London's most iconic Arts and Crafts movement properties, then on the market for £32 million. Irina was also intrigued by The Old Rectory, a magnificent nineteenth-century house on Chelsea's Old Church Street, owned by the Norwegian shipping magnate John Fredriksen, complete with an extensive art collection. The couple initially offered £40 million for the house and the art collection, even though the latter was not actually for sale. Her office then made an even higher offer before politely being told that no price would be high enough. In Belgravia Irina was also entranced by Hugh House on Eaton Square, owned by philanthropist and socialite Lily Safra. Again, nothing came of it.

It was not until June 2005 that Abramovich found the right home for his family: a £9.3 million Grade II-listed property in Chester Square, Belgravia. Once owned by the Duke of Westminster, it included a swimming pool and gymnasium and a mews house at the back. A year later he bought the next-door house in Chester Square and in the mews, thus creating an enclave of four houses. They were handed over to Irina as part of the settlement when the couple divorced in 2008.

While the family moved into Chester Square (and thus became neighbours of Lady Thatcher), Abramovich spent a further £10 million on four adjacent apartments in Lowndes Square to add to the two he already owned. In May 2008 he submitted plans to convert these flats (part of two adjacent town houses) into one grand London house, one with five storeys above ground level and three below. When finished, the 30,000-square-foot mansion (five times the size of an average five-bedroom house), complete with a football pitch-sized reception room, cinema, indoor pool, and steam room, was widely expected to be worth upwards of £100 million.

Abramovich's property empire extended beyond British shores. In 2008 he also owned an £8 million, 104-acre estate in Moscow – his principal home in Russia – the Tenisheva Palace on the banks of the River Neva near St Petersburg, a castle in Bavaria, the £10 million Ornellaia estate and vineyard in Tuscany, and a villa in St Barts. And then there was the £18 million Wildcat Ridge, a 14,300-square-foot mansion near Aspen, Colorado, sitting in 200 acres, and the Hôtel du Cap-Eden-Ros, an exclusive seaside hotel in Antibes between Cannes and Nice, a hotel complex in Cyprus, and a holiday home in Montenegro. There were also three homes in the South of France. And they are no ordinary homes. Take one of them – the Château de la Croix at Cap d'Antibes, which Abramovich bought in 1998 for £15 million. The chateau was not just the former home of the exiled Duke and Duchess of Windsor until 1949, but also of a succession of other former monarchs, from Leopold III of Belgium to Farouk of Egypt. In the 1980s it was owned by the shipping magnate Aristotle Onassis until it was devastated by fire in 1989. Abramovich and his ex-wife Irina spent millions restoring it to its former glory, grand enough for the requirements of a 'super-oligarch'. As well as twelve bedrooms, a swimming pool, and a tennis court, there is a dining room big enough to seat twenty-four and a drawing room whose walls are lined with expensive tapestries.

Once Abramovich had emerged from the shadows, security became paramount. Fearing that his family were targets for kidnapping, in autumn 2003 his UK management company, Millhouse Capital, hired Kroll Security International to provide bodyguards and close protection. Kroll commissioned Mark Skipp, formerly of the SAS, to manage the contract. He hired thirteen bodyguards on eight-hour shifts at £5,000 a month each. Three were based at his apartment at Lowndes Square, and ten looked after his family at his house in Chester Square and the country estate at Fyning Hill, West Sussex. Later an additional seven bodyguards were employed as fears of kidnapping increased.

In 2004 Skipp joined Abramovich's management company as head of security on an annual salary of £200,000. After Kroll's security wing was taken over by the multi-national Garda Worldwide, Skipp summarily sacked Garda and hired his former SAS colleague Bob Taylor. Skipp and Taylor were old friends and had served together in 22 SAS during the first Gulf War in 1991. Abramovich liked the idea of being protected by Special Forces. 'He loved having them around and did not mind that the ex-SAS officers charged a premium as long as he was being protected by Special Forces,' said one security source. But, in fact, many of his security staff were former RAF and army officers, because most former SAS officers ended up working for private contractors in Iraq and Afghanistan.

Nevertheless, Abramovich still developed one of the biggest private security operations in the world. In the South of France a team of four operatives armed with 9mm Glocks guards his vast villa. Another six protect his fleet of yachts. One of the boats, the *Pelorus*, is fitted with bullet-proof glass and a missile-detection system. In Russia security precautions were even more extensive: the oligarch recruited dozens of Russian

Right: FROM RUSSIA WITH LOVE
Roman Abramovich with his girlfriend Daria Zhukova on holiday in the Caribbean in 2008. His favourite island is St Bartholomew, where he owns a rambling villa and loves to jet-ski.

Below: CHELSKI
Roman Abramovich enjoying the benefits of his multi-million investment in Chelsea. Here he celebrates winning the Premier League in 2005 with John Terry (left), Frank Lampard (middle) and Eidur Gudjohnsen (right).

Above: PRISONER OF THE KREMLIN
Mikhail Khodorkovsky, former owner of
the Yukos oil company, on trial in Moscow
in 2005. The billionaire oligarch was convicted of tax evasion and money laundering.

Below: JOINT VENTURE
Prime Minister Vladimir Putin with
aluminium tycoon Oleg Deripaska (right).
One of Russia's richest men, Deripaska
has enjoyed a close relationship with
the Kremlin.

Above: BUSINESS AS USUAL
President Yeltsin with Boris Berezovsky (right), one of Russia's most controversial oligarchs, in Moscow in 1999. The following year Berezovsky fled to London.

Below: TO THE MANOR BORN
Boris Berezovsky in the well-manicured grounds of his estate at Wentworth Park, Surrey, which he bought in 2000 for £20.5m. The tycoon has spent an estimated £60 million on property in London and Surrey.

Left: RED PRESS BARON Alexander Lebedev (left), the former KGB officer and owner of London's *Evening Standard* newspaper, with former Soviet President Mikhail Gorbachev, and Bono of U2, at Hampton Court attending a party for the Raisa Gorbachev Foundation in 2008.

Right: A GOOD CAUSE Evgeny Lebedev (left), son of Alexander, with Gorbachev and Geordie Greig, editor of the *Evening Standard*, at the June 2008 fund-raiser for the Raisa Gorbachev Foundation.

Left: SUPER-MODEL, SUPER-RICH Naomi Campbell with boyfriend Vladimir Doronin, a Russian billionaire property developer, on his yacht in the south of France in the summer of 2008.

Right: WEALTH ON THE WATER
Pelorus, the pride of Abramovich's fleet of floating palaces, in St Petersburg with St Isaac's, the landmark Russian orthodox church, in the background.

Left: BLADE RUNNER
Most oligarchs love helicopters, mainly for commuting to and from the office. This one was used while Abramovich was on holiday in Sardinia in 2008.

Right: FLIGHT CAPITAL
This Boeing 767, which Abramovich bought for £55 million, has been compared to the US President's Air Force One. It has the same air missile avoidance system and has room for 30 seated dining guests.

Right: THE BROTHERS Christian Candy (left) and Nick Candy (right), the property developers, at the Royal Parks Charity Gala at the Serpentine Lido in Hyde Park in 2008. The Candy Brothers' success has been partly due to selling and renovating property to wealthy Russians in London.

Left: ROYAL FORTUNE Prince Michael of Kent, a fluent Russian speaker, next to his Bentley in Moscow's Red Square in 1999. The Prince was participating in a London-Moscow rally involving 12 vintage Bentleys.

Right: THE ULTIMATE SPIN DOCTOR Lord Bell, former media guru to Lady Thatcher while she was Prime Minister, has worked as a PR advisor to Berezovsky and other Russian exiles in London.

Above: BANKING ON RUSSIA
Nat Rothschild, the son of banking scion Lord Jacob Rothschild, attends a private dinner at Annabel's club in Mayfair in 2007. A friend and advisor to Deripaska, he is said to have made a fortune from his Russian connections.

Above: POLITICAL STORM
Shadow Chancellor George Osborne on 22 October 2008 – the day after he acknowledged that he made 'a mistake' in being involved in a discussion about a potential £50,000 donation to the Tory party by Deripaska. He strongly denied soliciting any donation.

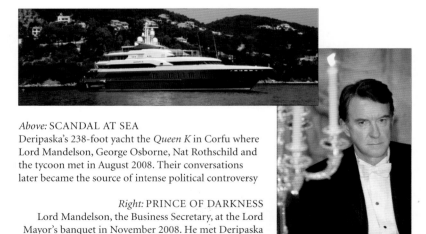

Above: SCANDAL AT SEA
Deripaska's 238-foot yacht the *Queen K* in Corfu where Lord Mandelson, George Osborne, Nat Rothschild and the tycoon met in August 2008. Their conversations later became the source of intense political controversy

Right: PRINCE OF DARKNESS
Lord Mandelson, the Business Secretary, at the Lord Mayor's banquet in November 2008. He met Deripaska while on holiday in Corfu as a guest of Nat Rothschild.

soldiers, some serving officers, as hired guns. As Russian infantrymen are among the worst paid in Europe, they are easily lured by the extra cash. In London his convoy of cars is armour-plated and his drivers are specially trained to deal with assassination attempts. Following the attack on Berezovsky in 1994, his security team continues to believe that Abramovich is a possible target for assassination or kidnap.

London is no stranger to wealthy foreigners heading to the UK with ambitions to buy up the nation's most prestigious addresses. Before the First World War, America's gilded elite bought houses in Kensington and Chelsea's most sought-after squares. In the 1970s a steady wave of oil sheikhs colonized entire areas of London, snapping up expensive homes and hotels in Kensington and boosting business in Harley Street. The Arabs were soon followed by super-rich Greeks, Italians, Japanese, and Nigerians, though not on the same scale, either in numbers or wealth. In the 1980s the flow of oil money was slightly reduced, and new foreign buyers included Americans (again), Hong Kong Chinese, and Singaporeans. Then, during the first Gulf War, the Saudi royal family bought no fewer than ten of the sixty-six properties that line The Bishops Avenue in north London.

Next it was the turn of the Russians. In the early 1990s some of the Russian arrivals started buying up property. Some came to live in Britain; some saw property as a great investment, while others bought for their children who they were planning to educate at British universities. In 1994 the *Financial Times* reported that at least £50 million worth of property had been purchased in the previous two years by buyers from the former Soviet Union.[2] Although apartments and small houses were popular, some were buying at the very top even then. By 1995, two houses in The Bishops Avenue were Russian-owned. Gary Hersham of Beauchamp Estates in Mayfair, and a specialist in the top end of the London market, remembers selling, in 1996, two consecutive properties in W14 to Russians within a month of each other. 'One went for £6.5 million, a record for the area at the time,' he remembers. 'That was rare, well before the later Russian influx. It was totally different from what happened after the millennium.' Even in the mid-1990s, it seems, Russians were outbidding British buyers in the central London sites. One of those buying property in London at the time was Vladimir Gusinsky. His wife and son spent much of their time in London from 1994 and he used to shuttle back and forth between Moscow and London for business so often that he once quipped 'it was like catching the metro'.[3]

Most of these transactions were exceptionally discreet, with the buyers often demanding anonymity, sometimes using inter-mediaries or pseudonyms to disguise their identity. Media coverage was the last thing they wanted. Even then the Russians started to show a distinctive taste. According to a director of one upmarket estate agent at the time, 'They like to keep themselves pretty anonymous, but they do like houses that make a bit of a statement. The amount of marble that might appeal to a Russian would perhaps be a little over the top for some Western European buyers.'[4] Often the money changing hands came via offshore accounts. In 1994 one estate agent was so excited by the influx of wealthy clients that he even started talking to a bank based in the Isle of Man about establishing a special offshore payment system for Russians.

Despite Abramovich's purchase of two flats in Lowndes Square in 2000, there was little wider awareness of Russians in the immediate post-millennium years. In March 2002 the London *Evening Standard* ran an article on the 'Top 50 residents of Kensington & Chelsea'. The list contained a number of super-rich foreigners, from the Swedish Tetra Pak entrepreneur Hans Rausing to the Norwegian oil and shipping magnate John Fredriksen (he of The Old Rectory), as well as a long list of

British tycoons and celebrities, from Sir Richard Branson to Stella McCartney. There was not a single Russian on the list.[5]

The real Russian assault on London's property hotspots followed Vladimir Putin's increasingly tough stand against the oligarchs and Abramovich's purchase of Chelsea Football Club. In early 2004 London witnessed its first super-rich bidding war when a property became available in Kensington Palace Gardens, W8. With some of the capital's finest houses, imposing stucco mansions, many the size of office blocks, the street oozes wealth, power, and privilege, perhaps more than any other in Britain. Only the super-rich and nations in search of embassies (Kensington Palace Gardens boasts more foreign embassies – the Russian, the Japanese, the Israeli, to name but a few – than any other in the capital) can compete for property here, and in 2006 the makers of the popular board game Monopoly dumped Mayfair as the most expensive square on the board and substituted Kensington Palace Gardens instead.

Past residents have included Baron de Reuter, founder of the eponymous news agency, family members of the Rothschild merchant banking empire, and the Sultan of Brunei. During the Second World War, No. 8 Kensington Palace Gardens was used as a top secret British interrogation camp that was known as the 'London Cage'.

In early 2004, No. 15 – next door to Kensington Palace, the former home of the late Diana, Princess of Wales – was put up for sale. Immediately, four of the richest men in the world, all foreign-born, London-based multi-billionaires, declared an interest. Three – Berezovsky, Abramovich, and the industrialist Leonid Blavatnik – had been born in the former Soviet Union and one – Lakshmi Mittal, since 2005 the richest resident in Britain – was Indian.[6]

In the event the sumptuous ten-bedroom Queen Anne mansion went to Blavatnik for £42 million, beating Berezovsky's offer of £37.1 million. As the agent who was lucky enough to handle the sale, Andrew Langton of Chelsea-based Aylesfords, stated: 'Blavatnik said, "I've got to have it", and he bid more than the others.'

Blavatnik, fifty-one, known to his pals as Len, was born and raised in Russia and moved with his family to the United States in 1978 at the age of twenty. He gained an MBA at Harvard and moved into business. Although a Cold War émigré and a US citizen for thirty years, he made his substantial fortune from post-communist Russia, taking significant stakes in oil and in the aluminium group Sual. By 2008, he was a major player in oil, aluminium, and petrochemicals. With a personal fortune close to £4 billion, he had joined the *Sunday Times Rich List* as Britain's eleventh richest resident.

From the millennium, foreign buyers came to dominate the top end of the London market. An extraordinary two-thirds of Savills' London sales over £4 million in 2006 were by international buyers, compared to only one-third by Britons. In 2004 it was the reverse. By 2006, the Russian super-rich, awash with money, had overtaken the traditional foreign buyers – the Arabs, Americans, and Europeans – to become the biggest overseas players in the London property market.

Fuelled by increasing fears generated by the incarceration of Khodorkovsky in November 2003 and uncertainty about Putin's second term, Russian money just kept pouring into London. Gary Hersham of Beauchamp Estates tells how he met a Russian friend around Christmas 2006.

'Gary, how are you?' asked his friend.

'Fine. How are you?' replied Hersham.

'I'm fine. I'm alive.'

'How's business.'

'Well, I made a couple of billion last year,' he said almost casually.

For Hersham that conversation put the issue into perspective. 'Do you think it makes a blind bit of difference to them whether they spend £20 or £50 million on a unit, £20 million or £22 million, £7 or £10 million?' he has said. 'It makes no difference to them. What's most important to them is time, efficiency of time. "This is what I want, I'm not going to be stingy, I'll pay the price, and if I have to pay a little more, I'll do that too." They're taking that to a different level, but that's what they are doing.'

In 2006 Hersham sold twenty properties ranging from £1 million to £25 million – mostly in Belgravia – mainly to Russians but also to Eastern Europeans from former Soviet states such as Uzbekistan and Kazakhstan, both enjoying booming economies. While working for Harrods Estates, Russian-born Tatiana Baker sold twenty-five to thirty properties between 2005 and 2007, ranging up to £7 million, all in Knightsbridge, Mayfair, or Chelsea. It was these central London 'trophy addresses' – along with certain parts of Hampstead and The Bishops Avenue – that make up the elite areas referred to as 'prime' and 'super-prime' by agents.

To meet the soaring demand, Knight Frank set up a 'Super-Rich Team' to handle clients worth over £100 million. They also published a glossy thirty-page brochure in Russian with guidance on all aspects of property buying in Britain. It covered not just the mundanities of conveyancing and rules on freehold and leasehold but issues such as 'UK money-laundering regulations' and 'the effect on taxation of buying offshore'. Such was the competition to secure Russian buyers that top-end agencies all launched into Russia with active marketing campaigns while some established offices in Moscow and St Petersburg.

According to Knight Frank, one-fifth of the houses they sold costing over £8 million in London in 2006 were bought by Russians. In that year alone Russians bought 240 homes while the agents estimated that, at the end of 2006, Russians owned £2.2 billion worth of property in London and the Home Counties. This was up from £93 million in 2000, a staggering increase.

In the next two years that figure would have grown still further. As the oligarchs rarely register properties in their own name, the genuine figure is likely to be higher still. The Russians often use intermediaries such as banks, employ company names or relatives, or buy through companies registered overseas to disguise the real buyers. According to one agent talking in 2007, 'When it comes to the top end of the market, properties over £10 million, you invariably deal with an intermediary, a bank, or a search agent, so you wouldn't necessarily know you are selling to a Russian. One house I am selling at the moment on behalf of a Russian, for £12 million, I have only dealt with an offshore trust in Jersey and the solicitor, I've never spoken to the vendor and apart from his nationality, I don't know who he is.' When Russians hire top London designers like Nicholas Haslam for major refurbishments, they often insist on their names remaining a closely guarded secret.

At the height of the top-end London property boom in 2006 and 2007, super-rich Russians were, according to Natalie Hirst of search agency Prime Purchase, 'not interested in paying at the lower end, from £1 to £3 million. They're really only interested in properties from £5 to £10 million and over.' They were also very specific about location. Even the prime locations have a pecking order. Properties in the most prized areas like Kensington Palace Gardens, The Boltons, or The Bishops Avenue were mostly, though not exclusively, snapped up by wealthy foreigners. The next most popular locations were the 'garden squares', especially Eaton, Chester, Belgrave, and Lowndes Square, the latter known to long-term residents as 'Red Square'. The Russians can mostly be distinguished from other residents by their cars and chauffeurs: Russians have a particular preference for Rolls-Royce Phantoms, Mercedes Maybachs, and Bentleys. Even Cadogan Square is regarded as 'Inner Mongolia' and one existing owner of a luxury flat in Lowndes Square was not amused to be told by a Russian's lawyer that these properties were really for 'staff accommodation'.

While location is also important in terms of convenience – the favourite haunts of Kensington and Chelsea are just across the river from Battersea heliport, a key transport hub for the super-rich – they are also happy to be near their favourite hotels and restaurants, while their wives of course love shopping in Knightsbridge. According to Tatiana Baker, 'People would get very excited about Harrods. It's something of a legend in Moscow.'

But the concentration in central London is also, as one agent put it, 'A snob thing. Certain addresses will be known to foreigners. Typical English squares like Eaton and Lowndes will be known about in top circles in Moscow.' That may also be down to the herd instinct, what Natalie Hirst describes more politely as 'their comfort zone'. Valerie Manokhina explained, 'The Russian rich all know each other, even if many have fallen out. They are not especially confident in London. Many don't speak other languages and they are not familiar with Britain, its history, and culture. So they stick together for security. The wives in particular like being near each other.'

For Abramovich's business partner Evgeny Shvidler, former chief executive of Sibneft, his London residence was built almost from scratch. The man sometimes known as 'Abramovich's representative on earth' has been very close to his boss since they first met at a synagogue. A trusted ally, he helped Abramovich negotiate the purchase of Chelsea FC. They are inseparable. Shvidler has degrees from the Gubkin Russian State University in Moscow and Fordham University in New York and in the 1980s worked for Deloitte Touche, gaining American citizenship and becoming known in America as Eugene. He returned to Russia in 1994, teamed up with Abramovich, and built a fortune of some £1.7 billion, with investments in Moscow real estate, steel, and a Russian meat processor. He keeps a private jet at Farnborough in Hampshire and flies regularly to his Moscow office.

Although he is an American citizen, Shvidler built his house in Caroline Terrace, Belgravia, for £20.5 million. The site had previously been occupied by a warehouse, which was sold in 2000 for £4.7 million and developed into a grand town house. Just two miles from Stamford Bridge, the property has an underground swimming pool, sauna, and a study with leather floors. It is five times the size of adjacent houses in the terrace where his neighbours include Viscount Rothermere, custodian of the *Daily Mail*, the actor Sean Connery, and the power couple Nigella Lawson and Charles Saatchi.

Like many Russians, Shvidler became obsessed with privacy, and the new house was set like a fortress behind high walls, reached only through a pair of tall, locked, and guarded iron gates with twenty-four-hour security. In order for him to build the gated archway, Shvidler bought out a neighbour for £1.3 million. When he leaves the house, he is driven in a black bullet- and bomb-proof Mercedes with VIP number plates. In Moscow he uses the Zil lane, once reserved for use by the ruling elite of the Politburo, and has a flashing blue light on the roof of his car while his bodyguards and retinue travel with him in four separate 4x4s.

High-level and expensive security is a trademark of the Londongrad set, many of whom enjoy better security than the British Prime Minster. Yuri Shlyaifstein, once dubbed the 'King of Aluminium' in Russia, bought a house in St John's Wood in 2006 and had all the windows reglazed with bullet-proof glass. Following a series of assassinations of high-ranking bankers in Russia, Petr Aven, head of Russia's largest private bank, Alfa, surrounded his house on the Wentworth Estate in Virginia Water, Surrey, with an 'intelligent' electronic fence, even though he lives mostly in Moscow. His security arrangements extend to a bomb-proof shelter and a two-storey guard house. It has been described as 'KGB-proof'.

The postcodes favoured by the Russians also carry great social significance. As the ceramic blue plaques scattered across the neighbourhoods show, they have long been areas favoured by some of the richest, most powerful, and colourful members of British society. The seventeenth-century chronicler of London, John Bowack described Kensington and Chelsea as a place 'resorted to by persons of quality, inhabited by gentry and persons of note'. What the Russians have been buying into is a large slice of British history.

The Russians have also showed, as one agent put it with characteristic understatement, 'less than modest demands'. When it comes to extravagance, they are even outgunning their aristocratic predecessors. Not that long ago, 4,000 square feet would have been a big house. Now 'big' means 20,000 square feet.

Size became necessary to accommodate today's new essentials – an indoor swimming pool, fitted gym, staff accommodation, computerized mood lighting, and extensive garaging. According to Knight Frank, 'Some clients have been known to spend up to £400,000 just on advanced electronics. One had a system that enabled him to see who was knocking on his door in London from anywhere in the world, via a video clip sent to his mobile phone.' Many wanted separate rooms for their growing art collections, a library, a billiard table, or a home cinema – or in some cases, all of them. If these didn't already exist, then they would be added – often through excavation of the basement – at a cost that might well have equalled or exceeded the purchase price.

What was happening in London was a process of 'megagentrification' that was reversing a hundred years of history. Kensington and Chelsea's prime locations were once more being colonized by the super-rich taking over the very properties built in the eighteenth and nineteenth centuries to house the landed gentry.

The effect of the foreign invasion on London's super-prime property market was dramatic. Just after the millennium prices in prime locations rose broadly in line with all other property across London. Then, in the two years from 2005, foreign demand brought rocketing prices. According to Savills, prices for prime central London properties they sold costing over £5 million grew by a remarkable 50 per cent in the year leading up to March 2007, six times faster than for houses in general.

Part of the explanation for the boom was Britain's own wealth explosion. Record City bonuses in the early 2000s fuelled demand for homes in the £1 million to £3 million range but, for homes above this level, the main driving force was international money from the global economic boom. 'The more expensive the property, the higher the density of overseas buyers,' Liam Bailey, head of research at Knight Frank said in late 2007. 'The top end of the market has become an increasingly international market. While the principal European buyers have been French, Italians, and Germans – typically bankers in financial services, working in the City or Canary Wharf – at the top end it is the Russians who have outstripped all other nationalities apart from the British, well ahead of the Indians and Chinese, who have been late arrivals in comparison.'

Payment by cash also became the norm. As one agent described it, 'I had this buyer approach me wanting to spend £64 million on three properties, two in prime central London and one in the country or in Scotland. I asked him for a banker's reference, and he said, "No need, I will pay cash".' One agent told us that it was not atypical for a client to buy a 'stop-gap property for about £15 million while waiting for the perfect purchase'. At the peak of the market in the late summer of 2007, top-end properties saw queues of frenetic cash buyers. There was an air of panic with properties being increasingly bought 'off-plan'. 'One foreign buyer bought a house off-plan in Eaton Square, a prime location next to the church, for £17 million', according to Savills. 'He didn't view the property, he just liked what he saw in the brochure.' By June 2007, one-third of the apartments at Candy and Candy's One Hyde Park, the most expensive development in London, had been sold, this despite it being no more than a large hole in the ground and not due to be completed before 2010.

Natalie Hirst at Prime Purchase recalled representing a Russian client in a competitive bid. 'The bidding got higher and I advised my client that he was overpaying by a significant amount and he looked me in the eyes and said, "Don't lose the property, Natalie". I carried on bidding and made sure I kept bidding until we won it. My client didn't want to lose it even if we were paying way over the odds.'

When the right property came on the market, especially in the most exclusive addresses, it created a frenzy of interest. Jonathan Hewlett at Savills explained how 'In 2007 we took on an unmodernized house in Mayfair and put it on the market for £15 million. Before we even had a floor plan, we had forty-six people viewing it in the first week.' Andrew Buchanan of John D Wood said, 'In mid-2006 I had seventeen registered buyers wanting to spend over £20 million; in mid-2007 I had sixty buyers willing to pay over £20 million.' Even after a sealed bid had taken place, it was not uncommon for a rival buyer to come back with a better offer.

As colder economic conditions began to bite in 2008, feverish conditions at the top end of the market showed no sign of abating. In the spring Liam Bailey of Knight Frank reported that 'The market for £5 million-plus homes had expanded to the point where the "super-prime" threshold had now risen to £10 million.' Only by the autumn did the prices for homes above £5 million start to slip.

Fuelled by the foreign influx, in 2007 London overtook New York as the most expensive residential market in the world. Prime London property cost £2,300 per square foot on average, compared to £1,600 in New York. In contrast, prime properties in Tokyo, Hong Kong, and Dubai were less than half the cost of London.[7] A year later, by September 2008, London had begun to feel the effect of the carnage in financial markets – but only just. Monaco – where prices rocketed 30 per cent in a year in the crowded Mediterranean tax haven – had pushed it into second place.

While super-rich Russians seeking a foothold in the UK headed initially for London's 'oligarch belt', they soon began to follow Abramovich's example by buying up country mansions as well. In Russia the rich have long enjoyed their own suburban and rural dachas and it wasn't long before they started trying to emulate that style of living by looking for country properties in England.

One of the first to do so was Eugene Tenenbaum, a former head of corporate affairs at Sibneft, a director of Chelsea FC, and Abramovich's closest aide as Managing Director of Millhouse Capital. In 1999 the Ukrainian-born banker and Canadian citizen – who moved to London in the 1990s – bought a country house with a swimming pool in Walton-on-Thames, located conveniently near the head office of Millhouse. In 2005 Andrei Melnichenko, the banker and industrialist billionaire, bought the 27-acre Harewood estate near Windsor to add to his London home.

In 2007 Sunninghill Park, a wedding present from the Queen for the Duke and Duchess of York, was sold for £14 million – considerably more than its asking price – to a Kazakh tycoon. The 5-acre estate, built in 1986 in Tesco-style red brick, was not widely admired but still carried the cachet of being a former royal residence.

Despite Britain having a long history of foreign residents buying homes in the countryside, only in the last decade have they once again become dominant players. The number of

Russians buying outside London rose more than sevenfold between 2005 and 2007, with a concentration on the gilded enclaves of Esher, Cobham, and Weybridge in Surrey, and Windsor and Ascot in Berkshire.

When an £11 million house near Guildford in Surrey was sold by Knight Frank in March 2007, half the viewers were Russians, as was the eventual purchaser. When the same agents sold a house on the Wentworth Estate for just under £10 million, 43 per cent of viewers were Russian. When another house near Virginia Water was marketed for £7 million, one-third of the viewers were Russians. In 2006 Russians accounted for more than half of the properties bought by foreigners costing more than £5 million in the Home Counties.[8]

One senior property agent, who worked only with Russian buyers, said in 2007, 'I will quite literally drop everything (day or night) to ensure they get the service they want. I have four of the best helicopter companies and a number of chauffeurs on speed dial in order that viewings can be arranged at the drop of a hat. I once spent two days in a helicopter with my prospective super-rich buyers touring country estates.'

The wave of foreign money that broke in the UK slowly changed the social and architectural map of parts of rural Britain. Expensive country homes were once the province of the landed aristocracy and the commercial barons of the Industrial Revolution. Then, from the end of the First World War, they were joined by high-earning professionals, such as stockbrokers and lawyers.

From the 1960s, the original owners and post-war newcomers of exclusive, gated estates such as St George's Hill near Esher found themselves sharing their plush surroundings with a diverse new group of neighbours. John Lennon bought Kenwood, a seven-bedroom mock-Tudor house set in secluded grounds in 1964, where he is said to have written 'Lucy in the Sky with Diamonds' and recorded two albums. He set a trend that saw the subsequent arrival of a wave of rock stars and celebrities, from Tom Jones and Cliff Richard to Ringo Starr and the comedian Eric Sykes. They, in turn, were joined in the 1980s by top celebrities and sporting stars as their earnings soared to take them into the rich lists.

By the height of the noughties boom, however, the stockbrokers and all but the top celebrities found themselves being priced out, as some of the outstanding country properties were bought up by stars of film, music, and the fine arts, such as Kate Winslet, Madonna and Guy Ritchie, and Damien Hirst.

But it was new money – home- (British financiers, tycoons, entrepreneurs, heads of investment banks, hedge fund and private equity partners) and foreign-grown – that was displacing the moneyed classes of the past. It was a Russian who ended up buying Torpoint on St George's Hill from Tom Jones. As one local upmarket developer put it, 'Once St George's Hill was the favoured haunt of celebrities and pop or football stars. Today you are more likely to find a Russian than a pop star or a Premier League footballer.'

The Russians became especially keen on areas close to Windsor Great Park, such as St George's Hill and Wentworth. Wentworth, which offers a period feel with modern living, has many Middle Eastern residents but also a scattering of recent Russian arrivals, among them Boris Berezovsky. One of his neighbours is Mikhail 'Micha' Watford, a Russian 'mini-oligarch' who made a fortune in energy with business interests in Russia and Ukraine. He then set up High Life Developments, a luxury property development and design company, based in the King's Road, Chelsea. Watford's £7 million high-security house on the Wentworth Estate has grounds which contain a five-a-side football pitch and cricket pavilion.

St George's Hill is a large private estate near Weybridge built as Britain's first gated community by local developer W. G. Tarrant in 1911 to provide 'large country retreats for the wealthy gentlemen of London'. The 200 original homes built in the Arts and Crafts style on 900 acres around a private golf course, most of them with several acres of garden, were originally snapped up by London's super-rich. With its breathtaking views of the local countryside, the estate became one of the most exclusive parts of the Surrey stockbroker belt in the mid-post-war years.

The first Russian believed to have bought in St George's Hill was Tanya Dyachenko, Yeltsin's daughter, in the late 1990s. She bought Hamstone House, a white-and-cream Art Deco house and the only listed building on the estate. There are also plenty of 'big boys', as one agent describes them, including Oleg Deripaska and Evgeny Shvidler. According to another agent, the latter was 'always on the prowl' for other properties in the area.

The impact of the surge in wealth did not only show itself in soaring prices on St George's Hill. Increasingly, houses that had lost their former appeal, or had simply become outdated, were demolished and replaced by modern and grand, often ostentatious styles: mock-this, neo-that, a Spanish-style hacienda. New money would appear to have few qualms about history or heritage. While minimalism is not in the Russian psyche or lexicon, it is not possible in today's property market to define a single Russian 'taste'. Some bought traditional period properties, but the great majority wanted a period style or feel. In the summer of 2007 forty-eight sites were under development, more than 10 per cent of the entire estate. Another factor driving demolition was scale. Just as for a London town house, the super-rich wanted large properties, returning to the scale of mansions that were often commonplace in the nineteenth century. 'Extravagance', according to one estate agent, 'is now the norm.'

Most of these new developments were finished to an exceptionally high standard. Take Hartlands, a super-luxury home built in 2005 on the site of one such property not considered up to scratch. The newly built seven-bedroom house, complete with staff flat and 12-metre indoor swimming pool, was bought by a Russian in 2006 and sold a year later, in the spring of 2007, for £14.5 million. The purchaser never even occupied the house. The property boasts a walnut-panelled study with a large handmade walnut desk to match. It comes with a range of gadgets that include a place to hold Rolexes and a plasma television screen that can be hidden behind a painted panel at the touch of a button. 'No one in the UK,' said the agent who handled the sale, 'would spend that kind of money on a study. It is going back to the Edwardian era.'

While most Russian émigrés seeking a retreat preferred the Home Counties for their proximity to London, some ventured further afield. In 2007 a Russian bought a house near Falmouth in Cornwall for £3 million. In 2005 Leon Max, the Russian-born fashion designer, paid £15 million for Easton Neston near Towcester, in Northamptonshire. It had been the ancestral home of the Hesketh family for nearly 500 years. Max attended an English school and then emigrated to New York at twenty-one, building a worldwide fashion retail empire with 300 Max Studio shops around the world.

Easton Neston, a Grade II-listed building, was designed by Nicholas Hawksmoor and is considered a masterpiece of the English Baroque style. It came with two lodges, a stable, and 550 acres of parkland. Max spent millions renovating outbuildings and converting the Wren wing of Easton Neston, which was badly damaged by fire in 2002. According to newspaper reports, the new owners were welcomed onto the estate with a gift from Lord Hesketh – a bottle of vodka.

Leon Max has used part of the stately home as a base for his expanding European business, living there half the year and the rest in California with his American model wife. Shortly after moving in, he told the local newspaper, the *Brackley and Towcester Advertiser*, 'I love the area. I have visited the local butcher, baker, and pub and feel that everything we need is here. I am hoping to lure some people away from London to this beautiful place.' He is already well integrated into British life and counts the Earl of Dartmouth, Sir Elton John, Richard Littlejohn, Lily Safra, and Conservative MP Nicholas Soames among his friends.

Of the Russians buying rural properties, few, if any, have lived in them permanently. Many have one or more homes in London as well as one or more country homes, a place in Moscow, *and* in the South of France. Some are global business-men who will spend more time abroad than in the UK. Some are Moscow-based entrepreneurs who will use their homes partly as an investment opportunity and partly for occasional spring and summer retreats. Other buyers have continued to work in Moscow but have moved their wives and children to the United Kingdom.

Just as some of the oligarchs, notably Boris Berezovsky, seemed keen to cultivate members of the aristocracy and the British royal family as contacts, so others were seen trying to emulate the lifestyles of the British nobility – 'Playing lord of the manor', as one property agent put it – quickly developing a taste for British rural and sporting traditions, even buying Scot-tish castles and estates. Berezovsky himself was said to have been 'sniffing around the Highlands' and has been an occasional visitor to Skibo Castle in Sutherland. Originally built by the Scottish-born American industrialist and philanthropist Andrew Carnegie, it later became a sporting and leisure club for the super-rich.

'Scottish trophy properties – sporting estates, castles, and islands – soon attracted international interest', according to John Coleman of Knight Frank in Edinburgh. 'Very few in top condition come onto the market, maybe three or four a year, so when they do they are real trophies. They offer international buyers looking for a way to unload their wealth on something special and scarce. The buyers themselves may not spend that much time here, maybe a month a year, but they buy them to entertain in and to use as a sanctuary to escape the world now and again.'

One Scottish property broker liked to promote the Highlands as 'Siberia without the cold'. 'What has been driving the market has been money coming out of Russia. The Russian interest – some real, some perceived – fuelled demand elsewhere and raised expectations,' says John Coleman.

Apart from the sheer size of the estates, Scotland had another great advantage. Trophy properties came relatively cheap: up to 2008, nothing sold for over £20 million – small change for oligarchs. In December 2005 Vladimir Lisin, then the fifth-richest man in Russia, paid £6.8 million for the sixteenth-century Aberuchill Castle, a sprawling 3,300-acre grouse-shooting, deer-stalking, and game-fishing estate overlooking Loch Earn, near Comrie in Perthshire. Lisin bought the property 'off the market'. He put in a knockout bid, sufficient to kill off the competition.

Lisin worked as a welder in a coal mine in Siberia in the 1970s. He acquired the steel giant Novolipetsk during the 1990s by buying shares in the metals sector and then sold a small stake on the London Stock Exchange in 2005. At the beginning of 2008 he was estimated to be worth some £7 billion. Married with three children, he enjoys clay pigeon shooting and smoking Cohiba cigars. He reportedly used some of his wealth to sponsor the Fitasc Sporting British clay pigeon shooting Grand Prix at the Southern Counties shooting grounds in Dorset in 2004.

Nikas Safronov is another who has acquired a Scottish estate. A celebrity painter, he has made big money producing portraits of the rich and famous in the guise of lords, dukes, popes, and emperors from throughout history, a style that greatly appeals to his subjects. Close to the Kremlin, he has painted President

Putin as a dashing Francis I of France. It is now *de rigueur* for the Russian elite to have their portraits painted, and Safronov charges some £40,000 to paint the wives (and sometimes the mistresses) of the rich.

Scottish estates offer the usual security, privacy, and isolation much sought after by so many Russians. How long those who bought into the dream will stay in Scotland is another matter. John Coleman doubts if they are in Scotland for the long term. 'The ones I have sold to are not really here because of a deep-seated desire to live a feudal life. It is more of a matter of "What can I spend my money on?" They love and enjoy the experience of a large Scottish estate but it wouldn't surprise me if in five years' time they moved on and sold up because they had found another interest. They are likely to have a much more short-term interest than the original Victorian developers had in mind for their beautifully crafted estates.'

The arrival of the Russians had a dramatic impact on Britain's top property landscape, both in the capital's 'golden postcodes' and in the Home Counties. But the impact of Russian money did not stop at the acquisition of some of Britain's finest town houses and rural estates. The steady outflow of Russia's historic wealth helped to fuel a much wider spending boom on a scale not seen since the 1920s.

CHAPTER 6

Boys with Toys

'It is size that matters. It's all down to boys' toys, surrounding yourself with ever more super-luxuries. You have to remember that all these guys know each other from the 1990s and it's a man's world; they compete with each other by showing off. The ladies go to a restaurant with the latest bag, but the boys do it with boats and planes. The guys are very competitive and ruling and one of the ways of beating the competition is to have something that is bigger and better than anyone else's'

— VALERIE MANOKHINA

THE FIRST ITEM ON THE LIST of 'must-have toys' for serious members of the Billionaire's Club is the private jet. This is a relatively recent phenomenon. In the 1980s international tycoons were content with the corporate jet. Today, despite their massive running costs in an age of high oil prices, the super-rich buy their own. You can see why. There is guaranteed privacy, the ability to bypass the world's increasingly congested hubs, and no baggage restrictions. And then there is the exclusive access to 5,000 airports – rather than the 500 suitable for commercial carriers and mere mortals.

Most London-based oligarchs soon acquired their own jet, including Boris Berezovsky, Evgeny Shvidler, and Oleg Deripaska. Most got by with one. Not Roman Abramovich. He was once content with a £40 million Boeing 737 – expensive enough to take him into the premier league of jet owners – but by 2006, he had added two more to his collection: a Dassault Falcon 900; and the crown jewel among private jets, a personalized Boeing 767 he calls the the 'Bandit'. He is in elite company: there are believed to be only a dozen privately owned 767s in the world.

Both Boeings are kept at Farnborough Airport, only thirty minutes' flying time from Battersea heliport and Fyning Hill, where he also keeps a brace of helicopters. One of them, a large, orange £6 million Sikorsky, has been sound-proofed so that Abramovich can watch videos and listen to DVDs in the passenger cabin. It is one of only five in the UK, three of which belong to the Metropolitan Police. The cost of running a jet does not stop at its purchase, however. Abramovich spent some £10 million equipping the interior of the 'Bandit' and even added missile-jamming technology similar to that used on the US Presidential aircraft, Air Force One. Originally designed to seat 360 people, the new airborne toy was finished in walnut, mahogany, and gold and fitted with every possible luxury: a gym, bathrooms, and plasma-screen TVs. Irina is said to have bought the cabin's crockery at Thomas Goode in Mayfair.

Each jet requires two crews consisting of a pilot, co-pilot, and two air hostesses. The cost over and above fuel and maintenance will run to several million pounds a year. Not that Abramovich doesn't put them to good use: in November 2003 he flew in 100 Russian friends to watch Chelsea play at home.

Not that long ago, most of the super-rich would have been content with renting a yacht for the summer, but today the super-yacht has become the next ultimate indulgence; an apparently mandatory status symbol that often turns out to be even more expensive than the jet. But, as with jets, even yachts in the super-league come with their own hierarchy, based on speed, power, luxury, and, above all, size.

Initially, Abramovich seemed content with his two relatively modest yachts – *Stream* and *Sophie's Choice* – both bought from Berezovsky in 1999. But it was not long before yachting, or owning yachts, became an obsession. By 2008, nobody could match his 'personal fleet'. In early 2003 he paid an estimated £50 million for the 370-foot *Le Grand Bleu*, one of the highest-tech boats afloat. The prestigious vessel requires a crew of sixty-five and carries a large aquarium, an arsenal of tenders, and water toys, including a 22-metre sailing yacht, two 60-knot Buzzi sports boats, and a landing craft to carry a 4x4 Land Rover. The boat leapfrogged Abramovich overnight into the ranks of the super-yacht owners, up there with Microsoft's Paul Allen, with Oracle founder and racing yachtsman Larry Ellison, and with Prince Sultan bin Abdul Aziz, the Crown Prince of Saudi Arabia.

You might think that owning one of the world's most impressive super-yachts would be enough even for an oligarch, but a few months later in 2003, in conditions of the utmost secrecy, Abramovich completed another deal, one that propelled him into the 'mega-yacht' league. In October 2003 he took possession of *Pelorus*, which, at 377 feet, made it the tenth-largest private yacht in the world. The boat had been commissioned by a Saudi Arabian businessman, Sheikh Modhassan, but Abramovich spotted it and made the Saudi a multi-million-pound offer he couldn't refuse.

The yacht, built by the leading German yacht-builders Lürssen, at its Rendsburg yard on the Kiel Canal, is the work of two internationally renowned British designers, Tim Heywood and Terence Disdale. After a major refit, it is the epitome of luxury. As Disdale described the design, 'We try to do beach house now rather than penthouse – lots of natural materials like rattan, leather, and stone instead of marble. It's nickel taps instead of gold.' It has a swimming pool with an artificial current, a spa pool, and an owner's cabin with 180-degree panoramic views and a private deck. The boat comes with top-of-the range engineering. Its six decks can accommodate twenty guests, attended by a crew of forty-two, and has a range of 6,000 nautical miles and a top speed of 20 knots. As well as the bullet-proof glass and a missile-detection system, it also has two helicopters and a submarine.

The deal may have been done in top secrecy, but it was only a month before yacht-watchers spotted Abramovich aboard his new acquisition on his way to Italy to watch Chelsea beat Lazio in the European Champions League. Photographs were helpfully posted on www.yachtspotter.com, which charts the movements of the world's classiest boats. The secret was out.

After acquiring *Pelorus*, Abramovich bought two more yachts. In 2006 he took delivery of *Ecstasea*, also designed by Disdale, who introduced a Chinese theme with lots of bamboo. At 282 feet, it is the only one of his 'fleet' that he personally commissioned. Built in conditions of extreme secrecy under the codename 'Project 790', it is the most stylish of his boats, is propelled by five engines, has a top speed of 35 knots, and cost £70 million. Next came the smallest and fastest of his personal fleet: *Sussurro*. Small it may be, but there is nothing basic about the boat. It was once lent to Chelsea midfielder Frank Lampard as a reward for being voted the club's player of the year in the 2004–5 season. 'We had ten staff, including a chef, five fantastic bedrooms, and five-star food,' said Lampard. 'Then you are pulling up in St Tropez and you feel half-embarrassed. I was absolutely blown away by all the facilities.' [1]

In November 2006 Abramovich gave away *Le Grande Bleu* to Evgeny Shvidler. As a result, Shvidler – who already owned the £28 million *Olympia* – jumped into the two super-yacht category. But a top oligarch is not easily satisfied. Rivalry among the super-rich goes back centuries, and owning the world's biggest yacht seemed to become something of an obsession for the Russians. To the delight of builders and designers everywhere, they started to commission bigger and ever-more luxurious ones every year – as ever, in conditions of the utmost secrecy.

According to Valerie Manokhina, this infatuation with possessions such as yachts is down to the Russian male's obsession with competition: 'It is size that matters. It's all down to boys' toys, surrounding yourself with ever more super-luxuries. You have to remember that all these guys know each other from the 1990s and it's a man's world; they compete with each other by showing off. The ladies go to a restaurant with the latest bag, but the boys do it with boats and planes. The guys are very competitive and one of the ways of beating the competition is to have something that is bigger and better than anyone else's.' Some question the claim that it is about the pleasure of sailing and the sea. 'When a yacht is over 328 feet, it's so big that you lose the intimacy, said Tork Buckley, editor of *The Yacht Report*. 'On the other hand, you've got bragging rights. No question that's a very strong part of the motivation.'

Abramovich is only too aware of what one industry figure describes as the 'battle for size'. In 2006 conscious that his position in the rankings was slipping as other multi-billionaires commissioned ever-larger yachts, he ordered yet two more vessels. One was a 120-metre boat with lots of toys to replace *Le Grande Bleu*. The other, *Eclipse*, built by the German shipyard Blohm & Voss, was due for delivery in 2009. It is said that this boat will be the last word in luxury and, for an owner obsessed with security, will also come with heat-and-motion sensors to detect intruders and missile-detector systems. Abramovich has also commissioned a 65-foot Nomad 1000 submarine, which will dock on *Eclipse*. This is smaller than his other submarine, a 116-foot Seattle 1000, which cost £13 million to buy and costs £1 million a year to run.

Eclipse's cost, according to one well-placed insider, will be in excess of £300 million, making it by far the most expensive boat ever commissioned. At an estimated 160 metres, it is one and a half times the length of a football pitch and, unless someone else gets there before him, will easily catapult Abramovich into first place.

By 2009, Admiral Abramovich will have five boats, four of them in the mega- or super-class league, and two submarines. Why he needs a private navy bigger than some entire nations' has been a source of much industry speculation. One head of a major charter firm described it as 'a nonsense; he doesn't need that many. That's what you do when you've got everything; you've already got the super-yacht, the amazing ski chalet in Aspen, you've got a *Gulfstream*. You have to go one step further, get a bigger yacht, get a Boeing. Next it will be an Airbus.' Another industry insider commented, 'It's clear. It's to upstage everyone else. Nobody needs a boat that size.' And one broker said it was to have 'a boat available at a moment's notice in every major yachting location – the Med, the Caribbean, South America, and the Pacific'.

Of course, a fleet of private jets, helicopters, and yachts ensures he can meet anyone anywhere at short notice and never needs to miss a Chelsea game. On one occasion he travelled to Stamford Bridge via helicopter and plane from one of his yachts off Alaska. But the fleet is also motivated by the need for asset diversification: by transferring cash into assets via SPVs in different offshore jurisdictions all over the world, his wealth is protected from sequestration and seizure.

On the road Abramovich's fleet contains top-performance cars, among them two customized bomb-proof Mercedes Maybach 62 limousines and a £1 million Ferrari FXX racing car, one of only thirty produced. In the five years after buying Chelsea, his capital outlay on property, jets, yachts, and cars alone would have exceeded £1 billion. The annual cost of running his yachts, his homes, and his jets alone would have easily topped £100 million. And then there is his expenditure on football. Its accounts in 2007 to 2008 showed that Chelsea carried debts of £736 million, more than £500 million of which was owed to Abramovich in a series of loans after he had bought the club.

Spending on this scale would be beyond any but about one hundred people on the planet, but it will barely have dented Abramovich's fortune. Between 2000 and 2003 alone, dividends from Sibneft totalled over $2 billion while, since 2000, he has netted billions more from asset sales. In 2003 his holding company, Millhouse Capital, not only held a substantial stake in Sibneft but also a 26 per cent stake in Aeroflot, a 50 per cent share in the world's second-largest aluminium producer Rusal, as well as stakes in car manufacturer GAZ, the Orsk-Khalilovsky Metal Combine, Avtobank, insurance giant Ingosstrakh, a hydroelectric plant in Kraznoyarsk, and the Ust Llinsky pulp and paper plant. In early 2003 he sold his shares in Aeroflot and then, following Khodorkovsky's arrest in October 2003, offloaded a large chunk of his stake in Rusal to his business partner, Oleg Deripaska. In the next two years he sold off most of the rest. Most significantly, in 2005 he sold his remaining stake in Sibneft to the state combine Gazprom for a massive £7.5 billion.

In 2008 the *Sunday Times* estimated his wealth to be £11.7 billion, almost 70 per cent more than that of the richest Briton, the Duke of Westminster. After the sale of Sibneft, he invested widely in Russia and Europe, adding a 41 per cent holding in the Russian steel group Evraz and a 44.6 per cent stake in Eurocement, Russia's largest cement and construction conglomerate. In September 2008 Eurocement Holding AG, its Swiss affiliate, bought a 6.5 per cent stake in Holcim Ltd, a Russian construction material company with a Swiss subsidiary. Like Berezovsky, he has gone to great lengths to ensure his financial deals and holdings have been kept secret. To ensure this, most of his assets have been registered in the British Virgin Islands.

Despite Abramovich's immense wealth, not everyone succumbs to his offers when he goes shopping. In 2003 he tried to buy a chalet in Courchevel, the luxury French ski resort invaded by nouveaux riches Russians every January. After flying in by helicopter with his wife and bodyguards, he asked to see the best private homes in the area. He then asked the resort's director of tourism, René Montgrandi, to telephone the owners and offer whatever it would take to persuade them to sell. 'I knew what they would say in advance,' said Montgrandi. 'We have no more land that can be developed and our owners are very happy to have a house. Mr Abramovich said he would pay double or triple, but each owner declined.'[2]

This is not the only time Abramovich has missed out. His purchase of Chelsea FC came with access to two of the special millennium boxes at the stadium that sit on the halfway line. The others cost up to £1 million a season to rent. As he often invites a crowd of friends to watch the games at Stamford Bridge, Abramovich tried to buy the special box next to his own. He offered considerably more than £1 million. The owner refused and so he upped the price several times. The answer was still no. Some hot property is simply not for sale – even to Abramovich.

The irony is that at least one of Abramovich's personal boxes is often empty, even more so in 2007 and 2008. One prominent PR consultant who was at Stamford Bridge for a big match asked a Club executive why the box was empty. 'I could have filled it several times over,' said the PR man. It was empty, the executive explained, because Abramovich liked to keep it in case he needed it at the last minute. 'To Abramovich, throwing away the £30,000 fee he could have received by letting it out was neither here nor there,' said the PR consultant.

* * *

It has often been asked why Abramovich has been allowed to strut the world's stage with his private armies of bodyguards, fleet of yachts, and squadron of jets while other oligarchs have been forced into exile or incarcerated in Siberia. After all, the Chelsea owner was also a beneficiary of the questionable privatization deals of the 1990s.

In the early days of Putin's presidency, Abramovich's relationship with the Kremlin was somewhat ambiguous. While others seemed initially to be favoured over him, the astute billionaire soon learnt to play by the rules. Abramovich's biographers describe him as a man with multiple fronts, 'With as many personas as there are figurines in a Russian doll'.[3] The answer is relatively simple: he has learnt to play a dual role – a London-based émigré and a Russian patriot. Under Putin, he had to develop another side to his personality. He turned himself into the model oligarch. Trading subservience for freedom is the primary reason for the leeway he came to enjoy.

Unlike Berezovsky and Khodorkovsky, he has steered clear of politics. 'As long as he does what he's told, he will be fine,' one Putin adviser explained. He agreed to stand as governor of Chukotka, in Siberia's far east on the Arctic Circle. When his term was up in 2005, he sought to relinquish the post, but in a personal meeting at the Kremlin he reluctantly yielded to Putin's request to stay on. He has handed over his assets to the Russian state when asked to do so. It is even claimed that Abramovich was always reluctant to divorce Irina and only agreed to do so under pressure from Putin. According to Chris Hutchins, one of the oligarch's biographers, 'Abramovich and Putin are incredibly close. Putin regards Abramovich as something of a favourite son. When the rumours about Abramovich's private life started surfacing, Putin told him to get his act cleaned up. Putin is a real family man and did not approve of Roman's relationship with Daria or the publicity it has generated. He … made it clear Abramovich should settle his personal affairs.'[4]

On top of this, Abramovich has spent lavishly on patriotic and social Russian projects, contributing to various political authorities, notably £200 million to Chukotka. As Putin set up a number of tax havens inside Russia, the investment also brought generous tax breaks in return.

David Clark, special adviser to former Foreign Secretary Robin Cook and Chair of the Russia Foundation, says that Abramovich's lifestyle has been tolerated because he has made himself useful. 'There is a sense in which Abramovich is the acceptable face of Russia, a global businessman who is non-threatening, and thus helpful to the Russian authorities by portraying an image of football and fun,' Clark said. In this way he can be seen as Russia's public relations globetrotter offering a more acceptable image of the typical oligarch.

Abramovich's exalted status is also in part due to his purchase of Chelsea FC. 'What better way to cover yourself in protective armour than to buy a high-profile British football club?' commented one Russian analyst. 'It was a masterstroke, a brilliant piece of public relations. He doesn't need a PR company. He has Chelsea.' Another called it 'the cheapest insurance policy in history'. He was the first Russian to buy into British football, acquired an international reputation by doing so, and thus bought himself a degree of protection not enjoyed by others.

When Abramovich bought Chelsea FC, however, he received considerable criticism within Russia. Yuri Luzhkov, the mayor of Moscow, called the move a 'slap in the face for Russian football'. The head of Russia's Audit Chamber said he was lavishing too much money on English football at the expense of the Russian game. The criticism may have stung Abramovich because, through Sibneft, a few months later he invested £30 million in CSKA Moscow. He later gained more political kudos when he bankrolled Russia's football federation, contributing heavily to the £4 million salary of the national coach, the Dutchman Guus Hiddink, and investing in a new Russian football academy. When Russia beat England 2–1 in Moscow in October 2007 in a critical qualifying game in the European Championship, Abramovich was seen cheering Russia on and was much in evidence congratulating the team as it left the pitch, a patriotic gesture not lost on the Kremlin.

While Abramovich ostensibly remains the Russian patriot *par excellence*, he has also expanded and cemented his roots in London. In 2005 he transferred the ownership of most of his UK properties from Caribbean offshore companies into his own name – a highly unusual move for any Russian oligarch and one designed to improve his image as the most secretive oligarch. But, unlike Berezovsky, he has largely shunned the London social scene and English high society – and not for want of opportunities. The purchase of Fyning Hill offered him the perfect entrée into the world of polo but he never mastered the sport (despite hiring the captain of the English polo team to tutor him) and is rarely seen at the polo festivals during the season.

Another route into English society was provided by a well-connected private banker, Roddie Fleming. In 2001 Fleming assembled a group of aristocratic investors, among them Lord Daresbury and the Earl of Derby, to buy a 34 per cent stake in a Siberian goldmine. Called Highland Gold, Abramovich acquired a large stake in the company, an investment that paid off handsomely as the value of their original stake grew fivefold in eighteen months. It provided a golden opportunity for Abramovich to cultivate a circle of establishment contacts, but it was one he declined. 'We invited him in and that's the only time I've met him,' said Fleming.[5]

Abramovich prefers privacy to high-profile socialising. Staff at Chelsea say they find him distant, while others say that if you approached him he would often stop you dead with his bland, almost ghosted look. Although this may be partly down to his poor command of English, he is clearly not comfortable in social situations, especially with people he does not know.

His ex-wife, Irina, by contrast, is a natural socialite, so much so that the pair often led relatively separate lives. She loved shopping on Sloane Street, being ferried around in limousines, jetting off to St Tropez, and lunching in Mayfair restaurants with celebrities. With the advantage of speaking better English, she threw herself into society in a way her former husband could not. She was a regular on the social calendar and even retained a PR company, Platinum Entertainment Services, to advise her, provide introductions, and secure invitations. It was Irina who was believed to have encouraged Kristin Pazik, the model wife of superstar AC Milan striker, Andriy Shevchenko, to persuade her husband to move to London to play for Chelsea (an ill-fated move: the Ukrainian failed to make his mark at Chelsea and returned to the *rossoneri* in 2008).

Abramovich could occasionally be seen, bodyguard in tow, at top London restaurants such as Marco Pierre White's Luciano's in St James's, Nobu on Park Lane, and the River Café in Hammersmith, but otherwise he rarely made public appearances, stayed behind tight security, and limited his socializing mainly to a small circle of wealthy, fellow London-based Russians. These included Oleg Deripaska, Ralif Safin, one of the founders of Lukoil, as well as the trusted Evgeny Shvidler and Eugene Tenenbaum. He also remained close to Tatyana Dyachenko and could be seen dining with her at Raymond Blanc's Le Manoir aux Quat' Saisons in Oxfordshire.

Abramovich had developed British associates, some of whom could be espied in the directors' box at Stanford Bridge. One regular was Lord Jacob Rothschild, while other visitors included Formula One boss Bernie Ecclestone, Gregory Barker, former investor relations manager at Sibneft and Conservative

MP, and Mohamed Al Fayed (owner of Fulham Football Club, Chelsea's near neighbours in west London), who was introduced by Irina after one of her marathon shopping expeditions to Harrods.

Despite his property empire, Abramovich's interest in London has not ranged much beyond Stamford Bridge, City investors, and his children's education. His national loyalties have remained with Russia alone. London has been used as a base for football and for depositing and growing his wealth. Although Irina and their children became more firmly based first in Fyning Hill and then Chester Square, when the two oldest children started to attend London schools from 2004 and 2005 respectively, Abramovich spent more time in Russia than in London. A court judgement in 2008 revealed that he spent little time in London before he bought Chelsea (ten full days in 2000, seven in 2001, and only one in 2002). After that he spent an increasing amount of time there, rising from sixty-seven full days in 2004 to 110 in 2006 before falling back to fifty-six in 2007, a year when a combination of tensions in Russia and his new relationship with the Russian fashion designer Daria Zhukova meant he missed an increasing number of Chelsea games. He has remained a Russian citizen and has entered Britain on a business visa. In a rare interview in December 2006 Abramovich implied that he does not regard London as his home. 'I live on a plane,' he said.[6] A comment no doubt designed to please Vladimir Putin, who was beginning to display a growing coolness towards a Britain he accused of 'harbouring criminals and terrorists'.

A main London attraction has been his children's education and security. 'I want my children to go to school in England,' Abramovich said in August 2003. 'I'm satisfied they will get the best education in the world here.' He sent his eldest daughter to a prep school in Belgravia from 2004 and then to an all-girls' independent school in London. In 2006 he made a substantial donation to the school.[7] He once looked into Charterhouse, near Godalming in Surrey, for his sons.

The Russian interest in British public schools began in the 1990s, though not all Russian students were welcome then. At the time some of those arriving were the offspring of members of Russia's burgeoning criminal gangs whose tentacles reached into big business and politics. Huge volumes of money were being made by the Russian mafia from narcotics, people trafficking, prostitution, bribery, and the ongoing fleecing of state businesses.

More than one British school came to suspect that at least some of the fees paid were the product of criminal activity. In 1994 a representative of Isis – the Independent Schools Information Service – that had started running recruiting trips to Moscow admitted, 'We don't screen the mafia out because you can't. You don't know where their money is coming from.'[8] From the mid-1990s, there were several reports of problems arising with pupils from families of the Organizatsiya – the Russian mafia, those involved in the big crime rings. There were even alleged incidents of mini-mafia infighting between pupils. On one occasion a head teacher in East Anglia asked the local police to investigate whether two Russian pupils' fees had been paid through a money-laundering operation.

During the 1990s, stories of parents turning up at the beginning of term with large bundles of cash in payment for the entire year circulated regularly at gatherings of teachers and headmasters. One head teacher of a small public school stated that 'Students from Russia and the former Soviet Union always seemed to have plenty of cash to splash around. They were all from affluent backgrounds and were never without the latest gizmo.' Headmasters, including John Rawlinson of Oakley Hall prep school in Cirencester, Gloucestershire, tell of how they used to turn parents away who arrived at the school with cash in hand. For most Russians, of course, this was not about buying favours – it was merely the way Russians conducted their affairs: they simply preferred paying the school fees in cash.

In 1990 the number of Russian children in British schools could be counted on the fingers of one hand and these were mostly children of government ministers. In 1994 the Russians made up only 3 per cent of overseas students at private schools. By 1999, that number had swelled to 20 per cent, a remarkable rise. One pupil who used to shuttle between London and Moscow during the school holidays recalled travelling on the first and last days of term, 'The British Airways flights were like school buses filled with unruly Russian children, commuting between their English public school and their Russian home.'

Among the Russians, the oligarchs proved especially keen on a British education. Berezovsky's four children from his first two marriages attended schools in Britain. Oleg Deripaska's wife Polina was educated at Millfield School in Somerset. Mikhail Gutseriyev, the billionaire former President of the Russian oil company Russneft, who was forced to flee Russia in 2007, sent his two sons to Harrow. Tatyana Dyachenko sent her son, Boris, Yeltsin's grandson, to Millfield and then to Winchester College in the mid-1990s.

Like British estate agents, the public schools themselves soon spotted the Russian potential. Shrewd headmasters started advertising their schools in Russian newspapers in the 1990s. Some schools took their marketing to Russia itself with a steady stream of representatives attending events in Moscow and St Petersburg recruiting students. John Rawlinson attracted eighteen Russian pupils for the autumn term of 1993 after giving a seminar in Moscow and advertising in a Russian financial newspaper. The parents of those pupils included a banker, the owner of a pharmaceuticals company, and the director of a Siberian factory and hailed from Kazakhstan and Ukraine as well as Moscow and Siberia. As Rawlinson explained at the time, security was a key factor: 'People are getting killed for having a lot of money in Moscow. Coming to school in England removes a child from the dangers.'[9]

Other schools that have sent missions to Russia include Roedean, Harrogate Ladies' College, and Dulwich College. Marianne Sunter, Deputy Headmistress of Box Hill, a small coeducational independent day and boarding school in Mickleham, Surrey, for children aged eleven to eighteen, made three marketing trips to Russia between 2005 and 2007.

In 2006 there were about a thousand Russian pupils being educated in British public schools, though the schools themselves are cagey about how many Russian students they have on their books. While Russian parents like British education for the quality of the schooling and the opportunity to learn English, that old bugbear security remains a key factor. In Russia it is still not unusual for the children of wealthy parents to be kidnapped and held to ransom. In 2005, 15-year-old Elizaveta Slesareva, newly enrolled at St Peter's, a boarding school in York, died along with her parents when their Mercedes was sprayed with bullets during the mid-term break back in Moscow. Her father was the owner of Sodbiznesbank, which had its licence withdrawn by the Central Bank amid accusations of money laundering.

Another British aristocratic tradition that has attracted the Russians to Britain is the 'season' – the extended series of spring and summer social and sporting events. Today it is more 'open season' where old money and minor royals mix openly at events like Ascot with Britain's new business elite, celebrities, and assorted hangers-on. The people who get most excited about it, however, are often those with foreign money.

While some of the season's appeal may have been lost on the old money in Britain, the Russians, long deprived of such 'aristocratic' tradition, are especially enthusiastic. For them, the season offers a chance to rub shoulders with assorted members of the British establishment, something that brings a good deal of cachet.

Today the season attracts not only many British-based moneyed Russians but also a small army of visitors from the ranks of the country's emerging professional middle classes – bankers, financiers, and entrepreneurs. 'The Russians are very taken with British high society,' reiterated Aliona Muchinskaya, who arranges trips for groups of sixty or more Russian clients at a time. In 2005 her company Red Square organized a dinner party for seventy guests at Spencer House, the eighteenth-century mansion in London's St James's Place. The four-course dinner was prepared by the Rothschild's private chef and was served with Dom Perignon and £300 bottles of cognac. Later the guests enjoyed a private concert by Liza Minnelli.

That same year, Red Square launched the first of what was to become the annual Russian ball. In June, some 400 guests, many arriving in limousines, vintage Rolls-Royces, and Bentleys, gathered for a sumptuous evening in the grounds of Syon House in west London. It was an opportunity for the London-based Russian community to mingle with the Moscow jet set, many of whom had flown in for the occasion, as well as British high society. For a 'diamond table' for ten costing £3,000, guests got to meet Count Nikolai Tolstoy (a historian related to Leo Tolstoy), Prince Gregory Gallitzin, producer of Gallitzin champagne, Alsou Safina, singer and daughter of Ralif Safin, and Nat Rothschild, the son of Lord Jacob Rothschild and close friend of Oleg Deripaska, who arrived in his private helicopter with his Russian girlfriend Zhenya.

London and the Home Counties soon became an integral part of Russia's social map, offering a UK-based parallel Russian social calendar. This involved balls, charity auctions, exhibitions, exclusive parties, and events that often brought the Russian and British elite together. Kensington Palace, a royal residence for 300 years, was regularly hired by Russians for wedding receptions, lavish parties, and charity events, such were its upper-crust connections.

The 'new Russians' loved nothing more than to be a guest at one of the season's glitziest gatherings – the Cartier International Day at the Guards Polo Club in Windsor Great Park, held on the last Sunday in July, which attracts its fair share of aristocrats and international celebrities. Indeed, several Russians have gained entry to the polo set. Vladlena Bernardoni-Belolipskaia, a professional polo player for the Royal Berkshire Polo Club who set up her own team called Vladi-Moscow, has become a Cartier regular. Another enthusiast is Sergei Kolushev, the Managing Director of a Canary Wharf-based events company that hosts the annual Russian Economic Forum, once the largest gathering of Russian business leaders outside Moscow and St Petersburg. Kolushev arrived in London in 1989 with little money and built up a business that also organizes social events such as the Russian Winter Festival. He claims that 200 Russians attended the Cartier in 2005 and many more would have liked to.

'The Russians want to show off,' said one Russian living in London. 'They love all that pomp and ceremony and the dressing up, and are desperate to be seen hobnobbing with members of European royal families, the British aristocracy, and the new moneyed elites.' Another Russian émigré, a jewellery designer whose clients include the American actress Sharon Stone and who came to Britain fifteen years ago and lives in St John's Wood, described her first visit to Ascot as 'magical'. 'It was like a scene from a novel – *Anna Karenina*, to be precise,' she recalled. 'I felt like Anna in nineteenth-century Russia, in the time of the tsars … I felt great nostalgia for all the beautiful events that were banished during the Soviet era.'[10]

Such is the interest and excitement it generates among Russians that at least two documentaries were filmed for

Russian television at Royal Ascot in 2005. According to one well-placed Russian commentator, the presence of Russian television crews at such events is usually enough to frighten off the richest Russians, especially those whose fortunes are 'a little vulnerable'. They are afraid that they may be spotted by the Russian authorities that have been trying to track them down for questioning over the source of their sudden wealth.

London has already hosted a number of society weddings involving Russians and Britons. Assia Webster, who came to London from St Petersburg in the mid-1990s to work at Christie's, married the top London jewellery designer Stephen Webster, who made Madonna and Guy Ritchie's wedding rings. Later Assia set up her own PR company, Rocks. Savile Row tailor Ozwald Boateng is married to six-foot-plus Russian model Gyunel. Natalia Vodianova, the supermodel and wife of the British aristocrat and billionaire property heir Justin Portman, commutes between Britain and New York with their two young children.

In another British/Russian liaison, *fashionistas* have also been intrigued by the relationship between another supermodel, Naomi Campbell, and the Russian billionaire Vladimir Doronin, a property magnate with a towering ego who has been called Moscow's version of Donald Trump.

Doronin was educated in St Petersburg, the home city of Russia's former and current presidents, Vladimir Putin and Dmitri Medvedev. A close friend of the present Mayor of Moscow, Yury Luzhkov, and his wife Yelena Baturina (at the last count, Russia's only female dollar billionaire), Doronin is another plutocrat who likes to ensure that he keeps in with the political in-crowd. He made his first money as a raw cotton distributor in the former Soviet republics of Tajikstan and Uzbekistan and in 1993 set up Capital Group, a Moscow-based property company specializing in 'luxury design property projects', among them grandiose 100-apartment high-risers,

Yacht City (a development on the Moscow River), and elite housing at Barvikha Hills, which is close to the Kremlin.

Despite her reputation for a dark side and a propensity for uncontrollable rages – throwing a telephone across a hotel room, beating her assistant with her Blackberry – Naomi Campbell has been sweetness and tenderness in her relationship with Doronin. When the tycoon invited her for a rowdy all-night dinner party on his yacht *Lady in Blue* off St Tropez, her friends were amazed by her serenity.

Like Berezovsky, many of London's rich Russian community became preoccupied with status. As Russian journalist Nicholas Ageyev put it in 2006, 'It is interesting how many fervent capitalists were born behind the Iron Curtain.'[11] Through a mix of corporate hospitality, hosting lavish social gatherings, and making generous charitable donations, wealthy Russians have steadily bought their way into the upper echelons of London society. Leonid Blavatnik is on the Council of the Serpentine Gallery and is a benefactor of the Hermitage Rooms at Somerset House. In 2006, Russia's London-based business elite threw an expensive gala at the Royal Opera House attended by guests from the British establishment and the arts. They paid £1,000 a head to celebrate the eightieth birthday of Moscow-born ballet icon Maya Plisetskaya.

A connection with the Royal Family is another major aspiration. This appears to have been achieved by Russian billionaire Sergei Pugachev, who has enjoyed close ties with former President Putin. Pugachev made his money through shipyards and property deals and became friendly with Viscount Linley, the son of Lord Snowdon and the late Princess Margaret and the Queen's nephew. In September 2007 the two men spent a long weekend on a bear-hunting expedition in southern Siberia, where Pugachev is a senator and has mining interests. In return, Linley invited the oligarch for a pheasant shoot in Windsor

Great Park that December. Shortly afterwards, talks got underway about Pugachev buying a large stake in Linley's luxury
furniture and interiors business, which has refurbished suites at
Claridge's.

Some Russians organized their own charity events. In 2006
former KGB spy turned banker Alexander Lebedev paid at least
£1.3 million to host a lavish party at Althorp, in Northamptonshire, the ancestral seat of the Spencers and childhood home of
Diana, Princess of Wales. It was the most extravagant ex-pat
party of the year, a fundraising event to launch the Raisa
Gorbachev Foundation to fight leukaemia. The guest list
included not only the former Soviet President Mikhail
Gorbachev (the foundation was established in his wife's name
after she died of the disease in 1999) but also Hollywood heart-
throb Orlando Bloom, supermodel Elle Macpherson, Lady
Gabriella Windsor, the daughter of Prince and Princess Michael
of Kent, author Sir Salman Rushdie, and model Jemma Kidd.
Indeed, Britons at the event nearly outnumbered the Russians.

This was the first time that Althorp had been opened to a
private party on this scale, and it is testimony to the influence
wielded by Lebedev in the British establishment. Connections
were key. It was arranged by Geordie Greig, then editor of
Tatler, who later took a swipe at the Russian super-rich for
leapfrogging the British upper classes in the intensified competition for the best schools and homes.

The event was built around extravagant Russian themes,
including Cossack horsemen and grey wolves from the steppe
roaming the estate's lawns with their attentive handlers. Two
years later the charity party – a white-tie gala dinner – was
repeated at a new venue, Hampton Court Palace. This time it
was attended by some 400 guests, including Lady Thatcher and
Naomi Campbell. Each paid £1,000 to attend and enjoy a
concert by Sir Elton John, who missed his annual jaunt at the
Cannes Film Festival. After dinner, guests bid for a catalogue of

prizes, topped by an all-night party at Annabel's nightclub for 160 guests.

The most notable absentees were the oligarchs. Lebedev's 27-year-old son Evgeny, who organized the party along with the well-connected Geordie Greig, admitted that he failed to persuade a single one to attend. 'Wealthy Russian people seem to be quite interested in their own causes and not very helpful to others,' he acknowledged. 'That seems to be a problem with Russian society as a whole, not just philanthropy. People at best don't help each other; at worst they make it worse for each other. They compete with each other.'[12]

An extravagant and eccentric dresser, Evgeny Lebedev was educated at Holland Park School, Mill Hill School, then the LSE, and also studied art history. In 2006 *Tatler* listed Lebedev as the third most eligible bachelor in Britain. Later that year, at a George Michael concert at Earl's Court, he sat alongside Kate Moss and Bob Geldof in the VIP enclosure. Charismatic and an energetic late-night socialite, the young Lebedev owns and operates a Japanese restaurant, Sake No Hana, in St James's Street, just a few doors down from White's, the epitome of British establishment private clubs.

His father, Alexander Lebedev, had been born into a Moscow academic family, studied economics, and gained a PhD on Russia's foreign debt. He joined the KGB in the early 1980s and was dispatched to London in 1988 as an intelligence officer, operating out of a flat on Kensington High Street on a monthly salary of £700. Working under the cover of an economics attaché, he was tasked with obtaining intelligence on capital flows but also on whether or not Britain was planning to activate its nuclear strike force.

When he left the KGB in 1992, Lebedev held the rank of lieutenant colonel and returned to Moscow with savings worth just £400. But as well as having a doctorate in economics, he had carefully studied the City's and Western commercial practices.

Nicknamed the 'Spy who came in from the gold', Lebedev initially made money as a consultant to foreign firms. He then used the fees to buy up the ailing National Reserve Bank, bought shares in Russian utilities, and by 1997, his assets hit £680 million. His recovery was based on astute investments in the energy giant Gazprom and Aeroflot.

By 2008, Lebedev had acquired an estimated fortune of £2 billion and still headed the bank, whose executives include former KGB colleagues. None of this made him disloyal to his former employer. In his bank's headquarters in Moscow there is a statue of Felix Dzerzhinsky, the brutal founder of the Soviet secret police, which was toppled and removed from its previous location when the Soviet system collapsed. It is likely to be a private joke because he was a vociferous critic of Putin's policy of promoting former KGB officers into power and influence. 'People in the security services are not always that educated,' he told the *Spectator*. 'They will do anything for a million dollars.'

Lebedev also owns *Novaya Gazeta*, Russia's last independent newspaper, jointly with Mikhail Gorbachev. This was the paper for which crusading anti-Putin journalist Anna Politkovskaya worked before her assassination in October 2006. A former deputy in the State Duma for the pro-Putin United Russia Party since 2004, he is unusual in that he is equally critical of what he regards as the selfishness and extravagance of the oligarchs and the authoritarianism of the Kremlin.

In London Lebedev acquired a taste for the high-society life. 'I like it when there's substance to it,' he told the *Spectator*. 'When you're sitting at a dinner with Tom Wolfe on one side and Tom Stoppard on the other, then obviously it's enjoyable.' But he also has a rebellious streak. By 2008, aged forty-seven, he looked more like a rock star with his designer-chic rimless glasses, casual outfits, and short, fashionably cut grey hair. In his campaign to persuade the Russian government to restrict betting, he appeared on television wearing a T-shirt reading, 'Who the fuck needs gambling?'.

Lebedev's stunt against gambling has been part of a wider campaign against the Russian mafia, including tougher laws against drug trafficking. He also called for a ban on wealthy bureaucrats and businessmen in Moscow from putting sirens on their cars and using the ambulance lanes – a practice that has caused delays for ordinary people being taken to hospital. Within a few weeks he was the subject of an assassination attempt in Moscow, when two bullets missed his head by inches.

In line with their social aspirations, most wealthy Russians take their personal appearance very seriously and since 2000 Britain's luxury retailers have learnt fast how to separate Russia's frenetic shoppers – a mixture of visitors and residents – from their cash.

One by one London's luxury department stores and Old Bond Street boutiques started to hire Russian-speaking staff. In 2005 Harrods' personal shopping department – Harrods by Appointment – employed its first Russian speaker: the oligarchs' wives are especially addicted to the 'personal shopping' service. On one occasion a Harrods personal shopper was even asked to furnish a private jet.

By 2005, Harvey Nichols employed six Russian-speaking assistants on its shop floors to cope with the influx of new, high-spending consumers. As the shop's marketing manager put it in 2005, 'The Russians are to this decade what the Japanese were to the 1990s and the Arabs were to the 1980s. They come to shop and they pay in cash. They have money and want to spend it. There are women who come in with pages from Russian *Vogue* and when they shop for the latest handbag, they buy seven.'[13]

Such is the demand from Russian shoppers that Elena Ragozhina of *New Style* magazine started publishing *Exclusive*

London, a bi-annual tourist guide to London's most exclusive shops and boutiques: one article in 2006 she called – tongue only partly in cheek – 'How to Spend a Million Pounds in One Hour'.

For the men, shopping means cars. In 2007 Russians spearheaded rising sales of the £285,000 Rolls-Royce Phantom, the seventh-most-expensive car in the UK. Rodney Turner, director of London's Rolls-Royce H. R. Owen dealership, says that he first started to notice the Russians in a big way in 2005 and that by 2007 they accounted for about one-fifth of his clients. They are one of the nationalities known within the trade as the 'big hitters'. 'Russians mostly don't stop at one car,' according to Turner. 'They will often buy a Phantom and the new Drophead Coupé [first introduced in 2007 and selling for £400,000] for the wife or for fun. Sometimes they will ship one or more cars to the South of France as well as keep one or two in England.'

Sometimes the Russians would come themselves with an interpreter and security. But more typically the cars would be bought by an agent. It was not uncommon for the agent to turn up with what Turner describes as a 'shopping list'. In the two years up to early 2008 he dealt with nearly thirty Russian customers, each of whom bought six or seven cars in one go, typically including a Rolls-Royce, Bentley, Ferrari, Lamborghini, and, on one occasion, a Bugatti Veyron, the world's most expensive limited edition car and very difficult to get. 'What they are really saying is: I have the money I want the best.' Those buying were mostly families who had bought a very expensive house and had hired an expensive, top-notch designer responsible for the complete package. 'Their job would be to design and manage the refurbishment of the house, select the furniture, décor, flooring, make sure the staff are in place and the cars are in the garage,' said Turner. 'The designer will be given a deadline and everything will need to be in place right down to the flowers and the garden before the family arrives. It would often be the designer who came in with the "vehicle shopping list" and who was commissioned to oversee the purchase and delivery of the fleet.'

As with buying property, the Russians' innate impatience meant that they were rarely willing to wait. In early 2008 the waiting list for a Phantom Drophead Coupé was at least two years. This led to a 'grey market' in which customers would jump the queue by paying another client about to take delivery a premium of up £75,000. Wealthy Russians were quite happy to pay a commission to secure first option on a sports car. In some Moscow restaurants they had become used to paying a premium of as much as £1,000 just to secure a reservation.

Renowned for their heavy vodka drinking, the Russians also quickly acquired a taste for fine wine. One dealer admitted that some of his clients were spending enough to support a small wine merchant single-handedly. As one butler to a Russian explained, 'Wine is one way they express themselves. Those with mansions sometimes buy up whole collections of wine, putting in cellars in the process. They want to drink what is perceived to be the very best – Cristal, Krug, Château Petrus, or Margaux – and then it has to be the premier years of each one. That's the year they want; they won't buy either side of it. If it's 1982 it has to be that year, nothing else.'

Wine writer Tim Atkin remembered watching four cigar-smoking Eastern Europeans order a 1996 Château Petrus at the Michelin-starred Hakkasan in London one night in June 2007. Two of the men proceeded to dilute the wine – which cost £1,560 a bottle – with Diet Coke. Petrus certainly has status value for Eastern Europeans.

Restaurant managers would rub their hands with glee when a Russian party made a booking. Top restaurants favoured by Russians have included Le Gavroche and Cipriani in Mayfair. And around the corner, the boutiques and jewellers became particularly grateful for the arrival of the 'rouble revolution'.

Moreover, while the economic downturn in 2008 started to affect mainstream retailers, it initially had a limited impact on some top-end retailing. In January 2008 Stuart Rose, the beleaguered chief executive of Marks & Spencer, commenting on the tough Christmas suffered by the store, added somewhat acidly, 'But London can't get enough diamonds.' Again it was the Russians who led the way.

Bond Street jewellers first spotted the Russians in the 1990s. In the second half of 1993 Tiffany and Co. saw an influx of Russian customers. According to the shop's manager, 'We've had people looking at stones worth tens of thousands. They're mainly interested in diamonds. It's odd seeing them wearing poor quality jewellery and coming into Tiffany's to buy a gem the size of a pigeon's egg.'[14] Diamond-encrusted watches were in particular demand. Cartier said at the time that Russian customers 'Sometimes employed bartering tactics. They obviously have a lot of money to spend but they try to get cash discounts. They like to know they're getting a bargain.'[15]

Like a celebrity or a royal princess, the Russians expect special treatment. 'There was one occasion when a Russian walked into a top Bond Street jewellers, asked for the manager, and said he wanted the store to open next Sunday because he was bringing a client who wanted to buy diamonds worth £1.5 million,' recalled Alexander Nekrassov. 'The jewellers never opened on Sunday but made an exception on this occasion. The Russian duly arrived and promptly handed over the promised payment.' A decade on, the Russians had become even better customers for top jewellery retailers.

In 2007 Elena Ragozhina started hosting regular parties for subscribers of her magazines at London's most exclusive fashion and jewellery boutiques such as Tiffany and Co. and the newly opened Old Bond Street showrooms of the Lev Leviev diamond empire. According to the store, prices ranged from an 'entry-level' diamond ring at £25,000 to a £4.2 million diamond necklace. Born in Uzbekistan and raised in Israel from the age of fifteen, Leviev became a billionaire courtesy of the controversial world of diamond trading. By 2007, the 51-year-old was rich enough to spend £35 million on one of the most expensive new houses in Britain, a Hampstead mansion that boasts a Versailles-style stone staircase, indoor pool and spa, and a carved replica of a chimneypiece at Cliveden House in Buckinghamshire.

Even by the summer of 2008, there were only minimal signs of a slowdown in the diamond trade. In June, as the credit crunch was starting to be felt and property and share prices plunged, Chopard launched London's most expensive cocktail at the Westbury Hotel in Mayfair. At £225 per glass, the Chopardissimo – a vodka martini with Beluga caviar – was served up to 100 of the company's best customers.

There are few areas of London's highly developed consumerist culture that have not been touched by the Russians. Chauffeur firms thrived. Michelin-starred chefs found themselves in great demand. Companies established to cater for the rouble invasion were inundated with requests from luxury goods industries in their attempt to target Russian spenders. Aliona Muchinskaya said that whenever her company gained publicity for organizing a big Russian event in London, she would be 'flooded with e-mails, letters, and calls from agents representing celebrity singers, famous chefs offering to cook in private houses, private chauffeur companies, agents selling properties from Dubai to the Seychelles, even companies selling private islands. On several occasions we have been contacted by titled Britons offering their homes to clients for events.'

The sustained spending frenzy that overtook London from the mid-noughties is not, however, just down to the billionaire oligarchs and their wives, daughters, and mistresses. In fact, it is no surprise to learn that the oligarchs have mostly preferred to keep themselves out of the limelight. Rather, the frenzy was led by the next socio-economic group down in the wealth stakes – those who were merely multi-millionaires. These comprised a much larger group of former KGB officials, businessmen hired by the oligarchs, and a newer generation of Russian entrepreneurs who started to make money out of the consumer boom that emerged in Russia from the millennium. This group may not be billionaires but they are equally addicted to a turbo-charged lifestyle and luxury living, something that Tom Ford, creative director of Gucci until 2004, has described as being 'in the hard drive of Russian people'.

In the 1990s the new moneyed Russians became known for their designer clothes, dark, sharp suits, jewellery, and heavy partying. They were not, however, the idle rich. Many were tireless, energetic, frenetic deal-makers – always hustling, trading gossip, and boasting about their profligacy. They seemed only too happy to conform to their emerging stereotype – vulgar, spendthrift, and indiscriminate buyers of the flashiest clothes, brands, and diamonds. 'It's the head-to-toe, total-look designer dressing,' one fashion observer said. 'Think chilled vodka, caviar, extravagance, cash, and bling. They acquired so much money so quickly; it went to their heads. They are like teenagers on heat.'

The more contemporary Russian super-rich have mostly displayed greater discretion during their spending binges. Wary of too many questions being asked about the origins of their wealth and obsessed with security, apart from their wives, the husbands have mandated their butlers, secretaries, PAs, and other third parties to choose the properties, negotiate with contractors, and do their spending for them. Even the wives started to show discretion. They may have continued to live high-octane social lives while donning Bulgari jewellery, but they did so more discreetly, thus preserving a new desire for public anonymity.

The days of conspicuous, vulgar displays of extravagance were less in evidence as the end of the first decade of the new millennium approached. 'They are more discriminating consumers nowadays,' said one member of the set. 'You won't see Russian women buying left, right, and centre the way they did during the nineties.' Their new style was described by one as 'discreet opulence', with the use of personal shoppers or benefiting from roped-off sections in the smartest shops. According to Marina Starkova, a director of Red Square, 'Their style is not as flashy as it used to be, all Versace and gold chains'. Aliona Muchinskaya claims that by the mid-noughties, conspicuous excess was fading. 'In Moscow you expect friends to ask how much a new bag or jacket cost, but in London the trend is towards British understatement,' she said.

Russian women, rarely worried about the price tag, have had a huge impact on the London fashion scene. In 2005 the designer Julien Macdonald claimed that most of his sales had been to Russians. 'Russians are every designer's dream,' he said. 'They are the saviour of almost every glamorous fashion brand in the world. Without them, a lot of us would have gone bankrupt a long time ago.'[16] It is a process fuelled by the emergence of new Russian models such as Natalia Vodianova. In 2005 *Vanity Fair* featured a number of Russian models on its cover, heralding 'the new supermodels from behind the Iron Curtain'. In the same year Russian *Vogue* devoted an entire issue to the Russian influence, much of it shot around Red Square.

One woman who has emerged as a force in the international fashion world is Roman Abramovich's girlfriend, Daria Zhukova. Her label, Kova & T, launched in Harvey Nichols in December 2007, sells in more than seventy stores around the world. It is a deliberately 'casual luxury' and consciously unglitzy brand – which includes plain jeans, vest tops, T-shirts, miniskirts, leather shorts and jersey dresses, and, most famously, latex leggings. The label is designed to counter what one fashion expert describes as the 'post-Soviet flashiness' that Russians seemed to embrace in the 1990s.

Zhukova's London circle included Lord Lloyd-Webber, Lord Freddie Windsor, Camilla Fayed, and Polina Deripaska. Typical of the new breed of young and successful Russians – a mix of entrepreneurs, designers, and models that make up the Russian jet set – she also became something of a celebrity draw herself. London became full of young, glamorous, and expensively dressed Russians. They could sometimes be spotted in London's stylish restaurants and tearooms or being chauffeured around their favourite shops in Old Bond Street and Sloane Street. This is a group that insists on looking immaculate and glamorous at all times. Their favourite designers tend to be Prada, Marc Jacobs, Alexander McQueen, Lanvin, and Chloé, and they holiday in St Barts at Christmas, Courchevel in January, and St Tropez in August. They strive for the most fashionable and know they will need to pay a premium. 'We get overcharged three times just for the accent,' said Katya, the stunning wife of Ruslan Fomichev, the former aide to Berezovsky.[17]

These then are the offspring of Russia's billionaires and multi-millionaires. They are the first generation to have come of age in the post-communist era and many have been raised in mansions with servants and chauffeurs. They want for nothing. Oozing with self-confidence and armed with limitless credit cards, many have been educated in British public schools and universities and so have the advantage over their parents of knowing the country and speaking good English.

Along with Evgeny Lebedev, a regular at events like Elton John's White Tie and Tiara Ball and Donatella Versace shows, another member of the Russian glitterati set has been Alsou Safina. She moved to London with her family when she was twelve, and was educated at Queen's College, a private school in Harley Street. While her father has returned to Russia, she has been granted British citizenship and lives in an apartment in St

John's Wood, overlooking Lord's Cricket Ground. She is a successful international singer, came second in the Eurovision Song Contest in 2000, and is now married with a young daughter.

The young Russian set may have parents or grandparents brought up under communism, but they remember little or nothing of the Soviet Union, or of the privations of the past. Many have bought apartments in the new blocks being built in Kensington and Knightsbridge, paid for by their parents. Local estate agents say that expensive new luxury flats have sometimes been bought by clients often barely out of their teens. Some have servants and could be seen parking their top-of-the-range cars ostentatiously outside their apartments or near fashionable nightclubs. 'Young men like nothing more than to change their cars almost every month – Ferrari today, BMW tomorrow, riding from one club to the next as if there was no tomorrow' as one who knows them puts it.

British universities – increasingly dependent financially on foreign students – have attracted thousands of Russians. In 2006, 20,600 Russians were granted visas to study in the UK. One lecturer in business studies at King's College London said that a number of the university's students from the former Soviet Union 'were distinguished by the wealth of their parents. Some of them have expensive apartments in nearby Kensington bought by their parents while some of the girls wear designer clothes even to classes'.

The Russian love affair with spending is confirmed by Ledbury Research Agency, a PR company that targets the wealthy. As they put it in 2007, 'Russia is producing today's most determinedly conspicuous consumers.' The obsession stems from their fatalistic approach to life. 'Russians like to spend. They have no concept of saving, just as they have no concept of tomorrow,' said Marina Starkova. Evelina Khromchenko, editor of the

Russian edition of *L'Officiel*, the leading French lifestyle magazine says, 'You have to realise the idea of saving for a rainy day is frowned on. Russians believe that if you keep money for a rainy day, you'll catch the rain. Instead they think you should just go out and buy a pair of Manolo Blahniks. Nobody allows a rainy day to happen to a girl in those kinds of shoes.'[18]

Valerie Manokhina, married to a relatively rich Russian, has a British passport and divides her time between London and Moscow. She remembers learning English at a London college in the mid-1990s. Because of the variety of nationalities in the class – Japanese, German, French, and Chinese – they were given a test in which they had to apply their respective characters to three circles. One circle represented the past, one the present, and one the future. They were then asked how much the circles, and what they represented, overlapped for them. 'The Russians in the class were the only ones who didn't connect all the circles,' she recalls. 'The past and present overlapped but the future circle always stayed apart. It is shocking but so true – we have nothing to do with the future, we don't refer to it, don't plan for it, don't think about it. I live my life just for the moment. As long as I can enjoy the moment I don't care what happens tomorrow. It is about being fatalistic, we live in the present, we use the present tense all the time.'

CHAPTER 7

The Big Game Hunters

'It's the logic of consumption. What is a rich Russian? It means you must have an apartment in Moscow, a Bentley, a dacha on Rublyovka, a house in London, a villa in Sardinia and a yacht. Then you must buy modern art'

      – JOSEPH BACKSTEIN, *artistic director for*
        Moscow's museums and exhibitions[1]

IN EARLY FEBRUARY 2007 Sotheby's in London's New Bond Street was preparing for its annual winter auction. All the signs were that it was going to be a frenetic few days. For the previous six months prices realized at fine art auctions had been break-ing records on both sides of the Atlantic. The third day of the sale was as tightly packed as ever with the usual gathering of art critics, dealers, and the international rich. The day had already started well with another set of ground-breaking prices.

Next up was *White Canoe*, a large landscape set in the Cana-dian Rockies by the contemporary Scottish painter Peter Doig. The painting, much admired by critics, was expected to fetch a maximum of £1.2 million. Bidding started briskly with six buyers still in when the price reached £2 million. At that point four dropped out while two continued bidding. First the £3 million threshold was passed, then the £4 million. Finally, as those witnessing the event gazed on in hushed anticipation, the painting was eventually sold for £5.732 million – close to five times its reserve price and a remarkable sum for a living painter relatively unknown five years earlier. Moreover, the painting did not go to one of the expected collectors or to a British or American buyer. Although his name did not emerge until months later, the buyer turned out to be an anonymous Russian.

This was not the first time a Russian had stolen the limelight in the art market. Eight months earlier, in May 2006, a middle-aged man in a blue blazer walked into Sotheby's in Manhattan, collected a bidding paddle, and was ushered to a seat near the back of the room for the auction house's sale of Impressionist and Modern Art. First the mysterious and unrecognized man bid $6.5 million for a Monet landscape, $2 million over the estimate. Then he steadfastly saw off the bids of three US billionaires to land Picasso's *Dora au Chat*, his 1941 portrait of his lover Dora Maar. It wasn't just the extraordinary $95 million price that stunned the array of hard-nosed art insiders, even though it was almost twice the estimate and the second-highest amount ever paid for an artwork at auction. 'He looked like he'd never been to a sale before,' sniffed one observer. Three days after the auction the *New York Times* carried the man's picture under the headline 'Recognize this man? The art world doesn't.' At the time the assumption in art circles was that, given his accent, bidding style, and willingness to pay so much over the odds, the mystery buyer had to be Russian.

The year 2005 had been quiet for the world's art markets. There were few extraordinary sales and nobody bid more than $100 million for a painting. Then came 2006, the year the international art market caught fire. In that year three paintings sold for more than $100 million apiece, including a Jackson Pollock drip painting and *Woman III*, by Willem de Kooning. In 2005, 487 works sold for more than $1 million. In 2006 it was more than double, at 810 works. It was not just Old Masters, Impressionists, and Picassos that started to break all-time records:

prices for contemporary artists, from Francis Bacon to Damien Hirst, also began hitting extraordinary heights.

What started in New York soon spread to London, and the reason for the booming market was, as one art critic put it, 'foreign money'. Prices were scaling new heights because of the desire of the new global billionaires to possess the world's most sought-after works. There was now an elite group of spenders, for whom multi-million-pound prices were small change and who were increasingly outbidding public galleries, charitable foundations, and the 'B' list of multi-millionaires for the rarest of works, both old and modern.

Even the most hardened of art insiders were aghast at the escalating prices and the question exciting the art world was how much higher prices would go. The answer was a lot. The first signs of a continuing boom came in the February 2007 sales in London. Then, in June, amid another round of bidding frenzy and tumbling records at sales by London's Sotheby's and Christie's, the market was catapulted into even higher territory. While much of the world was tinkering on the brink of recession, the rest of 2007 and the first half of 2008 saw that frenzy continue, and more records were smashed.

Because it is just the kind of art that appeals to the new buyers, contemporary art – works created since the late 1940s – proved especially hot. As one observer cryptically put it, 'It fits with the décor of a Chelsea loft.' Demand was again being driven by non-European and non-American buyers who were now regular fixtures at auction rooms and able to compete on equal terms with the more established names from Europe and the US. As Henry Wyndham, chairman of Sotheby's Europe, put it, 'At the top end of the market there's immense wealth. There's more wealth around than at any time in my lifetime. It's all over the world.'[2]

Although the new international players included collectors from China, the Middle East, and South-east Asia, the most prominent throughout 2007 were, according to experts, the Russians and those from former Soviet states. At Christie's June 2007 auctions, the biggest buyer was a Geneva-based Russian who bought ten lots worth a total of £23.4 million.

There was some sign of what was to come in the mid-1990s when a handful of Russians first started to show an interest in art at the London auctions. In 1994 Sotheby's reported interest from a number of Russians. Nevertheless, ten, even five years ago, it was unthinkable that the Russians would soon enter the ranks of the most powerful players in the global art market. Yet in 2007 they were behaving in the salesrooms with what one commentator described as the 'hot-headed madness of the Japanese in the late 1980s'.[3]

Leading art auction houses in London and New York for the first time started to add Russian roubles to the boards that display price conversions for the works carried. The boards, which help international buyers to keep track of the bidding, already showed US dollars, euros, sterling, Swiss francs, and yen. In June 2007 a London-based magazine for Russians, the *London Courier*, devoted an entire issue to the impact Russian money was having on the international art market. The private view at London's Frieze Fair that year was described jokingly as 'The October Revolution' so packed was it with wealthy Russians. So important had the Russians become that even the Tate joined other international museums and art collections courting the tycoons for their patronage. While some observers question the lasting impact of the recent Russian art frenzy, it is likely that some of the great collections of the twenty-first century will be found in Russia and Ukraine, just as some of the great collectors of the early twentieth century were Russians.

It is not just London and New York that have been targeted by Russians, a mix of those making big money in the 1990s and a younger group of art-loving entrepreneurs who have made money more recently from supermarkets, restaurants, or mobile phone businesses. The London sales at the end of June 2007 came after a month of frantic buying across Europe. When the Venice Biennale opened at the beginning of June, the Russians were there in force. Some arrived in their private jets, others in yachts. Many seemed to be there on a shopping spree, 'As if they had been buying cars', remarked one observer. This led some to complain that major international art fairs had less and less to do with art and more and more to do with the growing power and concentration of money. As one art critic covering the Biennale put it, 'The art may be rubbish but the parties are worth coming for'.

This seemed to be confirmed by the presence of Ksenia Sobchak, the young Moscow celebrity who courts publicity and has been dubbed the Paris Hilton of Russia. The host of a salacious Russian reality TV programme called *Dom-2*, Russia's equivalent of *Big Brother*, she drove a Porsche Cayenne and has hung out with, among others, Naomi Campbell. A former ballet student, she has been photographed for *Pravda* and the Russian edition of *Maxim*. She is sometimes called the 'Kremlin's cover girl' because her father, Anatoly Sobchak, once the Mayor of St Petersburg, was, before his death, close to Vladimir Putin and she is the goddaughter of the President. It was Sobchak who introduced Abramovich to Daria Zhukova.

From Venice the new collectors moved on to the Basel Art Fair in Switzerland, feted as the most important European fair for contemporary work, and then headed for London. One art critic who followed the crowds described it as like 'the eighteenth-century Grand Tour on speed'. William Cash, editor of *Spear's Wealth Management Survey*, called it a 'non-stop circus'.

The power of former Soviet money soon helped to switch the relative positions of New York and London. While London mostly took a back seat to New York, selling less and commanding fewer of the world's most sought-after paintings, that had changed by 2006. As New York-based Abigail Asher, one of the world's leading art advisers, explained, 'Take the London auctions. They were once poor cousins to those in New York, which was where all the blockbuster material ended up. It didn't feel that way in February 2007. The salesrooms were jammed and electric and – unlike New York – were buzzing with "*niet*" and "*da*". A new and energetic group of collectors seemed willing to pay any price for what they wanted.'[4]

Whether prices could just keep soaring was what kept dealers and collectors awake at night. The late 1980s saw a similar dramatic and frenzied boom. At that time it was led by the Japanese; when the well-heeled who had been burned in other markets began snapping up art, people suddenly appeared from nowhere to open galleries and unknown artists suddenly became somebody. The speculation ended in tears with the spectacular crash of 1990–91, when the market went into recession and many dealers went bust while paintings lost up to two-thirds of their value.

Some experts such as Cristina Ruiz of *Art Newspaper* argued that the ballooning prices of the time were unsustainable. 'Eventually the speculators will desert the market,' she wrote in 2006. 'The new galleries that have flourished in the East End [of London] will close. The really young dealers will crash. It happened in the early 1990s and will do so again.'[5] Another warned that the art market was behaving like 'froth on the cappuccino'.[6] Others dismissed talk of a bubble, saying that the 1980s were exceptional, a boom built mainly around Japanese buyers and a reliance on borrowing. By the end of 2007, it was claimed, the market was firmer, much more evenly spread across nations and less dependent on borrowed money. Indeed, demand continued to soar in the opening half of 2008, with both Christie's and Sotheby's seeing Impressionist and Modern paintings going for well above their expected prices. Again, the Russians were among those leading the charge.

In many ways the contemporary art market from 2005 had much in common with the market for top-priced housing. Demand was fuelled by speculation, a kind of desperation to buy. Buyers reported a surge in 'art gazumping' in which desperate collectors allegedly offered tens of thousands of pounds on top of an accepted price as bribes to secure work that had already been sold. In a duel over one painting in a sale of Russian work at Sotheby's in 2007, one private Russian buyer threatened to 'thump' his rival. One long-term observer of the art scene, asked when the boom might turn to bust, replied, 'I cannot speculate on how long it's going to last because it has nothing to do with the art any more. You could be talking about tulip bulbs.'[7]

The Russian interest stems from a number of motives. Some see investing in art as a way of making even more money: it's another place to put their cash, a kind of portable wealth. According to Janna Bullock, a Russian-born property tycoon and art collector married to an American, who now lives and works in New York, 'Most of the Russians are amateurs and just follow the trend.'[8] Fedor Pavlov-Andreevich, the head of a Moscow foundation that raises money for art projects, has said that 'Russian tycoons want to become the twenty-first-century equivalent of the nineteenth-century art patrons. We've had nearly a hundred years without such patronage. The Russians now want their names known through art.'[9]

Another, more basic, human instinct has also been at play – the need for tangible signs of success and social standing. For some, accumulating wealth is enough of a drive in itself. Many collectors prefer anonymity, but many of the mega-wealthy – not just the Russians – have an innate need to display the proceeds of their success and to be seen to be doing so. That sort of attitude is hardly new. In 1819 the English essayist William Hazlitt described it succinctly, 'Man is a toad-eating animal. The admiration of power in others is as common to man as the love of it in himself.'[10] The editor of the art quarterly *State of Art* wrote in the spring 2007 edition of the magazine that you cannot find anyone today quite so pleased with themselves as the top-end collector of contemporary artworks. 'During the last twenty-five years, major auctions of paintings, once the province of the professional dealer and gallerist, have become black-tie social events where a successful bid results in ecstatic applause. We were supposed to be impressed with the ever-increasing amounts paid for individual works as they unfolded, eulogised in newspapers and television reports … What is clear is that any individual prepared to pay large amounts of money for art in this new, highly public arena, would have society, the art trade and the media lining up to lick their boots. And this is the *irresistible* factor for those enjoying wealth without merit in our post rock'n'roll era.'[11]

Although great and memorable art has always been traded for its show power, this motive may have become even more dominant in recent times. It may be partly a financial game for today's 'quick rich', but it is also a statement of social arrival providing what one has described as 'bragging rights'. As William Cash describes the process, 'While much of the new art market boom is created by greed, an even greater motivation is social status. Many of the collectors who fly into Miami or London's Frieze are simply trophy hunting.'[12]

Russian art lovers also started investing at home. Such was the growing demand that Bonhams, Christie's, and Sotheby's began regular sales of Russian paintings along with artefacts ranging from Fabergé jostles to Imperial-era porcelain vases and Soviet propaganda plates. One of those leading the charge for Russia's artistic heritage was Yelena Baturina, the wife of Yuri Luzkhov, the Mayor of Moscow. A lavish investor in art and one of the world's leading collectors of Imperial-era porcelain, Baturina became a regular visitor to London.

The renaissance of the Russian collector brought a huge increase in the value of sales of Russian art in London. Jo

Vickery, a Senior Director at Sotheby's, said that the auction house sold $189 million worth of Russian art in 2007, compared with £4 million a decade earlier.[13] Petr Aven, known as the intellectual oligarch, and with one of the most prestigious collections of Russian art, summed the Russian attitude up as follows, 'I did care about prices but, believe me, when I wanted to buy something I didn't care about the price.'[14] According to Sotheby's UK chairman, Lord Poltimore, speaking in late 2006, 'Pretty well anything Russian is very hot at the moment and the buyers are 99 per cent Russians. The buyers are mainly oligarch-type people who have been buying houses all over the world and now want some art to put in them.'[15]

That may be only part of the explanation. London-based Russian journalist Margarita Stewart, the daughter of a former KGB colonel, has another theory. 'Buying up the world and buying precious Russian art is a substitute for the loss of empire,' she opined. 'Russians have had an empire since Peter the Great. Then there was the vast Soviet Empire. It's in the blood. Rich Russians are really showing the rest of the world how great we are again.'

The collectors include rich Russians and Eastern Europeans. Many of them move in the shadows and shun publicity, providing an opportunity for endless speculation in the art world. Buyers, often using intermediaries, may not even be known to the auction houses. With the Russians enjoying multiple homes on multiple continents, it is also far from clear where the artworks will end up.

Speculation continued for months about the buyer of Picasso's *Dora au Chat* and Peter Doig's *White Canoe*, until it was established, a year later, that it was the Russian mining magnate Boris Ivanishvili. The bidding for the Picasso had been undertaken by one of his employees, while his nephew Gher Ivanishvili was the intermediary for *White Canoe*. The dark-haired Gher relished inventing different names for his client to journalists to put them off the scent.

A billionaire Georgian-born financier from the Black Sea, Ivanishvili made his money initially through mining and banking. He then sold his metallurgical assets to other tycoons, netting around £1 billion. Ivanishvili is believed to be one of the twelve biggest private collectors in the world, the largest of whom is probably the American media mogul David Geffen, himself the son of Eastern European immigrants. When the Picasso masterpiece was flown back to Tbilisi, the airport was closed down to ensure the security and safe transfer of the painting.

There is another group of players active in the sudden surge in demand for historic Russian art – those buying back former prized pieces lost to the nation in the aftermath of 1917 when they were sold off to foreign buyers. This might be called the 'Putin factor'. In September 2007 Sotheby's was on the verge of auctioning the entire and much-prized collection of the late Russian musician Mstislav Rostropovich (exiled from the Soviet Union in 1974), which included a number of highly valued paintings, including *Faces of Russia* by Boris Dmitrievich Grigoriev, often seen as the greatest Russian work to leave Russia after the Revolution. Then suddenly, on the eve of the sale, the auction was cancelled, as the entire collection had been bought outright for some £25 million by a Russian billionaire who had promised to return it to Russia.

The auctioneers initially refused to reveal the identity of the buyer but he was later named as Alisher Usmanov, who only a few weeks earlier had invested heavily in Arsenal Football Club. Born in Uzbekistan, Usmanov had accumulated a fortune from metallurgy estimated at some £2.75 billion and planned to put the collection on permanent display at the Konstantin Palace near St Petersburg. He has a Tudor manor house set in 300 acres of Surrey countryside, as well as mansions in Hampstead,

Moscow, and Italy. Usmanov is another to come to Britain with a controversial past. In the 1980s he served a six-year jail sentence for fraud. He has always claimed he was the victim of a local KGB power struggle and his convictions were indeed later overturned by the supreme court in Tashkent in 2000. He told the *Guardian*, 'All the charges I faced in 1980 proved to be trumped up. There was a rehabilitation order by the Uzbekistan Supreme Court admitting that the alleged crimes never took place.'[16]

The purchase of the collection was widely seen as a deliberately patriotic gesture by an oligarch keen to keep on the right side of the President. In 2004 Usmanov was awarded the Presidential Medal of Honour by Putin for services to business and charity. In 2006 he bought the Russian paper *Kommersant*, once owned by Boris Berezovsky, for a reported £100 million, a purchase that looked like yet another example of the Kremlin taking control of the media.

Usmanov was just one of the oligarchs currying favour with Putin. One by one they started buying up art that had been lost to Russia and investing in Putin's favourite social projects, all designed to counter criticism that the oligarchs enriched themselves and exported their wealth abroad without giving anything back.

Buying the world's rarest and most expensive paintings has always been a privilege open only to the mega-rich. Once you have the mansion, the diamonds, the jet, and the yacht, making a statement requires moving on to possessions that not only inspire envy but are both unique and precious. As Joseph Backstein put it, 'It's the logic of consumption. What is a rich Russian? It means you must have an apartment in Moscow, a Bentley, a dacha on Rublyovka, a house in London, a villa in Sardinia, and a yacht. Then you must buy modern art.'[17]

The Russians may appear to be relative novices at the trophy asset game, but they have certainly not been slow in catching on. One leading art collector calls them the 'big game hunters'. The process began in Russia itself, where, in the 1990s, both Vladimir Gusinsky and Boris Berezovsky consolidated their power by building big media empires: in Berezovsky's case following in the footsteps of his hero Rupert Murdoch. The Russians have done so with rather more mixed results. All of the major oligarchs have lost their former media empires and most former independent television stations are now back in the hands of the state.

None of this means that the super-rich easily throw money away. George Orwell once remarked of Charles Dickens' character Mr Jarndyce that nobody who has spent so much effort making a fortune would give it away so easily.

For the oligarchs the trophy asset does not stop at media empires, the rarest works of art, or the world's top football clubs. It appears that money brings another perk: not just the beautiful blonde wife, invariably half their age, but the model mistress as well. In 2007 television host Oksana Robski and society girl Ksenia Sobchak published a light-hearted book, *Married to a Millionaire*, a tongue-in-cheek, do-it-yourself manual on how to ensnare an oligarch. Both authors are pictured on the front cover in risqué evening dresses toting machine guns. As the back cover blurb puts it, 'There are enough oligarchs to go around'. The book begins by wishing readers 'happy hunting' and advises girls to start planning for divorce on the wedding day itself, reflecting the fact that most oligarch marriages end in divorce. Abramovich and Khodorkovsky have had two wives, as has Berezovsky. They tend not to introduce their spouses as their wives, rather, 'This is the mother of my children'.

Russian women know the rules only too well. Lena Lenina, a woman who once made it to number thirty-two in *FHM* Russia's 'babe rankings', claims in her book *Multimillionaires* that 80 per cent of wealthy Russian men have mistresses, often with their wives' knowledge. As the French have in certain circles for centuries, so the wives tend to turn a blind eye. According to Lenina, who lives in Paris, Russian wives rarely complain for fear of losing their social position. 'The wives will be socially and financially dependent on their rich husbands,' she writes. 'They are terrified of divorce – Russian courts often favour the husband and the wives could end up with nothing.'

For some oligarchs, ruthlessly trading in their wives for a younger model is like buying a new car. Because Russian men are notorious for making miserly financial settlements, Russian women are advised to acquire a marriage contract to protect themselves. One wife of a rich Russian, Tatyana Ogorodnikova, said that many Russian women tolerate infidelity by husbands who maintain multiple mistresses and order up glamorous prostitutes as if they were takeaway pizzas. In her novel *A Marriage Contract* Ogorodnikova explains that Russian wives need to be in a position of power by increasing their value to their husband. She tells her readers that they must surround themselves with powerful men to keep their husband jealous and pursue a career as a pop star or actress to remain high profile.[18]

Impatient, frenetically busy, and impulsive, some newly-rich Russians prefer to buy their women. When one Russian businessman was asked why he spent £12,500 for sex for just one night, he replied, 'Because she will leave in the morning.' One escort service in Moscow matches models with multi-millionaires. If the woman is hired by the agency, it is her ticket out of deprivation into the good life. But she needs to be staggeringly beautiful. The agency charges $10,000 just for an introduction, $20,000 if they meet in person, and $50,000 if the relationship develops. It is also customary for the businessman to give the woman a car such as a BMW X5 or a Porsche Cayenne as a thank you after their first meeting. In the autumn the manager of this agency scouts the fashion shows in New York, Milan, and London in order to recruit new models.

In Russia the life of a 'sponsored woman' does not carry the same social stigma as it does in the West. They want a comfortable life of luxury and this is often the only way to obtain it. They also know that after the age of thirty they are likely to be surplus to requirements and so they need to acquire as much jewellery, and as many cars and flats, as possible. Russian women sometimes claim that the line between mistress and prostitute is very thin for the rich. 'If a woman marries or has an affair with a man purely for his money, does that make her better than a call girl? I don't think so,' one lawyer who worked in Moscow commented. For some Russian women, being a mistress offers liberation from poverty and a possibly loveless marriage to a Russian man who is often drunk, lazy, and unemployed. Many move abroad for a new life. In the winter they flock to Courchevel. In the summer they descend on the Côte d'Azur and Dubai.

But London remains the prize destination for the ambitious statuesque Russian woman. Wealthy English tycoons are sitting ducks for these strikingly beautiful but calculating seductresses. One well-heeled private banker had a long-standing affair with a London-based Russian businesswoman and she was given a flat in Knightsbridge. But when she demanded that he should leave his wife and marry her, the banker refused, whereupon negotiations began. The mistress consulted a lawyer who had once worked in Moscow but left to 'represent' such women in London. After some acrimonious, blood-curdling conversations, the businesswoman was paid off to keep quiet.

Based in her vast house in the capital, the same lawyer, who used to work in the City, developed a new career. After taking the children to school, she would spend the rest of the morning on the telephone to the mistresses. The negotiations were often crude, the mistress threatening to go public or to tell her lover's wife and the tycoon offering a monthly retainer to buy her silence. The only issue was how much.

Of course, most Russian women in London are neither mistresses nor predators. Many are educated, elegant, and erudite, albeit with irresistibly long legs and high cheekbones – a lethal combination. For the ladies of Londongrad, the English complement the qualities they themselves possess. 'There's something about the English sense of tolerance and love of tradition that marries very well with Russian passion,' said Oksana Kolomenskaya, a charismatic art dealer.[19] 'Russian men are absolutely fascinating,' said one London-based Russian woman. 'They're men of extremes. If they love you, they love you forever. They like magic, fantasy, romance, champagne. And they always find the right words. If you want true romance, go out with a Russian. But if you want a good marriage, find an Englishman.'[20]

One of those living up to the reputation for 'trading in' is Roman Abramovich. Some considered his divorce from Irina in the spring of 2007 inevitable. Sooner or later, it was said, he was bound to hitch up with a new and younger woman, and when he did, it was with art lover and successful fashion designer Daria Zhukova – 'Dasha' to her friends. Until she met the Chelsea owner, Dasha spent most of her time at a £1.5 million penthouse in York House, a Kensington mansion block apartment bought for her by her father, Alexander Zhukov. Zhukov started out as an assistant film editor, made his money in oil in the early 1990s, and then, along with a number of other oligarchs, founded his own bank. Once close to Mikhail Gorbachev and Boris Yeltsin, he is now a British citizen and operates from offices in Park Lane, distinguished by the brace of Rolls-Royces parked outside.

Dasha's mother is a molecular biologist who lectured at Oxford and then UCLA after separating from her husband when her daughter was young. Dasha was sent to a British private school, holds a degree from the University of California, and first captured the public's attention as the girlfriend of Russian tennis ace Marat Safin. She featured in a special edition of *Vogue* in 2006 along with a number of other glamorous young Russians. But despite her connections with young, hedonistic, international socialites like fellow Russian Natalia Vodianova and the British aristocrat Sophia Hesketh, she resents the 'party-girl' tag. She did a homeopathy course at the London College of Naturopathic Medicine near Oxford Street, before launching her leisurewear line Kova & T.

Some say that Abramovich went to great lengths to keep the relationship a secret, others that he flaunted it just as much as he does his wealth. He took her everywhere with him. The two were spotted together in the twelve months after they met in Moscow, Spain, London, Tel Aviv, and Paris and were soon being photographed together. She had also been to watch Chelsea as his guest. Abramovich may have hoped to juggle Irina with Dasha but neither Putin nor Dasha's father approved. Irina was reportedly devastated by the revelations and was not prepared to stay in a dual relationship.

Irina responded by going her own way, jetting off to the South of France with girlfriends or dining at smart West End restaurants. According to Abramovich's biographer Chris Hutchins, she then got her own personal trainer who came to their house at Fyning Hill every morning to oversee her workout.[21]

Despite his links with London, Abramovich insisted on the divorce taking place in Moscow where, as oligarchs' wives have found to their cost, the courts are indeed much more generous to the husband than to the wife. One industrialist, estimated to be worth £350 million, was said to have left his ex-wife with just a council flat and a Lada. By executing his divorce in Moscow, Abramovich would have saved himself a good deal of his fortune. But Abramovich was anxious to ensure that his children were well looked after. As part of the highly secret settlement, he handed over the Chester Square house, the Fyning Hill estate, and the use of his Boeing 737 and his yacht *Pelorus*. Indeed, Irina was using the jet regularly to fly between Moscow and London before the divorce, and it was not until eighteen months later that she finally broke the silence, describing her life with her billionaire husband as 'no fairy tale'. She told the Russian edition of *OK!* magazine that she hated being surrounded by bodyguards and lived in fear of their children being kidnapped. 'For my security and that of the children we hired bodyguards. We changed mobile phone numbers once a week so nobody could trace my whereabouts.'

Another benefit for the rich of divorcing in Russia is that the courts do not delve too deeply into a couple's business dealings. If it had taken place in Britain, Abramovich would have faced the prospect of having his assets and the source of his wealth formally recorded, with the media salivating over every detail.

At first Abramovich's relationship with Dasha Zhukova ran far from smoothly. After all, he would appear to be the last person to be interested in art and fashion. Although Irina is interested in art, her husband was rarely seen at the kind of exhibitions enjoyed by his former wife. It is even claimed that when he bought his first big flat in Moscow in the early 1990s, he told the interior designers that he didn't want any space for books, but just to install panels that looked like them. Not so long ago he was commissioning the legal forger Daniel Ermes Donde to paint a fake van Gogh and a fake Gustav Klimt.

However, his new girlfriend appeared to penetrate his philistine armour. In the summer of 2008 Abramovich joined the ranks of the art world's biggest spenders, splashing out £43 million for Francis Bacon's *Triptych*, £17.2 million for Lucian Freud's *Benefits Supervisor Sleeping*, and, reportedly, £7.5 million on a bronze sculpture by Giacometti. Not exactly a modest start for a first-time art buyer. Although the acquisitions are likely to end up in Abramovich's grand London home, this sudden arousal of interest in art was influenced by the cultured and hard-working Dasha. In the same year she opened her own upmarket gallery – the Centre for Contemporary Culture, also known as the Garage – in Moscow.

The gallery, set in a former bus depot designed in 1929 by the celebrated architect Konstantin Melnikov, is a work of art in its own right. Dasha, with wealth from the success of her fashion label as well as her inheritance, has poured money into the project, which is being coordinated by Molly Dent-Brockle-hurst, Damien Hirst's agent and a former Senior Specialist at Sotheby's. The gallery was also taking advice from Tate Modern's director, Sir Nicholas Serota, the most powerful man in the British art scene, and was opened at a lavish launch in June 2008. By all accounts it was some party, attended by 300 members of the art and fashion world's most powerful figures, including conceptual artist Jeff Koons, designer Marc Newson, and international gallery owner Larry Gagosian. According to one guest, 'Everyone was knocking back the vodkas but Dasha remained composed.'[22]

The launch culminated with a private performance by Amy Winehouse for a fee close to £1 million. A short while before Abramovich also splashed more than £200,000 on a sixteenth birthday party for his daughter at the London nightclub Paper, hiring top Mercury prize-winning indie band The Klaxons and the Brazilian electro band CSS to provide the entertainment.

Hiring rock stars has become something of a trait among the Russians. In 2005 Alexander Lebedev flew Rod Stewart to Moscow for a concert at the Kremlin. For his wedding in the South of France in 2005, Andrei Melnichenko hired Whitney Houston and Christina Aguilera. Guests included President Putin at the weekend ceremony at one of the coal magnate's six homes in the Cannes region. The chapel of a Russian Orthodox Church was taken apart bit by bit, flown to Cannes and reassembled for the service. Catering was provided by

Michelin-starred chef Alain Ducasse, who charges £7,000 an hour. Despite costing a reported $40 million, it would not have burnt too much of a hole in the billionaire's pocket.

Two years later, in April 2007, Melnichenko went one better and hired Jennifer Lopez to perform for forty minutes at a lavish party at his Harewood estate in Berkshire. The singer reportedly received a fee of £600,000, while a further £400,000 went on flying in her entourage and putting them up at a top London hotel. The party was to celebrate the thirtieth birthday of Melnichenko's wife, Alexandra Kokotovic, a Serbian pop singer and former Miss Yugoslavia who herself has a passing resemblance to J-Lo. The sixty guests at the heavily guarded party – said to have cost £3 million – included Abramovich and Dasha, as well as other Russian and Serbian tycoons.

In the summer the Côte d'Azur is a favourite haunt of the hedonistic oligarchs. Although there are plenty of yachts owned by fellow billionaires, Mohamed Al Fayed, Saudi Arabia's Prince Alwaleed, and Bob Manoukian, the Armenian businessman based in Belgravia, it is the Russians who have dominated the moorings on France's southern coastline in prime marinas such as the Cap d'Antibes. These moorings cost around $100,000 a week for super-yachts. In 2004 Dame Shirley Bassey complained that Abramovich's 370-foot yacht *Le Grand Bleu*, moored in Monte Carlo Bay, was ruining the view from her apartment.

The most expensive villas in the area – which cost upwards of £12 million – have in recent years been increasingly snapped up by Russians, and not just Berezovsky and Abramovich. In March 2007 London-based Leonid Blavatnik bought the legendary Grand-Hôtel du Cap-Ferrat, a magnificent white palace in one of the world's most exclusive resorts. The hotel's guest list reads like a who's who of European royalty, celebrities, and political leaders, and past guests have included Winston Churchill, Leopold II of Belgium, Charlie Chaplin, and Pablo

Picasso. Blavatnik snapped up the seven-acre hotel, as well as the five-star Hôtel de Vendôme in central Paris for a reported combined total of £146 million.

Locals have become used to the ostentation and excess of Russian money: the yachts, convoys of black limousines, chauffeur-driven Bentleys, Michelin-starred restaurants, wild champagne parties, and high-class hookers. Not for nothing has St Tropez become known as a 'twenty-first-century Sodom and Gomorrah'. During August, much of the Russian glamour set decamps from their Knightsbridge and Moscow apartments to descend on the French Riviera. Today the club scene has become increasingly international. Part of the ritual is the annual beach party in Ibiza over the August Bank Holiday organized by Boujis nightclub, all part of a global scene in which international clubbers flit between London's West End, St Tropez, the Maldives, and the Caribbean.

During the winter, the Russian nouveaux riches would flock to Courchevel, the luxurious French ski resort in the Alps. Several members of the 'family', including Berezovsky, Tatyana Dyachenko, and Abramovich, have been regular visitors since the mid-1990s. In 2007 an estimated 15,000 Russians visited in the winter season, concentrated in the first two weeks in January during the celebration of the Russian Orthodox New Year. Menus in the more exclusive restaurants and hotels are printed in Russian, as are signs to hotels and ski slopes. The Russians have greatly outspent other holidaymakers, colonized the most expensive chalets, hotels, and restaurants, and hired the best ski instructors.

Since the start of the new millennium, profits at the top hotels, restaurants and bars, designer jewellers, and boutiques have soared based on what one local describes as 'an annual orgy of conspicuous consumption'. Quickly learning Russian taste, jewellers at Courchevel would ensure a ready supply of watches and mobile phones encrusted with diamonds.

No expense has been spared when it comes to partying. Renting a top chalet in the resort would cost £25,000 a week. The favoured haunt of the Russian business elite has been the five-star Byblos des Neiges, which stands at Courchevel 1850, the highest of the four villages in the exclusive resort, and where prices would start at £1,200 per night. The hotel attracts film stars like Bruce Willis and supermodels like Naomi Campbell as well as Russian billionaires. The hotel's famous nightclub, Caves du Roy, charges £2,000 for jeroboams of Cristal and Krug Grande Reserve, while a portion of Beluga caviar costs £500. As well as the visitors, armies of young women are flown in for the 'season', while Russia's top rock bands like Zveri are also hired by the billionaire guests.

Others viewed this circus rather more darkly. Writing in January 2004, nearly three years before she was murdered, the journalist Anna Politkovskaya contrasted the fate of orphans in Russia with the antics of her super-rich fellow citizens: 'Meanwhile, our nouveaux riches are skiing this Christmas in Courchevel. More than two thousand Russians, each earning over half a million roubles [£10,000] a month, congregate for the "Saison russe". The menu offers eight kinds of oysters, the wine list includes bottles at £1,500, and in the retinue of every nouveau riche you can be sure of finding the government officials, our true oligarchs, who deliver these vast incomes to the favoured two thousand. The talk is of success, of the firebird of happiness caught by its tail feathers, of being trusted by the state authorities. The "charity" of officialdom, otherwise known as corruption, is the quickest route to Courchevel.'[23]

The arrival of the Russians in Courchevel has long divided local opinion as well. In the early days the Russians gained a reputation for vulgarity and lavish spending at a level never before seen in the resort. Hoteliers remember how they would knock back Château Petrus at several thousand pounds a bottle, often laced with vodka. 'They were quite a problem to start with,' said one hotelier. 'Every day we worried ourselves sick about what their next demand might be. They might want the pool opened at midnight, caviar delivered to their room at 3.00 a.m., or a limo in front of the hotel in three minutes. In the restaurant they would order all their dishes at the same time, send back what they no longer felt like eating, and query the bill. And if we didn't meet their requests, they made a terrible fuss, screaming and threatening to leave the hotel immediately. They drove us up the wall.'[24]

But gradually things began to change, with some Russian visitors realizing that throwing their weight about was bad for their image. They started to behave themselves. Later Russian visitors, many of them members of the newly emerging business elite – senior executives, entrepreneurs, and international bankers – have tended to behave less boisterously and more discreetly. This does not mean the partying and spending have stopped, far from it; but it is mostly less conspicuous and less riotous. It also does not mean they are popular with everybody. Many chalet staff refused to work with Russians, such was their reputation for rudeness.

One of the most notorious visitors to Courchevel has been Mikhail Prokhorov. Sometimes described in Russia's tabloid newspapers as 'Nickel to Knickers Prokhorov', the oligarch, who also has a home in London, built his multi-billion-pound fortune through mining with a substantial minority stake in Norilsk Nickel, the former state-owned company he acquired with Vladimir Potanin. The company produced one-fifth of the world's nickel, a key alloy in stainless steel, and in 2006 had profits of some $6 billion.

On the night of 7 January 2007 the mining tycoon, dubbed the 'most eligible bachelor in the country', was living up to his playboy reputation, partying in the company of stunning young women. Out of the blue the nightclub was raided by fifty French police, who snatched the man known locally as 'Our Gatsby' on suspicion of running a ring of high-class prostitutes. Prokhorov was taken to police headquarters in Lyons together with twenty-four others, including seven Russian women aged about twenty. Although all those arrested were later released without charge, news of the incident soon appeared in *Le Progress*, a Lyons newspaper. Prokhorov told police that he liked the company of intelligent women and had met the women in restaurants and nightclubs in Russia.

Prokhorov's winter jaunts had got him into difficulties before. According to officials in Ottawa, the Canadian government had refused to grant visas to a group of female companions accompanying him on a winter vacation to Canada two years earlier. Prokhorov was offered a visa, but his entourage was not.[25]

Prokhorov was not very pleased with the publicity but he could hardly complain. After all, partying is in the Russian blood. As the oligarch once told an interviewer, entertaining embodied his personal philosophy. But fortune seemed to be deserting the billionaire, for the revelations did not play out quite so well back at home.

The story was splashed across Russian newspapers and television stations. Soon Prokhorov was a household name and everyone knew about his extravagant international lifestyle. Two months later the event was even satirized in an advertisement for fruit juice shown on state-controlled television. The ad, which of course did not name Prokhorov, featured a newscast of police escorting a line of young women wearing lingerie and fur hats, followed by a tycoon in a bathrobe. The ad cut to a woman in a Russian apartment watching the news. The tagline was: 'Some enjoy fantasies of the good life. Others drink juice.'

Across Russia the antics and excesses of some of the oligarchs, so disdainfully dismissed by the late Anna

Politkovskaya, have been treated with weary contempt by ordinary people. While parts of Moscow have been turned into another super-rich playground hosting millionaire fairs and exhibitions such as the Extravaganza Show, the international spending spree has been a world apart from the experience of ordinary Russians. The great majority of the population have walked a spending tightrope, forever worried about how to pay for the doctor if they are ill or how they can afford to pay the military to keep their sons out of Chechnya. According to the World Health Organization, male life expectancy has declined since the Soviet era to the age of fifty-six. The country has one of the lowest minimum wages in Europe and is one of the most unequal countries in the developing world. In contrast to the unrestrained international spending of Russia's billionaires and multi-millionaires, the bulk of Russia's population remain pitifully poor.

CHAPTER 8

The Curse of Yukos

'This wasn't Mother Teresa versus Mike Tyson. These were two big tough guys at it with each other and one of them won. Putin won, Khodorkovsky lost, but it was a fair fight. He certainly didn't deserve the pity of some type of political prisoner because all the things he did basically disallow him from claiming that'

– BILL BROWDER, *Hermitage Capital Management*[1]

WHEN BRITISH SECURITY consultants arrived at the Moscow headquarters of the Yukos oil company in late summer of 2003, they were shocked by its size, opulence, and almost military atmosphere. The 'office' turned out to be an imposing Victorian castle with huge bronze letters declaring its presence. It was surrounded by a tall, wrought-iron fence with sharp spikes and barbed wire and armed security guards patrolled the grounds.

As the consultants walked through the endless labyrinth of doors, rooms, and bunkers, it was as if they had entered the command and control HQ of a private army. After a bewildering number of corridors, they finally entered the private office of Leonid Nevzlin, Director of Corporate and Political Affairs at Yukos and a close confidant of its majority shareholder, Mikhail Khodorkovsky. There was a Zen-like atmosphere about the

a different taxi and taken to another, an underground station. After a brief tube journey, they went in yet another cab to a restaurant where they were reunited with Burganov.

That protection ended in January 2005. Burganov had applied for political asylum and been handed over to a specialist immigration lawyer who secured his UK residency. The Russian authorities requested his extradition for fraud offences but it was too late. Foreign citizens granted asylum in the UK are usually automatically protected from extradition requests. At his extradition hearing the request was discharged by the judge because he had already been granted asylum.

As soon as his status was secure, Burganov moved into a much more comfortable flat in St James's Square and settled into a new life. The property had been bought by a British Virgin Islands-based company called Vengrada Estates, which has offices in Geneva and Mayfair. Burganov's finances were secure and held in an offshore company called Lutton Invest and Finance, also registered in the British Virgin Islands, and set up by wealth management company the Trident Trust. The following year he moved into a new apartment in Bayswater, bought for £520,000 and registered in his own name.

The next smuggling case was more challenging. Known as Operation Maltesa 2, this involved using the same procedure to move Natalia Chernysheva, a senior Yukos executive and adviser to Khodorkovsky. She had been accused by the Russian authorities of embezzlement in relation to the privatization of a state-owned chemical company. A prime target for the prosecutors, she also needed to be moved quickly.

Indiscreet and outspoken, Chernysheva was more difficult to manage during the risky journey in the late summer of 2003. She was also a habitual name-dropper, which irritated her security handlers.

When Chernysheva arrived in London, she was taken to the Grosvenor House Hotel on Park Lane. When asked if she wanted security, she refused. 'I know the right lawyer,' she snapped and walked off into the Mayfair night. Her bodyguards were mightily relieved. 'She argued about everything,' said one of the security consultants. But going it alone was a high risk for Chernysheva. A year later, in September 2004, the Russian authorities issued an arrest warrant and requested her extradition. But she could indeed afford the best lawyers – Edward Fitzgerald, QC, and solicitors Corker Binning – and in March 2005 the presiding judge rejected the extradition request – on the grounds that it was politically motivated – and the former Yukos executive was a free woman. She continues to live in London.

A number of other Yukos executives also entered the UK from their secret base in southern Cyprus. Known as Operation Olive Grove, this was a safer and easier route and had been used by one of Khodorkovsky's associates who settled in a safe house in London, just off Piccadilly.

The costs of Operations Maltesa 1 and 2 and Olive Grove were paid from a Yukos offshore account in the Isle of Man by bank transfer. Hundreds of thousands of dollars in cash from the transfer were stashed in safety deposit boxes in Knightsbridge and Mayfair. These were then used to disperse the fees and expenses. As for their predecessors in the 1990s, paying in cash was routine for the new arrivals, as commonplace as having a bodyguard, but it was a practice that would become more difficult after 2 June 2008. On that day Metropolitan Police Specialist Crime officers raided a Mayfair safety deposit centre on Park Street, the culmination of a two-year undercover anti-money-laundering operation. They found vast quantities of cash and sensitive documents belonging to at least one former Yukos executive and a prominent Georgian businessman – as well as handguns, fake passports, and cocaine.

* * *

Unlike Boris Berezovsky, the oil billionaire Mikhail Khodorkovsky was strategic, modest living, and methodical. Highly focused and intense, he often appeared oblivious to his immediate surroundings. A classic boffin-type intellectual, he once arrived for a business meeting wearing only shoes, socks, trousers, and jacket, having forgotten his shirt and tie. None of this, however, should disguise his single-minded, ruthless streak – he was known to install CCTV cameras to spy on his own staff. Like Berezovsky, Khodorkovsky was merciless in his pursuit of wealth and power. One journalist who interviewed him in Davos in 2003 remembers 'rarely meeting anyone with such hard and unforgiving eyes'.[2]

As Russia faced bankruptcy in the late 1990s, Khodorkovsky became obsessed with protecting the value of his multi-billion-pound fortune. Like some of his fellow oligarchs, he had obtained lucrative state assets cheaply, but in the volatile atmosphere of the time his windfall wealth was far from secure. Knowing that the authorities might one day claw back the nation's wealth by reversing the privatizations or imposing retrospective taxation, the tycoon had already taken contingency measures.

As his business empire expanded in the 1990s, Khodorkovsky, like most tycoons, developed an aversion to paying tax. Fortunately, there was a neat solution that would enable him to both protect his assets and avoid paying tax: he could move his assets offshore and into hard currencies. With advice from Western European financial experts, they developed a complex network of offshore companies and accounts.

However, parts of Khodorkovsky's business empire may, it seems, have had quite a cosy relationship with certain elements of the Russian state. This was confirmed in testimony to the US Senate Banking and Financial Services Committee in 1999, which described a 'KGB money-laundering operation with stolen funds that were passed through Khodorkovsky's

Menatep Bank as a KGB-controlled front firm'.[3] In effect, the committee was told the bank was being used by Kremlin insiders and top KGB officials as their paymaster. The reward for the oligarch was a large pot of gold, which one source described as 'a platinum parachute'.

Bank Menatep – registered in a PO box in Gibraltar – was at the centre of all Khodorkovsky's business operations. It was through Menatep in 1996 that he acquired his biggest prize of all, Yukos oil, in the 'loans for shares' auctions.[4] The potential flow of money from the oil business was huge and required an even more complex set of arrangements.

As Khodorkovsky's empire escalated and his offshore base expanded, friends suggested that he might need specialist legal advice. The lawyer he turned to was Stephen Curtis.

In the summer of 1997 Khodorkovsky arrived at Luton Airport in his private jet. Surrounded by three bodyguards and amid intense secrecy and security, he was driven to Curtis's offices at 94 Park Lane. Soon Curtis had signed up his first oligarch client and set about masterminding the restructuring of Yukos and its offshore network.

Excited by the challenge, Curtis's first task was a major one: the creation and setting up of Group Menatep, which was incorporated on 5 September 1997. Menatep became the vehicle of ownership for the oligarch's legal control of Yukos, but its primary purpose was to protect Khodorkovsky's assets from being frozen and seized by the Russian authorities. This could only be done by setting up an elaborate offshore network.

Also registered in a PO box in an anonymous suite in Gibraltar, Group Menatep Ltd's (GML) original share capital was just five million shares, despite controlling assets worth billions of dollars. These were held equally between Stephen Curtis and a senior accountant based in Cyprus. All but one of these five million shares were then transferred to a trust called the Palmus Foundation and offshore companies in Liechten-stein, Cyprus, and Gibraltar. The one remaining share was retained by Curtis.

However, GML was ultimately controlled by Khodorkovsky. His majority shareholding was administered by a special offshore trust of which he was the sole beneficiary. This was set up by Curtis, who was given voting rights in the event of Khodorkovsky's arrest or death.

In effect, Curtis had become the custodian and protector of Yukos's and Menatep's assets. He was not the beneficial owner of the shares, but he held them in trust. He was the firewall that investigators later hit when they tried, mostly unsuccessfully, to penetrate the bewildering maze of interlocking companies and trusts that had been established.

Khodorkosvky both trusted and liked the sociable Curtis, who was honest and did not steal from him. The oligarch also liked the way the Mayfair lawyer kept most of the sensitive details in his head and the paper trail to a minimum. Although this helped maintain secrecy, it was also a reflection of Curtis's computer illiteracy and chaotic filing system (he preferred to dictate his letters and attendance notes verbally). Like an absent-minded professor, Curtis often carried about him scraps of paper with scribbled notes of information relating to hundreds of millions of pounds. And on the rare occasions when he could not recall data, he would telephone his staff at 3.00 a.m. for the answers.

Sometimes minutes were kept. Indeed, the scale of the oper-ation was revealed in the minutes of a meeting in June 1999 at Curtis's offices. These showed complex and impenetrable financial networks that stretched across the globe. Hundreds of millions of dollars of Russian oil profits from Yukos were spir-ited away via offshore accounts in Gibraltar, the Cayman Islands, and the Isle of Man.[5] However, exactly how much will never be known.

The network that handled the oil flow was code-named Jurby Lake, named after a stretch of water in the Isle of Man. Some of the revenue from Yukos oil exports flowed through Jurby Lake into a range of companies in Switzerland, Liberia, and the Republic of Ireland. It was these companies that accumulated vast sums in profits. Although they all had legally separate entities, they shared a common office in Geneva.

Placing money offshore in this way proved a huge financial bonanza, helping to save Khodorkovsky's fortune when the rouble collapsed in 1998. As the crisis turned into near catastrophe, Menatep found itself, at least publicly, in deep trouble. Consultants and staff went unpaid, and the bank blocked withdrawals and deposits and refused to pay its creditors. The Central Bank withdrew its licence and its giant name in letters was quietly removed from its façade at its Moscow headquarters while depositors queued up in their hundreds, largely in vain, outside the grand marbled building. Menatep might have appeared to have crashed but most of its assets, including Yukos, had already been safely deposited abroad in hard currency largely through the offshore networks set up by Curtis.[6]

The shuffling away by Khodorkovsky of these assets to offshore subsidiaries and bank accounts was not just a mass tax avoidance device. During the second half of the 1990s, Western investors sensed the potential profits to be made and poured money into Russia. Many were so keen to get involved in the newly privatized companies that the normal process of due diligence was often carried out only superficially. By hiding the assets in this way, some minority shareholders in Yukos claimed that this structure was used to hide profits and hence avoid making their dividend payments.

One of the minority investors was Bill Browder, who set up Hermitage Capital Management, once the largest private foreign investor in Russia. From 1997 to 1999, the share price of Yukos crashed precipitously from a high of $6 to a low of 8¢.

Although the fall was mainly down to the economic crisis rocking Russia at the time, this was not the only reason. 'While some of the drop in the share price – from $6 to about $1.25 – was down to the market, the rest from $1.25 to 8¢ was as a result of the asset stripping plan,' said Browder.[7]

Browder was just one of several Western casualties. Among Menatep's creditors were the German Bank West LB, Japan's Daiwa Bank, and South Africa's Standard Investment. Between them they had lent Menatep, with deeply unfortunate timing, a total of $236 million just a few months before the crash in 1998. As collateral, the lenders were pledged shares in Yukos – the equivalent of 30 per cent of the company. The shares would be reclaimed by Menatep when the loan was repaid. On paper the deal looked pretty robust.

When, following the crisis, they inquired about the state of their loan, the overseas banks were given a remarkable runaround. Repeated requests for information were met with contradictory answers. At one point a truckload of Menatep documents being shipped out of Moscow ended up in the Volga River. Moreover, to hide the true state of the bank's finances, Khodorkovsky embarked on a series of new financial manoeuvres, effectively playing a game of hide and seek with both the bank's and Yukos's assets.

On one occasion shares were sold on Khodorkovsky's behalf in two of Yukos's main petroleum-producing units to a group of offshore subsidiaries. Menatep claimed that it did not know who owned these companies, but it emerged that one of the subsidiaries was owned by close advisers of Khodorkovsky. Yukos's minority investors claimed that profits were being siphoned off into anonymous offshore accounts and at least one shareholder hired private detectives to find out what had happened.

The effect of the share offloading was that Menatep's assets were further diluted. As a result, the overseas banks owned 30 per cent of a company that was little more than an empty shell.

While Khodorkovsky and Curtis set up elaborate offshore arrangements, they had not reckoned on the emergence of whistleblowers. One was Elena Collongues-Popova, a Russian living in Paris who managed another network of offshore accounts for Menatep from 1996.

Collongues-Popova, once married to a KGB colonel, became involved in Menatep following a party for elite Russian businessmen in St Tropez in 1995. She claimed that she was eventually managing twenty to thirty companies, registered in her name – in Switzerland, Luxembourg, the British Virgin Islands, the Seychelles, Panama, and the Bahamas – involving transfers of some £150 million a year. Some of the transactions allegedly passed through major London-based British and American banks.

Working in what one observer described as the 'seedy back streets of global finance' also offered a bonus: a glamorous lifestyle. 'I could have bought an English football club,' joked Collongues-Popova. 'It was like the soap opera *Dallas*. It meant executive jet flights all the time – to the Caribbean, to the Seychelles, and to the Isle of Man. It was a life of luxury hotels, top restaurants, and endless supplies of cash to bribe the right people. I cannot remember how many pearl necklaces – at £80,000 apiece – I bought to win over the wives of our go-betweens.'[8]

Like the methods used by spy rings and terrorist cells, the complex network of companies linked to Menatep and Yukos was run by different people, each deliberately kept at arm's length from each other to preserve secrecy. 'It was like a big building block in which there were many apartments, everybody had his own key and was doing his own business with his own premises,' admitted Collongues-Popova.[9] The network only emerged during an investigation by the French tax authorities, which had uncovered large amounts of cash moving in and out of Collongues-Popova's bank accounts.

During the investigation into Yukos, she was asked to go to Moscow to testify but refused because she feared for her safety. In an attempt to clear her name, in August 2003 she sent the Russian prosecutors boxes of documents including corporate papers, trading reports, and bank statements dating from 1996 to 2000.

While some of the billions that flew out of Russia and into foreign bank accounts were the result of tax avoidance, a great deal also disappeared through wire transfers, phony import-export documents, oil shipments, and other devices.[10] It mostly came from what should have been highly profitable companies providing the backbone of the Russian economy. There is even evidence of the looting of international loans from the IMF made to help prop up the rouble.[11]

Despite his growing business empire, Khodorkovsky also sought political influence to protect his interests after Putin came to power. 'It makes me weep when Boris Berezovsky talks about this group of people having 100 per cent political influence,' Khordorkovsky said in 2000. 'If we had just 10 per cent of the political influence that Berezovsky claims, we would never have allowed the government to impose the unbearable tax burden on business that it has.'[12] His own influence at the Kremlin was in decline. He had been extremely influential at the Ministry of Fuel and Energy under the Yeltsin regime but, as Putin's star rose, so Khodorkovsky's declined.

Unwilling to be cowed by Putin and his new tougher line on the oligarchs, Khodorkovsky turned to a new tactic. He now realized that for Yukos to become a global energy power and attract foreign investors he needed to clean up his commercial reputation. To his credit, he did not attempt to deny a chequered business past. 'We started out as robber barons, but you have got to understand that rules were hazy in those early days and we changed ourselves as we became familiar with what was expected of us,' he said in December 2001. 'I don't think I actually violated the law but it took me some time to realize that above and beyond the law there were also ethical laws.'[13]

Realizing the deep-seated damage to his reputation from a run of exposures and the potential risk from the Russian investigators, Khodorkovsky set out to reinvent himself as a responsible businessman and to rebrand Yukos as a law-abiding company. In May 1999 the oligarch paid a whirlwind visit to Washington, DC, and New York. He toured the New York Stock Exchange, met newspaper editors, and attempted to defend his business methods.

By the end of 2000, the Yukos boss was well into his international charm offensive. He realized that transparency and efficiency were now in his own financial self-interest. He was, as *The Economist* put it, 'The first of the Yeltsin-era tycoons to see that there was even more money to be made by going straight'.[14] He ended some of the more controversial aspects of the offshore scams, brought some income back onshore, used profits to reinvest, and even started to pay taxes. Suddenly, he was a model of corporate transparency, released financial records, paid dividends, and even repaid, at least in part, some depositors who had lost their money when Menatep collapsed in the 1998 financial crash. To meet his new goal – to create 'something huge', a Western-style quoted company listed on the London or New York Stock Exchange – he knew he would have to play by their rules.

Accordingly, he set up company towns like Nefteyugansk, where even the Christmas lights on Lenin Street were in the shape of the Yukos corporate symbol – a green and yellow triangle. In a desolate town where temperatures reach –40 degrees C in mid-December, Yukos supplied everything, from new computers to fresh water. The company provided a hospital, welfare, and even a police force. Based on the Japanese business model, drugs or drinking were forbidden and there were early morning exercise sessions.

In July 2001 Khodorkovsky sat in his nineteenth-century-mansion HQ in Moscow under a sign with a slogan that read, 'Honesty, Openness, Responsibility' and told the *New York Times* of his conversion to business transparency. Having once denied that he owned any shares in Yukos or Menatep, he now confessed details of his controlling stock and published accounts to international guidelines. Khodorkovsky hired American and French executives from Western oil companies and banks and appointed prominent politicians as non-executive directors. 'He was trying to protect his rear,' according to one British academic who knew him well. The change of heart was rewarded by investors. In the years after 2000 Yukos's share price soared, boosting the value of the company and Khodorkovsky's personal fortune, although the rising demand for world energy was the major factor.

To help improve his image abroad, Khodorkovsky hired Western PR experts and contributed generously to conservative think-tanks linked with the Bush administration. He turned to APCO Worldwide, the savvy American lobbying company and a subsidiary of the global giant Grey Advertising. The lobbying company was paid an upfront fee of $4 million, a monthly retainer of $25,000 for website design and maintenance, and an annual fee of $90,000.

It was APCO that advised him to create the Open Russia Foundation, modelled on George Soros's Open Society Foundation. It was launched with much fanfare in London's Somerset House on the evening of 10 December 2001. Khodorkovsky flew in from Russia and told guests at the launch, 'I am launching the Foundation in London to highlight the international nature of the Foundation's aims and to create an infrastructure from which the next generation of Russia's leaders will emerge. Yukos oil already supports various educational programmes in

Russia and I view this as the next step towards encouraging further cooperation between our country and the West.'[15]

In the same week Khodorkovsky held court at the Dorchester Hotel, a venue long associated with controversial foreign tycoons and royal families. Even in the grandeur of the Dorchester tearoom, there was little that was flashy or ostentatious about Khodorkovsky or his presentation. The diffident executive was escorted by a press officer and interpreter, but there was not a bodyguard in sight. When asked whether he was uncomfortable about being so rich in a country where poverty was widespread, he answered, 'A wealthy person is not very comfortable in Russia.'[16]

Describing itself as the 'first Russian international corporate philanthropic foundation', the Open Russia Foundation was launched in the US in September 2002 in the elegant hall of the Library of Congress in Washington, DC. The launch was attended by America's political and business elite and addressed by James Wolfensohn, President of the World Bank. Many of those present no doubt smelt new and lucrative networking opportunities. With APCO's help, the foundation recruited powerful figures as trustees, notably Henry Kissinger, Dr Mikhail Piotrovsky, Director of the St Petersburg's fabled State Hermitage Museum, and Lord (Jacob) Rothschild.

The multi-millionaire scion of the banking dynasty, Lord Rothschild is a close friend of Prince Charles and one of the best-connected bankers in the world. Khodorkovsky first met him in the 1990s when he was invited to a party at his country home at Waddesdon Manor, Buckinghamshire. Unsure about navigating his way through Western corporate governance waters, Lord Rothschild became a confidant of Khordorkovsky's and allowed his offices in St James's to be used as the London address of the Open Russia Foundation. He was so trusted that he was assigned the voting rights behind Khodorkovsky's Yukos shares in 2003. That meant that the veteran banker could vote at board meetings and AGMs as a surrogate for the oligarch in his absence.

Henry Kissinger was also an admirer and even travelled to Moscow to support a joint project with the foundation to promote 'Russian democracy'. But not everyone was so enthusiastic. Former Senator Bill Bradley of New Jersey was invited but declined. Although the foundation funded projects inside and outside Russia, including exhibitions of Russian art at Somerset House and a programme to bring together young British, American, and Russian leaders, it always had a modest $15 million budget. According to the American journalist Lucy Komisar, 'Open Russia Foundation's grants seemed aimed more at cultivating powerful friends than promoting democracy. A book of photographs of Russia by Lord Snowdon was commissioned. The Foundation also gave $100,000 to the National Book Festival, a favourite charity of Laura Bush, the wife of President George Bush.'[17]

Khodorkovsky also pumped money into the powerful investment fund Carlyle Group, run by Frank Carlucci, a former deputy director of the CIA and US Defense Secretary under Ronald Reagan. These moves all helped to secure the oligarch goodwill among powerful US political figures. Hoping to win over public opinion, in 2001 he invited a handful of prominent journalists on what became an infamous champagne-fuelled junket around Russia by private jet. The trip, organized by Prince Michael of Kent, became known among Moscow correspondents as the 'plane of shame'.

The Open Russia Foundation also donated $1 million to the Open World academic exchange programme, championed by the Librarian of Congress and Russian scholar James H. Billington. In September 2002 Billington organized a dinner at the Library of Congress at which he described Khodorkovsky as a 'visionary'. Later, in the grand setting of the Members Room of the Thomas Jefferson Building, Khodorkovsky and

Lord Rothschild mingled with congressmen, State Department officials, businessmen, and Russia experts. The rebranding and relaunch of the oligarch had been an 'enormous success', according to Lord Rothschild.

In Britain Khodorkovsky's foundation also paid for Somerset House to retrieve paintings once owned by Sir Robert Walpole, Britain's first Prime Minister, which had been sold off to Catherine the Great by Walpole's eccentric and flamboyant grandson. In 1779, 204 of the finest paintings in the Walpole Collection were shipped to the State Hermitage Museum in St Petersburg. Khodorkovsky's money funded the return of thirty-four of the paintings back to London. Entitled 'Passion, Painting and Politics', the exhibition was displayed in 'The Khodorkovsky Room'.[18]

To win influence, the oligarch indirectly donated to the Foreign Policy Centre (FPC), which has close links with the Labour government, and whose patron was Tony Blair. Such politically connected think-tanks are, according to the FPC's former Communications Director Rob Blackhurst, beholden to their corporate sponsors. 'The FPC has accepted more than £100,000 from an unnamed Russian oligarch to establish a programme on Russian democracy,' Blackhurst stated in January 2005. 'The money does not come directly. It is channelled through London PR companies presided over by a retinue of former New Labour special advisors. The PR people want to shift public sympathy away from Vladimir Putin and they are no doubt delighted that the project has led to a paper criticizing Downing Street's closeness to the Russian President.'[19]

Like most oligarchs, Khodorkovsky was enamoured of the House of Lords and cultivated influential peers. In late 2000 he was invited to lunch at the Lords by Baroness Smith, the Labour peer and widow of former Labour Party leader John Smith. The Baroness was a consultant to BP, which was then starting to invest in Russia, and the country fascinated her. As part of his cultivation of the New Labour establishment, Khodorkovsky donated to the John Smith Memorial Fund, which was why he was invited. As Khordorkovsky does not speak English, he was seated next to Lord Skidelsky, distinguished academic and biographer of John Maynard Keynes and a fluent Russian speaker. The peer asked the oil baron what he thought of Putin. 'He is a perfect representation of [mainstream] Russian opinion,' he replied dismissively, alluding to the fact that the President understood the basic instincts of Russian people. Khodorkovsky's generosity to the Fund was further rewarded when he was invited to 11 Downing Street and thanked personally by the then Chancellor of the Exchequer, Gordon Brown.

Khodorkovsky also hired Lord Owen, one of the founders of the Social Democratic Party. Lord Owen had already been involved in Russian business as a Director and figurehead for Middlesex Steel, owned by the oligarch Alisher Usmanov, since 1995. The former Labour Foreign Secretary was retained as a paid consultant to Yukos.

Khodorkovsky also retained the lobbying company Public Policy Partnership, owned by Lord Gillford. Known as Paddy, he is the only son and heir of John Meade, the 7th Earl of Clanwilliam. Educated at Eton and Sandhurst, Gillford is a former Coldstream Guardsman and became head of the public affairs (i.e. lobbying) unit of Hanson Plc, Lord Hanson's construction conglomerate. He has all the attributes of an aristocrat: monogrammed signet rings, tailored pinstriped suits, and a cut-glass accent straight out of P. G. Wodehouse.

A consummate political networker, Paddy Gillford joined the notorious lobbying company of Ian Greer Associates, which he left in 1993 to form his own consultancy, Westminster Policy Partnership, later renamed the Public Policy Partnership. One of his clients was Vladimir Potanin's investment vehicle Interros in London. With his aristocratic bearing, Gillford, one of the more unorthodox political lobbyists networking in Westminster on behalf of Russian clients, was precisely the type of spin doctor that appealed to Khodorkovsky. As well as Yukos, Gillford's clients included Russian Axis Ltd and several foreign regimes and he was close enough to Prince Michael of Kent to host lavish receptions for oil and gas companies at Kensington Palace.

The Russians fell in love with the titled lobbyist. And Lord Gillford loved to play up to his aristocratic image, inviting his Russian clients to his Scottish estate every year for a spot of hunting, shooting, and fishing.

To cement his cultivation of the British establishment, Khodorkovsky set up the Khodorkovsky Foundation. Registered as a UK company on 8 December 2003, it received $500 million from Group Menatep Ltd, roughly twenty-five times the amount given to Open Russia. Its objectives were 'to advance education in the Russian Federation through the provision of scholarships to students and the making of donations to educational establishments'.

The Khodorkovsky Foundation was a philanthropic and academic organization. Its initial board members were: Alistair Tulloch, a Mayfair lawyer who represented several Yukos companies and entities; Charles Young, Bursar of Magdalen College, Oxford; and Anthony Smith, the former President of Magdalen College. Boris Saltykov, the former Russian Deputy Prime Minister, joined the board on 11 March 2004. For its first year, the foundation was a commercial operation and not registered as a UK charity until 19 November 2004, a year after Khodorkovsky was arrested. And it did not make any donations until 2005, when it provided over £400,000 to St Antony's College, Oxford, over four years and £500,000 to the Oxford Russia Fund, which provides scholarships. The latter was another charity set up with the same trustees as the Khodorkovsky Foundation.

Although the oil tycoon invested heavily in the West to improve his corporate image, he was taking no chances back home. He may have enjoyed relaxed security in London but in Moscow his security manifested itself in something more resembling a small private army and was dominated by specially trained former Special Forces operatives. A normal convoy consisted of four cars – bomb- as well as bullet-proof, and all with blacked-out windows – and a motorbike, and bodyguards armed with French machine guns and side pistols. Run on military lines, security was staffed by Russian officers and soldiers left unemployed after the collapse of communism. Highly-trained and in prime physical condition, they were mostly in their thirties and bored, with little money. They were not difficult to recruit.

Gradually, Khodorkovsky picked up where Berezovsky left off. Now Russia's richest man, and increasingly arrogant, he believed that he no longer needed protection or to pay political godfathers for a '*krisha*' (Russian for roof). By 2003, Khodorkovsky was expressing vociferous criticism of the Kremlin and was becoming more than just a pestilential nuisance to Putin. The tension between the two culminated in one of the regular meetings at the Kremlin between the President and businessmen. This particular one occurred in February 2003.

Usually, such meetings were mundane affairs, but this one crackled like a log fire, with Khodorkovsky accusing Russia's bureaucrats of corruption. Ignoring the advice of his colleagues, he singled out a murky deal involving the purchase of the Northern Oil Company by the state-owned Rosneft a few days earlier. His own company had been outbid by Rosneft, which paid $622.6 million – three times what Yukos considered a reasonable price. Frustrated at losing out, Khodorkovsky complained that Rosneft executives had paid an inflated price and received kickbacks from the state in return. He demanded that Rosneft be investigated. 'Your bureaucracy is made up of bribe-takers and thieves,' he told the President.

Bristling with irritation, especially given Khodorkovsky's own track record, Putin icily reminded him of how he himself had made billions through manipulated government auctions and tax evasion. 'Rosneft is a state company and needs to increase its insufficient reserves,' he said. The President then stared at Khodorkovsky with such hostility that he turned pale. 'And a few companies like Yukos, for example, have good reserves. The question is, how did they get them?' he added sharply. 'So I am returning your puck.'[20]

The meeting was the catalyst for the impending showdown between Russia's richest man and its most powerful. Khodorkovsky had consistently ignored Putin's stark warning not to meddle in politics. He funded opposition parties hostile to Putin, publicly criticized the government, and hinted at his own presidential ambitions. He even acted like a sovereign power, negotiating with the Chinese government directly to build a pipeline through Siberia to China.

Despite his outward self-confidence, Khodorkovsky knew he was taking risks. In early 2003 he made secret contingency plans to avoid arrest. His business partner Leonid Nevzlin devised a plan whereby oligarchs would live on a ship that sailed around the world in international waters. A Cyprus security company was commissioned and it bought a mini-*QE2* cruise liner for the operation. The 100-cabin ship was dismantled, refitted, and refurbished and its cabins reduced to twelve luxury suites. Named *Constellation*, the plan was for the ship to fly an international flag, in the manner of Liberia, and remain in international waters, thereby avoiding extradition and international arrest warrants. While Khodorkovsky was on board, other oligarchs would be flown in by helicopter and plenty of food and drink would be provided.

Plans for military, anti-radar, and security systems were agreed and commissioned. The basic idea was for Khodorkovsky and the other oligarchs to move from port to port, a sort of floating anti-Putin vessel. This may have helped to explain Khodorkovsky's continuing bravado. He may have thought that he would be immune from extradition but, in fact, he was legally misinformed – no territorial waters are immune from extradition.

Meanwhile, Putin, urged on by the leaders of the newly empowered FSB, was running out of patience. On 2 July 2003, the same day the value of Yukos reached £16 billion, Platon Lebedev, Khodorkovsky's business partner, was arrested. Warrants were also issued for other executives, notably Yukos's Security Chief, Alexei Pichugin, who was later found guilty of murder and given a life sentence. It was this move that triggered the rapid flight of Yukos executives to the UK via Malta and Cyprus.

Two days later Khodorkovsky attended Spaso House, the official residence of the US Ambassador in Moscow, to celebrate American Independence Day. He briefed the Ambassador on the situation and the implications of Lebedev's arrest, then he flew to Washington, DC, for meetings with Democratic Congressman Tom Lantos and Energy Secretary Spencer Abraham. During his trip, he began negotiations to sell a substantial stake of Yukos to ExxonMobil, the US oil giant. These discussions further infuriated Putin, who was not consulted.

Khodorkovsky could have stayed in exile and the Kremlin privately gave him three opportunities to leave Russia while the investigation was underway. Putin even sent messages via intermediaries that he would not pursue the oligarch if he stayed away from Russia. But Khodorkovsky thought he was untouchable, that his wealth would protect him. 'With money, you can ultimately buy anything', he once said.[21]

But even the steely Khodorkovsky was now beginning to show uncharacteristic signs of nerves. Later in July, after Lebedev's arrest, the self-confessed former robber baron gave a lecture to the Moscow School of Political Studies, which he had helped to finance. During the session, he was asked about the pressures on Yukos. 'I would rather rot in a Russian jail than make compromises with these criminals,' he replied bluntly. 'It is my right as a citizen to use my money to organize political opposition.' One of those present, Lord Skidelsky, recalls, 'He was clearly having no part of the Putin deal. I gained the impression he had developed a martyr complex. He was courting danger. He was certainly tense – he was chain-smoking and I had never seen him smoke before.'

Three months later, on 25 October 2003, Khodorkovsky arrived in his private jet at Novosibirsk Airport in central Siberia to refuel. It was the day the Yukos owner had been summoned to appear before the prosecutors for questioning. Once it had taxied to a halt, two carloads of masked FSB officials, armed with sub-machine guns, stormed the plane. The country's richest man had reached the end of his journey to untold wealth.

The dramatic arrest of Khodorkovsky was designed to send a chilling message: the state was more powerful than the oligarchs. The former KGB officers had been let off the leash and were now exacting their revenge. As Vladimir Kolesnikov, the Deputy Public Prosecutor explained, 'Let those who are not yet jailed think hard about what they are doing.'[22] One former KGB official close to the Kremlin, who headed a state-owned oil company, revelled in the arrest, 'Three days in Buttrke prison and they will understand who is the master of the forest.'[23]

Khodorkovsky was charged with grand theft, fraud, forgery, and corporate and personal tax evasion. The charges related primarily to his acquisition of the Apatit chemical company (in the 'loans for shares' auction in 1994). Soon after Khodorkovsky's arrest, Aleksandr Voloshin, who was seen as the oligarch's patron within the Kremlin, resigned as Putin's Chief of Staff.

The move against Khodorkovsky caused a panic among investors and a short-lived run on the Russian stock market. It also sent a shudder down the spines of the other oligarchs. Few had expected Putin to take such drastic action, and the talk was of 'who's next'.

As for Russia's business elite, they might have won more friends if they had reinvested more of their wealth in Russia and, as Putin demanded, paid for social welfare projects. Asked in prison what he had done wrong in the 1990s, Khodorkovsky replied, 'My biggest mistake was that I established a company and invested in industrial plants – but it would have been necessary to build up the country and create social institutions. This was the general problem of the liberal reforms. Business forgot about the people, their interests, their problems and opinions.'

Most oligarchs, for their own self-interest, had by 2003 started to reinvest in their own industries. Aware of the dangers of alienating an entire population, some funded social projects, though initially at largely tokenistic levels. Some were buying back the lost national heritage. To avoid being the next target, none of the oligarchs except Berezovsky (in London) stood up for Khodorkovsky.

Up to this point Roman Abramovich – a canny political operator – had played his cards much more carefully than either Berezovsky or Khodorkovsky. Understanding that Putin's ultimatum to the oligarchs was deadly serious, he steered clear of politics and complied with Putin's wishes. He willingly agreed to stand for the governorship of Russia's remote and impoverished Siberian province of Chukotka, an area where living standards could not have been in greater contrast to Abramovich's own lifestyle. He also quickly responded to the Kremlin's overtures to make large-scale investments in social projects. As a result, he continued to climb up the world's rich list, just as Berezovsky slipped down it.

But despite being on his best behaviour, even Abramovich was not immune from growing Kremlin pressure. Shortly after the arrest of Khodorkovsky, Evgeny Shvidler, then Chief Executive of Sibneft, was summoned to the Interior Ministry to face questions about whether Sibneft was paying enough tax. The wider message was clear: the days of tax loopholes were over.

Within seven weeks, the Audit Chamber announced it was reviewing all privatizations of the past decade, including the 'loans for share' auctions. One Audit Chamber report stated that Sibneft had been sold off in a 'fake auction' with the winner chosen in a 'premeditated agreement'. Fellow oligarch Vladimir Potanin smugly remarked, 'Everything is not going well for Abramovich. It is not turning out the way he wants.'[24] Nearly two years later Abramovich sold Sibneft to Gazprom for $13 billion, another in the steady round of state renationalizations.

Following the arrest of the company's principal owner, the state soon moved to crush Yukos. First its assets were frozen. Then, in December 2004, the government announced that the bulk of Yukos was to be auctioned off. Only two companies were allowed to bid and the winner was a mysterious company called Baikal – later found to be registered to a twenty-four-hour grocery store in the provincial town of Tver, 150 miles north of Moscow.

On the day of the auction, to which Yukos's lawyers were refused access, Baikal bought the company for a fraction of its real value. Two days later the government announced that Baikal, clearly set up to act as a front for the state, would sell the main production arm of Yukos to Rosneft, the giant state combine. If Rosneft had made a direct bid for the company, it might have been the subject of international lawsuits for recovery of Yukos's foreign-owned assets. Even in a country accustomed to rigged auctions and double dealing, the seizing back of a company the state had earlier given away was still a remarkable charade. Khodorkovsky and his fellow shareholders were left with one oil refinery and a handful of petrol stations. The oligarch's global ambitions were over.

After the auction, the once powerful oligarch's attorney, Robert Amsterdam, declared, 'Well, we will have to eat more reasonably now. We have a much smaller company. The share value of Yukos when we first met Khodorkovsky was $16. Now, I think, it's under a dime. They [the Russian government] behaved like gangsters. This is a dirty war carried out by a corrupt system.'

This enforced renationalization of a company was just as controversial as the privatization a decade earlier. Until the arrest of Khodorkovsky, foreign investors had been nervously moving into Russia. Now, at least for a while, capital flight accelerated. 'Putin paid a high price for going for Yukos – it was a big setback internationally for Russia,' said Lord Skidelsky.

Back at 94 Park Lane, the dual incarceration of first Lebedev and then Khodorkovsky had dramatic implications for Stephen Curtis. By the time of Khodorkovsky's arrest, the lawyer had already moved from being a moderately successful Mayfair solicitor to a multi-millionaire and an international businessman.

The sudden wealth, however, was accompanied by intense pressures. While Curtis retained his generous spirit and honesty, he was no longer the easy-going personality he had once been. Now he behaved more like a typical oligarch himself – quick-tempered and impatient. He started tipping doormen £20 every time he walked into a hotel, and entertaining lavishly at Chinawhite – an increasingly popular haunt for rich Russians and celebrities – where he was given a special VIP room. During one epic night at Stringfellows with some Russian clients, he went through £20,000 in cash – for the best table, vintage champagne, dinner, lap dancers in private rooms, and tips. For the

Russian businessmen, such hospitality was a sign that they were being accepted by London and Curtis was providing it all – legal services, advice on property and schools, and, in some cases, nocturnal entertainment.

Nothing was too good for his new Russian clients. He hired executive boxes at Manchester United for Berezovsky, Abramovich, and Yukos executives. It was at one of these matches – the Champions League tie match between Manchester United and Real Madrid on 22 April 2003 – that Abramovich decided to buy a major English football club. Curtis himself never attended but it was all part of the service. Typically, Berezovsky was the most demanding and often asked for tickets for sought-after theatre and sporting events that were long sold out. Curtis would use all his contacts and occasionally spend £5,000 on tickets. He was both exasperated and amused when Berezovsky paid up but then failed to attend. 'Perhaps he was testing me,' he told a colleague.

As the big Russian money poured in, Curtis's hourly rate for his legal services rocketed while his colleagues still worked on the flat rate. In November 2002 he became a tax exile in Gibraltar, operating separately from Curtis & Co. and took the Russian clients with him. He set up a new company, the New World Value Fund Ltd, an investment fund whose clients included Berezovsky and Patarkatsishvili. He moved into the Penthouse Suite at the Elliott Hotel in Gibraltar at a cost of £5,000 per month. He became the sole director of Group Menatep Ltd, and was now managing Khodorkovsky's global business empire – all from his hotel suite in Gibraltar.

Based in Gibraltar, Curtis was forced to decline dinner invitations because – as a tax exile – he could only spend ninety days of the year in the UK. He only came into the Park Lane office once a month and staff were told that their former boss was preparing to transfer ownership of the firm and instructed that no correspondence was to leave the firm bearing his name.

They were told that whenever anyone called for Curtis, they should say he was 'out of the country' but could be contacted on his mobile phone. Everything else was done on the telephone from his Gibraltar hotel suite. Computer-illiterate, Curtis lived on the phone: his mobile phone bills ran to between £15,000 and £30,000 a month. He would call Russia and Israel and talk for an hour or dictate letters to his secretary in London.

Curtis's finances also started to bear comparison with those of his wealthy clients. At first his assets were held in his wife's name but he later arranged a network of offshore companies and trusts, just as he had for his oligarch clients. Fees from Khodorkovsky's Group Menatep Ltd were paid into a Gibraltar-based company, Corfe Holdings Ltd, which was 100 per cent owned by Curtis. His fees from Berezovsky and Patarkatsishvili were also paid into this company.

In the month of Khodorkovsky's arrest, October 2003, Curtis received fees of $6.49 million from the New World Value Fund and $33.9 million from Group Menatep Ltd for overseeing a $20 billion corporation. These funds were, in turn, channelled into other companies that held Curtis's personal property. His helicopter – bought for £1.5 million from the Hon. Charles Pearson, brother of Lord Cowdray, and, through his family trust, a shareholder of the *Financial Times* – was owned through a British Virgin Islands company, Island Spice Overseas Ltd. And his home of Pennsylvania Castle, formerly held in his wife's name, was transferred to a new company called Fezan Ltd. Other assets were held by various companies in the British Virgin Islands and Gibraltar. He even planned the acquisition of a UK bank. In 2003 he bought himself a villa in Ibiza and divided his time between there, Guernsey, and Gibraltar, where he now applied for a passport.

Everything changed when Khodorkovsky was arrested. 'The shit has hit the fan,' he told his colleagues. During his occasional visits to the London office, the atmosphere was cooler. Curtis was now a much more serious man. 'I cannot go back to Russia now. I will be arrested immediately,' he said. Gone was the friendly banter of old. Now conversations were all about business and he became impatient and demanding. 'This has to be done. That has to be done,' he snapped.

The pressure mounted further when, in early December 2003, Curtis agreed to replace Platon Lebedev as chairman of Menatep. His job was to protect Khodorkovsky and the Yukos assets along with the company's deepest secrets. Matters intensified yet more when the Russian government claimed, as part of its ongoing investigations, that the Yukos restructuring was illegal. Curtis's response was that it may have been Byzantine, opaque, complicated, secretive, and offshore but it was perfectly legal. 'I worked closely with Stephen,' said one banker, 'and he was scrupulous about not doing anything illegal. It may not have been transparent and good for corporate governance and minority investors, but it was not criminal.'

Fearing that he was a target for prosecution and investigation, Curtis increased his physical security. He could not resign because he was a shareholder and a trustee of the shares, but he could protect himself and his family. Security had always been tight. Now it was paramount.

Curtis already 'owned' a private security company, ISC Global. In order to disguise his and Khodorkovsky's connection, the company was 100 per cent owned by Kilmarsh Ltd, a Gibraltar-based company, which, in turn, was owned by another Gibraltar-based company, Zampa Holdings Ltd. Both were owned by Curtis, but only as a nominee on behalf of Khodorkovsky. The original plan was for ISC to service all of Curtis's clients, but it ended up working mainly for the two oligarchs. Berezovsky paid ISC an estimated £2 million a year in fees – mainly for physical security for his family – but gradually Yukos became the most prominent client. In effect, ISC Global became the intelligence and security arm of Yukos and Menatep. The main contact at Yukos was Leonid Nevzlin.

Nigel Brown was head of ISC Global. A former police officer, the calm, quietly spoken Brown had a reputation for honesty and professionalism. He was joined by Keith Hunter, talkative, hyperactive, smart, and extrovert, the very opposite of his more considered and strategic partner. Hunter was also a gambler who owned racehorses and bet on his own horses. Always the centre of attention, he was popular and he enjoyed entertaining his Russian clients when they were in London. Business meetings often took place in expensive and exclusive restaurants rather than at their sober offices in Cavendish Square, Mayfair.

Secrecy was Brown's motto. 'The best security is not to know what was happening,' he said. The secrecy encouraged a strange atmosphere in the office. Brown was insistent on strict confidentiality because of the sensitive business of their two Russian clients. Operatives rarely knew what the others were doing. Reports were often deleted from the computer. Documents were written in code and then shredded after distribution to the client. It appeared as if Russian paranoia had been caught by their British minders.

Curtis relied on ISC Global heavily for his own security. The lawyer not only switched pay-as-you-go mobile phones on a regular basis, but the Park Lane office was swept for bugs every day. And for good reason. Despite his infrequent visits to London, he was under surveillance by business intelligence agencies working for commercial competitors to Yukos. In just one day in 2003 there were 7,000 attempts to hack into the computers at Curtis & Co.

Bugging of meeting rooms was also a concern. 'The problem with any listening device is the battery,' said one top professional. 'The power is the key to any successful bug. That is why you should always look for the device inside your television set. Whenever we had meetings, Stephen would always turn on the radio or turn on a CD with opera with a soprano voice, because that is the nearest thing you get to white noise and that made it very difficult for eavesdroppers to pick up their conversations.'

Much of the security work was put in the hands of Israelis. ISC liked using Israelis – superb surveillance and counterespionage technicians who used the most sophisticated devices – and it helped that both Brown and Berezovsky were Jewish. ISC bought an Israeli company just to obtain their contacts. They also hired a German former Mossad officer to conduct polygraph tests of employees, and likely suspects as well, after information leaked from ISC or Curtis's office.

The Mayfair lawyer believed that he was an assassination target. He even moved his desk away from the window on the first floor overlooking Park Lane because he was convinced that someone would shoot him in the back of the head. Curtis spent £40,000 on counter-surveillance equipment and special bugs were placed in cars. He used mobile phones to record meetings with clients because mobiles have long memories and could be left open on the meeting-room table. But despite the elaborate security, the lawyer would sometimes resort to more primitive methods to avoid being bugged: he would buy a mobile phone, use it for a couple of conversations, and then throw it away.

On one occasion ISC discovered that a hostile intelligence firm had informants that enabled them to obtain Curtis's telephone, bank, and credit card details. About six months before he died, a printout of Curtis's calls was obtained by that security firm. ISC responded by buying him new unregistered pay-as-you go mobile phones, which made it impossible to identify the numbers.

Mostly, Curtis revelled in the intrigue, but when the Russian authorities started to investigate Yukos from early 2003, he too began to feel the pressure. As well as investigations by the Russian state, many companies were suing Yukos and Curtis was the custodian of its secrets. One of the litigants was Kenneth Dart, who had invested heavily in Yukos subsidiaries – and lost equally heavily – and who was now leading a class action lawsuit against the company on behalf of minority shareholders. In 2003 Dart hired a private security firm in the US to investigate Curtis – the firm's first move was to approach UK business intelligence agencies. One such company that it initially approached was ISC itself – unaware that it was owned by Curtis. They offered ISC $1 million to unravel the restructuring of Yukos and the ultimate beneficiaries.

The US security firm then turned to private investigators, tasking their operatives and Russian journalists to track Curtis's movements, as well as those of his staff. Vast fees were offered for revelations about the secret, complex ownership structure. But the private detectives were clumsy and were soon spotted in rented cars. 'We knew we were being followed,' said one employee. 'At first we thought it was a laugh and so we bought Stephen a wig, hat, beard, and glasses for his birthday, but then it became more sinister. We actually caught one of them and he turned out to be a reporter from the *Moscow Times*. Another followed a secretary back to her house.' On the surface Curtis was unfazed and, on one of his London visits, he walked over to the watchers to tell them where he was going. On another occasion he even offered them a cup of tea. But, despite the humour, he confided to friends that he was concerned.

When Khodorkovsky was arrested and Curtis became chairman of the holding company, Menatep, he himself became a target of the Russian investigators. Business was now being done in even greater secrecy and in an atmosphere of heightened paranoia. In early 2004 a memo was sent to all staff at Curtis & Co: 'We have had a major security problem with the office.' It reminded staff not to open the front door to anyone they didn't know and to 'shred all unused documents *every night* [including drafts, old note pads and Post-it notes]'. Such was the secrecy and discretion required that one Curtis & Co. lawyer flew to Russia in the middle of the night and arrived in an obscure location, remote even by Russian standards. He walked straight through immigration at Tolmachevo Airport, drove to a remote forest in Siberia, delivered a document, waited for it to be signed, and then returned to the UK.

As a further indication of his apparent desire to show that his operations had been above board, Curtis also established contact with law enforcement agencies in Gibraltar and London. In early 2004 he met an official in the Gibraltar Criminal Intelligence Agency and gave him copies of Menatep documents. He also liaised with Matthew Porter, a Foreign Office civil servant responsible for international financial services, and Alan Kalbfell, a City of London police officer then assigned to the Foreign Office, to pass on information about the oligarchs. (When approached by the authors, all three declined to comment about their dealings with Curtis.)

Meanwhile, Khodorkovsky remained in jail in Krasnokamensk, Siberia, anxiously awaiting trial. To some extent his earlier charm offensive had paid off. On his arrest in October 2003, the reaction in the West was mostly one of outrage. The move was widely seen as a further sign of Putin's autocratic tendencies while Khodorkovsky was portrayed as another victim of Russian injustice. Newspapers warned of a return to Soviet-style despotism.

While waiting for the trial, Khodorkovsky's lawyers tried a new tactic – that of turning the man seen as a robber baron into a political martyr. From jail, he took to issuing letters renouncing the way he had made money and attacking what he called 'the tyranny of wealth'. 'I stopped worrying about material goods a long time ago,' he wrote. He claimed that he had never paid himself more than enough to lead an ordinary life and that he simply ploughed most of his great fortune back into his company. It is true that, compared with his fellow oligarchs, he led a relatively unflamboyant life, holidaying with his family in Finland, living in a comparatively modest house, and managing without expensive yachts or a football club. He told a Russian interviewer early in 2003 that you had to be born wealthy to get much pleasure from hobbies such as indulging in fine wine.

In March 2004, a year before he was sentenced, he wrote, 'We have made many mistakes because of our stupidity, ambitions, and lack of understanding. Forgive us if you can and allow us to redeem ourselves.' Russia's leading opposition newspaper, *Novaya Gazeta*, supported Khodorkovsky with a mass poster campaign and found itself deluged with support. As a result, the crushing of Yukos turned into almost as much a trial of Putin as it did of the oligarch.

At the trial his attorney Robert Amsterdam condemned the proceedings, 'This is not a trial. It is a show; a show to legitimize what is one of the largest thefts in recent history. My client will be found guilty. It is a show trial.' In May 2005 – eighteen months after the arrest – the panel of judges, sitting without a jury, finally announced a guilty verdict. The judgement ran to 1,000 pages. Khodorkovsky and his partner Platon Lebedev were both sentenced to nine years in jail. In a final, ironic twist Khodorkovsky was sent to YaG-14/10, a Soviet-era prison camp in eastern Siberia, a region once the source of his great wealth. He soon acquired a new skill: sewing police uniforms for a few roubles a day.

Although Putin's tactics almost turned Khodorkovsky into a national hero, most oligarchs remained hate figures for ordinary Russians. As a member of the Moscow Chamber of Commerce put it at the time, 'Any mention of the word "oligarch" had the average Russian reaching for a gun.'[25] In a 2003 poll 88 per cent of Russians believed that all large fortunes were amassed in an illegal way, 77 per cent said that privatization results should be partially or fully reconsidered, while 57 per cent believed that the government should launch criminal investigations against the wealthy. In a 2004 poll only 18 per cent of Russians opposed wholesale renationalization of the country's resources. Interviewed by the *Independent*, Vladimir Potanin recognized that the oligarchs 'had to learn not to be loved by fellow-Russians. People live in difficult conditions. I should not blame them for their lack of love for me.'[26]

Despite his lawyer's vehement protestations, Khodorkovsky always knew he was at risk of losing his empire to the state. Only a couple of years after he had acquired Yukos in the rigged auction, he declared, 'I don't own anything. I rent it.'[27] Some Western investors were also unconvinced about Khodorkovsky's corporate makeover and PR tactics. 'Khodorkovsky was doing an enormous amount of asset stripping,' said Bill Browder in 2006. 'He had pretended he was reformed, but in fact was trying to do the same kinds of dirty tricks politically that he was doing in business.'[28]

The indignant reaction in the West had less to do with a sudden concern for international human rights and more to do with the perceived new threat to Western economic interests. The West had turned a blind eye to the mass sell-offs of the 1990s because they were seen as the route to cheap oil and gas and opened up the door to foreign investment. British and American banks, PR companies, accountancy firms, and investment fund managers marched into Russia like an invading army intent on grabbing some of the spoils for themselves. In London the City's investment banks and fund managers could hardly believe their luck as much of Russia's secreted wealth flooded into Britain.

The reaction to Khodorkovsky's incarceration reflected at least in part the fear that the party was over. As Professor Michael Hudson, an independent Wall Street financial economist, put it, 'The hypocrisy of American pretence to help Russia create an honest and fair market economy was laid bare late in

2003, when Putin's government finally began to roll back the most crooked privatizations by moving against the largest tax evaders and embezzlers. The US response was a series of hand-wringing complaints that "private enterprise" was being threatened by a renewed statism. It was as if … Mikhail Khodorkovsky was an heroic entrepreneur, not an insider dealer and kleptocrat.'[29]

Khodorkovsky ended up behind bars for one simple reason: he challenged Putin politically. The message being sent out was that making large amounts of money in Russia would be sanctioned if it was accompanied by political conformity. That is where Khodorkovsky went wrong. Putin was furious that the recalcitrant oligarch mobilized support in the Duma to vote down a bill set to raise taxes on the oil industry. Khodorkovsky considered such lobbying, so common in the United States and the UK, integral to a modern democracy. 'I really don't see the difference, politically, between Yukos and General Motors,' he said shortly after Putin's election as President. 'Both have about 2 per cent of [their country's] GDP. Both lobby in parliament for their interests. Both propagandise in the press.'[30]

Khodorkovsky also supported human rights groups and bought the weekly newspaper *Moskovsky Novosti*, appointing an outspoken Kremlin critic as its editor. He paid $100 million to the opposition parties, the Union of Right Forces and its sister party, Yabloko. He even hinted that he would run for President in the 2008 election. If he had succeeded, it would have been highly risky for those then in power. He knew much about where the nation's wealth had gone, and who among the state and KGB apparatchiks had benefited. 'If such a man decides to go into politics, he is a danger,' said one Menatep insider.[31] He was not merely an irritant; he was a potentially dangerous one. His arrest was an effective way of silencing him.

Most significantly, at the time of Khodorkovsky's arrest, Yukos was in the process of merging with Abramovich's Sibneft, a deal that would have created the world's fourth-biggest oil company after ExxonMobil, BP and Shell and worth some £22 billion. Khodorkovsky's plan was then to sell off part of the merged giant to one of the two giant US oil majors, ExxonMobil itself or Chevron Texaco. Within the Kremlin, relinquishing even partial control of Russia's major natural resource conglomerate to a foreign power – and not just *any* foreign power – would have been viewed as tantamount to treason. Khodorkovsky was well known for his pro-American views. Asked by *BusinessWeek* if Putin was aware of them, he replied, 'He knows where I stand. It's not a secret ... I am well known in Russia for my pro-Americanism.'[32]

Putin knew that once the oligarchs started selling off their stakes to foreign interests, there was little he could have done to prevent money from leaving Russia. 'Selling off part of Russia's strategic assets without consulting Putin was a big no-no,' said a Yukos executive. 'Nobody really knows, but there are lots of people who believe that was the real reason the Kremlin went after Khodorkovsky.'[33]

The man working on the new merger was Yuri Golubev, a senior Yukos executive and one of Khodorkovsky's most trusted lieutenants. In January 2007 Golubev, one of the Yukos executives later sought by the Russian prosecutors, was found dead in his London apartment. His death was treated as 'non-suspicious' by the British police. He was recorded as having died of a heart attack.

Khodorkovsky was also planning another move, one seen by the Kremlin as even more arrogant. Only about 18 per cent of Yukos stock traded publicly; the rest was held by insiders. While the tax evasion investigation was proceeding, Yukos's board of directors declared an extraordinary $2 billion dividend distribution, an increase of 400 per cent on the previous year. 'Rather than use this money to modernize the industry, they appeared to be planning to strip the assets before letting it go,' according to Michael Hudson. 'There was no market justification for the huge dividend.'

The action against Khodorkovsky may have been an example of 'selective justice', according to Paul Klebnikov, later editor of *Forbes Russia,* but he added, 'This is still better than no justice at all … The Khodorkovsky arrest does not signify the triumph of the rule of law. The brutal way in which the detention was handled shows how far Russia has to go before it develops a civilized law-enforcement system … But I think we'll look back on this event and conclude that it actually strengthened the foundations of Russian property rights.'[34]

'This wasn't Mother Teresa versus Mike Tyson' was how Bill Browder of Hermitage Capital Management described the epic battle. 'These were two big tough guys at it with each other and one of them won. Putin won, Khodorkovsky lost, but it was a fair fight. He certainly didn't deserve the pity of some type of political prisoner because all the things he did basically disallow him from claiming that. For anyone who knew the past … he made a lot of people's lives very difficult when he was sitting on top of the heap.'[35] Even those in his own circle knew that he was playing a dangerous game. As one Yukos executive said, 'It was clear to me that we were signing our own death warrants.'[36]

In Moscow's political circles they like to talk of the 'curse of Yukos' when referring to the remarkable personal fallout from the Yukos case. One of those who may have been a victim is Stephen Curtis. If Khodorkovsky and Lebedev had not been arrested in 2003, Curtis would probably have continued as their secret back-room lawyer. The arrests changed all that, moving Curtis from the hidden world of offshore banking into the heart of one of Russia's biggest business and political dramas.

Many people have been touched by the Yukos curse: three are in jail, several linked to the company have died – some in suspicious circumstances – and others have simply disappeared.

Most senior Yukos executives were forced to flee Russia. At least twenty ended up in exile, most of them in London. In May 2003 the second in command at Yukos, Leonid Nevzlin, fled to Cyprus, where many of the Yukos- and Menatep-owned offshore companies were registered. The following month Nevzlin summoned Nigel Brown, his head of security, for an urgent meeting. Nevzlin was extremely nervous and convinced that the FSB were planning to assassinate him. He tasked Brown with organizing his move to Israel.

Within days Brown flew to Israel to make the arrangements. But Nevzlin remained paranoid about being kidnapped or shot while in Cyprus. Never one for cigarettes, he became a chain-smoker almost overnight. In the event, the operation went relatively smoothly and, in October 2003, the Yukos executive arrived in Israel on a tourist visa. Within two weeks he had been granted citizenship. Some Israeli opposition MPs were sceptical about the speed with which this was expedited. 'Suddenly, overnight, he [Nevzlin] became a dedicated Zionist and he got citizenship in a speedy manner,' said one MP. Another MP, Colette Avital, asked internal affairs and immigration ministers whether Nevzlin used influence and his friendship with Israeli government officials to secure his citizenship so quickly. In response to the controversy, the spokesperson for the then Prime Minister Ariel Sharon said, 'He got citizenship because he has no criminal record. As a Jew, his citizenship is automatic.'[37]

Nevzlin settled into a comfortable, if not overtly luxurious, lifestyle in Israel. He moved into a walled compound in Herzliya Pituach, an exclusive coastal neighbourhood north of Tel Aviv that was also home to ambassadors and business tycoons. His split-level villa featured a manicured garden with lemon, grapefruit, and olive trees and a small crescent-shaped swimming pool. It had marble floors, a wrought-iron spiral staircase, and a downstairs lounge dominated in his first two years in exile by 'Free Khodorkovsky' posters. After 2006 they became less prominent.

A tall, thin man with an angular face, Nevzlin lived frugally, eschewing drugs and vodka. He drank green tea. He had a number of girlfriends. His office was simple, stark, and minimalist. In business meetings he rarely seemed to notice what other people were saying. Instead, he would send text messages, speak on his mobile phone, or read books of Russian poetry. He often seemed to have about three things on his mind at the same time, which made him difficult to understand when he spoke. 'He just talked in riddles the whole time I was there,' said one Israeli visitor to his office.

Shortly before Curtis's death, Leonid Nevzlin fell out with ISC over his security arrangements. Brown had arranged a large, modern, private jet to carry Nevzlin from Tel Aviv to London, but, when advised at the last minute that the chartered plane was actually an old aircraft and would need to stop to refuel en route, Nevzlin became furious. 'I trusted you!' he shouted at Brown. But Nevzlin, believing that he was being set up to be kidnapped, returned to his Tel Aviv apartment, refusing to speak to Brown again. Curtis was forced to act as intermediary. Neither Curtis & Co. nor ISC survived Curtis's death. Brown retained his Israeli clients and set up a new company, GSS Global, while Hunter set up Risc Management and continued to work for Berezovsky.

While some prominent former Yukos personnel hid in Israel because they knew that they would not be extradited, most settled in London. As well as Ranil Burganov and Natalia Chernysheva, ten other former executives have been granted asylum in the UK; the most prominent of whom is Alexander Temerko, a former Director, Vice-President, and Head of Government Relations at Yukos. Despite his high-profile role as a company spokesperson, he is a highly skilled engineer and technician, and was another Yukos executive targeted by

Russian state prosecutors. In early 2004 Temerko's Swiss bank accounts were frozen by Swiss authorities at the request of the Russians. Then, soon after being questioned by state investigators in Moscow in October 2004, he fled to London.

On his arrival Temerko gravitated to the 'oligarch belt'. He first rented a flat just off Belgrave Square and then moved into a modern luxury apartment in a mansion block in Palace Gate, overlooking the south-west corner of Hyde Park. Highly intelligent and technically gifted, he is also demanding and impatient. Every day the former Yukos executive was driven by his chauffeur from his Kensington apartment to his office at New Broad Street House in the City. But, increasingly exasperated by the traffic jams, he asked an associate if he could buy 'blue lights' for his Mercedes – the flashing blue lights used by VIPs and oligarchs in Moscow. Placed on top of their cars, these enabled Moscow's financial and political elite to burst through grinding traffic ahead of other vehicles as if they were emergency ambulances. His aide had to explain that such privileges were not afforded executives in London.

Temerko had access to several million pounds to invest. In 2007 he set up his own private UK-based 'investment research and consultancy', BST Link, of which he is the sole shareholder. He set his sights on SLP Engineering, based in Lowestoft, Suffolk, which provides consultancy services in oil and gas extraction technology. After successful ventures in Mexico and Iran, SLP developed a presence in Russia and the Caspian Sea region. Given Temerko's track record at Yukos, he was a natural choice to join the board. But the Russian also had plans to manage the company and invested hundreds of thousands of pounds in SLP. He was then dismayed to learn that his shares were non-voting ones and so he was forced to pour more money into the company to secure management control. It was a clear illustration of the different corporate cultures in Russia and the UK.

Nothwithstanding his technical background, Temerko has also been politically active on behalf of Yukos and against the Putin regime. He hired Bell Pottinger on a substantial retainer and through them wrote articles for the *Guardian*, *Daily Mail*, and *Wall Street Journal*.

With Temerko keen to cultivate and to ingratiate himself with the British establishment, Lord Bell introduced his client to a number of peers in the House of Lords. This kept Temerko happy for a while but the relationships were tense and never developed beyond an ad hoc basis. On the evening of 11 December 2006 he hosted a private drinks party at Kensington Palace, organized by Inna Vainstock, daughter of the president of Transneft, a state-owned business running oil pipelines in Russia. The party took place under the auspices of Prince Michael of Kent, and was attended by a mixture of art historians and Russian businessmen. No expense was spared and the reception was followed by dinner at Mark's Club, the exclusive Mayfair dining club, where a four-course dinner including *fois gras* and lobster was specially prepared by a French chef.

While Temerko is not regarded by the Kremlin as public enemy number one, he remains on the wanted list of those to be extradited. On 25 October 2005 he appeared at Bow Street Magistrates Court before Senior District Judge and London's Chief Magistrate Timothy Workman. At the hearing Temerko was represented by the top criminal solicitor Ian Burton and the experienced QC Julian Knowles from Matrix Chambers. During the proceedings, Professor Bill Bowering, a specialist in Russian law, testified that the extradition request was politically motivated. After giving the first part of his testimony, Professor Bowering flew to Moscow but was held at the airport for six hours. After intense questioning, he was refused admission to Russia and deported back to London.

On 23 December 2005 Chief Magistrate Workman dismissed the extradition application. In his ruling he said that he was 'satisfied that the request for Mr Temerko's extradition is in fact made for the purpose of prosecuting and punishing him for his political opinions'. Although the possibility of an appeal by the Russian government was mooted, this did not materialize.

Timothy Workman has heard and dismissed all the extradition applications for the former Yukos officials who moved to London. In January 2004, just as Yukos personnel were fleeing to the UK, an 83-year-old widower named Robert Workman was shot dead at the front door of his home in the Hertfordshire village of Furneux Pelham. The police described the killer as a 'professional hitman'. The victim, a retired army officer, may have been another victim of the Yukos curse: a Russian website later claimed that the murder was a case of mistaken identity and that the real target was, in fact, Chief Magistrate Timothy Workman.

The murder has not been solved and the case remains open as a 'cold case'. Hertfordshire police said that they investigated the claims made on the Russian website but could find nothing to substantiate them. A police spokesperson said that the incident was like an episode of *Midsomer Murders*.

CHAPTER 9

Plotting Revolution

'At the height of Berezovsky's influence, when his name came up in people's office's in Moscow – including in or near the Kremlin – my hosts would sometimes point to the walls and start whispering or even, in a couple of cases, scribbling notes to me. This was a practice I had not seen since the Brezhnev era in furtive encounters with dissident intellectuals'

— STROBE TALBOTT, *former US Deputy
Secretary of State, 1993–2000*[1]

IN HIS GILDED CAGE in London and the Home Counties, Boris Berezovsky could have settled for a quiet life, indulging in the sybaritic and hedonistic lifestyle of a retired tycoon. But he could not resist his favourite drug – political intrigue – for this was a man who listed his hobbies in Russia's equivalent of *Who's Who* as 'work and power'. And so, from the security of his fortified Mayfair office, surrounded by hidden cameras, the oligarch set out to plot a new Russian revolution. His modern-day Tsar Nicholas was former President and now Prime Minister Vladimir Putin.

By 2001, Berezovsky's finances were secure and, like Napoleon on Elba, he began plotting, turning himself into Putin's most bitter opponent, dedicating his days in exile to removing the Russian President from office. Most of his energies and fortune became devoted to one cause: blackening Putin's name in the West and destabilizing him in his own country.

Even by tycoon standards, Berezovsky is a demanding and eccentric individual. A short, wiry, if slightly stooping figure, he has drooping eyelids and an intense stare. It is a demeanour that disguises an intense intelligence, fertile curiosity, and analytical mind. 'He is chaotic, destructive, brilliant, impatient, and sometimes impossible,' said one source who worked closely with him in his London office. 'His brain is always in 100 per cent overdrive. He cannot finish a sentence before changing his mind or the subject. He is constantly shouting and making outbursts. He is hyper all the time and like a child with attention deficiency syndrome. But he can also be suave and turn the charm on and off whenever it is expedient.'

Sitting at his desk, the fugitive oligarch is often in a world of his own, lost in thought. Then, unexpectedly, he will launch into a burst of hyperactivity: jamming his finger on the intercom button repeatedly and yelling in such fast, impenetrable Russian that he needs to repeat himself constantly. He lives on the telephone, often holding two mobiles and conducting two conversations at the same time.

Berezovsky is also a perfectionist. Every document that comes out of his office must be perfect in style and layout. He often seems more concerned about style than substance. 'What is worse is that he is also a perfectionist about things that he knows nothing about,' recalled a former business partner.

Additionally, he has an apparently high tolerance for alcohol. At his Surrey country house he likes a glass of St Emilion or Ornellaia '95 served by a white-gloved English butler. At his Mayfair office he may indulge in something heavier: some Sasakeli, an expensive and very strong Italian wine. For most people, one glass would knock them out for the rest of the week, but Berezovsky could get through more than that and still remain sharp at his desk.

Berezovsky has made every effort to integrate into English society and has been unfailingly polite to his new hosts, but initially he found it difficult to break Russian habits. When his children first turned up at their private school near Cobham, Surrey, with a cavalcade of burly bodyguards, it raised eyebrows. After that incident, their Swiss nanny accompanied the children to school instead.

While Berezovsky has been devoted to his family and generous to his friends, he is extremely self-absorbed. Unlike most oligarchs, he is very conscious of his looks, spending a fortune on clothes. He wears black silk shirts, bespoke suits, rarely wears a tie, and loves shopping on Sloane Street and New Bond Street, where his favourite fashion designer is 'Black Zhenya'.

No longer the Machiavellian Kremlin insider, instead now isolated from Russia, Berezovsky has become intensely concerned about his image and reputation. He regards himself as a major international political superstar and celebrity. 'He would love to be an insider in the British establishment; nothing would excite him more,' said a former aide. 'That's why the other people at private dinner parties he attends are very important to him.' He loves to be the centre of attention, sees himself as a high-calibre VIP, and has a thirst for newspaper column inches.

Despite his relatively poor English, Berezovsky has shown an insatiable appetite for delivering speeches, campaigning, and talking to the press. Often turning in an eighteen-hour day, he would spend up to 80 per cent of his time on media and propaganda activities. Every newspaper and magazine article was cut out and put into scrapbooks in his office. By 2008, he had assembled a three-volume, 1,800-page compilation of press cuttings and transcripts of interviews he had given since the 1990s. He called it *The Art of the Impossible*. As well as power, the two things that Berezovsky has craved more than anything in his remarkable life are attention and publicity. For him, the media has been his personal channel to political power and the governing institutions.

A highly contentious figure, Berezovsky was regarded as just another shadowy Russian businessman when he first arrived in London in 2001. To succeed in destabilizing and discrediting Putin, he first needed to transform himself into a credible political figure. He may have mesmerized the Yeltsin government for a while when he operated like a cross between Lenin and Mephistopheles, but could he perform the same magic on the British establishment?

He soon came to realize that spending time with aristocratic companions provided little more than introductions to other aristocrats and invitations to prestigious parties and was not the conduit to opinion formers he was seeking. Instead, Berezovsky turned to the PR industry – a key route to influence in Britain during the Blair government. More secretive oligarchs such as Oleg Deripaska retained City PR firms like Finsbury and Financial Dynamics, but for damage limitation rather than in order to give out a positive message. Most Russian businessmen regard the media with disdain. Roman Abramovich once told *Le Monde* that the difference between a rat and a hamster was public relations. Abramovich's affable spin doctor John Mann, an articulate American living in Moscow, is renowned for saying as little as possible on behalf of his client, even protesting that his boss is not a public figure and is entitled to his privacy.

Berezovsky, however, sees the role of the press very differently. He regards it as a crucial political weapon and relishes the attendant limelight. On his own admission he is a media manipulator, 'I use the mass media as a form of political leverage.'[2]

In the court of Tsar Boris, no one has been more important in transforming the fugitive oligarch from obscurity to prominence than Lord Bell, the PR guru who helped to mastermind Margaret Thatcher's three general election victories. Appointing Lord Bell was one of Berezovsky's shrewdest moves. A smooth operator, Bell has proved adept at representing foreign clients, notably the Saudi royal family and, more controversially, President Lukashenko of Belarus and the late President Pinochet of Chile.

Lord Bell first met Berezovsky in 1996 when he was parachuted into Russia to rescue President Yeltsin's ailing re-election campaign. Working closely with business insiders and American spin doctors, he reinvented Yeltsin's persona. Lord Bell is a master of the personal touch and has a soothing bedside manner. He is credited with transforming Yeltsin from a dour, aggressive, hard-line, mechanical politician into a smiling, accessible populist. Berezovsky was clearly impressed by the man who had honed his skills at the advertising agency Saatchi & Saatchi in the 1970s and whose personal allure led one former colleague to comment, 'He was so charming that dogs would cross the street just to be petted by him.'

Berezovsky was impressed by the spin doctor's energy, charm, and guile, and even more so by the leading figures he had advised: Lady Thatcher while she was Prime Minister, Rupert Murdoch, his business hero, and former President F. W. de Klerk of South Africa. Optimistic, articulate, and well connected, the chain-smoking Lord Bell was also a power broker and Berezovsky hired him as much for his contacts book as for his PR skills. 'Using Tim Bell is the communications equivalent of dialling 911,' said one industry executive.

After leaving Saatchi & Saatchi, Bell moved into public relations. He specialized in advising accident-prone, high-profile figures – among them Lady Thatcher's son Mark Thatcher; the coal industry boss Ian Macgregor during the 1984 miners' strike; the BBC Director-General Lord Birt over allegations of tax avoidance; British Airways Chairman Lord King over claims of dirty tricks against Virgin Airlines; and David Mellor during the media firestorm that broke over his affair with the actress Antonia de Sancha in 1992. He was therefore tailor-made for

Berezovsky, who has poured millions of pounds into commissioning anti-Putin advertisements, PR stunts, political lobbying, and promoting his personal message.

Since late 2001, most of his media profile has been facilitated by Bell's company, Bell Pottinger, to whom Berezovsky pays a retainer of £25,000 per month plus expenses. These invoices – which run into hundreds of thousands of pounds – are always paid in full and on time, a measure of Lord Bell's importance.

During their meetings at the oligarch's Mayfair office, Lord Bell rarely disagreed with his client's endless stream of ideas for propaganda, appearing to be as much an admirer as a mere advocate. He has his own take on his client. 'The trouble with this world is that one man's freedom fighter is another man's terrorist,' he has said. 'There is some kind of dirty tricks campaign being waged against him [Berezovsky]. To attack him, physically intimidate him, and to mount media attacks on him at every level. And where he approaches authorities in other countries, he discovers that there is a file on record put there by the Russians questioning his integrity and financial and political status ... I think Boris Berezovsky is a very important person because he believes more profoundly in democracy and in human rights than almost anyone I have come across.'[3]

Lord Bell has been responsible for ensuring that there is a place for Berezovsky at Britain's top tables. As well as speaking at the Reform Club, Berezovsky has lectured at Chatham House, addressed Eton schoolboys, spoken at the Oxford University Russian Society (in 2004), and was once quizzed by a group of senior EU policy-makers. He has enjoyed favourable coverage in the *Sunday Times* – even penning several articles under his own byline – and been interviewed regularly by BBC2's *Newsnight*. He took to calling impromptu press conferences, paying to hold them in the grand auditoriums of the Royal United Services Institute on Whitehall and at Chatham House in St James's Square.

Right: THE MAN WHO KNEW TOO MUCH
Stephen Curtis, the 45-year-old Mayfair-based lawyer who worked for Khordorkovsky and Berezovsky. Originally from Sunderland, he died in a mysterious helicopter crash in March 2004.

Below: FORTRESS
Pennsylvania Castle on the Isle of Portland, Dorset. The 18th century £3 million home was a haven to Curtis. Guests attending his parties at the castle were told that there was only one rule: no cameras.

Bottom: CRASH LANDING
The remains of the Agusta 109E helicopter which spiralled out of control while taking Curtis home from Battersea heliport. It crashed near Bournemouth airport.

Above: CREDENTIALS
The Russian Security Service
badge of Alexander Litvinenko
when he joined the FSB in 1988.

Right: A SPY IN LONDON
Former Russian FSB officer
Alexander Litvinenko fled to the
UK in 2000 after publicly
criticising his former spymasters.

Below: DEATH OF A MAVERICK
Litvinenko in his bed at University
College Hospital, London. As he lay
dying - from a lethal dose of polonium -
he claimed that his murder was
orchestrated by Vladimir Putin.

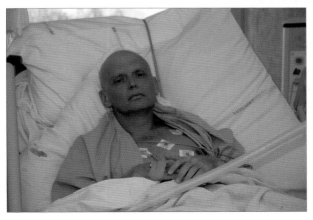

Right: MURDER OF A DISSIDENT
Anna Politkovskaya, the courageous Russian journalist renowned for exposing state atrocities in Chechnya. In 2006 she was shot dead near her apartment in Moscow.

Left: CONTRACT KILLING
American business reporter Paul Klebnikov in early 2004 with a special *Forbes* edition on one hundred Russian billionaires. Later that year he was murdered in Moscow by unknown assailants who fired nine shots from a slowly moving car.

Left: IN THE FRAME
Private security consultant
Andrei Lugovoi (right)
who has been accused by
Scotland Yard detectives of
poisoning Alexander
Litvinenko. Now living in
Moscow, British
prosecutors have
requested his extradition.
Lugovoi has vigorously
protested his innocence,
even claiming that MI6
was behind the killing.

Right: THE PARTNER
Georgian billionaire Badri
Patarkatsishvili (right)
with his business partner
and closest friend
Berezovsky. The Georgian
oligarch died of a heart
attack at his mansion near
Leatherhead, Surrey, in
February 2008.

Above: COUNTRY REFUGE
Fyning Hill, the sprawling country estate in West Sussex which Abramovich bought for £12 million in 1999.

Below: PIED-A-TERRE
The Belgravia house which Deripaska bought in 2003 for £17 million. The Grade I listed mansion, decorated in a Regency style, used to be the home of Sir Henry 'Chips' Channon, the society host, diarist and Conservative MP.

Above: FESTIVAL
Russian women celebrate their country's winter festival in Trafalgar Square, London in January 2007.

Below: MOSCOW-ON-THAMES
More Russians gather in Trafalgar Square to participate in the 2007 winter festival which celebrates Russian culture, music and dance.

Above: HOW TO MARRY AN OLIGARCH
Society girl Ksenia Sobchak gives a press
conference on her and television host
Oksana Robski's book offering tongue-
in-cheek advice on how to ensnare
a Russian tycoon.

Below: THE FAMILY
Oleg Deripaska's wife Polina (left) with
Tatyana Dyachenko, the daughter of
former Russian president Boris Yeltsin,
with her husband Valentin Yumashev, at a
music premiere.

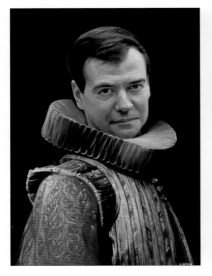

THE NEW TSARS
President Medvedev (*left*) and Prime Minister Putin as portrayed by Russian painter Nikas Safronov, who also paints portraits of oligarchs' wives.

RICH CHOCOLATE
A group of Russian business magnates in chocolate as displayed in one of Moscow's cafes in December 2003. Organizers of the display declared: 'You may live a sweet life, but you might be eaten any time.' (*Left to right*) Vladimir Potanin, Roman Abramovich, Boris Berezovsky, Mikhail Khodorkovsky, Mikhail Fridman, Anatoly Chubais and Oleg Deripaska.

In June 2007 he was a panellist on BBC1's *Question Time*, the only Russian so far to have appeared. His message was always the same: Putin was creating an authoritarian government, seizing the mass media, stifling opposition, and renationalizing privately owned companies. Unsurprisingly, Russian authorities questioned how a fugitive such as Berezovsky could gain access to such venerable British institutions and be afforded such a respectful reception.

As well as securing platforms from which to wage his high-level campaign, money was also spent on lavish self-promotion and media stunts. Lord Bell was tasked with organizing a demonstration outside the Russian Embassy in Kensington Palace Gardens in October 2003 when fellow oligarch Mikhail Khodorkovsky was arrested, and in May 2004 he was further responsible for the presence of dozens of limousines that drove past the Russian Embassy bearing large signs accusing Putin of running a police state. 'Free Khodorkovsky', 'Russian Business vs KGB', and 'Russian Business vs Police State', some of them read, a clear indication of the strength of Berezovsky's opposition.

Just before the 2004 Russian presidential election, Berezovsky commissioned a full-page advertisement – at a cost of some £250,000 – that appeared in the *New York Times*, the *Washington Post*, *The Times*, the *Financial Times*, and the *Daily Telegraph*. Headed 'Seven Questions to President George Bush about his friend President Putin', it accused Putin of genocide in Chechnya and of whipping up 'militaristic hysteria similar to Germany under the early Nazi regime'. It urged Bush to 'look into the eyes of your friend again'. Joining Berezovsky as signatories were several Soviet-era dissidents.

At the St Petersburg summit of G8 nations in July 2006, Bell Pottinger planned to place an advertisement on behalf of Berezovsky's civil liberties foundation in the official programme. The advertisement contained a photograph of President Putin, who was chairing the summit, made up to look like Groucho Marx. It carried the comedian's famous line: 'I wouldn't want to be a member of any club that would have me as a member.' The organizers ordered its removal and it was never used. 'What seemed to upset him [Putin] was the word "Marx",' Lord Bell remarked.[4]

Berezovsky rarely missed an opportunity to denounce his arch foe or plot his downfall. By now the two men had a deep-rooted loathing for one another. Asked his views on Berezovsky by a journalist in 2002, Putin replied, 'Who's he?' In September 2004 Berezovsky declared, 'Putin is the terrorist number one … He is a war criminal making genocide.'[5]

Desperate to return to Russia, unseat Putin, and reverse his legacy became an obsession. According to Andrei Vassiliev, the editor of *Kommersant*, 'He is not addicted to gambling or drugs, but to politics. He has fallen ill with politics.'[6]

Steadily, the vast outlays on security, public relations, and legal fees began to make inroads into Berezovsky's personal fortune. By being forced to sell most of his assets, he also missed out on the post-2000 rise in oil and gas prices and the soaring Russian stock market. However, he remained the richest refugee in Britain. In 2008 he still had an estimated fortune of some £700 million.

It was inevitable that Putin would retaliate. Between 1999 and 2008, the Russian prosecutors filed a string of charges against the renegade billionaire for fraud and embezzlement. They issued one demand after another for the extradition of Berezovsky to Moscow to face trial, all the while adding to the charge sheet. The first of these arrived in March 2002.

Berezovsky's effectiveness depended not just on the size of his war chest but also, crucially, on the British response towards his request for political asylum. In Britain, while asylum requests are considered in secret by immigration authorities and are ultimately decided on by the Home

Secretary, extradition requests are reviewed in open court, independent of government. In most circumstances an extradition request is not heard if asylum has already been granted as the presumption is that the person would be in danger if sent back to his home country. In the case of extradition the presiding judge has to decide not on the guilt or innocence of the charge being levied by the requesting nation, but on whether the defendant can demonstrate that the request is politically motivated or if he or she would face an unfair trial, or worse, if extradited.

The political sensitivity of Berezovsky's case was demonstrated by a high-level meeting held at New Scotland Yard on 29 November 2002. It was attended by senior officials from the Foreign Office, the Crown Prosecution Service, the Fraud Squad, and the police. 'There is significant involvement and interest from Tony Blair and Jack Straw [then Foreign Secretary],' said the Foreign Office representative at the time. The consensus at the meeting was that Berezovsky's application for asylum would be refused and he would be told to take refuge in Israel where he has citizenship. But they accepted that his appeal would be successful. 'The British government is trying to show Russia that we are trying to help them in their political moves against Berezovsky,' said the same official. 'Yes, but we can only push this so far because there are no circumstances in which we can extradite back to Russia,' interjected the police officer. 'The reality is that he will not receive a fair trial if he returns to Moscow.'

Berezovsky's extradition hearings eventually began in the spring of 2003, at the height of his propaganda campaign against Putin, and before a decision on his asylum application. At Bow Street Magistrates Court in April he was released on bail of £100,000 pending a full hearing. Court documents reveal that half the bail money was posted by Lord Bell and the rest by Stephen Curtis.

At the preliminary proceedings Berezovsky pleaded that his life would be in danger if he returned to Russia and that he would not receive a fair trial because of the politicized judiciary. The hearings were attended throughout by FSB officers, mostly looking gloomy and stern. The court resembled a scene from a gangster movie: FSB officers mingling with and staring down Berezovsky's bodyguards and MI5 agents and police officers brushing shoulders with staff from Stephen Curtis's law firm. None of them exchanged words because they did not want anyone to know that they recognized each other. Just outside the courtroom Berezovsky's bodyguards were anxious to keep him away from anyone who represented a threat – in effect, most of the people in the room.

The somewhat comic atmosphere was encouraged by the oligarch. On one occasion upon leaving the courtroom, Berezovsky pulled on a paper mask of Putin to demonstrate his opinion that the request for his extradition was little more than a farce. It is said that Putin, watching the news on television, was absolutely furious and so enraged that he let rip with a stream of expletives. 'I have never seen him so angry,' said a source close to him.

In the event, the extradition hearings were never concluded. On 11 September 2003 the then Home Secretary David Blunkett granted Berezovsky's request for asylum on the grounds that he was being pursued for 'political reasons'. The following day Chief Magistrate Workman rejected the extradition request based on his new asylum status. Berezovsky was ecstatic. 'This could only happen in England,' he gleefully remarked to an aide as he accepted a glass of wine back in his Mayfair office.

Throughout the hearings, the application by the Russian prosecutors was unimpressive. The Russians were unable to demonstrate that their judiciary was not under state control. One opinion as to why the application failed was that, if the prosecutors detailed all the evidence against Berezovsky, it would have implicated senior Kremlin officials and politicians. But the truth is likely to be more prosaic. The request was based on the Russian judicial system whereby there is an assumption of guilt and 90 per cent of defendants are convicted, whereas in the UK the opposite is the case. The Kremlin simply presumed that Berezovsky would be extradited and prepared its case accordingly.

Shocked by the judge's ruling, the Russian prosecutors came to believe that there was something sinister, even underhand, about the way that Berezovsky had resisted extradition. 'He is being protected by the establishment and the Security Services,' said one Putin adviser. The Kremlin accused the judge of 'playing Cold War politics'. But even Berezovsky's enemies disagreed. 'He spent a fortune on hiring the best lawyers who worked extremely hard on his behalf,' commented one.

But the Russian prosecutors were not going to give up and turned instead to Europe for assistance. Since 1999, Swiss authorities had already been assisting them in their pursuit of Berezovsky, much of whose fortune was held in Swiss bank accounts. They handed over quantities of documents relating to the allegations surrounding Aeroflot, granted Russian requests for legal assistance in the extradition hearings, and on occasion agreed to freeze his accounts. In November 2003 Swiss authorities then went a step further and launched their own criminal investigation into Berezovsky's dealings. This focused on allegations that he had fraudulently transferred millions of dollars from Russian car companies into Swiss banks accounts. 'We are concerned with criminal justice, not politics,' said a spokesperson for the prosecutor's office. 'We just want to know which ones of Berezovsky's activities in Switzerland were legal and which ones might have been illegal.' The move was part of Switzerland's attempt to clamp down on money laundering and improve the image of its financial sector. Protesting his innocence, Berezovsky dismissed the move as 'an anti-Semitic act'.[7] Ultimately, no further action was taken.

Even the French police became involved, focusing for their part on Berezovsky's properties. On 7 May 2003 officials searched his villa in Cap d'Antibes as part of an ongoing two-year investigation into money laundering. Two years later, almost to the day, twenty armed police arrived by helicopter at the same villa. Based on a warrant from a Marseilles judge, they searched the premises to determine the origin of the funds used to buy his two villas in the Côte d'Azur. In his defence, Berezovsky made a bold claim. 'I only rent the villas and so I could not have laundered money through them.' His lawyer Semyon Aria added, 'Mr Berezovsky never owned that property. It was not he who took the money, and he never signed any papers. He is accused of being the one who secretly inspired this.'[8]

At the time of the raid his formidable 81-year-old mother, Anna Alexandrovna, was still living in the villa. Watching television, she was getting ready to go to the opening of the Cannes Film Festival – it took place a short distance from the villa. Suddenly, out of the blue, 'a helicopter landed near the house and masked, armed men stepped out of it,' recalled her son. 'She even thought it was a show in honour of the Film Festival, because she was in Cannes already.'[9]

Convinced that the FSB were constantly plotting to kill him, Berezovsky not only took expensive and elaborate security precautions but he even commissioned the building of a heavily protected yacht known as Project X. The vessel, which was still running trials in the summer of 2008, had underwater cameras to identify bombs or anything attached to the underside of its hull. Built in Poole, Dorset, the yacht also carried anti-missile devices while living quarters were protected by bullet-proof glass and meeting rooms were equipped with white noise emitters to disrupt bugging.

While it is illegal for his bodyguards to carry guns, the yacht contained an armaments room of legally registered weapons, including small machine pistols and even sonic Air Zula weapons that are capable of knocking people backwards. There was also a weapon that fired rushes of air on a military scale and the same hi-tech sonic device used by cruise ships when faced with pirates on the high seas. According to his staff, Berezovsky also installed 'toffee guns', for use by his bodyguards, which fired a jet of glue and disorientated intruders and slowed down their movements. Sometimes his minders also carried 'dazzlers', giant flashguns that can temporarily blind people.

During its sea trials in 2008, the vessel was deliberately moved around from port to port throughout the UK and the Mediterranean, while the design details were kept in a safe house in a remote part of Dorset. 'It is like a mobile castle,' said a visitor. Berezovsky invested millions in the yacht, which, at the end of 2008, was still being modified. He even bought a $1 million vintage Rolls-Royce just so that he could drive it onto the yacht. Project X is so big that Berezovsky's current yacht, *Thunder*, could comfortably fit onto it.

Back in Russia, in a parallel and coordinated operation, jailed fellow oligarch Mikhail Khodorkovsky also launched a plot to destabilize Putin. 'He [Khodorkovsky] did not think that the President was personally financially corrupt, but he believed that there was evidence that his advisors and ministers were taking kickbacks on government contracts and abusing their public office,' said Nigel Brown, of ISC Global. From exile in Israel, Khodorkovsky's close colleague Leonard Nevzlin masterminded the plot, hiring ISC Global to coordinate the investigation.

'Operation Fab' was hatched in early 2004 and it aimed to investigate a number of officials and tycoons close to Putin. The hope was that, if they could find evidence of compromising behaviour by Putin's allies and supporters, they could damage the President by leaking their findings to the Western media. 'We were going to create a media frenzy which would have been irresistible,' said a source close to the operation.

The investigation was discussed at several meetings and budgets were agreed, with Nevzlin authorizing £37 million for the first phase. Funding was to be channelled through Stephen Curtis.

One ISC Global memo to a Yukos lawyer showed how the media was to be used in the strategy: 'The BBC *Newsnight* team are hoping to carry a story on Mr A and Operation Fab ... The BBC programme on Mr A is a great opportunity to maximize full exposure on this particular individual, the companies he represents, and, without question, his association with Mr P.'

'Mr A' was, of course, Roman Abramovich. 'Mr P' was Vladimir Putin. 'Nevzlin thought that if we could find some damaging material on Abramovich and get a lever on him, then he could persuade Putin to lay off the oligarchs and even release Khodorkovsky,' said a source directly involved. 'The idea was to go to Abramovich and say, "We won't expose you if you go to Putin and say let's call a truce. Why do we need a fight with the oligarchs?"' Neither the material nor the programme ever materialized.

A second project, code-named 'Operation Come to Me', intended to undermine Putin by mobilizing the international student movement, whereby operatives would visit student campuses, secretly fund their publications containing articles highly critical of Putin, and persuade them to agitate against him all over the world. It also aimed to promote the plight of Khodorkovsky globally in the media. Two anti-Putin demonstrations duly took place in London and one in Israel in late 2003. Plans were drawn up for further protests in London, Israel, South Africa, and New York City to coincide with the Russian parliamentary elections.

In the event, the plots were only implemented at their most primitive stages. A short list of state officials and oligarchs was drawn up and investigators were sent to Russia. In 2005 Nevzlin confirmed that if Khodorkovsky was found guilty, he would publish material exposing corruption in the Kremlin. 'I want to tell about the people who are running the country and stealing from it,' Nevzlin told the press. 'I will tell everything: about corruption in the Kremlin, about connections to business, about what kind of money Kremlin officials get, and on what kind of yachts they spend their vacations.'[10]

Ultimately, because of a breakdown of trust between ISC Global and Nevzlin over the latter's personal security, the convoluted plots came to nothing. Although Nevzlin agreed to fund the plans on a contingency basis, many of the informants demanded upfront payment and the so the operations were aborted.

Just as a mix of business and political insiders surrounded the oligarch in his days of power at the Kremlin, so Berezovsky soon gathered a new group of dependants and admirers from the steady stream of fellow exiles and dissidents fleeing Putin's Russia. One of those smuggled out was Alexander Litvinenko. It was Berezovsky who persuaded Litvinenko, a former FSB agent who had fallen foul of the Kremlin, to flee Russia and run his own anti-Putin campaign from London.

Another member of Berezovsky's inner circle was 58-year-old writer Yuli Dubov, one of his most influential political advisers based in his London office. He was so close to the fugitive billionaire that in 2000 he was able to write *Bolshaya Paika*, the thinly disguised memoir of Berezovsky's early years in business, which was later made into the film *Oligarkh*. Dubov became Chairman and a Director of *Kommersant*, the Russian newspaper owned by Berezovsky until 2006.

While living in London, Dubov wrote another novel, *The Lesser Evil*, about an oligarch in exile, which was published in

Russia in 2005. *The Lesser Evil* is, according to Nick Paton Walsh, the *Guardian*'s Moscow correspondent, part social treatise, part crime novel, part political pamphlet, 'It addresses the rise of a former KGB officer, through the mysterious bombing of Moscow's international trade centre and the influence of a conglomerate known as "Infokar". It's a series of barely disguised references to Berezovsky's accusations, denied of course, that Putin engineered apartment bombings in Moscow to justify sending troops into Chechnya, a move that won the former KGB spy an election and led to Berezovsky fleeing the country. Safe to say that Putin is not the "lesser evil" Dubov is referring to, rather his nemesis Berezovsky. The politics of the Russian court remain as transparent and subtle as ever.'[11]

A long-term ally, Dubov is one of Berezovsky's last links to his commercial Russian past. A former Director of the car dealership LogoVaz, Dubov was also accused of fraud by the Russian authorities. In 2000 he fled Russia for Great Britain and became another target for extradition. On 7 October 2003 Bow Street Magistrates Court dismissed the extradition case. His lawyers told the court there would be 'collateral damage' if he was returned to Russia.

Perhaps the most controversial figure in Berezovsky's inner sanctum has been Akhmed Zakayev, a bearded, mild-mannered former actor who became an important activist in Chechen resistance. Born in 1959, Zakayev played many leading roles at the state theatre in Grozny, including Hamlet. He became a field commander in the first Chechen war and, under the Chechen leader Zelimkhan Yandarbiyev, headed the rebel group's security service. Later, after the assassination of Yandarbiyev in 2004, he became a close confidant of his successor, Aslan Maskhadov, and was his Vice-Premier and Minister of Education, Culture, and Media. He also conducted negotiations with Moscow on behalf of the de facto Chechen government.

Zakayev left Chechnya after he was wounded in the second Chechen war and took refuge in Turkey until he was forced to leave. The Russians pursued him and he was arrested in Copenhagen by Danish police on 30 October 2002, while attending the World Chechen Congress. The Russian authorities accused him of planning the bloody seizure of a Moscow theatre in that same year and of taking part in other earlier terrorist activities. Denmark's Justice Ministry refused his extradition due to lack of evidence but he was arrested again on his arrival in the UK on 5 December 2002. He was freed after the actress Vanessa Redgrave put up £50,000 bail. An activist in the Workers' Revolutionary Party and a campaigner for human rights in Chechnya, Redgrave worked closely with Lord Bell to orchestrate media campaigns in the run-up to the extradition proceedings for Zakayev. His extradition was duly rejected on 13 November 2003 by Chief Magistrate Workman. 'There is a substantial risk that Mr Zakayev would be subject to torture' was the conclusion.

With a safe haven in London, Zakayev continued his campaigning and media work, all the while bankrolled by Berezovsky. They had met in 1997 when Berezovsky was President Yeltsin's negotiator in Chechnya. In London Alexander Litvinenko worked closely with Zakayev in identifying Russian soldiers allegedly involved in war crimes. The two men's families also became friends. Living opposite each other in Muswell Hill, north London, Litvinenko and his wife were regular guests at Zakayev's house and were favourites of the Chechen's grandchildren. When Litvinenko and Zakayev were granted political asylum by the British courts, the decisions were greeted with fury in the Kremlin.

In response to the steady stream of dissident arrivals in London, Putin expanded and intensified his intelligence presence in London. By 2007, there were more than thirty Russian intelligence officers based in London; working for the SVR or the GRU (the main foreign intelligence agencies of the Russian Federation), they maintained a presence not seen in Britain since the Cold War. Some of these officers were working officially – the senior intelligence officer, or 'Resident', is always identified to the Foreign Office, as is his British counterpart in Moscow. But others, under the guise of the diplomatic or trade missions, worked undercover, investigating and monitoring political events in Westminster and Whitehall and at military installations, just as they had during the Soviet era. The scale of the Russian presence was heavily criticized by the head of MI5, Jonathan Evans, in a speech in November 2007: 'It is a matter of some disappointment to me that I still have to devote significant amounts of equipment, money, and staff to countering this threat [of covert Russian intelligence activity].'

Russian spies were also targeting the oligarchs and dissidents making London their home, as well as those of their British associates. In 2005 Vanessa Redgrave was confronted with a sizeable demonstration outside her north London home, organized by a pro-Putin group called 'Marching Together', which was campaigning for the extradition of Zakayev. The group, run from Moscow, advertised in a London-based Russian newspaper for young Russian immigrants to take part in demonstrations and then paid them each £15 to turn up. The actress was targeted because of her championing of Zakayev and her closeness to Berezovsky. Following the demonstration, she invested in extensive security and counter-surveillance equipment at her home.

'Marching Together' held at least six demonstrations in London during 2005. In a larger protest in Trafalgar Square that October, they carried banners declaring, 'Merry Xmas, Mr Zakayev. Stop Your Bloody Business' and 'Get Out of the UK'. According to *Novaya Gazeta*, the group – which claims 100,000 members in Russia – is funded by Gazprom, the giant state-owned gas and energy conglomerate that acts, in effect, as an arm of the Kremlin.

Berezovsky's criticism of Putin is that he has turned Russia into an authoritarian state, smothering opposition, controlling the media, and centralizing power. There is no doubt that Putin has weakened the democratic process, stamped on press freedom, and emasculated the power of the country's governors and Parliament through a process described by one expert as 'stealth authoritarianism'.[12] But as one analyst put it, Putin set out to modernize Russia, not democratize it.

Apart from independent newspapers like the business daily *Vedomosti* and the liberal radio station *Ekho Moskvy* – which together reach only a tiny audience – most of the Russian media became either state-controlled or pro-Putin. Putin seized control of the formerly combative television stations ORT and NTV because he understood the power of television in managing his own image. From then, state-run television – the main source of information for 85 per cent of Russians – enjoyed a near monopoly, rarely giving a voice to opposition figures or reporting anti-Putin demonstrations.

There was another, darker side to the dissent. Between 2000 and 2008, at least thirteen dissident Russian journalists – most investigating state corruption and its links with organized crime – were killed, of which the gunning down of Anna Politkovskaya in October 2006 was the most high profile. None of the murders has yet been solved. Other notable assassinations have included those of Eduard Markevich, Editor and Publisher of the newspaper *Novy Reft*, known for its strident criticism of local officials, and Valery Ivanov, Editor-in-Chief of *Tolyatinskoye Obozreniye*, who was shot eight times. Eighteen months later his successor at the independent newspaper was stabbed to death. In 2007 the New York-based Committee to Protect Journalists identified Russia as the third most dangerous place to work in the world after Iraq and Algeria.

Another prominent murder was that of 42-year-old Paul Klebnikov, the Manhattan-born, Russian-speaking investigative business reporter who launched the Russian edition of *Forbes* in 2004. A descendant of Russian émigrés who left after 1917, he wrote *Godfather of the Kremlin*, a biography of Berezovsky.[13]

The first edition of *Forbes Russia*, published in May 2004, drew up the first-ever list of Russia's 100 richest people. Written by Klebnikov, the study – entitled 'The Golden Hundred' – uncovered thirty-six dollar billionaires and estimated that Moscow alone had thirty-three, more than any other city in the world, including New York. If anything, these figures probably understated the actual number of billionaires, since many of them had hidden away so much of their true wealth.

Forbes Russia found something even more significant: Russia had more billionaires in proportion to the size of its economy than any other country in the world. The combined wealth of the top 100 was the equivalent of 25 per cent of Russia's GDP at the time.[14] This gave Russia the world's highest concentration of wealth. By contrast, in the United States, which traditionally tops the developed world's inequality league, the combined wealth of the country's 277 billionaires only amounted to 6 per cent of its GDP.

The publication of 'The Golden Hundred' was not popular among those listed: the last thing many of the oligarchs wanted was to highlight details of just how rich they were. Many of them protested about their inclusion. Some questioned the size of their identified fortunes. While some were high-profile individuals, they had made extensive efforts to keep details of their personal wealth very private. '*Forbes* couldn't find a worse time and place,' said one oligarch. 'The only reaction I get from discussing personal wealth in our country is high blood pressure.'[15]

Executives at the Sibneft oil company were especially displeased. 'The ratings have no connection with reality, the numbers are wildly speculative, the methodology used by the magazine is clouded in darkness,' said its head of public relations. In contrast, the image-conscious Berezovsky protested that his listed fortune of $620 million was actually *understated*: 'In the middle of 1995 *Forbes* estimated my wealth at $3 billion,' he complained. 'That means that I've either spent $2.5 billion or their current estimates are incorrect.'[16]

For Paul Klebnikov, the first edition of *Forbes*' Russian edition also proved to be his last. Six weeks later he was dead, shot four times at point-blank range in a gangland-style killing as he left his office in central Moscow. Although it was a contract killing, the culprit and his paymasters will probably never be known or brought to justice.

Since the end of communism, there has been little effective political opposition in Russia. During Putin's reign, most opposition parties were forced to close while many were excluded from standing by the tightened electoral rules. The only real opposition has been the Russian Communist Party and a coalition called The Other Russia, whose leaders include former world chess champion Garry Kasparov. Although The Other Russia has organized the odd demonstration, it has effectively been unable to operate freely. Kasparov only travels with armed bodyguards and has been the subject of constant harassment, raids, and police intimidation.

In 2006 the World Bank ranked Russia one-hundred-and-fifty-first out of 208 countries in terms of political stability, democratic voice, the rule of law, and control over corruption. Despite this, polls suggested the majority of the population appeared to continue to support Putin and his malleable successor, Dmitri Medvedev, even if this support was relatively shallow. Backing for Putin is partly a product of the nation's cultural affinity for authority and strong leadership. But for most Russians, the

Western-style democracy of the pre-Putin era became synonymous with corruption and the enrichment of the few.

In Russia the oligarchs have long been the butt of popular satire. While campaigning for the 2007 parliamentary elections, Gennady Zyuganov, the long-standing leader of the Communist Party, liked to tell a joke about Abramovich, 'Roman arrives in heaven and is met by St Paul. The saint asks Abramovich, "Is it true that you own Chelsea, five yachts, and a five-kilometre stretch of beach in the South of France?" "Yes," replies the oligarch. "Well," says St Paul, "I don't think you're going to like it here."'

Some describe Russia's political system as a 'managed democracy' – part market economy, part centralized state. Robert Amsterdam, Khodorkovsky's attorney, has likened it to 'market Bolshevism'.[17] The opposition's critique is blunted by its own lack of democratic credentials. Berezovsky likes to quote Sir Winston Churchill, who said that democracy was 'the worst form of government, except for all those other forms that have been tried from time to time'.

But Berezovsky is hardly one to take the moral high ground on democracy, for it was his brazen and partisan use of his own media empire that helped engineer the re-election of Yeltsin in 1996 and Putin's ascendancy to the Presidency in 2000. What he chooses to ignore is that he and his fellow oligarchs were central players in the creation of modern-day Russia.

In 2001 Berezovsky formed a new opposition party, Liberal Russia, jointly led by himself and Sergei Yushenkov, intended to unite leading businessmen and supporters of the free market. The plan was to run candidates in the 2003 Duma elections but the party was plagued by internal dissent. In April 2003 Yushenkov was shot dead by an unknown gunman in front of his house.

Some of Berezovsky's campaigning has been channelled through the International Foundation for Civil Liberties, his political lobbying group. The foundation, established in 2000, is based in New York City and run by the dissident biologist Alex Goldfarb, who was employed by the billionaire investor George Soros to head a programme combating tuberculosis worldwide. Goldfarb met Berezovsky when Soros was investing in Russia during the Yeltsin era and became one of the oligarch's closest confidants.

Once potential business partners, Berezovsky and Soros collided over Soros's financial backing of a rival, Vladimir Potanin, in the bitterly contested auction for Svyazinvest, the giant state telecommunications company. They soon became irreconcilable and at the annual World Economic Forum in Davos in 1996 they clashed badly over Berezovsky's business methods. In the 1990s Berezovsky outstripped even his fellow oligarchs in the vigour of his business techniques. Soros himself had long warned of the severe dangers of no-holds-barred markets and regarded many of the oligarchs as the architects of the 'robber capitalism' of the time.[18] On one occasion he claimed that he started to fear Berezovsky. 'His anger gave me the chills.'[19]

Berezovsky's foundation funded a range of protest groups in Russia, from anti-war activists to local human rights watchdogs. Its organizer in Russia once told the paper *Komsomolskaya Pravda* that money was also used to fund 'rallies and street marches' and that a demonstration of 3,000 people would cost a few thousand dollars. It also funded several websites, underwrote films alleging that the FSB were involved in the Moscow apartment bombings, and financed expensive advertisements in the *New York Times* and the *Financial Times* attacking Putin's civil rights record. For Berezovsky, the International Foundation for Civil Liberties was an integral part of his operation – 'a grassroots network that could evolve into an anti-establishment political party'.

Much of Berezovsky's political networking has been filtered through the little-known Global Leadership Foundation (GLF), which comprises a group of former political leaders who provide confidential advice to current rulers, notably in emerging markets. The GLF was set up by Graham Barr, an associate of Lord Bell and an executive of Chime Communications (Bell's holding company), and former South African President F. W. de Klerk. The foundation was launched in March 2004, at Chevening in Kent, the official country residence of the British Foreign Secretary, an indication that the GLF was sanctioned by the government.

Prominent members of the GLF have included former International Development Minister Baroness Chalker, former adviser to President Reagan, Chester Crocker, and former British diplomat Sir John Shepherd. Berezovsky was a founding member of the GLF's International Council, making a donation and maintaining involvement through his own International Foundation.

Berezovsky believed that he could destabilize Russia by stirring up opposition in its former satellite states. To encourage this, he has channelled money to opposition groups in Ukraine and Latvia. In his November 2004 speech to the Oxford University Russian Society he claimed that he had spent some $25 million in former Soviet states, all aimed at weakening the power of Russia. He also substantially underwrote the 'Orange Revolution' in Ukraine in 2004–5, which led to the victory of Viktor Yushchenko over the Moscow-backed Viktor Yanukovich. It was a major setback for Putin.

Berezovsky's legal status meant that his movements were severely restricted. He could only fly openly to Israel, where, as a Jew, he knew that he would never be extradited. In the UK those granted asylum are allowed a new legal name as a way of giving them extra protection from their pursuers. They are then provided with new British documents registered in that new name, including a passport. Berezovsky chose the name Platon Yelenin: Platon was the first name of the character in the 2002 film *Oligarkh*, Yelena the name of the woman with whom he has been living for many years.

In late 2003, after Berezovsky was granted asylum, he flew to the Georgian capital of Tbilisi in a private jet owned by Badri Patarkatsishvili, his friend and former business partner. In order to get into Georgia, he used the Yelenin passport to avoid being arrested. This was not a name known to the Russians and therefore did not appear on the international wanted list provided by Interpol or Russian prosecutors. Despite the subterfuge, Georgian officials recognized the fugitive and could have arrested him but refused to do so. The Russians were furious about the visit and issued high-level protests to both Georgia and Britain.

When the two men were carving up Russia's natural resources in the 1990s, it was Patarkatsishvili who took the lead while Berezovsky pulled the levers of political power in the Kremlin. A man who had spent his life hiding from the spotlight, it was entirely out of character when, in late 2003, Patarkatsishvili suddenly emerged from the shadows to become involved in Georgian politics.

Forced into exile in Georgia (which refused to extradite him to Russia), Patarkatsishvili helped to finance the 'Rose Revolution' of 2003, which toppled the pro-Kremlin Eduard Shevardnadze and brought the pro-Western Mikheil Saakashvili to power. He then invested heavily in Georgian business: buying Dinamo Tbilisi Football Club; oil terminals; and a holiday resort on the Black Sea. He became Chairman of Georgia's Olympic Committee and funded charities, an amusement park, and a monastery.

In 2006 Patarkatsishvili bought all of Berezovsky's assets and shares in their joint enterprises. These included *Kommersant* (which he then sold to Alisher Usmanov) and businesses in Serbia and Georgia. In May of that year he also purchased a country house in the UK, the £9 million Downside Manor in

Leatherhead, Surrey, a Palladian-style mansion set in extensive grounds, with a swimming pool, tennis courts, and ornamental gardens. According to locals, Patarkatsishvili bought the property from the Qatari Ambassador to London. Eight months later, in December 2006, he bought Broadlands on the Bagshot Road in Ascot for £20 million.

Patarkatsishvili was drawn reluctantly into the political arena by Berezovsky. He had fallen out with the new Georgian President he had helped into power and, together with Berezovsky, launched a high-profile opposition campaign against Saakashvili. In late 2007 he had a secret meeting in London with a Georgian Interior Ministry official. Patarkatsishvili outlined his plans for a *coup d'état*. During the conversation, recorded by the official, he also offered the minister a £50-million bribe if he would remove the Interior Minister, Vano Merabishvili.

The tape was leaked and Georgia's Prosecutor-General's office launched a criminal investigation against Patarkatsishvili, charging him with conspiring to overthrow the state. He admitted to the authenticity of the tape and wisely remained in London and Israel. Later that month the government plotted revenge: a Georgian official and a contract killer discussed 'options for making Badri disappear' and their conversation was also recorded. 'I know about the tape and I was told that it is very serious,' said Patarkatsishvili. 'I have one hundred and twenty bodyguards but I know that's not enough. I don't feel safe anywhere and that is why I'm not particularly going to Georgia.'[20]

In November 2007, when Patarkatsishvili became a presidential candidate in the Georgian elections, he was given immunity from prosecution and the criminal investigation against him was suspended. But, as an absentee candidate, he only won 7 per cent of the vote and in January 2008 he was once again charged over the illegal conspiracy.

A month later, on the afternoon of 13 February 2008, Patarkatsishvili attended a meeting at Bell Pottinger's offices at

Curzon Street, Mayfair. In attendance were his lawyer, Lord Goldsmith, the Attorney-General until June 2007, his PR adviser, Lord Bell, and some Russian exiles, notably Nikolai Glushkov (another exile in Berezovsky's intimate circle, who had by this time been released from jail in Russia), and Yuli Dubov. At 6 p.m. Patarkatsishvili started to feel unwell and left the room for some fresh air.

At 7.30 p.m. his chauffeur-driven car took him back to Downside Manor. After dinner with his wife and children, he went upstairs and immediately collapsed. An ambulance was called but he was soon pronounced dead. At 3 a.m. his widow called Berezovsky and told him the bad news. His public statement did not reflect his private anguish. 'This is a huge loss for all of his family and friends,' he said. In fact, he was devastated. His staff had never seen him so depressed and so desolate.

At first Surrey police treated the Georgian's death as suspicious, purely because it was so sudden and there had been no prior warnings of ill health. The investigation was transferred to the major crimes unit but post-mortem results subsequently suggested that he had died of natural causes.

None of this high-level international plotting stopped Berezovsky from enjoying himself. On 23 January 2006 he celebrated his sixtieth birthday – in style. He hired Blenheim Palace, the ancestral home of the 11th Duke of Marlborough and the birthplace of Sir Winston Churchill. Although the FSB tried to stop its departure, he also chartered a private jet to fly some journalists in from Moscow. Guests – a mix of Berezovsky's inner circle and Western dignitaries – were greeted by a huge ice sculpture, flanked by bottles of frozen vodka and bowls of caviar. Berezovsky's favourite singer, Cesaria Evora, performed a dozen of her ballads.

The guest of honour was Rupert Murdoch (Berezovsky had himself been one of the eighty-two guests at Murdoch's wedding to Wendi Deng on board his yacht in New York Harbor in June 1999). But the real surprise of the evening was the appearance of an infamous oligarch and Berezovsky's once bitter rival, the fugitive Vladimir Gusinsky. He arrived with a giant cake out of which Berezovsky's 13-year-old daughter jumped to dance for the guests. Before falling out badly, the two men had at one stage been the most powerful media barons in Yeltsin's Russia. Exile seemed to have changed all that, as the two now shared a new common enemy.

A year later Berezovsky told the Moscow radio station *Ekho Moskvy*, still owned by Gusinsky, that he wanted to see Putin overthrown. 'President Putin violates the constitution and any violent action on the opposition's part is justified today,' he said. 'That includes taking power by force, which is exactly what I am working on ... The regime is doomed and I want to see it collapse before Russia collapses.' A few days later a letter arrived at the Home Office. It was a renewed extradition request for the outspoken Berezovsky. This time the charges had been extended from fraud and embezzlement to include 'attempting a coup against the Russian government'.

Russian prosecutors still believed that Britain was protecting a businessman indicted on numerous fraud charges and now openly plotting the violent overthrow of a foreign state. Privately, the Foreign Secretary Jack Straw was furious at Berezovsky's outburst, warning him that advocating the violent overthrow of a sovereign state could see him stripped of his refugee status. Straw told the Commons that the government 'would take action against those who use the UK as a base from which to foment violent disorder or terrorism in other countries'.

Knowing that the courts would be unlikely to grant the new extradition request, the provocative Berezovsky ignored Straw's warnings. A few months later he repeated his clarion call. 'We need to use force to change this regime,' he told the *Guardian*. 'It isn't possible to change this regime by democratic means.' When pressed, he admitted that he was fomenting an insurrection.[21] Three days later he told Radio Free Europe, 'I am in collusion with people from Putin's close circle with the intention of overthrowing Putin's anti-constitutional regime.' He added that he was bankrolling people close to the President, members of Russia's ruling elite, in order to mount a coup. This coup included members of Garry Kasparov's opposition party, The Other Russia.

The Home Office was again forced to investigate Berezovsky. A Home Office spokesman told us, 'We were very much aware of the comments made by Boris Berezovsky in the *Guardian* and officials in the Border and Immigration Branch Agency of the Home Office have studied the comments attributed to him. However, we cannot reveal the outcome of that review.' Nevertheless, Berezovsky later backtracked, claiming that he was not in favour of a violent overthrow.

Unsurprisingly, the FSB kept a close eye on his activities. Announcing the issue of another international arrest warrant in December 2001, a Russian police official warned, 'We know what he eats for breakfast, where he has lunch, and where he buys his groceries.'[22] According to Alex Goldfarb, the FSB checked his every move, bugged his telephone conversations, checked his emails, and mounted surveillance.

Despite his long and expensive campaigns, Berezovsky's achievements have been limited. He has kept Putin's excesses in the public eye, endlessly repeated the allegation that it was the FSB that bombed the Moscow apartments, and has kept human rights in Russia on the media agenda. His funding of the 'Orange Revolution' in Ukraine was undoubtedly influential, and his campaigning, orchestrated by Bell Pottinger, contributed to increasingly common anti-Putin sentiments in the Western media. Indeed, the Kremlin has long complained about Britain's Russophobia.

But Berezovsky has enjoyed very little genuine credibility as a substantial political figure and has developed no popular base for his 'democratic revolution'. His foundation may have succeeded in winning support from a tiny minority of Russians who have been helped, but he has remained a figure derided by most ordinary Russians. Not that this bothers him. 'I know that most Russians don't like me but I don't care what they think,' he once admitted.[23]

Berezovsky's supporters have likened him to a twenty-first-century Leon Trotsky, who used his time in exile to organize opposition against Stalin. But, unlike Trotsky, Berezovsky's attacks have been little more than skilfully orchestrated acts of bravado. The level of support enjoyed by Berezovsky among Russia's elite – even among anti-Putin activists – has been minimal. Opposition figures have mostly shunned his advances. One analyst referred to the clique around Berezovsky as the 'party of oligarchic revenge'. Another analyst dismissed his attempts at destabilizing Russia as 'the usual bluff'.[24]

In Britain Berezovsky may have proved an irritant to the Foreign Office and Britain's own security services but others defended his right to free speech. 'Although Berezovsky's outspoken attacks on Putin may have contributed to deteriorating relations with Russia, that is mostly Russia's fault,' said David Clark of the Russia Foundation. 'Britain should not deny the right of free speech for reasons of improving international relations; that would be wrong. However inconvenient we find it, we can't trample over our own democratic standards just to mollify Putin and those like him.' Others have taken a contrary view. Labour MP Ken Purchase asked the Commons' Foreign Affairs Committee, 'Why do we not send him back to Russia? He has called for the overthrow of the Russian government.'[25]

The British courts' decisions to grant asylum to the oligarch and other Russians, such as Litvinenko, Zakayev, and a number of Yukos executives, certainly strained relations between the two countries. Putin raised the matter personally with Tony Blair while the latter was Prime Minister. That deteriorating relationship was demonstrated only too vividly by the way in which the former British Ambassador in Moscow, Sir Anthony Brenton, was repeatedly intimidated by a nationalist youth movement called Nashi ('Our People'). The group – obviously well informed about his movements – trailed and heckled the Ambassador through the Moscow traffic, organized anti-British demonstrations outside the embassy, and triggered a violent incident outside his residence.

Founded by the Kremlin, Nashi is reminiscent of *Komsomol*, the former Communist Party youth movement. Its members like to parade in T-shirts emblazoned with Putin's portrait and are involved in regular anti-Western actions, notably burning literature considered too liberal and disrupting meetings organized by Russia's beleaguered opposition.

Berezovsky's tirades against Putin have enjoyed a wide audience in the UK and have chimed with the views of most of the foreign policy establishment. His wealth has brought him access to influence. While the British government has occasionally chided Berezovsky over his more outrageous remarks, it has turned a blind eye to his background, apparently only too happy to have his money in the country.

Some of those who know Berezovsky believe that he deserves the same fate as Khodorkovsky. Others argue that, despite a chequered past, his reinvention of himself as a democratic campaigner deserves to be taken seriously. Berezovsky sees himself as a victim of Putin's authoritarianism. In truth he is the architect of his own fate. He helped create the conditions that saw not just the rise of Putin but also the revival of Soviet-style policies. As he once admitted, his actions have always been self-serving: 'I view the world through the prism of the New Testament. Freedom is the most important thing. Whatever I do in life, I do it for myself. That doing-it-for-others type of hypocrisy isn't for me. I don't understand it. I believe that I do everything for my own sake. It's another matter entirely that what I do for myself frequently happens to benefit others. Remember the Bible? Where it says "Love thy neighbour as thyself. Not as you love your mother or your child, but as you love yourself".'

Berezovsky's long campaign against Putin has eluded most of the British public. Few believed that the world of the oligarchs had much impact on London other than through the power of their wealth. That was all about to change in the most dramatic of circumstances.

CHAPTER 10

Murder Inc.

'As I lie here I can hear the beatings of the wings of the angel of death at my back. I may be able to give him the slip but my legs do not run as fast as I would like. I think, therefore, that this may be the time to say one or two things to the person responsible for my present condition. You may succeed in silencing me but that silence comes at a price. You may succeed in silencing one man but the howl of protest from around the world will reverberate, Mr Putin, in your ears for the rest of your life. May God forgive you for what you have done not only to me but to beloved Russia and its people'

— ALEXANDER LITVINENKO

AT 4.30 P.M. ON 1 NOVEMBER 2006 three Russians gathered in the Pine Bar of the Millennium Hotel on Grosvenor Square, just across from the American Embassy in Mayfair. Two of them – Andrei Lugovoi and Dmitri Kovtun – had flown into London from Moscow that week. Both had once worked for the FSB, the Russian security services. The third man was 43-year-old Alexander Litvinenko.[1]

When Litvinenko arrived at the bar, the former FSB officers offered him an alcoholic drink despite knowing that he was teetotal. When he refused, Lugovoi poured him a cup of green tea from a pot already on the table. 'Won't you at least drink tea with us?' he asked. Litvinenko took one sip of the tea but no more, as it had an unpleasant taste.

Litvinenko did not stay long. He was under strict instructions from his wife Marina to be home in time for dinner. The first of November was a special day for the family – it was the sixth anniversary of their flight from Russia. They had another reason to celebrate: a week earlier Litvinenko had been granted British citizenship. To celebrate, Marina was cooking his favourite meal – chicken and pancakes in a herb sauce.

But when Litvinenko arrived at his north London house later that evening, he started vomiting uncontrollably. 'I think I've been poisoned,' he said. He asked Marina for some permanganate of potash (potassium permanganate), a Russian folk remedy taken to cleanse the system, which he drank with several glasses of water. It had little effect. By now, convulsions had started. As they continued, the pain becoming increasingly unbearable, his wife drove him to their local hospital in Barnet. As his condition continued to deteriorate and no diagnosis was forthcoming, he was eventually moved – with a police escort – to University College Hospital in central London. There he died a slow and agonizing death in the full glare of the international media.

It was one of the most bizarre, perplexing, and incredible murders ever to occur on the streets of London. The poisoning of Litvinenko, straight out of a John Le Carré novel, would have seismic repercussions not just for the oligarchs but also for Anglo-Russian relations. For the first time it thrust the uglier side of the previously hidden activities of Londongrad into the spotlight.

Like his two companions in the Pine Bar that afternoon, Litvinenko had once been a loyal and committed member of the KGB and then the FSB. For a while he had been stationed in Chechnya before joining URPO, a special FSB unit with fully independent authority to investigate and, in some cases, eliminate leading criminals. The KGB had been reformed under Yeltsin into three separate groups: the FSB, which handled internal security and criminal investigations; the SVR, the foreign intelligence service; and the GRU, responsible for military intelligence.

Alexander Valterovich Litvinenko was born on 4 December 1962, in Voronezh, a university town 300 miles south of Moscow. His father Walter was a medical student specializing in paediatrics and had married a fellow student, Nina, at college. They separated when Litvinenko was young and both subsequently remarried.

From the age of three, Litvinenko was raised by his paternal grandfather in the small town of Nalchik in the north Caucasus. Known as 'Sasha', he was a sickly infant, prone to pneumonia and colds. But he grew into an open, gregarious child and was shuttled between maternal homes in the north Caucasus, where his grandparents still live. 'I thought it would be easier for him to get into university there [Nalchik]. He wasn't brilliant at school,' said his mother. 'It was hard to get into university then. You had to have an exam but they took students in without an exam if you excelled at sports.'[2]

In his early years Litvinenko was drawn to collecting objects that could be ordered, controlled, and catalogued – such as bright postage stamps, badges, toy soldiers, and miniature tanks. His mother bought recruits for his small armies as gifts when she returned from trips to Moscow, and the young Sasha spent many hours lovingly assembling the platoons.

His grandfather took him to the zoo and to the history museum. He told his grandson, the future FSB officer, about his experiences in the Red Army fighting the Nazis and said that he too should defend Russia one day. 'His grandfather was a pilot in the Second World War and he grew up listening to all his stories,' recalled his widow, Marina. 'Sasha modelled himself on him: he could be strict, but he was a very upstanding, moral person.'[3]

At school Litvinenko was interested in sport and athletics and became obsessed with the pentathlon. In 1980, when Sasha was seventeen, his father moved back into his grandfather's house with his new wife and children. Litvinenko graduated from school and left to join the army. In 1988 he successfully completed the highest level military courses of the KGB.

In his early career Litvinenko was friendly, honest, and law-abiding to the point of pedantry. Former colleagues describe him as 'easy-going', only occasionally displaying the sternness and aggression that was mandatory for his job. His wife Marina says that he was terrible about making or managing money and, unlike his FSB colleagues, had no interest in luxurious living or possessions. When she first met Litvinenko, she thought he was 'jolly, witty – quite boyish, really'.[4] 'Others have described him as 'child-like'. 'He was a very honest man,' said his friend Vladimir Bukosky. 'I mean very straightforward. He had some kind of boyish chivalry.'[5]

Litvinenko developed into a very serious young FSB officer: earnest and intense, he had little social life. But he also developed a reputation for living in a world of fantasy and conspiracies. He later claimed, for example, that FSB agents had trained al-Qaeda operatives in Dagestan and were involved in the September 11 attacks. Specialist Eastern Europe writer Thomas de Waal revealed another side of Litvinenko; he found him to have a 'manic personality' with 'a taste for public theatrics'.[6]

Litvinenko's speciality was not internal security but organized crime, involving investigations, stakeouts, and the interrogation of Russian mobsters. It was during his posting to URPO that, in December 1997, he and four other officers were summoned for a high-level meeting. It was to prove a fateful afternoon. As the five men assembled, they were told that they had been chosen for a special assignment: the assassination of

Boris Berezovsky. Then one of the most powerful men in Russia, he was also proving to be a thorn in the side of certain high-ranking FSB officials who resented his influence over President Yeltsin and saw him as a threat to their own power.

The five men knew only too well that the assignment was high risk and involved significant personal danger to themselves. Their dilemma was an acute one. One option was to refuse to carry out the order. They calculated that if they murdered such a high-profile citizen, they might be arrested and charged or even killed themselves. On the other hand they did not know whether the order had been sanctioned at a higher level. After three months of nervous indecision the men decided on an alternative plan: the best way of saving their own skins was to warn Berezovsky directly of the plot. In fact, Litvinenko and Berezovsky already knew each other. They had met when the FSB officer had earlier been sent to investigate the car bomb attack on Berezovsky in 1994, during which the two had struck up a fleeting friendship.

At first it appeared that Litvinenko had made the right call: Berezovsky used his influence to have URPO closed down and Litvinenko returned to his day job. But the ambitious FSB officer was regarded as 'flaky' and spent much of his time carrying out mundane duties, such as escorting prisoners from one jail to another. The purging of URPO also had quite an unintended consequence, one which may have sealed Litvinenko's fate. For, shortly afterwards, Yeltsin appointed Vladimir Putin as head of the FSB.

From that moment, matters spiralled out of control. Litvinenko later claimed that by this stage he was already disillusioned with widespread corruption within the security services. Prompted by Berezovsky, he asked to see Putin and, in a tense meeting, informed him of the assassination order and presented him with a file containing evidence of questionable FSB activities – from protection rackets to illegal businesses being run by senior FSB figures. Berezovsky and Litvinenko had miscalculated, however: Putin was not impressed either by the dossier or by Litvinenko's presentation and did not investigate the allegations.

After this meeting Berezovsky took a high-risk decision that he came to greatly regret. He persuaded Litvinenko to go public with the allegations. On 17 November 1998 five men gathered before representatives of the Russian press and media. All but Litvinenko wore ski masks to hide their identity. During the press conference, they did not merely gave details of the assassination plot but also made accusations of extortion, kidnapping, and murder against top FSB officials; an astonishing list of allegations that was later broadcast in detail to the nation on Russian television. Their actions were both unprecedented and audacious. All the men, especially Litvinenko, knew that they were taking high personal risks. To their fellow FSB agents, such high-level whistle-blowing was treachery of the worst kind.

If Berezovsky and Litvinenko thought that this would force Putin into investigating the FSB and curb its power, they had got it badly wrong. Putin, a loyal spy, was being asked to treat his own colleagues like criminals. He did not like the way in which he was being boxed into a corner by Berezovsky. Although Putin and Berezovsky were friends, the incident would have sowed in Putin the seeds of doubt about Berezovsky, despite his value to him.

In public Putin said that he would investigate the allegations, but this was simply a cover for dealing with Litvinenko. Within a few weeks Litvinenko had been fired. Two months later, in March 1999, with Berezovsky's influence at the Kremlin waning, Litvinenko was arrested on a series of flimsy charges and thrown into Moscow's notorious Lefortova prison, where he was held for six months before being released.

The FSB had exacted its revenge, but Litvinenko knew that a short term in prison would not be the end of it. By now a high-profile enemy of the intelligence services, and even of Putin himself, Litvinenko was strongly advised by Berezovsky to leave Russia. With his mentor's help, he fled the country in October 2000 and tortuously and clandestinely made his way, via the Black Sea and Georgia, to Antalya on Turkey's Mediterranean coast. A few weeks later his wife Marina and young son Anatoly joined him. There they spent a few uncertain and nervous weeks, convinced that they were being watched by Russian and Turkish agents. Then finally, on 1 November 2000, with the help and advice of Alex Goldfarb, they flew – without a passport, in the case of Litvinenko – to the UK. Because the UK does not require transit visas, the family booked airline tickets from Istanbul to Russia via Heathrow. It was a clever ploy. When they reached Heathrow, Litvinenko presented himself to the authorities, requesting asylum. The defection was news for two days in Russia and, much to his frustration, attracted no media attention in the UK, apart from a brief report in the *Sun*. Eight months later the former FSB agent was granted asylum and the relieved family believed that they would finally be safe.

Berezovsky soon co-opted the exiled Litvinenko into his inner circle, hoping to recruit him as an ally in his campaign against Putin. Initially, the family rented accommodation in central London but Berezovsky then bought them a house in Muswell Hill – through a front company in the British Virgin Islands – and paid Litvinenko a £5,000 monthly retainer. He also paid for his son to attend a private school.

There is no doubt that Litvinenko remained of interest to the Russian authorities. In December 2001 Marina's mother, who had visited her daughter in London, had been stopped on her return to Moscow and strip-searched. The authorities found the address of her daughter and, a short while later, Litvinenko and his wife were visited by officials from the Russian Embassy and summoned to appear in court in Russia.

Litvinenko was not slow to join the propaganda war. Feeling secure in the protection of Berezovsky, he was soon accusing his former FSB masters of corruption and of running a criminal state. Together with Yuri Felshtinsky, a Russian historian living in New York, he wrote a book that accused the Russian secret services of bombing the apartment block in Moscow in September 1999 in which 246 people were killed. He alleged that it was a state-sponsored act that enabled the government to justify a second Chechen war, as the Russian authorities pinned the blame on Chechen terrorists.

The allegation was nothing new and the book, *Blowing Up Russia*, contained mostly circumstantial evidence. Extracts were printed in *Novaya Gazeta* but no Western publisher could be found. As a propaganda weapon, it failed. Completed in 2002, 5,000 copies were privately printed and paid for by Berezovsky, but most were seized by Russian police en route to Moscow. The book was only published in the UK after Litvinenko's death.

Unperturbed, Litvinenko started work on another book called *The Gang from Lubyanka*, a personal memoir that alleged that the FSB was a criminal, mafia-type organization that targeted select Russian people for assassination. Numerous cases were cited: apartments were bombed; money was laundered; individuals were assassinated; and shadowy businesses started up and closed down in the interests of a secret intelligence elite called the St Petersburg Chekists. The master plan of this secret FSB cabal was to install one of their own – Putin – in power (neatly forgetting that it was Berezovsky who had engineered Putin's ascendancy in the first place).

According to Litvinenko, it was this group of FSB officials close to Putin that emerged as the new elite: driving the luxury cars; owning the best houses; managing the most profitable companies; and being propelled into safe seats in the Duma. Once again Western publishers shunned the book. Although never translated into English, 10,000 privately printed copies were successfully smuggled into Russia.

Litvinenko has been presented as a principled defector waging a moral war against the evil FSB because he became disillusioned with the role he was being asked to play. The truth is much more complicated. He may well have become opposed to some of the dirtier FSB operations, but people who knew him say that many of his actions were more motivated by self-survival and a desire for the limelight and attention. 'Why else did he appear at the press conference [in 1998] attacking the FSB without a mask,' said a former colleague. 'That was crazy. It was purely to attract attention to himself and create recognition.'

Litvinenko's personal record is also far from unblemished. During his time in Chechnya as a member of the feared URPO, he was involved in inhumane, brutal acts, including torture and murder. Gary Busch, a businessman who worked in Russia and knew Litvinenko over many years, described him as a 'thug'.[7] Throughout his relentless attacks on the FSB, it is likely that Litvinenko was driven more by an obsessive desire to get revenge on Putin, a man he had once trusted but who he now blamed for his enforced exile.

Steadily, Litvinenko's allegations against Putin became increasingly sensational. They included claims that the then Italian Prime Minister Romano Prodi was a KGB spy and that Putin was a paedophile. Even Berezovsky was 'increasingly exasperated with his former protégé, whose flights of fancy he felt were undermining his own credibility', according to Martin Sixsmith, the BBC's former Moscow correspondent.[8]

According to Berezovsky's staff who encountered him in the London office, by early 2006, Litvinenko had become a sad, ineffectual, unhappy individual. He was a conspiracy theorist, a fantasist, unable to differentiate between gossip, speculation, conjecture, and evidence. He would drop by the office and claim information about death threats to Berezovsky but his staff did not take them seriously. At first the oligarch felt sorry for him and continued to pay his substantial monthly retainer.

Then, in March 2006, now something of a liability, Litvinenko's retainer was cut to £1,700 a month. Living in London on £20,000 a year with a wife and child to support was not easy and Litvinenko became desperate for money. He began fabricating bizarre conspiracy theories and death threats in the hope that Berezovsky would rehire him. To some extent, the oligarch encouraged him, but he did not trust the former FSB officer because of his incapability of telling the truth and his indiscretion. 'If he had any information, he would leak it within three seconds,' one former Berezovsky aide said.

As Litvinenko become alienated from Berezovsky, the more he sought a new role in the murky world of corporate espionage and business intelligence. He began to boast about his expertise in investigating Russian organized crime and started consulting for London-based security and commercial intelligence companies specializing in investigating Russian businessmen. Their clients were international companies, law firms, and banks that needed due diligence to be carried out on Russian individuals and the Kremlin. By networking the 'Circuit', as it was known, Litvinenko secured occasional assignments and offered advice to certain European law enforcement agencies.

One of his new business partners was Andrei Lugovoi. The two men had known each other from the 1990s when Lugovoi was working for Berezovsky. They came to an arrangement whereby Litvinenko would be paid 20 per cent of the price of any intelligence material he was able to sell on that had come from Lugovoi. Litvinenko had the contacts and Lugovoi, who travelled regularly to London, had the expertise.

One of Litvinenko's new clients was Titan International, a security and intelligence firm based in Grosvenor Street, Mayfair, and run by Major John Holmes. Both successful and effective, they had secured contracts in Iraq. In 2006 they were hired by a British aircraft manufacturer to investigate a lucrative contract whereby a Russian aviation company was planning to commission new long- and short-range missiles. It was worth billions of pounds to the firm and inside intelligence was invaluable to help them to secure the contract. Titan's brief was to investigate eight Russian individuals linked to the aviation company and the Kremlin.

Titan hired Litvinenko on a £50,000 contract and the former spy was excited by the assignment. It was the ideal job for him: investigating Russians connected to Putin and making some cash in the bargain. With no idea where to start, however, he subcontracted the assignment out to Yuri Shvets, a former major in the KGB and now a well-connected private investigator with a substantial number of American clients. Based in Washington, DC, he was a resourceful operator with excellent contacts who had testified before the US Congress on Russian money laundering and organized crime.

Shvets tapped into his sources in Moscow and soon discovered incriminating information about one of the businessmen involved with the Russian aviation company. He then produced a comprehensive and highly professional eight-page report, complete with glossy cover, and, on 20 September 2006, handed it to Litvinenko. Litvinenko had no idea how to present, let alone research, such a report but put his name to it and handed it to Titan. Their client was delighted and offered Litvinenko and Lugovoi a one-year contract.

Pleased with himself, Litvinenko also gave a copy to Lugovoi in order to show him how such reports were compiled under Western corporate governance requirements. This was a serious mistake. Investigators into Litvinenko's death believe that this may have sealed his fate. According to Shvets, on his return to Moscow, Lugovoi showed the highly damaging document to one of the targeted businessmen, a senior figure with close ties to the

FSB. 'Sasha [Litvinenko] said that he gave the report to Lugovoi and I believe that this triggered the entire assassination,' said Major Shvets, who claimed that Lugovoi was an FSB informant.[9]

Even though the British company that had hired Litvinenko and Lugovoi was awarded the contract by the Russian company, they withdrew because the due diligence report was so damaging. The confidential report was potential dynamite. It contained devastating personal and business details about one individual, which, according to a BBC Radio 4 investigation by Tom Mangold, 'marked him as a powerful, dangerous, and vindictive' man. 'Many representatives of the new generation of Russian leaders view him as a remnant of the past who fits more to Josef Stalin's times than modern Russia', stated one section of the report.[10] The report not only killed the deal, but it also prevented the Russian businessman from making lucrative commissions and fees.

The document was later handed over to Scotland Yard officers, who took the allegations seriously enough to fly to Washington, DC, to interview Shvets. If the former KGB major was right, it would explain the growing animosity towards Litvinenko within some sections of the Kremlin. Apart from the fury at losing a multi-million-dollar project, there was also the fear about what the indiscreet Litvinenko might do with the information contained in the dossier.

Litvinenko's horrific death was to become a very public and international event. The disturbing photograph of the former FSB officer on his deathbed, wired up to a life-support machine, gaunt, and gazing defiantly with those penetrating blue eyes, was shown repeatedly around the world.

The use of what soon became an iconic photograph – of a hairless and physically wasted Russian émigré three days before he died – is a powerful example of the way in which Berezovsky, aided by Lord Bell, used the tragedy of Litvinenko's death in his campaign against Putin. When Litvinenko first complained of severe stomach pains after his meeting at the Millennium Hotel, Berezovsky's initial reaction was to dismiss his fears that he had been poisoned. But when it became clear that he was seriously ill, Berezovsky was quick to take advantage of the situation, though not without Litvinenko's approval. Alex Goldfarb, who had known Litvinenko for many years and had helped him to escape from Russia, quickly flew in from New York.

The full propaganda operation – with all its guile and relentless energy – produced a blitzkrieg of global publicity. Goldfarb placed calls to journalists at several newspapers, the BBC, and *Channel 4 News*. For several days he gave regular press briefings at the hospital on Litvinenko's condition and the latest theories on how he had been poisoned. Throughout, the handling of the Litvinenko story was run and coordinated behind the scenes by Lord Bell and his team at Bell Pottinger. Both Berezovsky and Goldfarb instantly pinned responsibility on the Kremlin.

The iconic photograph of Litvinenko was taken and released by Bell Pottinger, who retained its copyright ownership. Two days before he died, Litvinenko purportedly dictated a final statement to Goldfarb. The widely quoted passage blaming Putin is but part of a much longer and more powerful piece of prose:

> As I lie here I can hear the beatings of the wings of the angel of death at my back. I may be able to give him the slip but my legs do not run as fast as I would like. I think, therefore, that this may be the time to say one or two things to the person responsible for my present condition. You may succeed in silencing me but that silence comes at a price. You may succeed in silencing one man but the howl of protest from around the world will reverberate, Mr Putin, in your ears for the rest of your life. May God forgive you for what you have done not only to me but to beloved Russia and its people.

The day after Litvinenko's death, Alex Goldfarb read extracts from the note on British television and radio as if it had been composed entirely by Litvinenko. Yet the authenticity of the note and who had actually written it became the subject of speculation and scepticism. *Izvestiya* accused Lord Bell of writing it. In fact, it was subsequently admitted that it had been composed by Goldfarb and Litvinenko's lawyer, George Menzies.

The media campaign was immensely effective in helping to turn public opinion against Putin. Litvinenko's death was presented almost universally as an international espionage scandal, with the Kremlin in the dock. The British press erupted in a frenzy of anti-Putin rhetoric. Whoever was behind the murder, media manipulation ensured that the man who gained most from the death of the 45-year-old Litvinenko was Boris Berezovsky.

The exploitation of the Litvinenko story continued well after his death. On 7 December 2006 he was buried at Highgate Cemetery in a specially sealed casket provided by the Health Protection Agency. A few days later Berezovsky, with Lord Bell at his side, gave a press conference directly challenging Lugovoi to face trial for Litvinenko's murder. Within days another story was fed to the press: Berezovsky himself had become the target of a potential Kremlin murder plot just a few weeks earlier. Then, as the Kremlin tried to turn the tables by claiming that Berezovsky himself was behind the Litvinenko killing with the aim of discrediting Putin, the fugitive repeated his assertion on BBC's *Newsnight* that the President was behind the murder and that Lugovoi was merely the front man carrying out orders. Berezovsky even offered to stand trial himself, not in Russia but in an independent country such as Germany or Holland, if Lugovoi would do the same.

As a former government information officer, Martin Sixsmith witnessed spin doctoring first hand. In his investigation into the murder, *The Litvinenko File*, he concluded: 'Anyone paying attention could see there was some fairly cynical news management going on to keep the story constantly in the public eye. Berezovsky's PR professionals have turned Sasha Litvinenko's agonizing death into much more than a human tragedy. Now it is a weapon, a piece of ammunition that can be exploited over and over again in the propaganda war against the Kremlin.'[11]

Initially, the cause of Litvinenko's illness eluded the doctors and consultants who were treating him. For a while experts attributed it to thallium poisoning, which acts by slowly destroying nerve cells. It was only in the closing days it was confirmed that he had been poisoned by a lethal dose of polonium-210, a terrifying, deadly, and highly radioactive chemical. Polonium is a little-used isotope, employed sparingly in spark plugs, nuclear warhead triggers, and rocket engines. Only one nuclear laboratory in Russia produced polonium. The discovery was only made because University College London had a medical physics department with a strong radiation physics group that was able to assemble a network of experts to help solve the mystery of his illness.

If Litvinenko had died more quickly, as his assassin expected, the real cause of his death would have gone undetected forever and the murder would merely have been deeply suspicious. Polonium-210 was described by Professor John Henry, the toxicologist hired by Litvinenko's family, as a 'perfect assassin's tool'.

The assassination of Litvinenko was not just an audacious crime with tragic consequences. It had a much deeper – and continuing – political and diplomatic fallout. It was the first known incidence of radiation poisoning in the world and set alarm bells ringing within the British government and its intelligence agencies and those of its allies. Using military alpha counters to detect radiation, specially trained forces from the police and the Health Protection Agency embarked on a frantic search across London. There was a nationwide and then an international hunt for contamination. By Christmas of 2008, traces of polonium had been found at thirty sites in the UK and in Europe, while at least 140 British residents, from hotel and restaurant staff to airline personnel, were reported by government health advisers to contain low levels of contamination. Those with the highest levels were warned that they faced a higher risk of developing cancer in the future because of the radiation. Security services around the world were left wondering if such an attack might happen again.

Up to this point, the seedier side of Londongrad – the commercial vendettas, activities of intelligence agents, human trafficking – had mostly been hidden from public view. The police and intelligence agencies monitored and investigated the oligarchs and Russian organized crime but rarely carried any cases forward. The high-profile death of Litvinenko thrust this shadowy world into the limelight and law enforcement agencies were now under pressure to be seen to be doing something.

In the immediate aftermath of the murder there were severe diplomatic and political repercussions. When news first broke about the poisoning of the former Russian FSB officer, the Kremlin was swift to deny that the Russian state was involved. 'Mr Litvinenko is not the kind of person for whom it would make sense to smear bilateral relations,' said a spokesman. The media quickly focused on allegations by Litvinenko, whose deathbed statement had laid the blame for his murder firmly at the door of Putin. To counter this, the President's Deputy Chief Press Secretary, Dmitri Peskov, was dispatched to Britain to quell increasingly shrill press speculation. 'It is Cold War thinking,' he said. Meanwhile, the Kremlin played down the importance of Litvinenko. They denied that he had ever been a spy and instead portrayed him as a low-level operative who had spent most of his career as a border guard and prison officer.

They claimed that he was a questionable character who had no access to any state secrets worth passing on.

In December 2006 British detectives travelled to Russia to interview Andrei Lugovoi and Dmitri Kovtun. In return, the Russian authorities demanded the right to a reciprocal visit. They requested that Russian police be allowed to visit the UK to inspect sites and interview designated people – witnesses and suspects in the Litvinenko case and exiled opponents of Putin whom Moscow had long tried to get extradited. This occurred in March 2007, when Russian prosecutors flew to London and interviewed Berezovsky and Zakayev. Putin saw his opportunity for an old-fashioned Cold War exchange: Lugovoi and Kovtun would only be extradited if the UK handed over Berezovsky and the Yukos executives wanted by Russia. Berezovsky responded by accusing Russia of 'blackmailing Scotland Yard'.[12]

By early February 2007, the police investigation into the murder had narrowed its focus, with Lugovoi as the prime suspect. In an attempt to steady nerves, the Trade Secretary, Alistair Darling, flew to Moscow ostensibly on a trade mission. The government was undoubtedly worried about the implications of the assassination for business between the two countries and was anxious that Britain should not suffer economically because of increasing tension. The Litvinenko case was discussed but Kremlin officials also repeated their requests for the extradition of what they called 'Russian criminals' in exile in Britain.

Two months later, just a few days before it was due to open, Putin forced Russia's business and political leaders to boycott the Russian Economic Forum, which was to have been held in London. For several years it had been the world's largest Russian business gathering but that year few Russians of significance turned up. One regular who did, State Duma Deputy Alexander Lebedev, joked to the *Moscow Times* that, 'Some people told me, "You are the only one who was allowed to come, but will you be able to go back?"'[13]

The police investigation arrived at a number of key conclusions: the deadly poison had been administered via a dissolving capsule or sprayed into the pot of green tea that Litvinenko drank in the Pine Bar at 4.30 p.m. on 1 November 2006; according to expert calculations, Litvinenko swallowed a dose of at least three gigabecquerels of radioactivity – the equivalent of around 100 lethal doses – this despite taking only one or two sips of the tea, which he later said tasted odd; that a trail of polonium was left at a number of locations before and after the poisoning took place; that the fatal attack had been preceded by at least one earlier attempt during the previous two weeks. The polonium, a terrifying substance and dangerous to all who came into contact with it, had been smuggled into Britain aboard passenger planes from Moscow, probably on more than one occasion.

Six months later, in May 2007, Scotland Yard announced that the chief suspect was Lugovoi, but that there was insufficient evidence to charge Dmitri Kovtun. The hunt for the trail of polonium by squads of specialist officials had revealed traces in a number of locations where Lugovoi had been present: in top London hotel suites and bars, in offices, restaurants, and on the two British Airways flights in and out of London. Following the announcement, Britain sought the extradition of the former Soviet spy to stand trial, despite knowing that extraditions were banned by the country's constitution. The Russians duly refused to release him, claiming that if they were provided with the evidence they would try the suspect in Moscow, a proposal not acceptable to the British government.

From that point, the drama gathered pace. The murder created a major diplomatic headache for the British government. Relations between the two countries were already severely strained because of the standoff over the sheltering of Berezovsky and other exiles. Russia argued that Britain was protecting an enemy of the state and was furious about the refusal to hand over twenty-one other businessmen whom they were trying to extradite. This refusal was regarded as a hostile act. But with Britain increasingly dependent on Russia for oil and gas supplies, the then Prime Minister Tony Blair was anxious not to further antagonize an already prickly Putin. And yet such a shocking event that took place in broad daylight in the very heart of London could hardly be ignored.

Blair's initial instinct was to be conciliatory, but this was always going to be an untenable position and relations deteriorated. In July 2007, as the stalemate continued, Britain expelled four senior Russian intelligence officers in retaliation for Russia's refusal to hand over Lugovoi, reducing the complement of Russian diplomatic staff in London from seventy-seven to seventy-three. It was not just the first such set of expulsions since the end of the Cold War, it was also the first major foreign affairs decision taken by Gordon Brown who had taken over as Prime Minister just two weeks earlier. According to former Foreign Office adviser David Clark, 'Blair had invested a lot in developing a personal relationship with Putin while Brown felt less constrained by personal closeness. He also had fewer illusions about Putin than Blair and was less reluctant to see Putin for what he was.'

The raising of the stakes by Britain reflected this harder line: a clear message needed to be sent to President Putin that Britain would not put up with Russian espionage wars being fought in London. 'We will not tolerate a situation where a British citizen is assassinated on British soil,' said Brown. 'Our first duty is to protect our citizens and prevent there being lawlessness on the streets of London.' Nevertheless, to some the expulsions were too feeble a response to what had been the first example of nuclear terrorism in London. Hawks in the Foreign Office argued that what was needed was actually a much tougher stance on a visa policy that currently seemed to allow any Russian into the country.

In retaliation for the expulsions, a Kremlin adviser, Sergei Markov, said that 'the mood within the Russian government was cold and angry' and accused the British government of behaving in a high-handed and 'imperial' manner.[14] There was also a fear that the murder of Litvinenko could have been just the beginning of espionage-related attacks. Indeed, in the same week Berezovsky added to his earlier claims, announcing that only a few weeks before Scotland Yard had advised him to leave the country because of an alleged attempt on his life. Once again the location for the attempt was Mayfair. Scotland Yard confirmed that a Russian 'hitman' had been arrested at the Hilton Hotel on Park Lane, less than half a mile away from the Millennium Hotel, in June 2007. The hitman was suspected of a plot to murder Berezovsky and handed over to immigration services for deportation after his visa was cancelled. The plot had been uncovered as a result of 'eavesdropping', according to one source, and the man was released because there was not enough hard evidence to charge him.

A few days later Russia reacted to the expulsions in kind: they deported four mid-ranking Moscow-based British diplomats, halted cooperation on counter-terrorism, stopped issuing visas to British government officials. There is nothing new about tit-for-tat expulsions, but in the past most of these took place in the Cold War era when spying was rife on both sides, notably in 1970 when 100 Soviet officials were expelled by the Heath government. This time the circumstances were very different. The relationship between Britain and Russia had become warmer, both diplomatically and in business. Now they were at freezing point again. 'It is the big chill,' remarked one observer.

As the mutual recriminations continued, many conflicting theories emerged about the motivations for the murder. One such theory was that the murder was linked to the role played by Litvinenko in the compiling of the dossier on the aviation industry and its sensitive and incriminating information about a senior Russian businessman. It is certainly plausible that Lugovoi was hired by Kremlin insiders to suppress the evidence, though that in itself does not provide hard evidence of murder.

Another theory was that Litvinenko was killed because of research he had done on the Russian government's campaign against the Yukos executives who had fled to Britain after the imprisonment of Khodorkovsky. Indeed, in the summer before his death, Litvinenko flew to Tel Aviv and met Leonard Nevzlin, the former deputy chief executive of Yukos, and a wanted man in Russia. This was a business pitch, an attempt to sell his information to Nevzlin. During their meeting, Litvinenko warned Nevzlin of a plot to claw back the money from exiled Yukos officials and handed over a seventeen-page dossier allegedly containing details of the way the Kremlin was handling the Yukos investigation. Nevzlin said at the time that Litvinenko's information may have been the reason for his assassination and passed on his dossier to Scotland Yard.

The main doubt about the involvement of commercial forces is how they could have gained access to such a high degree of technical sophistication and huge resources, as well as to the polonium itself. Given its sensitivity, say business intelligence investigators, there must have been knowledge and cooperation at a senior level in the Russian government.

Conventional wisdom remains that the FSB – or a freelance agent not traceable to the FSB – was running Lugovoi and authorized the operation. MI5, however, is adamant that the Kremlin was responsible. 'It was the Russian state, not a rogue element,' an intelligence source told *Newsnight*. 'The polonium itself is evidence itself of state involvement.'[15]

Unsurprisingly, Lugovoi has continued to protest his innocence, even claiming that MI6 tried to recruit him. In another twist he embarked on a new career as a politician and successfully stood for Parliament for the Kremlin-backed ultra-nationalist Liberal Democratic Party in the elections of December

2007. As a member of the Duma, Lugovoi automatically enjoyed immunity from prosecution. This was clearly a Kremlin-inspired move that offered the prospect of the accused man projecting himself as a Russian patriot fighting off false allegations by the West.

Meanwhile, the Russian government continued to pin the blame for Litvinenko's death on Berezovsky. Two days after the expulsion of British diplomats, Russian prosecutors challenged Britain's version of events, claiming that the poisoning might have been the other way round – that Litvinenko had actually tried to poison Lugovoi. Kremlin officials were also quick to remind journalists that Lugovoi had once worked full time for Berezovsky – after leaving the FSB he became head of security for the oligarch's television channel, ORT. The two remained friends. They often met in London and Lugovoi attended Berezovsky's sixtieth birthday party. They even shared a bottle of wine at Berezovsky's office the night before Lugovoi's fateful meeting with Litvinenko. While Berezovsky benefited substantially from the death and the attendant anti-Putin publicity, there is no evidence that he was involved in any way. Nevertheless, Litvinenko's death provided yet another chapter in the ongoing war between the two arch-enemies, Putin and Berezovsky.

By 2008, many questions about Litvinenko's murder still remained unanswered. Who had administered the poison – was it Lugovoi or Kovtun, or, as was widely suggested, a third, unknown party, a professional killer who joined the others at a later point in the meeting?[16] This theory has been reinforced by a man who appeared on airport surveillance video footage, which shows him talking to Kovtun as the two men arrived at Heathrow in the days before the killing. Litvinenko told friends while he was dying that he had been briefly introduced to a man at the hotel bar during his meeting with Lugovoi and Kovtun. Police have been unable to trace the man, his passport details, or when he left Britain.

Then there is the critical question of who issued the orders. Was this a decision taken at the highest level – by Putin himself – or by senior FSB officers at a level senior enough to enable them to acquire and pay for such a quantity of polonium? If Lugovoi was one of the assassins, what was his motive for getting involved? He was, after all, already a very rich man with a successful security agency, Ninth Wave, which provided bodyguards for wealthy Russians. If he was working for the FSB, was it out of loyalty or because he was being blackmailed?

We may never know the answers. The British police certainly believe that the murder was orchestrated by Lugovoi. One theory is that Lugovoi had been acting as a double agent – employed by the FSB to spy on Berezovsky and Litvinenko while remaining friends and business associates of both. Lugovoi's attempt to secure joint business deals with Litvinenko was almost certainly a cover, but his role – if any – in the assassination plot has not been proved. One theory is that, even if the poison was administered by a third party, Lugovoi must have been aware of the role he was playing to create an opportunity for the poisoning. Alternatively, he may have been in the pay of the FSB and made the introductions, but did not know that Litvinenko was about to be murdered.

In their book on the murder, *Death of a Dissident*, Alex Goldfarb and Marina Litvinenko argue that Putin was personally responsible but provide no convincing evidence.[17] 'One of the reasons for the Litvinenko assassination is that Putin was tidying up the loose ends from the apartment bombings and making sure that anybody who knew anything damaging about it would not be in a position to use it against him should he subsequently fall from grace,' said one former Foreign Office official. While this is no more than classic conspiracy theorizing, it would not be the first time that prominent critics of the FSB were poisoned.

* * *

In the autumn of 2004 Anna Politkovskaya, the courageous columnist for *Novaya Gazeta*, lost consciousness after being poisoned aboard the plane she was taking to the Chechen frontier to report on the Beslan school hostage crisis. She woke up in hospital several days later, claiming that she had been poisoned by the FSB. Politkovskaya was one of the most outspoken Russian critics of the Kremlin and had also been investigating the Moscow apartment bombings. Two years later, at the age of forty-eight, she was shot dead in the lift of her apartment block in central Moscow. A surveillance camera caught an image of her otherwise unidentified assassin, a shadowy figure in a dark baseball cap. She was murdered just a few weeks before Litvinenko.

In 2003 Yuri Schekochikhin, a Russian writer, anti-Kremlin Parliamentarian, and Deputy Editor at the investigative journal *Novaya Gazeta*, died from a mysterious illness during a trip to investigate a corruption scandal with links to high-ranking intelligence officials. His skin fell off and his internal organs swelled up, symptoms associated with radioactive thallium poisoning. The writer had also been working on the apartment bombings story. His death was put down to an 'allergic reaction' and his medical chart has remained 'classified'. His symptoms were identical to those experienced a year later by Viktor Yushchenko, the anti-Kremlin presidential candidate in Ukraine who fell seriously ill with abdominal pains in the run-up to the presidential elections in 2004. Doctors in Vienna later confirmed that he had been poisoned with TCDD dioxin. He recovered to win the election but his face remains severely disfigured from the poison. Most observers believe this was a classic old-style KGB act to knock him out of the race and to clear the way for the pro-Kremlin candidate Viktor Yanukovich.

The lurking doubt about Livinenko's assassination being sanctioned by Putin or the Kremlin is that he was such a marginal, insignificant individual. He was not a threat to anyone but himself. Even Berezovsky had disowned him as ineffectual and only paid him a retainer out of loyalty. Among Berezovsky's aides, he was always seen as one trying to exaggerate his own importance. Even his friends were surprised at how he became increasingly politically active. Before he died, he met Gary Busch, who asked him, 'When did you become so political.' Litvinenko replied, 'My circumstances made me political.'[18]

It is difficult to see what conceivable benefit Putin gained by ordering the murder of such an individual – quite the opposite, in fact. Indeed, when questioned at a G8 summit, the President became visibly angry and irritated. 'Litvinenko did not know any secrets,' Putin remarked dismissively. And why would the President have ordered such a controversial assassination at a time when he was engaged in sensitive diplomatic discussions and a year before the run-up to the presidential elections?

It is, of course, possible that it was organized by senior rogue FSB officers, acting without orders from the top but with access and funds sufficient to acquire polonium. Some sections of the FSB certainly used Litvinenko's photograph for target practice during training and he was a despised and derided figure. But why wait so many years after he had long ceased to be an effective opponent?

One theory is that Litvinenko was merely playing the role of 'Trotsky's dog', a reference to those comrades close to Leon Trotsky, Stalin's bitterest enemy, who were assassinated to frighten the exiled revolutionary. Later Trotsky himself was murdered in Mexico, killed with an ice pick while working at his desk. If Litvinenko's death was designed as a warning to Berezovsky to de-escalate his campaign, it had zero impact.

The 'rogue FSB theory' has been propagated by his friends, and even by Litvinenko himself. From the moment he arrived in the UK, he claimed that he was constantly being threatened by former colleagues and FSB agents, often by telephone. But his former colleagues in Berezovsky's office said that Litvinenko was 'incapable of telling the truth' and dismissed these threats. 'Nobody took him seriously.'

But some former colleagues argued that the very exaggeration of Litvinenko's outbursts might have irritated the Kremlin. Oleg Kalugin, the highest-ranking KGB officer to defect to the West, and who often spoke to Litvinenko on the phone from his home in the United States, called his murder an act of 'political retribution'. He added, 'I told him that he was too emotional in his attacks. Too personal. He called Mr Putin a paedophile, a mass murderer. So they obviously could not forgive him. That's it. That's the reason.'[19]

The KGB has a long history of exacting vengeance on defectors. Despite his lack of credibility, Litvinenko's relentless attacks on the Russian state made him a traitor in the eyes of his former employers, and his friendship with Berezovsky further alienated him from Russian officialdom. The murder also had the bonus of compromising Berezovsky. Yevgeny Limarov, another former intelligence agent now living in France, said, 'They're nostalgic for the greatness of the Soviet empire. They want to raise barriers between Putin and the West, between Putin and the pro-democracy opposition in Russia – thus reinforcing their own totalitarian positions. The overall message sent by this murder is about sowing fear among the opposition and other "enemies of the people", and announcing to the whole world: we're back, we're strong … The organizers allowed for two possible scenarios: if the polonium wasn't discovered, then the agonizing death would intimidate the appropriate people – and if the polonium was discovered, even more people would be scared.'[20]

Moreover, just a few months earlier, the state had effectively given a legal licence for such an assassination. In July 2006 the Duma passed a remarkable piece of legislation – Federal Law N 153-F3 – that allowed the President to use the secret services to eliminate 'extremists' in Russia or on foreign territory. A subsequent amendment expanded the definition to include those 'libellously critical of the Russian authorities'. This power could only be used with the authority of the President.

Well before this new law was passed, there was evidence of the government's willingness to target enemies abroad. In February 2004 Zelimkhan Yandarbiyev, a Chechen leader living in Qatar, was blown up while travelling in his SUV in Doha. Two Russian intelligence officers were tried for the murder and sentenced to life imprisonment. During the trial, the judge claimed the two had been acting under the instructions of the Russian state. The court's verdict caused such severe tension between the two countries that Qatar agreed to release the men to serve their sentences in their own country. When they arrived, they were freed and received a hero's welcome.

During his research for his book on the Litvinenko case, Martin Sixsmith secured access to the Prosecutor-General's office, responsible for all policing, investigation, and prosecution. During his interview with two detectives at their office in Moscow, he asked them about the new law. The two stared at one another and then retreated to 'seek clarification' from their bosses. After a prolonged delay and what Sixsmith describes as an 'air of mild panic', they returned to say, 'Yes, these laws were adopted but not with any evil intent. They were a response to the cowardly abduction and murder of five Russian diplomats in Iraq.' Then, as Sixsmith was about to leave, and thinking the tape recorder was turned off, the two detectives suddenly became more animated. 'Look, do you really think we would bother assassinating someone like Litvinenko?' said one. 'He just wasn't important enough. He didn't know any secrets that would be a reason for liquidating him.'[21] This was close to an admission that such operations did take place; but might it also have reinforced the view among former special forces sources that such high-risk operations would not have been wasted on Litvinenko?

If Litvinenko was killed by a KGB 'clan' operating at a senior level, it was further evidence of the restoration to power of the security services in the state hierarchy. Under Yeltsin, the most powerful Kremlin grouping was the clique built around the oligarchs and the 'family'. Under Putin, they were replaced by a quite different and much larger organization – the veterans of the KGB and its principal successor, the FSB. According to Olga Kryshtanovskaya, the leading academic expert on elites in Russia, the proportion of ex-military and security services personnel working in and around the President increased from some 5 per cent under Gorbachev to nearly 60 per cent in 2004. During Putin's first term, more than 50 per cent of his informal twenty-four-member politburo and about one-third of government functionaries were *siloviki*, as were 70 per cent of the staff working for the Kremlin's seven regional directorates.[22] Many of these were from the elitist KGB 'Chekist' clan from St Petersburg. The *siloviki* was mostly a hard-line group that numbered some 6,000 people and was once described by *Novaya Gazeta* as having all the signs of a 'domestic junta'.[23]

Under Putin, the security services penetrated all spheres of social, economic, and political life, a remarkable turnaround in the fortunes of the FSB. After the end of the Cold War and the demise of the communist state, the KGB/FSB had been marginalized. Real power lay with the oligarchs and with Yeltsin's 'family'. But now Putin had restored their supremacy and influence. 'Whereas in the past people from security backgrounds generally did jobs connected with state security, now they hold office in just about every ministry and government agency,' said Kryshtanovskaya. 'We are witnessing the restoration of the power of the KGB in the country from the regions to the top of the Kremlin.'[24]

The rise of the FSB to a position of such influence would have given their leaders the confidence to mount the Litvinenko operation without official authority. As Kryshtanovskaya has written, the *siloviki* was a 'very homogeneous group with a common mentality which thinks they act in the interest of the state and their aim is for Russia to be feared again'.[25]

CHAPTER 11

Showdown

'I don't need to defend myself. I am not ashamed and I don't
need to hide'

— OLEG DERIPASKA, *July 2007*[1]

ON THE AFTERNOON of Saturday 6 October 2007 Roman
Abramovich was browsing through designer clothing and
luxury accessories in the exclusive Hermès shop at 179 Sloane
Street, Knightsbridge. At that very moment his former friend
Boris Berezovsky was perusing the shoes and clothes in Dolce &
Gabbana, the Italian fashion house, just two doors down. It was
to prove an expensive day's shopping for Abramovich.

The two oligarchs were unaware of each other's presence
until one of Berezovsky's three bodyguards spotted the Chelsea
owner in Hermès and told his boss. Six months earlier Berezovsky had filed papers at the High Court, claiming multi-
billion-pound damages against Abramovich and was desperate
to serve the 'writ', necessary under British law, for the case to
proceed. He had been trying for months and had even hired
security operatives to catch him when Chelsea were playing at
home. But his former protégé had proved elusive. 'There was a
plan to ambush him with the writ when he went to watch
Chelsea play Hull in an FA Cup match, but Roman got wind of
it and didn't turn up', according to a Berezovsky spokesman.[2]

Now that Berezovsky's moment had finally come, he ran over to his armoured Mercedes Maybach. Shrewdly, he kept the legal documents in the limousine's glove department at all times. With the papers in hand and surrounded by his minders, he marched towards the Hermès boutique, but two of Abramovich's bodyguards noticed their approach and formed a human blockade at the entrance.

As astonished shoppers looked on, the respective body-guards faced off, staring each other down like boxers before a heavyweight bout. Then they started jostling. An animated Berezovsky tried to join the scuffle. Eventually, after much pushing and shoving, the wiry oligarch – clutching his writ like a rugby fly-half with the ball – charged through the scrum and handed the envelope to Abramovich. 'It's a present, from me to you,' he snapped. A startled Abramovich pulled away and put his hands in his pockets, allowing the envelope to fall to the ground.[3] 'I think that he'd been watching too much television, because he seemed to think that if he didn't have physical contact with it then the writ would not be served,' said a Berezovsky aide.[4]

This extraordinary showdown was captured on Hermès' CCTV and was later used in court as evidence in the case. It was a clear illustration of how the raw business methods of many of the new plutocrats – built on litigation, distrust, and security – had spilt over into the heartland of Londongrad.

The 'writ' stemmed from 2001 when Berezovsky claimed that he had been 'induced' into selling valuable shares in two companies they jointly owned – the oil and metal giant Sibneft and the aluminium combine Rusal – to Abramovich at knock-down prices. The exiled oligarch was claiming damages of '$4.3 billion arising out of allegedly wrongful actions committed by Mr Abramovich.' Berezovsky claims that Abramovich was 'a party to the explicit and implicit coercive threats and intimidation' against him and that he had lost out hugely as the value of

Sibneft soared off the back of escalating oil prices, enriching his former protégé in the process.[5] Abramovich hotly disputes each of Berezovsky's allegations against him.

Berezovsky had earlier said that he had no intention of suing. 'No, because I think it is useless,' he told Abramovich's biographers in 2004.[6] But the resentment continued to smoulder. His own fortune had been shrinking with the costs of his high-profile campaigns against Putin and a successful legal challenge against Abramovich might restore his pot of gold. The catalyst for Berezovsky was when Abramovich sold Sibneft – the oil company they had jointly acquired – back to the state in 2005 for £7.5 billion. The sale consolidated the power of the state-combine Gazprom, and its chairman Dmitri Medvedev who later became President, but also greatly inflamed Berezovsky, who wanted his own cut from the sell-off.

The Commercial Court in London confirmed that the case was ongoing as of December 2008. It is thought that neither will relish the prospect of being cross-examined in public about their pasts and the sources of their wealth. The question is: who will blink first? The Chelsea owner in particular will be uneasy about the idea of his alleged role as President Putin's agent being scrutinized so publicly by Berezovsky's lawyers.

Many of the oligarchs may have become near neighbours in London's smartest streets and squares, but the bitter, decade-old rivalries over media, business, and political deals have not gone away. In the 1990s business disputes were resolved in the notoriously corrupt Russian courts or through the barrel of the gun on the streets of small industrial towns. Some oligarchs hired private armies for protection. By 2007 and 2008, however, many of these rancorous and simmering disputes – involving billions of pounds of former state assets – had moved to the streets and the courts of London.

A year before Berezovsky's bizarre encounter with Abramovich on Sloane Street, another of his former business associates had also been singled out for legal action. On a misty evening on 26 November 2006 Oleg Deripaska flew into Luton Airport on one of his private Gulfstream jets, a routine visit for the aluminium magnate who had regular business meetings and a house in London.

What he did not know was that private detectives had been keeping tabs on him for weeks. They were employed by Michael (originally Mikhail) Cherney – the controversial founding father of the post-Soviet-era aluminium industry and a former business partner of Deripaska. A few days before, Cherney had filed a High Court claim against his former protégé but needed the document to be served before the case could proceed. The detectives' task was to check when Deripaska was in London and to alert Cherney's aides immediately.

That evening they struck lucky when they discovered that their quarry had landed at Luton. He was then flown to Battersea heliport in his Sikorsky helicopter and from there was driven by a Mercedes Maybach to his grand town house on Belgrave Square. After tracking him, the detective called the process server – hired to hand over the documents – who raced over by motorbike to Belgravia to await Deripaska's arrival.

He was just in time. When the armoured limousine pulled up at 10.40 that evening, the server made his move. He failed to reach Deripaska, who disappeared quickly into the house, and so he approached one of the security guards, explaining that he had an important document to be delivered to him personally. The guard agreed to pass on the A4 envelope. Without any idea of the potential legal implications of what he was doing, the guard duly passed the envelope containing the writ to Deripaska and told him it was from a 'courier'.

The connection between the two men went back to the early 1990s, when Cherney dominated the aluminium industry, largely through his contacts in the Kremlin. Deripaska was

Cherney's protégé and rose rapidly, in less than a decade, to overtake his mentor as the most powerful force in the industry.

Introverted and obsessive, Deripaska leads a relatively ascetic and frugal lifestyle. A workaholic, he works fourteen- to sixteen-hour days and even failed to attend President Yeltsin's funeral in 2007 because he was 'too busy'. He spends most of his time on his private jet travelling the world, often whiling away the hours with his favourite pastime – reading physics books. In business he is tough, smart, ruthless, and calculating. But in his private life he is quiet, abstemious, and very low key. His one cultural interest is ballet. 'He is motivated by power and deals and making his business as big and powerful as possible,' a former aide said.

Like his former business ally Abramovich, Deripaska likes his toys – private jets and yachts. He has also invested in a Moscow nightclub, but there his taste for luxury goods and trophy assets ends. Despite rumours of an interest in West Bromwich Albion, he has not to date bought a football club. Although he has been seen at Chelsea matches, that is because of his friendship with Abramovich rather than because of any particular enthusiasm for the game. Uncomfortable with the media and suspicious of people in general, he is a man of few words, as *Toronto Globe & Mail* journalist Eric Reguly found when he interviewed him in December 2007:

Mr Deripaska arrives casually dressed – it is Saturday – and pecks away at his food. He is slim and fairly tall with close-cropped hair. He gives little away about himself or his companies. His answers are usually short. 'Why?' or 'Why not?' are often the responses to questions. His English is good but his voice is soft and he sometimes places his hand over his mouth. He has a friendly smile … Deripaska does not smoke or drink, a rarity among Russian men. He stays fit by swimming.[7]

Despite being married, Deripaska has been one of the billionaires most ruthlessly targeted by female gold-diggers. In early 2008, for example, a group of 18-year-old Russian models claimed that he was the oligarch they would most like to meet. His wife Polina is twelve years younger than him and, despite her husband's aversion to publicity, something of a socialite. An Anglophile who insists on a British nanny for their two children, she was often seen at fashion and art events and was best friends with Abramovich's girlfriend, Daria Zhukova. The two planned to create a new social networking site. Although more colourful than her husband, she is not an extrovert. *Vedomosti* called her a 'fragile, modest young woman with a quiet voice'. Her husband invested in some media companies and she became head of the publishing house Forward Media Group, which publishes the Russian *Hello!*, as well as an owner of the gossip website www.Spletnik.ru.

Deripaska and his family have lived most of the time in a vast top-floor apartment in the most expensive area of Moscow, Ostozhenka, known as the 'Golden Mile'. In true oligarch-style he built an extra floor on top of the building despite opposition from local residents. He spent hundreds of thousands of pounds redecorating the apartment. He also bought an enormous dacha in the southern region of Khakassia, Siberia, based near a private skiing resort and a golf course designed by Jack Nicklaus.

In London Deripaska could not resist a Grade I-listed eleven-bedroom Regency house on Belgrave Square, a property he bought through a British Virgin Islands company in April 2003 for £17 million. Built in the 1820s and formerly the home of Sir Henry 'Chips' Channon, society host, Conservative MP, and notoriously indiscreet diarist who died in 1958, it was designed for entertaining royalty and diplomats with its grand staircase, reception rooms, Madame Recamier sofas, and flamboyant décor. By the light of a thousand candles, Channon's wife, Lady

Honor Guinness, treated the house like a theatre and became one of the great society hostesses of the 1930s and 1940s. When Harold Nicolson arrived at the house, he declared. 'Oh my God! How rich and powerful Lord Channon has become.' To maintain its grandeur and to forge his own links to the English political family tradition, Deripaska employed Graham Bonham-Carter, a cousin of the actress Helena Bonham-Carter, as the household manager.

In the Home Counties Deripaska bought a house on Surrey's St George's Hill, also overseen by the discreet Bonham-Carter. He paid £7.1 million for the property in September 2001, using a Cyprus-registered company, and installed a gymnasium and swimming pool. Not to be outdone in the oligarch property stakes, across the Channel, he bought three houses in France, as well as properties in Sardinia, New Delhi, Beijing, and Kiev.

Deripaska's other major luxury asset was his super-yacht *Queen K*. Built by Lürssen, by 2008, it was the forty-eighth-largest yacht in the world. Designed for long crossings, it had a range of approximately 5,000 miles at a constant speed of 12 knots.

By contrast, Michael Cherney, the man who issued the writ against Deripaska, has little time for the attendant luxuries of being an oligarch. He does not own a private jet, and his favourite pastime is watching boxing and his favourite Bulgarian football team on television. Born in 1952 in Ukraine, he grew up in Uzbekistan. He enjoyed significant influence and extensive contacts in the Russian government from the early 1990s. But he left the USSR with his family, finally settling in a suburb of Tel Aviv in 1994. A year later he was the target of an assassination attempt on Israeli soil.

Cherney started to trade in metals in 1989 and within a few years had stakes in raw materials, metallurgy, engineering, and seaports. Many of his businesses were registered in Liechtenstein, Switzerland, and Cyprus. In 1992 he and his brother turned to aluminium, creating the Trans-World Group (TWG) owned by Cherney, his brother Lev, and the Indian-born, British-based brothers David and Simon Reuben. TWG became the world's third largest producer of aluminium. The company's scope was so vast – from the Siberian steppe to the shores of Cyprus – that it became known as 'a state within a state'. Much of its business was with Russia, supplying aluminium ore from their refineries elsewhere to four smelters in Russia, building huge profits in the process. By the mid-1990s, Cherney, something of an instinctive entrepreneur, was a billionaire.

By Cherney's own admission, he is an unconventional businessman. As he spent so much time outside Russia, he delegated daily management to his partners, among them Deripaska. He did not retain or receive much in the way of routine documentation, preferring instead to close deals for enormous amounts with a handshake or primitive 'trust' agreements, a commonplace of business life in Russia.

Cherney first met Deripaska in 1993 at a metals conference at London's Dorchester Hotel. Deripaska was only twenty-five at the time but impressed the Uzbek oligarch with his technical knowledge and diligence. Like Berezovsky and Abramovich, their partnership was initially something of a father and son/mentor and student relationship. By late 1993, Cherney had already acquired a substantial stake in the Sayanogorsky aluminium smelter, partly through buying vouchers from the plant's workers. In 1994 he appointed Deripaska as his manager.

Deripaska took every advantage of his boss's frequent absences and steadily began to acquire his own stake in the plant. By the end of 1994, TWG, Cherney, and Deripaska had between them taken control of the whole plant. By then Deripaska had become Director General and swiftly set about boosting production. He had run-ins with the plant's communist-era bosses and learnt an early lesson about Russian business that remains true to this day: the state is stronger than the market. 'I was expecting they would treat me as a share-holder,' he recalled. 'But they said, "No, you have the shares, but we run our business. And it's separate."'[8]

Deripaska has rarely spoken about the violent gangster capitalism that dominated the industry in those days but he later admitted to the *Financial Times*, 'It was anarchy.'[9]

During one occasion, in a major assault on the Sayanogorsky facility, his commercial director was seriously wounded.[10] As the *New York Times* put it, Deripaska 'somehow survived the bloodbath that accompanied the privatization of the industry'.[11]

By 1999, after years of brutal rivalry and enforced takeovers and buyouts, the industry was dominated by a quintet of players owning two giant companies. Among those forced to sell up in the ongoing commercial battles were TWG, the Reuben brothers, and Lev Cherney. Two of the remaining players were Michael Cherney and Deripaska, who had competing claims to Siberian Aluminium (Sibal), which now owned the Sayanogorsky plant. The other three involved were Roman Abramovich, Boris Berezovsky, and Badri Patarkatsishvili.

Once again it was London – not New York or Moscow – that would become the arena for the next stage in the ongoing dissection of the multi-billion-pound industry. In March 2000 four of the gang of five – Deripaska, Patarkatsishvili, Abramovich, and Berezovsky – met at the Dorchester Hotel, according to Berezovsky's account. Despite an air of distrust, the four agreed to merge Sibal and Sibneft to form a single company: Russian Aluminium (Rusal).

In March 2001 Cherney and Deripaska met at the Lanesborough Hotel in probably the most critical meeting in the history of Russian aluminium. They had come to discuss the future of Sibal. After a brief exchange in the Library Bar, they retreated to the Presidential Suite. There Cherney claims he agreed to sell his share of the company to Deripaska for $250 million upfront, plus a 20 per cent share in Rusal.

Two years later, in 2003, Deripaska bought a large quantity of shares from Roman Abramovich, for $1.5 billion. At only thirty-two, Deripaska had squeezed out all the other players to become the dominant shareholder of Rusal and a premier league oligarch.

It was these events that formed the backdrop to the dramatic legal claim made by Cherney in November 2006: that Deripaska had swindled him out of billions of dollars a claim that Deripaska vehemently denies. In the ensuing legal wrangles, the two men have presented opposing accounts of their roles in the 'aluminium wars'. Despite having opportunities to settle out of court for a relatively small amount, Deripaska regarded the claim as 'a smear against his achievement', according to one aide. Cherney portrayed Deripaska as his precocious protégé, first making him a manager and then giving him a stake in the smelter, and insisted that without his help his young manager would not have risen to the top. Deripaska accepted that, by 1994, TWG and Cherney owned much of the Sayanogorsky plant between them, but he denied that his mentor had financed the purchase of his own shares. He claimed that he was already wealthy enough to invest in the plant himself.[12]

In a further show of defiance, Deripaska claimed that he operated independently but alongside Trans-World because of their dominance in the industry. 'This person [Cherney] had no relation to my business,' he told the *Financial Times* in 2007. But he acknowledged that cooperating with Trans-World was 'the only way to trade' because 'they controlled all the raw material supplies at the time'. According to Deripaska, 'These people [Cherney] pretended they were connected and helped build the business. But they were in Israel, London. What can you do from there?'[13]

The two men also bitterly dispute the nature of the deal at the Lanesborough Hotel in 2001. Cherney claims that although he was paid the upfront fee, Deripaska reneged on the 20 per cent agreement. Deripaska robustly denies any liability. He maintained that from 2001 he was Sibal's sole owner and that he owes Cherney nothing. He accepts that he signed an agreement to pay $250 million but denied that he promised to hold 20 per cent of Rusal shares in trust for Cherney. 'He was never a [business] partner in any normally accepted commercial meaning of the word,' Deripaska stated.[14] Deripaska goes much further: he alleges that, far from being business partners from the mid-1990s, his former associate had been running a protection racket and the $250 million was paid to 'buy Mr Cherney off'.[15] Cherney has always vehemently denied this allegation and pointed to a ruling from a court in Switzerland in January 2008 that found he had no connection with organized crime.[16]

After emerging as the dominant owner of Rusal, Deripaska went on to prosper. With rising international commodity prices and cheap electricity, he steadily expanded his empire. By 2008, his holding company, Basic Element, had 350,000 employees with interests in car and aircraft production, insurance, timber, and construction, as well as aluminium – and also had investments from Asia to Latin America. In the summer of 2008 he even showed an interest in acquiring Hummer, the struggling American automotive brand owned by General Motors.

But Deripaska's momentous rise to the top had been dogged by controversy over his business methods. In 2002 he was alleged to have bulldozed through a hostile takeover bid for a large timber company called Ilim Pulp, then part-owned by Dmitri Medvedev. If he had known that one of those he was crossing swords with would, six years later, become President of Russia, he might have been more wary. Deripaska always maintained that he had acquired the company legitimately. Critics argued that he only obtained the mill by – according to the *New York Times* – plucking 'away legal control of the mill in an elaborate legal maneuver – a takeover tactic he had perfected in the last three years of piecing together a vast business empire'.[17]

The much-publicized dispute between Deripaska and Ilim – racked by complex legal wrangles and accompanied by constant police raids – went on for two years, with grave consequences for investment in the industry. The Russian government eventually intervened and the two sides agreed a settlement.

Deripaska acquired many enemies en route to his billionaire status and from 2002 his aluminium empire was on the receiving end of a barrage of lawsuits. As Rusal was a private company almost entirely owned by Deripaska, he was often directly in the firing line. The legal bullets were fired by a succession of former partners, subsidiaries, and suppliers for breach of contract – their claims were mostly related to the turf wars of the 1990s.

One issue at stake was who owned Rusal – an amalgam of disparate assets from smelters to refineries and mines. As a private company with limited disclosure requirements, Deripaska combined their constituent parts in a complex and secretive web. This made it difficult to unravel much of the company's true ownership. As the profits rolled in, some former partners and rivals alleged that they owned some of Rusal's assets, while other former smelter bosses claimed that Deripaska had persuaded them into selling their stakes. In several cases Deripaska settled out of court, handing over millions of dollars to former partners, although never with any admission of liability.

The most far-reaching, long-running, and bitter dispute has been with Michael Cherney. Cherney's case against Deripaska finally reached the High Court in spring 2007 – five months after the delivery of the writ to Belgrave Square.[18] The first issue on the agenda was whether Deripaska was 'domiciled in England'. This was critical because if he was not UK-domiciled then the case could be moved in Moscow – to Deripaska's huge advantage, it being his home territory.

To establish Deripaska's London connections, the High Court provided rare official insight into his movements and lifestyle. It found that in 2005 Deripaska spent twenty-seven nights in his Belgrave Square house. In 2006 he spent nineteen nights there, while his longest continuous stay was six nights. Although his wife and children spent a few more nights a year there – thirty-three in 2006 – the couple only lived there together for seven nights in 2006. In contrast, he spent 179 nights in Moscow and eighteen nights elsewhere in Russia, where he has a number of properties.[19]

In the event, the judge ruled that Deripaska was not domiciled in Britain: 'In many ways its [Belgrave Square] use by Mr Deripaska resembles that of a private hotel. It is infrequent, intermittent, and generally fleeting. The house has the character of continuity and permanence; its use does not.'[20] It was a key victory for Deripaska, because it made the chances of the case coming to court in England seem slim.

Cherney pressed on with his efforts to have the case heard in England. In July 2008 he got his reward – when Mr Justice Christopher Clarke announced, 'I am persuaded that the risks inherent in trial in Russia – assassination, arrest on trumped-up charges, and lack of a fair trial – are sufficient to make England the forum in which the case can most suitably be tried.'[21] Indeed, in sifting through the evidence, the judge found that Cherney had already been the victim of at least one assassination attempt – in Israel in 1995. These assassins, concluded the judge, were 'possibly connected to the Russian secret services'.[22]

The court's judgment was not merely an indictment of the legal system in Russia, it also gave Deripaska a new problem to think about. It meant that he now faced the prospect of being cross-examined under oath in a public court by some of the

UK's best forensic lawyers who would not hesitate to rake over the nitty-gritty of his disputed past business relationship with Cherney.

Referring to the size of the claim, potentially worth some $4.35 billion, the judge commented, 'The payment of such a claim, if valid, would be beyond the reach of most individuals. But Mr Deripaska was, on his account, the beneficial owner of the majority of the shares of Rusal, together with many other commercial interests. The Rusal group employs some 100,000 people. Mr Deripaska's other companies employ over 250,000. He is said to be the richest man in Russia and ninth on the list of world billionaires.'[23]

If the $4.35 billion is eventually awarded to Cherney, it will be the highest award of damages ever granted in a British court. Deripaska, of course, has filed his own appeal against Mr Justice Clarke's decision and strongly disputes Cherney's case. It will now be well into 2010, or beyond, before this titanic legal battle is resolved.

Despite the succession of legal setbacks, Deripaska's global ambitions showed no sign of waning. In 2006, aged only thirty-eight, he began discussions to invest in Magna International, a Canadian auto parts company that then had designs on the giant US car manufacturer Chrysler. A stake in Magna would allow Deripaska's Russian auto business to start making Western-designed car parts.

Negotiations were proceeding smoothly but then hit a major obstacle: Deripaska was not granted entry to the United States. In November 2003 he had been due to speak at the Harvard University-Dow Jones US-Russian Investment Symposium, but a few weeks before the event, his name was mysteriously removed from the list of speakers. The reason for this was simple: Deripaska had been refused a visa to enter the United States. The US State Department has not disclosed the official reason for the ban.

The ban was a major impediment to his US commercial ambitions and so in 2003 Deripaska turned to two of Britain's best-connected bankers – Lord Jacob Rothschild and his only son Nat – for advice on how to lift it. They had met when the oligarch was visiting the London School of Economics periodically to learn English.

Deripaska, born in 1968 and raised without a father, often turned to mentors throughout his career. During his formative years, it was Cherney and then Arkady Sarkisyan, who later became a Russian Senator. From 2003, Nat Rothschild fulfilled the role. Deripaska became extremely close to the young Rothschild who, three years younger and equally driven and ambitious, was something of a kindred spirit.

The importance of Rothschild to Deripaska cannot be exaggerated and the two met regularly at an imposing house in Cleveland Row, St James's. Situated next to St James's Palace, the house is owned by the Rothschilds but was, in effect, Deripaska's London office. 'He [Nat] was consulted on everything,' a former Deripaska aide related. 'The joke in the office was that he asked Nat about the colour of the new toilet paper.' They met while both were serving on the board of a Brazilian company. Deripaska invited Nat Rothschild to join the advisory board of Rusal and consulted him on most of his deals, notably oil exploration in the Black Sea and investments in Ukraine and Kazakhstan.

It was the Rothschild name and the attendant connections invoked by that dynasty that mesmerized Deripaska. Unsure of himself in the City of London, Nat Rothschild's contacts with the banks were invaluable. A measure of Rothschild's importance was that he held shares in a Deripaska-controlled company in the UK called London and Russia Holdings plc, now dormant. 'He trusted Rothschild,' another former aide said. 'Trust was a very important issue for Deripaska. He did not trust many of his staff and he gave them meaningless job descriptions while he micro-managed the company.'

But Rothschild also needed Deripaska's contacts if his hedge fund, Atticus, was to exploit opportunities in the emerging markets of the former Soviet republics. Their fortunes had been inextricably linked, with the Rothschild heir making millions in fees and commissions from links with Deripaska.

But Nat Rothschild also played another significant role. In October 2004 he introduced Deripaska to Peter Mandelson, shortly after he had been appointed the European Trade Commissioner but just before he formally took up the post. They had dinner together at the Café Pushkin in Moscow, along with German Gref, the Russian Trade Minister. The former Cabinet Minister and confidant of Tony Blair had always been open to the blandishments of the wealthy and he struck up a rapport with Russia's richest man.

Trips to Moscow were a regular feature of Mandelson's schedule because the European Union was Russia's largest trading partner. He would occasionally have dinner with Deripaska, according to Benjamin Wegg-Prosser, former special adviser to Mandelson. During one evening, there was a 'fierce disagreement, to the point of raised voices, that both men had on two issues,' said Wegg-Prosser:

> First was Russia's entry to the World Trade Organization. Peter [Mandelson] wanted them to join, Deripaska didn't. Second, the tariffs which the Russians were imposing on Finnish timber imports. Peter said they were illegal, protectionist, and wrong. Deripaska argued that they were a necessary defence mechanism to protect a key national industry in an emerging economy. Their friendship was founded on these sorts of jousts and arguments.[24]

Three months after their first encounter the trio met again: Rothschild flew into Davos in his Gulfstream during the World Economic Forum, collected Mandelson, and off they went to

Moscow to meet Deripaska. The occasion was a private dinner at the Cantinetta Antinori restaurant hosted by Rusal, which was selling two aluminium plants to Alcoa, the US giant. The dinner, also attended by Alcoa boss Alain Benda, was taking place at a crucial time for the industry: companies claimed that tariff rates for exporting aluminium into the European Union were too high. While between 2005 and 2008 Mandelson reduced the tariff rates, the former Trade Commissioner has always denied he had either been asked for any favours by Deripaska, or had offered any, or that his decision to lower the rates had anything whatsoever to do with his relationship with the oligarch or Rothschild.* He has also stated that he 'never had a discussion with Deripaska, or anyone else from his company, about aluminium duties or any other matter relating to the EU.'

Mandelson often mixed business and politics with pleasure. In early August 2006 the European Trade Commissioner was again present at a Rusal-sponsored reception, this time a party held at the Royal Opera House, Covent Garden, to watch a performance of *Swan Lake* by the Bolshoi Ballet. There Mandelson once again met Deripaska but looked somewhat out of place among the aluminium traders, bankers, and industry analysts. 'He did not quite know what to do with himself,' said one fellow guest.

In his youth Nat Rothschild was renowned for his drinking and heavy partying. At Eton he is remembered for being scruffy, rebellious, and resentful of authority. A member of the

---

* Mandelson wrote to *The Times* on 25 October 2008, 'The Director-General for Trade in the European Commission, David O'Sullivan, confirmed ... that I made no personal intervention to support the commercial interests of Mr Deripaska. Mr O'Sullivan explained ... that in respect to both the nine-year debate in the EU over tariffs on raw aluminium and to anti-dumping duties on Russian aluminium, the decisions were made 'after the usual consultation procedures had taken place, including with industry and all 27 European member states, and were based on sound facts.'

notorious Bullingdon drinking club at Oxford University, he was an aimless playboy. In 1996, aged twenty-five, Nat Rothschild eloped to Las Vegas to marry the model and socialite Annabelle Neilson, whom he had met on a beach in Bali. The couple divorced after a turbulent two-year marriage.

When his marriage broke up, the heir to the fifth Lord Rothschild cut back on the partying, become teetotal, and left his reputation for self-destruction in the past. After working for the investment bank Lazards, he moved to New York and joined the fledgling hedge fund Atticus Capital. Helped – in part – by the Rothschild family connections, it grew, at its peak, to managing assets worth an estimated $20 billion. A near billionaire himself, Nat Rothschild commutes between his homes in London, Paris, New York, Corfu, and Moscow, although his main residence is in Klosters, Switzerland.

In the world of Nat Rothschild, connections have been priceless. In Deripaska he saw a vehicle to vast fees and contracts, and in Mandelson, the political conduit to the highly regulated markets of the European Union. The former European Trade Commissioner has known Nat and his father Jacob Rothschild since the early 1990s and has stayed at their villa in St Barthélemy, the idyllic Caribbean Island popularly known as St Barts.

'He [Mandelson] likes to use other people's planes and yachts,' said one source who knows Mandelson and Rothschild. 'He thinks that for a person of his calibre and experience, he is badly paid. He likes to spend time with people who have considerably more money than him … Peter has seniority and status, while Nat has money. Peter likes the comfort of flying on a private jet, staying on a nice yacht, and having the odd glass of champagne.'[25]

One Rothschild villa frequented by Mandelson was a ten-bedroom property in Corfu. Known as 'Chateau Rothschild', it is set on a rugged headland in the north-east of the island. A blue and gold flag flying from the battlements is decorated with a clenched fist with five arrows symbolizing the five sons of Mayer Rothschild who founded the banking empire. The family uses a military-style, gunmetal grey speedboat to transport guests at a speed of 50 knots from the airport to their villa.

It was to this exclusive setting that Deripaska sailed his yacht, the *Queen K*, in the last week of August 2008. It was to prove a fateful weekend. As it happened, Mandelson was in Corfu to celebrate the fortieth birthday of Elizabeth Murdoch, Nat Rothschild was at his villa, and Conservative MP, George Osborne, the Shadow Chancellor, and his wife Frances, were renting a nearby villa while on holiday.

On the afternoon of Friday 22 August, Mandelson and Osborne were invited onto Deripaska's yacht for drinks and that evening the three attended a dinner party at Chateau Rothschild. The Shadow Chancellor, the European Trade Commissioner, and the Russian oligarch all sat at the same table. They discussed Russian and British history and politics and Osborne appeared to be impressed by Deripaska.

The following evening Mandelson, Osborne, and Rothschild attended a special dinner at the Taverna Agni, a low-key restaurant in the quiet bay of Agni with spectacular views of the Albanian mountains. The occasion was to celebrate Elizabeth Murdoch's birthday. For the next two hours, over a mezé dinner with red wine, Mandelson and Osborne were locked in conversation. Later, reports emerged that during this dinner Mandelson had 'dripped pure poison' about Gordon Brown into the ear of Osborne, who was then fingered as the source for these damaging allegations (Mandelson insisted 'there was no poison being dripped').

By the following day, Sunday 24 August, the Osbornes had moved into Chateau Rothschild. The Shadow Chancellor had known Nat Rothschild since they were contemporaries at Colet Court preparatory school and then Oxford, where they were both members of the Bullingdon Club. Given the unpopularity of the Labour government at the time, Rothschild perhaps saw his old friend as a potential ally. That evening the investment banker invited Osborne, the Conservative fundraiser Andrew Feldman, and James Goodwin, a former adviser to President Clinton, for drinks. Then, according to Rothschild, Osborne invited Feldman to accompany him on Deripaska's yacht to solicit a donation to the Conservative Party. Later that evening Deripaska hosted Osborne, Feldman, and Goodwin on his yacht, where they talked and drank tea for an hour. In a letter to *The Times* on 19 October 2008, Rothschild wrote:

> George Osborne, who accepted my hospitality, found the opportunity of meeting with Deripaska so good that he invited the Conservatives' fundraiser Andrew Feldman, who was staying nearby, to accompany him onto Deripaska's boat to solicit a donation. Since Deripaska is not a British citizen, it was suggested by Feldman, in a subsequent conversation at which Deripaska was not present, that the donation was "channelled" through one of Deripaska's British companies (Leyland DAF). Deripaska declined to make any donation.

The Shadow Chancellor and Feldman vehemently deny that they solicited or were involved in the solicitation of what would, in effect, have been an illegal foreign donation. 'There was a discussion about British and Russian politics, education, and history', Osborne said. 'There was no mention or conversation of party funding or the possibility of Deripaska making a donation to the Conservative Party.'

This episode became a *cause célèbre* when, on 5 October 2008, Osborne decided to leak to the *Sunday Times* Mandelson's alleged derogatory comments about the Prime Minister. 'He [Mandelson] poured out pure poison about Brown,' said the Shadow Chancellor. 'It was not like a passing thing. He had really thought it through.' The timing of Osborne's leak was very deliberate. Just two days earlier Mandelson was restored to the cabinet by Brown as Business Secretary.

When Mandelson read the article he flew into a boiling rage. The accusation, he said, was a 'totally baseless piece of fiction made up by the Tory Party propaganda unit'. Soon afterwards a stark, dark message reached David Cameron's private office: tell your Shadow Chancellor to 'back off' because the new Business Secretary had something 'explosive on him'. Despite the warning, information about Mandelson's trip to Corfu continued to leak. When Nat Rothschild emailed his letter to *The Times*, the dam broke.

While it appeared that Rothschild had been defending one old friend, Peter Mandelson, against another old friend, George Osborne, he was in fact protecting his new friend and business associate Deripaska. As their respective fortunes had become so intrinsically linked, it was important to preserve – as far as possible – the oligarch's reputation. In 2008 this was still a major problem: he was still banned from visiting the United States.

Despite the power and prestige of the Rothschild name, attempts to remove the visa ban to the US proved frustrating, expensive, and, by the end of 2008, still unsuccessful. Deripaska spent millions on investigators, lawyers, and lobbyists but all to no avail. The key group he hired was Global Options Group Inc, a Washington, DC-based private security and intelligence-gathering company. Since 2000, they have investigated many of Deripaska's business rivals and provided litigation support. Global Options had, in turn, hired Alston and Bird – the Washington, DC law firm whose special counsel was former presidential candidate and Senate majority leader Bob Dole – specifically to lobby the US government on the visa issue. New documents obtained by the authors shed light on Dole's lobbying services for Deripaska. One invoice, dated 15 April 2004, was sent by Alston and Bird to Deripaska himself in Moscow for £45,000. The invoice was submitted for 'legal services in connection with … Immigration' while 'Robert Dole' was the designated lawyer. In 2008 Dole himself was still actively lobbying on the oligarch's behalf.

Global Options coordinated the whole visa ban operation, hiring personnel and arranging meetings with US State Department and Justice officials. A parallel operation by Deripaska involved hiring Rick Davis, the senior campaign manager for Senator John McCain, the Republican presidential candidate in 2008.[26] McCain and Deripaska have met many times. In January 2006, for example, they met for drinks, accompanied by their aides, and then at a buffet dinner at the World Economic Forum in Davos (where Deripaska owns a chalet). Later that year, in August, they met at a social gathering in Montenegro, where Deripaska owns a house and has extensive business interests, while McCain was undertaking an official Senate trip. And they both attended a social function at Spencer House in London, organized by Lord Rothschild and his son Nat to raise funds for McCain's presidential campaign.

Such high-level lobbying resulted in a long-running dispute between the White House, the State Department, and law enforcement agencies.[27] A respite came in mid-2005 when Deripaska was granted a multiple-entry visa, which would allow him to make regular trips to conduct business; this, however, was to enable US officials to interview the tycoon about his business dealings. Deripaska has always staunchly defended his reputation as a businessman and attributes criticism to false propaganda spread by business competitors in the US and Britain.

Then, in mid-2006, the visa ban was reinstated. This continued to have a damaging impact on Deripaska's commercial ambitions in the United States, notably his negotiations with Magna International. Magna reassured its shareholders that the delay was 'pending the resolution of certain unspecified questions that had arisen within the government'. Irritated and frustrated by the ban, Deripaska pinned the blame on what he called 'stupid and ignorant bureaucrats'. Until John McCain failed in his bid to win the 2008 presidential election, he seemed to be pinning his hopes on the Republican making it to the White House. 'Maybe I'll get the visa when the next [US] administration comes in,' he said, only half joking.[28]

In comparison with the much tougher entry requirements in the United States, most Russian businessmen with controversial pasts have sailed through the British immigration system with barely a whimper from the authorities. This is partly because the government has calculated that their wealth would help fuel a London-based and wider economic boom. As a result, it has mostly turned a blind eye to allegations concerning the tainted origins and source of their wealth.

The contrast with procedure in the United States is striking. Although the US took the lead in encouraging Yeltsin to implement a laissez-faire capitalist economy, they have been much more reticent about letting fleeing plutocrats settle in the US. Many Russian settlers in the United States, such as Alex Goldfarb and the former KGB General Oleg Kalugin, are high-profile defectors who were granted asylum during the Cold War years. From the late 1990s, the United States developed much stricter visa rules than the UK, especially when it came to Russian dissidents and businessmen.

This was partly due to the crackdown on money laundering and corporate abuse that followed 9/11, and the Enron scandal, which was revealed in late 2001. In addition, to avoid escalating tension with the Russian government, the Americans have not wanted to be accused of harbouring Russia's enemies. There was also concern about the intention of some Russian industrialists to enhance their economic and political clout in the West.

When Jim Pettit, the Consular General at the US Embassy in Moscow, was asked in 2007 whether there was a 'blacklist' of Russian businessmen, politicians, and other citizens trying to enter the US, he replied, 'I cannot address individual cases but it is true that we check all visa applications against a database of individuals who might be ineligible for entry to the US under our immigration laws.'[29] That can be taken as a yes.

Boris Berezovsky may not have found it so easy to gain asylum status in the US. When Litvinenko fled Russia via Turkey, he was advised not to try Italy, France, or Germany and first attempted to seek asylum in the United States by approaching the US Embassy in Ankara. He was interviewed at length by the CIA regarding his work for the KGB and FSB and was only then denied asylum, forcing him to turn to the UK instead.[30] And Deripaska is far from being the only Russian businessman to fall foul of these tougher rules. Because of his alleged involvement in the infamous 'aluminium wars' of the 1990s, Michael Cherney has also been banned at various times not just from entering the United States but also France, Austria, and the United Kingdom.

Despite being an Israeli citizen and living in Tel Aviv, Cherney regarded London as his future refuge. Even while he was barred from visiting the UK, his family lived in London and his children attended British schools. In early 2004, when he was fifty-two, the ban on his entry into the UK was suddenly lifted and he regularly began flying to London with British Airways. That spring he bought a vast luxury apartment in The Bromptons, the new deluxe, hi-tech, high-security complex in South Kensington, for £8.1 million for his wife, Anna – a Russian orthodox Christian – and his two daughters. And he purchased a much smaller flat in Knightsbridge for his chauffeur and cook.

Clearly, Cherney regarded London as a safe investment in which to park his wealth. In May 2004 he acquired two large apartments in The Knightsbridge, the contemporary apartment complex overlooking Hyde Park, for a total of £17 million. Later that summer he paid out another £11 million for Draycott House, a former hotel just off Sloane Square. The plan was to convert the property into luxury apartments but the development has been beset by legal disputes with consultants and contractors. And then, in 2006, Cherney invested a further £10.5 million for two grand flats on Arlington Street in St James's, just around the corner from the Ritz Hotel. All the properties were bought through offshore companies.

In November 2008 Cherney was asked by *Spear's Wealth Management Survey* whether Russia was closer to 'Capitalism or KGBtalism?' 'What the West ought to understand is that the choice that our country once faced has long been made', he replied. 'My former associates have all made it. My nomadic life has been a blessing in disguise – it has saved me from having to make it. Had I remained in Russia, I know I would have chosen wrong. These days, money is deadlier than polonium.'

This has not made Cherney – by now a fledgling member of the Londongrad community – back away from his billion-pound feud with Deripaska. Both are Teflon oligarchs – not much sticks to them and they both have thick skins. Very little appears to faze either of them. 'I don't need to defend myself,' Deripaska told the *Financial Times* in July 2007. 'I am not ashamed and I don't need to hide.'[31]

In August 2007 Deripaska appeared at a press conference in Toronto to talk about his proposed $1.54 billion investment in Magna, looking relaxed and informally dressed. Some Magna shareholders were less than enthusiastic about a buyout by someone with a controversial business reputation like Deripaska's.[32] Despite shareholder reservations, the deal was concluded in September 2007. Such is the financial muscle offered by the oligarchs and the promise of access to Russian markets.

Western unease did little to stop Deripaska's ambitions. In 2007 Rusal merged with its main Russian rivals, Viktor Vekselberg's Sual and the Swiss commodities trader Glencore, to form United Company Rusal, registered in the tax haven of Jersey. This turned it into the world's largest producer of aluminium, holding 12.5 per cent of the global market. Deripaska held a 66 per cent stake in the new company, Vekselberg 22 per cent, and Glencore 12 per cent.

A short while later Deripaska announced his intention to float a quarter of the newly merged UC Rusal – then potentially worth $30 billion – on the London Stock Exchange. If the flotation proceeded, Rusal would have entered the FTSE100, making it the first Russian blue-chip corporation.

For some years the London Stock Exchange had been playing host to Russian flotations. In 2006 Russian firms raised £5.8 billion in new capital, a substantial rise on earlier years. By early 2007, eleven Russian companies – some private, some state-owned – had listed, mostly partially. New York, in contrast, has raised very little from such IPOs.

The motives for floating Russian companies abroad were mixed. From the moment of Putin's strike against Yukos, many nervous Russian entrepreneurs started transferring their assets into hard cash – partly by floating shares – thereby reducing their vulnerability to the political whims of the Kremlin. 'It is their exit strategy,' said Pavel Teplukhin, the head of Russia's Troika Dialog Asset Management. 'By listing their shares in London, these companies are buying themselves political insurance.'[33] While some companies have issued new shares in order to reinvest in their business at home, others have offered only existing equity in flotations. This has brought money to the owners, which has almost certainly leaked out of Russia. 'It is like taking chips off the table,' said one investment banker.

The way in which the City has courted controversial oligarch clients has been a highly contentious subject in the UK. As Bill

Browder, once one of the West's biggest investors in Russia, warned, 'There are lots of corporate governance skeletons in the cupboard of all the Russian companies listed in London.'[34] In 2006, despite investing more in Russia through his £4 billion Hermitage Fund than any other fund manager, Browder had his own visa to Russia withdrawn during a trip to Moscow. He had long attacked Russia's murky corporate governance and accused state companies such as the energy giant Gazprom of 'asset stripping' and fraud. Although Tony Blair took up his case with the Russian authorities, the ban remains.

The most controversial flotation was Rosneft. The state-owned oil company raised £5.6 billion in London in July 2006 after the High Court overruled an attempt by Yukos to claim that Rosneft's public listing would amount to the 'laundering' of illegally acquired assets. Nevertheless, the Rosneft prospectus contained one of the longest sections ever devoted to 'risk factors', with extensive details of lawsuits the company was facing from Yukos and its former shareholders.

Billionaire international investor and philanthropist George Soros claimed that the Rosneft float raised 'serious ethical and energy security issues' and should not have been permitted by British regulators.[35] His criticisms were widely echoed. The Co-operative Insurance Society described those investing in such companies as 'speculators not savers'.[36] The *Independent* described the investment banks and accountancy firms that pocketed some £70 million in fees between them as having 'City snouts in the trough'.[37] While New York tightened the rules for Russian companies seeking to list their shares, London financial markets became what one critic described as a 'colossal boot sale for the crony capitalists of the Kremlin'.[38]

Deripaska's IPO plans for UC Rusal were dogged by both the ongoing issue of the visa ban to North America and the convoluted nature of the ownership of UC Rusal's assets. But these were sideshows compared with other obstacles described by one commentator as the 'hidden depth charges' lurking beneath Deripaska's plans.[39] The first was the unresolved dispute with Cherney and the continuing risk that Deripaska might face a $4.35 billion bill.

The second hurdle was the shadow of Putin. While the Russian Prime Minister broadly approved of Russian companies issuing shares in London and the respectability and kudos it brought to the Russian state, the question remained: was the flotation a pure business deal, or one that came with hidden political strings attached? In particular, was there a risk of a sovereign takeover similar to the state seizure of Yukos?

The shadow of the Kremlin was given added depth by the remarkable image of oligarchs such as Deripaska and Abramovich discussing such deals directly with Putin on television. The concern about the hidden hand of the state was given credence by Deripaska himself when, in July 2007, he said that he saw himself as little more than the custodian of state assets. 'If the state says we need to give it up, we'll give it up,' he said. 'I don't separate myself from the state. I have no other interests.'[40]

This was an astonishingly candid statement to make about the umbilical nature of his relationship with the state in the build-up to such a significant float, and his banking advisers were furious at such uncharacteristic indiscretion. Deripaska later claimed that he had been misquoted and was simply expressing his commitment to Russia as a patriotic businessman. But it is unlikely that someone as savvy as Deripaska would not have spoken as he intended. His remarks reinforced the views of those warning of the risk that Russian companies might suddenly be snatched back by the state. By the end of 2007, the Russian government had launched a number of 'stealth takeovers', notably that of VSMPO-Avisma, one of the world's leading titanium producers, and of AvtoVaz, the maker of Lada cars. On the other hand many Russian companies have bought foreign assets with no negative consequences.

Deripaska, like Abramovich, has managed to stay on the right side of Putin, enjoys more independence than other oligarchs, and has been asked to represent Russia abroad. Putin, who is very selective about membership of his inner circle, once visited the oligarch's Swiss-style ski retreat in southern Siberia. Being a Kremlin favourite is in part due to the protection afforded by his high-profile marriage into the Yeltsin family and spending his money on patriotic causes such as the restoration of Russian churches.

It has been a mutually beneficial relationship. Deripaska has offered Putin – who has long called for the creation of 'national champions' to project Russia's economic power – a way of expanding Russia's economic muscle westwards. In return, he has been given much greater freedom and flexibility than other oligarchs.

Without Putin's blessing, Deripaska's empire-building would have been curtailed. Before the Sual–Rusal merger was given the go-ahead, Deripaska was questioned in depth by Putin in August 2006. The President made it clear that the merger was dependent on the new Rusal remaining a Russian company and paying taxes to Russia, even if it was registered in Jersey.

Nevertheless, by the spring of 2008 Deripaska's hopes of a London float seemed to be dead in the water, sunk in the wake of uncertainty over the future of Rusal and the High Court's decision to allow the Cherney v Deripaska case to proceed in London. Instead, he decided to turn to Hong Kong to launch his IPO. There would be fewer 'legal' difficulties there than in London, he said. By the summer of 2008, a new cloud was appearing on the horizon – the unfolding economic fallout from the credit crunch. Among those swept up in the gathering global storm were the oligarchs.

CHAPTER 12

Paint the Town Red

'The bell has started to ring. If someone isn't able to buy a Bentley, or if some government bureaucrat has to sell his Gulfstream jet for $50 million of his hardworking money ... that's a good thing'

— ALEXANDER LEBEDEV, *November 2008*[1]

IN JUNE 2007 *Tatler*, the 300-year-old in-house journal for Britain's upper classes, published a splenetic attack on the arrival of the new foreign super-rich in London. 'The rise of London as the financial capital of the world has brought a huge influx of clever, competitive foreigners who want our schools and houses,' ran the article. 'They are over-here, over-paid, and making many people feel displaced and distressed, particularly hard-working middle-class professionals, many of whom can no longer afford to pay school fees or buy nice houses in the places they were brought up in and which they consider home. They have become exiles in their own country.'[2]

The critique of the way untold foreign wealth was 'squeezing out the Brits' was written by the magazine's well-connected and long-serving editor, Geordie Greig. He mixed freely in London's super-rich circles and used his extensive contacts book to ease the entry of several Russian émigrés into British high society, among them Alexander Lebedev, the former KGB spy turned banker.

Despite these connections, the Russians did not escape criticism. 'Take the Russian oligarch who recently wanted a new yacht and went to see one being made. "I like it and I wannit," he said. He was told it would take two years. "You don't understand – I like it and I wannit," he continued. The yacht broker blustered that the original owner had spent £95 million and was taking charge of it the following week. "Offer him £145 million," said the Russian. And so the original owner walked away with a £50 million profit.'

The article also expressed an apparently growing concern among parents about access to the best schools: 'Private schools are becoming notoriously difficult to get into … The fight for places for one's children has turned ugly and the sense of desperation is palpable'. And on London's best homes: 'In one street in W8, 80 per cent of properties were owned by non-Brits who were not paying full taxes.'

An elegant siren warning also came from Peter York, the co-author of *The Official Sloane Ranger Handbook*, first published in the 1980s: 'All these Sloane grannies are defenestrated. They are being forced out of their former territories and they are starting to resent it. Local elites are supplanted by a global elite.'[3] Equally outraged cries of anguish came from newspapers not normally associated with hostility to affluent tycoons. In April 2007 London's *Evening Standard* carried a front-page article under the headline, 'Blair's Real Legacy Is a Tax Bolt Hole for the World's Fat Cats.'[4] The following month, 'Why I Deplore the Billionaires who Contribute so Little to Britain' was the headline in the *Daily Mail*.[5]

What the astute editors had sensed was a developing bitterness at the heart of middle- and upper-class Britain. At dinner parties they had picked up a roll call of complaints, from the difficulties facing their adult children in joining the housing market to the way the tax system appeared to be rigged in favour of wealthy foreign nationals. Access to independent schools was also raising temperatures. Growing foreign competition, it was claimed, was contributing to school fees that rose by more than twice the rate of inflation between 2002 and 2007.

Similar views echoed around London's oligarch belts. In November 2005 Councillor Daniel Moylan, deputy leader of Kensington & Chelsea Council, claimed that local families were being priced out by fabulously wealthy invaders. He called for new rules to give preference to locals in what was already a packed borough: 'Families in Kensington & Chelsea are leaving because they can't afford to stay here. New property is being snapped up by people looking to make a quick buck or a fat investment, which is helping to drive prices up to levels which locals cannot afford. It does not help if flats go to foreign investors buying pieds-à-terre for their wives to go on shopping trips to Knightsbridge.'[6]

But the arrival of the Russian super-rich has been welcomed by some members of the political and business establishment. The former mayor of London, Ken Livingstone, went out of his way to applaud the Russian influx. At one time the former radical left-wing leader of the GLC might have had qualms about the questionable way Russian wealth had been used to help fuel the London boom, but now Livingstone expressed no such reservations. In 2006 he addressed 1,200 Russian government and business guests at the annual Russian Economic Forum held in the Queen Elizabeth Hall opposite the Palace of Westminster. The Mayor talked of the 'warmth and sympathy' Britons felt for an old ally against Hitler and was full of praise for the wave of business moneyed Russians were bringing to the capital. 'I would like Russian companies to regard London as their natural base in Europe,' he declared. The Mayor's Office at City Hall even established a small department devoted to attracting Russian investment into London.

Support for Russian investors was shared in Whitehall and the City and among the myriad retailers, luxury goods boutiques, and 'bag-carriers' whose livelihoods were transformed by the untaxed rouble invasion. Many British-born multi-millionaires owed their own march up the rich lists to the arrival of foreign, and especially Russian, money. Among those cashing in were the upmarket property agents and developers. While the multi-millionaire Candy brothers were the most high-profile winners, in 2007 top executives at London's elite property agents were rewarded with City-style million-pound bonuses after making record profits. As one of the new property search agents that sprang to life during the early twenty-first century observed, 'If foreign money dried up, so would we.'

Then there was the legal profession. Russians love litigation. One oligarch once shouted across the table during a tense business meeting, 'What you need to know about me is that I love litigation more than I like sex!' Not only was Bruce Buck, the American head of the European arm of the law firm Skadden, Arps, Slate, Meagher & Flom, handling Abramovich's growing list of legal challenges, he was also chairman of Chelsea FC. During her divorce negotiations, Irina Abramovich hired Raymond Tooth, the aptly named divorce lawyer, and inevitably nicknamed 'Jaws'. Tooth had famously represented Karen Parlour, wife of former Arsenal footballer Ray Parlour, and was responsible for acquiring for his client a substantial chunk of her husband's future earnings after the divorce. As soon as Alisher Usmanov, the Uzbekistan-born billionaire, invested in Arsenal, he hired one of London's most aggressive libel law firms, Schillings, to warn media outlets against 'any defamatory statements or invasions of his privacy'.

Russian oligarchs loved their trophy assets and so another winner was the private aviation industry. The number of private flights into and out of the UK doubled in the decade up to the end of 2007, twice the rate of increase of ordinary passenger travel. Private airports serving the private jet set, such as Northolt and Farnborough, expanded more quickly than Gatwick and Heathrow. Niki Rokni, marketing director of the British charter private jet company Ocean Sky, revealed that the company grew from a staff of four and one plane on launch in December 2003 to 126 staff managing twenty aircraft by mid-2008. 'Sixty per cent of our clients are Russians and we fly them all over the world in luxury private planes,' she said. 'These are a mix – most live in Russia itself but a significant number also live in London. Our charter clients are mainly entrepreneurs and businessmen, the new millionaires who are not rich enough to buy their own jet. They have created a massive boom in private air travel.'

Premiair became one of the largest private client helicopter operators in the UK. Based in Camberley, Surrey, it grew at 10 per cent a year post-millennium. According to one of its directors, David Langton, 'The Russians are significant players in the helicopter market in the UK. When the Russians buy a country home, for example, they look to the helicopter as their main form of transport. It's ideal for moving them from their country retreat to get to country sporting activities such as shooting parties or the yacht.'

At the height of the economic boom in the summer of 2007 the demand from foreign cash was creating lucrative 'grey markets' in areas such as private jets and specialist cars. With order books for private jets full for years to come, buyers were paying premiums of up to £5 million to jump the queue for the top-of-the-range £22 million Gulfstream G550 (Deripaska's jet). With a similar wait of three years for the Aston Martin AMV8, places on the waiting list were changing hands for tens of thousands of pounds.

Other winners included the Mayfair and Kensington art auction houses. Prices for contemporary art quadrupled in the decade up to 2007. The Russian interest in older mansions also rubbed off on the antique furniture trade. English country furniture, porcelain, silver, and books were especially popular. According to Mark Poltimore, UK Chairman of Sotheby's, Russians turned up 'at a 2006 sale of contents at Shrubland Park in Suffolk, a 40-bedroom stately home that used to belong to the de Saumarez family. Although the guide price was £2–3 million, the auction made £4–5 million, mainly due to Russian buying power. If the Russians turn up you can add a nought to the price of things.'[7]

Former prominent industrialists and politicians found themselves in great demand as non-executive directors of Russian companies. In 2005 the banker Gagik Zakaryan bumped into the former Chancellor of the Exchequer Lord Lamont at a party at Cliveden House. The two hit it off so well that the Russian entrepreneur immediately invited him on to the board of his bank, Unistream. To the bank, about to seek a listing on the London Stock Exchange, hiring a former Chancellor brought extra clout and respectability. Along with Lord Owen – who was chairman of Yukos International until Khodorkovsky's arrest in late 2003 – other peers recruited to Russian firms included Lord Robertson of Port Ellen, the former Defence Secretary and Head of NATO, Lord Powell, former adviser to Mrs Thatcher, and Lord Hurd, former Foreign Secretary.

On their arrival in London wealthy Russians soon signed up with new concierge agencies such as Quintessentially. Catering for every whim of the rich – from renovating their new multi-million-pound homes to obtaining tickets for sold-out sporting and cultural events – this 'lifestyle management' company has a £24,000 membership fee and a long waiting list. A lucrative business that offered 'dream-fulfilment', they kept reservations at all London's top restaurants, and, for a price, guaranteed a ticket for any opening night, the Wimbledon finals, and the most exclusive parties.

In 2008 an extraordinary 50 per cent of their elite membership was foreign – a mixture of Russian, Middle Eastern, and
Asian clients. When they started in 2000, Quintessentially had
eight staff. By 2008, they employed ninety-six at their London
headquarters and thirty-four offices across the world, including
Moscow. Their Russian clients were never shy of making
unusual requests. The wife of one wanted to buy the new £700
Roland Mouret 'Galaxy' dress, but it had sold out across
London. So Quintessentially found one for her in the right
colour and size in a department store in Canada. The client's
personal manager had it flown over to London in three days,
just in time for the party. On another occasion a Russian asked
the company to book nineteen rooms in a hotel in Mauritius
that only had five available. The hotel agreed – for a fee – to
displace fourteen existing reservations to another part of the
island.

Always concerned about personal safety, the Russians
brought boom times to the private security industry. One of the
capital's biggest security operators, Crown Protection Services,
provided private guard-dog patrols for forty streets in Kensington alone. Russians also started to hire London-based private
business investigators to provide litigation support and probe
other oligarchs and commercial competitors. 'Traditionally our
industry has been used by Western companies wanting information on Russian business people and companies,' said Patrick
Grayson, head of GPW Ltd, based in Mayfair, whose business
has grown rapidly in recent years. 'More recently, this has been
turned on its head with a significant increase in demand from
Russians wanting to check out British companies and businessmen for potential opportunities.'[8]

The oligarchs also breathed new life into one of Britain's
oldest craft-based industries – yacht building. Following his
design for the refit of Abramovich's *Pelorus*, Terence Disdale
was inundated with inquiries and even had to turn down new

clients. According to Jonathan Beckett, Managing Director of Burgess, the British yacht-chartering company, the Russians 'took the yachting business by storm. Between 10 and 20 per cent of our customers are Russian.' He reported in early 2008 that the Russians might not be the dominant players in the world market but 'they are the biggest spenders. They want the best design and the best materials. In the charter market too they are chartering the biggest and best for the longest. We are chartering more boats to the Americans but the Russians charter a boat that costs $100,000 a day while the Americans hire one costing $40,000 a day.'

Ten years ago there were 200 boats afloat of over 40 metres in length. At the end of 2007 there were over 260 of this size in construction and 600 afloat, greatly increasing the demand for berths across the world. 'Ten to fifteen years ago we were selling berths in the South of France for between $1.5 and three million for a twenty-five-year lease,' said Beckett. 'Now they cost $10 million; that's just for a stretch of concrete to tie your boat to.'

In the late 1970s London looked more like a bombsite than one of the world's leading capital cities. Thirty years later its restaurants, shops – its entire atmosphere – had been transformed, partly though not wholly because of super-charged foreign spending power. In 2005 *Newsweek* said London was 'leaving other European cities behind'. Two years later New Yorker Audrey Saunders, owner of the celebrated Pegu Club in downtown Manhattan, told the *New York Times*, 'I hate to admit it, but London is the best cocktail city in the world.'[9] And *Spear's Wealth Management Survey* concluded: 'If Paris was the capital of the nineteenth century and New York of the twentieth, London is shaping up to be the capital of the twenty-first.'[10]

By bringing new wealth, the giant geyser of foreign cash helped to promote new industries and boost profits, making

London a great club for those who could afford its membership fee. New jobs were created in retail, the City, and restaurants. Chauffeurs, bodyguards, and gardeners were in great demand. There were more butlers in London than in Victorian times.[11] Abramovich kept twenty-eight staff at Fyning Hill alone, and even though he only stayed there relatively infrequently, Oleg Deripaska's mansion in Belgrave Square was fully staffed all year round.

Most Britons could not afford to shop at the new luxury stores, dine at celebrity-chef restaurants, or buy penthouse suites overlooking Hyde Park. Much of the financial gain has been gobbled up in soaring salaries, dividends, and bonuses by those already at the top of the earnings and wealth ladders. Much of the spin-off work from the boom has gone not to British residents but to non-British workers – from highly paid American and European professionals in the City to low-paid employees in restaurants.

Some Britons also became worse off as a result of the arrival of foreign wealth. This extended well beyond the ranks of the upper middle class forced to pay premium prices for nannies, being shunted out of their child's preferred private school, and no longer able to afford the Mayfair town house.

Among the casualties were those trying to join the housing ladder. While the runaway house prices of the mid-decade were not just down to exploding foreign demand, the price boom would have been weaker without the multi-billion-pound overseas cash injection. Experts claimed that soaring prices in London's hotspots led to a ripple effect across and outside London, contributing to the squeezing out of thousands of first-time buyers. According to Professor Chris Hamnett of King's College London, the extra cash descending on the prime locations eventually drove up prices at the bottom. 'What you're getting is geographically displaced demand which ripples out all the way down.'[12] As one agent operating in Berkshire explained, 'We were London-driven. As soon as Kensington and Chelsea started to twitch, we felt it within three months.'

The extraordinary price boom also fuelled a wave of ultimately unsustainable property speculation. Buyers bought desirable properties at the top end of the market, kept them empty while waiting for markets to rise, and then sold them on for huge profits. This was all free of capital gains tax and stamp duty for non-domiciled residents, provided they were bought through an offshore company, the favourite means of purchase. Property agents invented a new term – 'buy-to-sit' – to describe the process. In one of many examples, in March 2006, an apartment in Hertford Street, Mayfair, just round the corner from Park Lane's Hilton Hotel, sold for £6 million. Eight months later, it was back on the market with Beauchamp Estates for £14 million.

Experts also claimed that the influx of foreign wealth was turning London into a more divided city, a place where only the affluent could live comfortably.[13] In a survey published in July 2007 four out of ten Londoners thought that the capital had become 'just a city for the rich'.[14] In Kensington and Chelsea new arrivals created what one active local resident called the 'fortress flat' effect. Most of the large new luxury developments in prime central London – from 199 The Knightsbridge to One Hyde Park – were fortified, gated communities with full security and twenty-four-hour concierge services.

Certain areas of wealthy London were turned into near ghost towns. For example, only a minority of apartments in the new luxury wharfs and marinas colonizing the Thames between Wandsworth and Chelsea bridges were occupied at any one time. Some of London's proudest squares barely had a light burning in the evenings. Many of the grand mansions in The Bishops Avenue, the street first dubbed 'Millionaires' Row' in the 1930s, were often deserted.

For many of the foreign invaders, their luxury properties were not just a second, but a third, fourth, or even fifth home. At 20 per cent the Royal Borough of Kensington & Chelsea – the true oligarch belt – had the second highest number of second homes in the country, many of them left unoccupied for months, sometimes years, at a time.

The Russians were also a significant part of a new worldwide phenomenon – the emergence of the nomadic super-rich. Many of them flitted between Moscow, London, and Switzerland, while shifting their money around at will. Unlike previous generations of the wealthy, they mostly had little or no loyalty to the places they chose to park their money. London won the intensified international competition to bag the rising volumes of footloose capital, in the process making Britain's economy increasingly dependent on financial services. This turned the capital into what *Prospect* magazine called 'a hyper-capitalist, deregulated, very unequal, financial services-driven, mass-immigration-driven city state'.[15] This may have helped to create the conditions for the post-millennium boom, but it also made the economy much more vulnerable to the whims of global wealth, contributing to the debt-driven speculative bubble that finally burst in the autumn of 2007.

By then, Britain had come to resemble what Ajay Kapur, head of global strategy at Citigroup in New York, called a 'plutonomy' – a society in which wealth and economic decision-making was heavily concentrated in the hands of a tiny minority while growth was powered by and largely consumed by an affluent elite.[16] The only other countries that conformed to this pattern were the United States and Russia itself. This was what Britain was in Victorian times, before the development of full democratic institutions and the emergence of a powerful middle class.

The tidal wave of Russian money into London helped inject new life into the luxury goods industries, fuelled a domestic wealth boom, and contributed, along with other foreign money, to the creation of Britain's plutonomy. But it also helped to distort the local and national property market, opened up new wealth gaps, and made the economy dangerously dependent on the vagaries of huge swathes of fugitive wealth.

Eventually, the government was forced to respond to the growing public unease about the tax advantages enjoyed by super-rich foreigners. When, in April 2008, the Chancellor, Alistair Darling, introduced a single annual payment of £30,000 on non-domiciles, there was a flurry of warnings from the City that it would frighten away foreign money and expertise. Yet a levy at this level – small change for billionaires and multi-millionaires – was unlikely to encourage the super-rich to pack their bags. There were too many advantages to living in Britain. By the beginning of 2010, despite the recession, there was little sign of the exodus predicted in some quarters. Those who had bought to invest appeared to be holding on.

In fact, far from selling up, some of the oligarchs showed every sign of strengthening their Londongrad roots. Abramovich's children continued to be educated in west London and in July 2008 they began taking lessons at riding stables, accompanied not merely by instructors but by bodyguards on bicycles. In the same month Abramovich was finally granted his request to stand down as governor of Chukotka. In September Kensington & Chelsea Council gave the go-ahead for the multi-million-pound makeover of the two adjacent four-storey town houses he owned in Lowndes Square. The 2005 transfer of the registered ownership of all his UK properties from offshore companies in obscure locations to his own name was also a sign of his intention of securing a more permanent base in the UK.

In May 2008 Oleg Deripaska cemented his links with the UK by buying two racehorses and enlisting the help of one of Britain's most prominent bloodstock agents, James Wigan.

Deripaska already owned a number of racehorses in stables closer to home, near the Black Sea. He had met Wigan, an Old Etonian employed by Lord Rothschild, through his friendship with Nat Rothschild.

Boris Berezovsky showed no sign of moving on from his bitter campaign against his country of birth. He continued to play the role of the slighted James Bond villain Ernst Stavro Blofeld from his fortified Mayfair offices. But, despite devoting the lion's share of his fortune to this defiant campaign, he was still no nearer to his dream of unseating Putin and his chosen successor, Medvedev.

Meanwhile, Russian prosecutors were continuing to investigate Yukos. Eighteen months earlier Mikhail Khodorkovsky and Platon Lebedev had been served with new charges accusing them of yet more money laundering and embezzlement, between 1998 and 2003, amounting to $25 billion. In the same year the assets of Khodorkovsky's foundation were frozen by the Russian authorities, a move that was heavily criticized by its beneficiaries in the US.

In July 2008 Khodorkovsky, still languishing in jail, applied for parole. If his lawyers hoped that the new President would be more flexible than his predecessor, they had misjudged Medvedev. 'Prisoner Khodorkovsky does not deserve the conditional early release,' said Judge Igor Falileyev at a court hearing in the Siberian city of Chita. According to the court, this was because of the former Yukos owner's refusal to take part in professional training and in sewing and for another alleged misdemeanour. Khodorkovsky was set to spend many more years in his Siberian cell.

Nevertheless, the wider spending boom that had raged during the middle of the first decade of the new millennium could not last forever. The first signs of the impact of the impending financial crisis came in the dying days of summer 2007, when the continuing surge in house prices nationwide first shuddered, came to a halt, and then went into reverse. There was one significant exception to this trend – the prime London market.

Even as the credit crunch began to take its toll on the domestic demand for housing, foreign wealth continued to come into the country. At least until the autumn of 2008, house prices at the top end of the market carried on 'defying the laws of gravity', as one agent put it. In the months straddling the Russian presidential election in March 2008, leading property agents reported a new surge of interest from Russians uncertain about the future of the country after Putin. At least for a while Russian and former Soviet citizens kept pouring money in, especially at the very top.

In February 2008, while average house prices were heading downwards, Viktor Pinchuk, a Ukrainian businessman, bought a ten-bedroom house in Upper Phillimore Gardens, Kensington, for £80 million, at the time making it the most expensive property sold in the UK. In May that year Alisher Usmanov spent £48 million buying Beechwood, a Regency-style estate set in 11 acres of woods and parkland in Hampstead, previously owned by the Emir of Qatar.

In July 2008 Yelena Baturina, Russia's richest woman, splashed out £50 million on Witanhurst in Highgate, the largest private house in London after Buckingham Palace. A ninety-room Grade II-listed Queen Anne mansion – with spectacular views over Hampstead Heath, it was once owned by leading members of the Assad family from Syria. With 40,000 square feet across three floors and twenty-five bedrooms, there was ample space for Baturina's extensive art and shoe collection. The mayor of Moscow's wife, who had accumulated a £1.3 billion fortune based on construction contracts, also bought a home in Holland Park.

For a while some Russians already well rooted in London even contemplated building larger property empires. Before the credit crunch started to seriously bite in the late summer of 2008, the residential division at Knight Frank received a number of inquiries from Russian clients wanting to do just that. 'For a while, some Russians were inquiring about buying a number of apartments, possibly several in a single block, for investment', according to an agent then working on the Russian desk at Knight Frank. 'This was a small group, still cash-rich, who had already put down roots in London; they felt comfortable here, their children had finished their education, and this was a natural next step for them. The arrival of the credit crunch put a stop to such ambitions.'

Meanwhile, there was new intrigue within the Londongrad community. In June 2008 the FBI launched an investigation into the disappearance and possible murder of London-based media tycoon Leonid Rozhetskin. The Russian-born multi-millionaire was a renowned socialite and was deeply embroiled in the cut-throat world of Moscow business. An American citizen, he made his fortune in Russia, and became a founding investor of the London business newspaper *City AM* and an outspoken critic of Putin. He vanished from his holiday home in Latvia on 16 March 2008, leaving behind a pool of blood. To this day no body has been found. One theory circulating among Kremlinologists was that he was murdered over a business dispute with a senior figure in Putin's administration. Others speculated that he was about to make public details of fortunes acquired by top Kremlin officials.

The mystery deepened further when, in October, his wife, the model Natalya Belova, and their three-year-old son also vanished. The pair was being protected by five bodyguards at their £3 million apartment in Mayfair. The unsolved disappearances had all the hallmarks of the way the sinister side of Russian big business had been exported overseas.

Meanwhile, despite the high-profile death of Alexander Litvinenko and the diplomatic chill still affecting relationships with the Kremlin, Downing Street continued to sanction an open-door policy to Russian exiles. Some of the steady, if slowing, stream of business émigrés and political dissidents joined the Berezovsky cabal.

One of the new arrivals was Elena Tregubova, a thirty-three-year-old journalist who had been sacked from the influential *Kommersant* newspaper, once one of the last media outlets regularly critical of Putin. She wrote a bestselling and unflattering portrait of the Kremlin, *Tales of a Kremlin Dagger*, which contained accounts of alleged embarrassing indiscretions by Putin. These included the claim that he once made a pass at the willowy six-foot blonde at a New Year's Eve gathering. Tregubova allegedly suffered an attempt on her life in 2004 and Berezovsky offered to provide her with security in Russia. After a smear campaign against her, she arrived in Britain in 2007 and went into hiding at an anonymous address. When Berezovsky, who supported her relocation, was interviewed by Russian investigators looking into the Litvinenko murder, he was asked repeatedly for her address. He refused to disclose it. Tregubova was eventually granted asylum in April 2008.

A few months earlier, in December 2007, 32-year-old Andrei Sidelnikov fled to Britain after slipping out of Russia via Belarus and Ukraine. He headed a small opposition movement, Pora (It Is Time), which advocated an Orange Revolution-style insurrection to overthrow the government and claimed that the Russian security forces tried to stop him leaving the country. He also met Litvinenko, two days before he was poisoned, in a café near Oxford Street, where they discussed the murder of Anna Politkovskaya. In something of a diplomatic slap in the face to the Kremlin, the Home Office granted him political asylum in June 2008, just before Gordon Brown held one-to-one talks with the new Russian President Dmitri Medvedev at the G8 summit in Japan.

Even those oligarchs who towed the Putin line were not necessarily secure. Mikhail Gutseriyev was a largely compliant billionaire. Then suddenly, on 31 July 2007, he slipped past the usually watchful eye of the authorities, took a flight to Minsk, the capital of Belarus, and then on to Antalya in Turkey. From there he flew to London and joined the queue of those requesting asylum at the Home Office.

By 2007, the 47-year-old owner of Russneft – with two oil refineries and a chain of 300 petrol stations – had risen to become Russia's thirty-first richest citizen. Then he was ordered to hand Russneft over to the authorities in exchange for 'compensation'. In an echo of the Soviet era he was told to show willingness by 'thanking the party and government'. Originally from Caucasia and known for his forthright and hot-headed manner, he refused to comply. He soon learnt that it did not pay to say no to the Kremlin.

It is likely that the authorities turned against Gutseriyev because he angered Kremlin insiders by attempting to purchase some remaining Yukos assets that had been earmarked for another recipient. Some saw it as part of the renewed struggle for control of assets being waged between different factions inside the Kremlin, powerful groups that had been steadily and covertly enriching themselves during the Putin era.

In early 2007 Gutseriyev's company offices were raided and senior staff were pulled in for questioning. Gutseriyev was then charged with 'illegal business activity' while Russneft was saddled with a tax bill for $800 million. In May he was released on bail. In a remarkable act of defiance Gutseriyev then published a damning letter in Russneft's newsletter accusing the Russian authorities of using the tax demand as a pretext to grab his oil assets. 'They made me an offer to leave the oil business, to leave on "good terms",' he wrote. 'I refused. Then, to make me more amenable, they tightened the screws on the company with unprecedented persecution.' The letter was the first serious public challenge to Putin from a prominent businessman since Khodorkovsky. Although Gutseriyev had never meddled directly in Kremlin politics, and had never challenged Putin, there were striking parallels with the actions of the two men. Russian newspapers soon dubbed him the 'second Mikhail' and predicted that Russneft would suffer the same fate as Yukos – dismantled, sold off, and absorbed into an existing state-run firm. A few days later Gutseriyev fled and the security services embarked on yet another international manhunt of a super-rich fugitive.

Within months of Gutseriyev's arrival in the UK, he entered the *Sunday Times Rich List* at number thirty with a fortune estimated at £2 billion. His membership of the swelling London-grad community hostile to their homeland added to the increased tension in the already embittered British-Russian relationship. 'Why do you allow the territory of GB to be used as a launching pad to fight Russia?' Vladimir Putin, by now Prime Minister, asked British journalists in September 2008. 'That's why it is not possible to build normal relations with Britain.' A St Petersburg taxi driver put it more robustly when he told a British tourist, 'You Brits have turned London into a brothel full of tarts like Berezovsky and Abramovich, so who do you think you are lecturing to?'

Back in Russia, Putin passed the presidential baton to his successor, Dmitri Medvedev, up to that point perceived as one of the more pliable of the contenders for succession. The oligarchs were only too aware of the transient nature of political favour in Russia. Those who had stayed onside within Russia not only had to woo the 43-year-old Medvedev and former Chairman of the all-powerful Gazprom, they also had to continue to keep a close eye on his predecessor. Few doubted that Putin was the man really in control.

Meanwhile, the economic storm clouds kept on gathering. In early October 2008 the global economy came close to meltdown. In the United States the giant investment bank Lehman Brothers went bankrupt, while AIG, one of the world's biggest insurance companies, had to be bailed out by the state. Recession started to sweep through one leading economy after another. Among those caught in the financial crosswinds were the oligarchs.

Earlier in April, the Russian business magazine *Finans* reported that the number of Russian dollar billionaires had soared to 101, double the 2007 figure. Russia then sat in second place in the world's billionaire league table – well behind the US with 415 but ahead of Germany with sixty. Oleg Deripaska topped the list with $40 billion, while Abramovich was in second place with $23 billion.

Six months later it was a different story. In September *Forbes* estimated that ten oligarchs had lost one-third of their wealth. A few weeks on, in October, the financial news service Bloomberg reported that Russia's richest twenty-five men had lost $230 billion (£146 billion) between them as world stock markets and commodity prices plunged. While such figures were at best rough estimates, and changeable by the day, one by one the super-rich Russians found their paper fortunes shrinking as the global slowdown saw plummeting oil, steel, gas, and aluminium prices. Between May and October, the Russian stock market lost a remarkable 71 per cent of its value from an all-time peak. On a number of occasions it was forced to close for business for several days at a time.

Many of the billionaires continued to hold large stakes in Russia's mining, petroleum, and industrial behemoths. Some had invested heavily in hedge funds, some of which, after years of staggering returns, were now close to collapse. Many had borrowed heavily from Western banks to expand their empires. It was high-wire financing with no safety net. According to Bloomberg, on paper Abramovich – who owned 40 per cent of Evraz, the leading Russian steel producer – lost millions as Evraz's share price fell over 80 per cent. Alisher Usmanov was also said to have lost heavily. In mid-October the Russian

Central Bank reported that collectively Russian companies were being asked to repay $47.5 billion to jittery foreign creditors by the end of 2008 and a further $160 billion by the end of 2009.

One of the biggest losers was Oleg Deripaska, caught in a lethal whirlwind of collapsing commodity prices, falling share values, and over-reaching ambition. To finance his international corporate spending spree, he had borrowed heavily from Western banks, using his assets as collateral. Now the beleaguered banks – under pressure to rebuild their badly depleted balance sheets – wanted their money back. In mid-October 2008 he sold his 9.9 per cent stake in Hochtief, the German infrastructure company, losing substantially as a result. He handed over to the creditors who financed the deal his $1.5 billion stake in Magna, the Canadian auto parts company he had acquired little over a year earlier. He also suffered a large loss with the fall in value of Norilsk Nickel, the giant mining group, in which he acquired a 25 per cent stake in April 2008.

Most of the oligarchs claimed Bloomberg's figures were based on exaggerated paper losses. Abramovich, through his indomitable press spokesman John Mann, dismissed the figures. But although his fortune was seriously depleted, by the end of 2008 his international property empire remained intact, along with his art, his jets, and his yachts. Alisher Usmanov denied speculation that he would be forced to sell his stake in Arsenal, despite its falling value, and compared his love for the club to that of 'a man for a woman'.[17]

At the end of October 2008 the Kremlin handed out cash to Russian businessmen struggling to repay loans to foreign lenders. During the years of feasting and soaring oil and metal prices, the state had built a substantial 'rainy day fund' and was now putting it to use to help the country's giant but struggling companies. There was much speculation that the state bail-outs would come with new strings attached, bringing even tighter control over the oligarch's empires or a new round of renationalization of strategic industries once dubbed the 'national champions' by Putin.

But not all the oligarchs were wringing their hands in despair. Despite, on paper, losing close to one-third of his $3 billion fortune, Alexander Lebedev, who owned 30 per cent of Aeroflot, seemed unperturbed. Long critical of the excesses of his fellow billionaires, he told *The Times*, 'The bell has started to ring. If someone isn't able to buy a Bentley, or if some government bureaucrat has to sell his Gulfstream jet for $50 million of his hardworking money … that's a good thing.'[18]

Three months later, in January 2006, Lebedev announced that, after a year of tough negotiations with Lord Rothermere, the owner of the London *Evening Standard*, he had bought three-quarters of the loss-making newspaper. In a remarkable cut-price bail-out, Lebedev paid a nominal sum for the 150-year-old paper. Football clubs, mansions, and rare art collections had already fallen into Russian hands, but this was in many ways a more significant moment in the story of Londongrad. A British newspaper had not merely been taken over by a Russian – an event that would have elicited a splenetic reaction from the British media and political establishment even a few years earlier – but by a former KGB spy to boot. A week after buying the paper, Lebedev announced that his close confidant Geordie Greig, editor of *Tatler* since 1999, had been appointed its new editor. He took over from Veronica Wadley, who left to pursue new interests in journalism.

During the years of super-charged spending by the new Russians – the billionaires and the multi-millionaires alike – Moscow became known as the 'new Rome', such was its reputation for excess and hedonism. For a while the shining new shopping temples and millionaire fairs, financed by oil cash and besieged by the world's luxury brands, from Louis Vuitton and Prada to Ferrari and Maserati, glittered with indulgence like a Gulf state. By the end of 2008, a more sombre mood had descended over Moscow's small army of luxury and bling (or *pafos* in Russian) retailers and the once-buoyant private jet and Rolls-Royce dealerships. There were fewer takers, too, for those former status symbols of the explosive consumer age, from diamond-studded mobile phones to designer dresses made of dollar bills. Moscow's top restaurants reportedly stopped accepting credit cards, and, in a sure sign of the times, elite nightclubs such as The Most – where the lavatory fittings are made of gold – were forced to relax their formerly tight entry rules.

Not that the partying came to a complete halt. On 15 October 2008 *Spear's Wealth Management Survey* launched a Russian edition of the exclusive magazine for the super-rich at Zolotoi, one of Moscow's top restaurants. The packed event was attended by plenty of Russia's business elite, and even by a sprinkling of oligarchs. The Russians, it appeared, were avid readers of such publications. In September the Russian edition of *Tatler* was launched at a star-studded party, while a few weeks later there appeared yet another magazine, the upmarket *Snob*, the brainchild of playboy oligarch Mikhail Prokhorov.

In London luxury goods retailers were also facing up to the falling spending power of their best customers. Once Hermès had had no difficulty selling £13,000 alligator-skin bags and £395 Mors de Filet cufflinks in London's designer malls, but in November 2008 the Paris-based fashion company, known for its resilience in tough economic times, was just one brand leader to report slowing sales. Among those issuing profit warnings were Bulgari, the jewellery and leather goods maker, and Theo Fennell, jeweller to celebrities and oligarch wives. In a sure sign of the new mood, in early December 2008, four Russian art auctions at Christie's and Sotheby's missed the dealers' own low overall estimates.

At the height of the consumer boom customers would pay huge premiums to jump the queue for a Gulfstream jet or a

Bugatti Veyron. By the winter of 2008, prices had already gone into reverse. One specialist car dealer reported that a Rolls-Royce Phantom Drophead convertible that could fetch a premium of £100,000 (and sell for a total of £400,000) at the end of 2007 was selling at £274,000 a year later. It was the same story with Bentleys, Lamborghinis, and Aston Martins. On Bloomberg's internal portal, on which the business community posts items for sale, almost-new Bentleys were being offered well below their retail prices.

Asset prices – which had soared to record levels – also started to plummet. Following years of almost continuous growth, the Live-ex index of the world's most sought after fine wines turned down – sharply. Bingeing on Château Petrus could be done at more affordable prices than a year earlier. In both London and New York the once-booming art market began to contract – for the first time since 1990. Roman Abramovich, it would appear, had got his timing badly wrong: choosing the peak of the market to decide to become a serious art collector.

For a while top-end, multi-million-pound homes seemed to buck the wider trend of tumbling values. Through the first half of 2008 house prices above £5 million in prime central London locations stayed firm, and only started showing signs of falling from the late summer. Even then properties at the higher 'super-prime' end of the market – those above £10 million – continued to change hands. According to Liam Bailey, head of research at Knight Frank, 'The super-prime sector maintained its strong run for the first half of 2008 but then peaked by late summer. Despite this, prices were still up 12 per cent over a year earlier.'

By October, it was a different story. One property agent specializing in the top end of the market said 'the Russians are in hiding'. Another commented that there was still some Russian cash around. Some were looking for bargains in London, while others were turning their sights elsewhere – New York, Italy, or the South of France. A spokesman for Savills in

Surrey said the speculative element had gone, but he still had several new Russian clients wanting to put down roots and looking for the right property at the right price. The frenzy of the past, the 'we can afford it, we must have it' attitude had been replaced with a new caution. Russian money had become more circumspect and savvy. None of this would have dented morale at London's top property agents. In December Knight Frank announced that bonuses to its fifty-six partners would average £780,000 for the year ending April 2008, only a little down on the £1.1 million paid the previous year.

Despite the retrenchment, London continued to play host to the world's super-rich. Airports catering for private jet owners continued to report thriving business. There was no lack of demand from global wealth for places at Britain's top schools. Even for Russians facing hard times, the last thing they would do is remove their children from British public schools.

In November, with the recession biting deeply in the retail trade, one French menswear shop, Zilli in New Bond Street, had its best month since it opened in 1983, all courtesy of well-heeled Russians. According to the store's spokesman, Arnaud Corbin, 60–65 per cent of their customers were from Russia or Kazakhstan. He counted several oligarchs among the shop's regular clients. 'Despite the credit crunch, the Russians are still buying. Our customers are a mix of London-based Russians and businessmen travelling through London on the way to the US or the continent,' he said in December. 'Only a few weeks ago a Russian came in and bought a crocodile casual jacket with a fur collar for £65,000. It was his first visit and he was only in the store for twenty minutes. Without the Russians, we would be in serious crisis.'

The concierge company Quintessentially agreed that the Russians remained important clients, although they were throwing less money around. 'Gone are the days of flash spending; it's not seen as right to be seen to spend huge sums in an ostentatious way, but people are still spending, just in a more subtle way. It's getting the tone right. There's still lots of requests for gorgeous parties, but you won't arrive to a champagne fountain any more.'

The fountains may have gone but the champagne was still flowing at some venues. On 24 November 2008 Partridge Fine Arts of New Bond Street hosted a special event to launch a collection of some sixty pieces of jewellery designed by a Russian husband and wife team based in New York. Partridge sells vintage jewellery from leading designers such as Cartier, and Russians, known for their love of high-end signature jewellery, have been their main clients.

The new items – selling at between £5,000 and £250,000 under the brand name ARK – were being modelled by Princess Michael of Kent, President of the gallery. Of the 150 British and international guests at the launch, about one-quarter were Russian, a mix of British- and Moscow-based. Although no oligarchs or their wives were present, there was no shortage of wealth on display in the main picture gallery. One well-heeled guest explained that he had just given a diamond necklace to a business associate. 'It was to repay a debt,' he confided to another guest.

Many in Russia and across the world rubbed their hands in glee at the looming calamity facing the Russian plutocrats, one *Guardian* headline calling it 'The Twilight of the Oligarchs'.[19] Experts predicted that in 2009 the number of Russian billionaires would fall by a half. The *New York Times* declared: 'Perhaps no community of the super-affluent has fallen as hard, or as fast, as the brash Kremlin-connected insiders whose wealth was tied up in the overlapping bubbles of the Russian stock market, commodity prices and easy credit.'[20]

But while the new Russian billionaires and multi-millionaires were not immune to the global economic meltdown, and were nursing heavy hangovers from the wanton partying of the roaring noughties, they were far from a spent force. 'The Russians may be losing money, but they still have huge financial empires. They are still sitting on fortunes most people can only dream about,' one property agent who worked only with Russians told us in 2009.

Throughout 2009, the flow of money into London might have slowed, but the property empire building, extravagant parties and the giddy hedonism were far from over. There was little sign of the predicted exodus of rich Russian settlers.

By early 2010, oligarch fortunes had started to bounce back from the global financial crisis. According to a survey by the business magazine *Finans*, the assets of Russia's top ten oligarchs had almost doubled to $139.3 billion from the previous year as equity prices, corporate assets and international oil and metal prices recovered from their lows of 2009. Oleg Deripaska's estimated wealth had recovered sharply. Abramovich's wealth had also risen well above the decline of 2009. Although he had slipped to third place in the rankings – the first time he had failed to make the top two in the list – the Russian magazine noted wryly that he was still wealthy enough to finance his Premier League team for the 'next 100 years'.[21]

Alexander Lebedev – who lived in London as a former KGB officer in the early 1990s – also saw a leap in his fortune, up an estimated 75 per cent over 2009 to more than $3 billion. Lebedev, the first Russian to own a British newspaper – London's *Evening Standard* – seemed determined to build his media empire. In March 2010 he purchased the *Independent* and *Independent on Sunday.*

Although the Russians still had shallower pockets compared with their record fortunes recorded in 2007, they were not far short of this peak. Just a year on from the deepest international recession since the 1930s, the oligarchs were on their way back as a global financial force. The epitaphs of their fall and of the death of Londongrad had proved premature.

BIBLIOGRAPHY

Matthew Brzezinski, *Casino Moscow: A Tale of Greed and Adventure on Capitalism's Wildest Frontier* (New York: Free Press, 2001)

Alan Cowell, *The Terminal Spy: A True Story of Espionage, Betrayal, and Murder* (New York: Doubleday, 2008)

Zita Dabars and Lilia Vokhmina, *The Russian Way: Aspects of Behavior, Attitudes, and Customs of the Russians* (New York: McGraw-Hill, 2002)

Chrystia Freeland, *Sale of the Century: The Inside Story of the Second Russian Revolution* (London: Little, Brown, 2000)

Alex Goldfarb with Marina Litvinenko, *Death of a Dissident: The Poisoning of Alexander Litvinenko and the Return of the KGB* (London: Simon & Schuster, 2007)

Marshall Goldman, *Oilopoly: Putin, Power and the Rise of the New Russia* (Oxford: Oneworld, 2008)

David E. Hoffman, *The Oligarchs: Wealth and Power in the New Russia* (New York: PublicAffairs, 2003)

Andrew Jack, *Inside Putin's Russia* (London: Granta Books, 2005)

Ian Jeffries, *The New Russia: A Handbook of Economic and Political Development* (London: Curzon Books, 2002)

Paul Klebnikov, *Godfather of the Kremlin: Boris Berezovsky and the Looting of Russia* (New York: Harcourt, 2000)

Nick Kochan, *The Washing Machine* (London: Duckworth, 2005)

Bibliography

Dominic Midgley and Chris Hutchins, *Abramovich: The Billionaire from Nowhere* (London: HarperCollins, 2004)

David Satter, *Darkness at Dawn: The Rise of the Russian Criminal State* (London: Yale University Press, 2003)

Martin Sixsmith, *The Litvinenko File: The Life and Death of a Russian Spy* (New York: St Martin's Press, 2007)

Elinor Slater and Robert Slater, *Great Jewish Men* (New York: Jonathan David Publishers, 1996)

Joseph Stiglitz, *Globalisation and Its Discontents* (London: Penguin Books, 2002)

Strobe Talbott, *The Russia Hand: A Memoir of Presidential Diplomacy* (London: Random House, 2003)

NOTES

Chapter 1: The Man Who Knew Too Much

1. Michael Freedman, *Forbes*, 23 May 2005.
2. Guy Adams, *Independent on Sunday*, 17 December 2006.
3. James Harding, *The Times*, 13 March 2007.
4. James Meek, *Guardian*, 17 April 2006.
5. Sergei Guriev and Andrei Rachinsky, *Ownership Concentration in Russian Industry*, mimeo, October 2004.
6. *Moscow Times*, 30 January 2008.
7. Ibid.
8. Elinor Slater and Robert Slater, *Great Jewish Men*, Jonathan David Publishers, 1996, p. 60.
9. *The Times*, 7 September 2002.
10. Jonathan Dee, *New York Times*, 9 September 2007.
11. *Forbes*, 16 November 2006.
12. Mark Milner and Luke Harding, *Guardian*, 1 May 2008.
13. Dominic Midgley, *Spectator*, 8 October 2005.
14. Robert Service, *Observer*, 22 July 2007.

Chapter 2: The Russian Billionaires' Club

1. D. Midgeley and C. Hutchins, *Abramovich: The Billionaire From Nowhere*, HarperCollins, 2005, p. 55.
2. From www.newyorkerfilms.com, October 2002.
3. BBC News Online, October 2002.
4. *Financial Times*, 1 November 1996.

5. Speech to the Frontline Club, June 2007.

6. Ibid.

7. WPS Monitoring Agency, July 2002.

8. Paul Klebnikov, *Godfather of the Kremlin*, Harcourt, 2000, p. 118.

9. Oliver Harvey and Nick Parker, *Sun*, 16 March 2007.

10. Dominic Midgley, *Management Today*, 28 October 2004.

11. P. Gumbel, *Time*, 2 November 2003.

12. Chrystia Freeland, *Sale of the Century*, Little Brown, 2000, p. 117.

13. Michael Gillard, 'From the Kremlin to Knightsbridge', BBC Radio 4, November 2006.

14. Strobe Talbott, *The Russia Hand*, Random House, 2003, p. 207.

15. M. Kramer, 'Rescuing Boris' *Time*, 15 July 1996.

16. A. Cowell, *The Terminal Spy*, Doubleday, 2008, p. 56.

17. Kramer, op. cit.

18. Ibid.

19. Klebnikov, op. cit., p. 218.

20. *Financial Times*, 26 April 2003.

21. Talbot, op. cit., p. 207.

22. Klebnikov, op. cit., p. 201.

23. Talbot, op. cit., p. 207.

24. D. Midgley and C. Hutchins, *Abramovich: The Billionaire from Nowhere*, HarperCollins, 2004, p. 56.

25. *Kommersant*, 16 November 1995.

26. Andrew Jack, *Inside Putin's Russia*, Granta, 2005, p. 83.

27. John Thornhill, *Financial Times*, 28 August 1998.

28. See, for example O. Kryshtanovskaya and S. White, 'The Rise of the Russian Business Elite', *Communist and Post-Communist Studies*, 38 (2005), p. 298.

29. Quoted in A. Osborn, 'The World's Richest Russian Is Sued for $3 billion in London', *Independent on Sunday*, 25 February 2007.

30. Interview with *Financial Times*, 13 July 2007.
31. P. Boone and D. Rodionov, 'Rent Seeking in Russia and the CIS', Brunswick UBS, Warburg, Moscow, 2002.
32. Naomi Klein, *The Shock Doctrine: The Rise of Disaster Capitalism*, Allen Lane, 2007, p. 249.
33. Interviewed in *Counterpunch*, 27 February 2004.
34. 'Question Time', BBC Television, 7 June 2007.
35. M. E. de Boyrie, S. J. Pak and J. S. Zdanowicz, 'Estimating the Magnitude of Capital Flight Due to Abnormal Pricing in International Trade. The Russia–US Case', CIBER Working Paper, Florida International University, 2004.
36. Michael Freedman, 'Welcome to Londongrad', *Forbes Global*, 23 May 2005; see R. Skidelsky, *St Petersburg Times*, 4 January 2003; David Satter, *Darkness at Dawn: The Rise of the Russian Criminal State*, Yale University Press, 2003, p. 55.
37. Thomas L. Friedman, *New York Times*, 19 April 2000.
38. Nick Kochan, *The Washing Machine*, Duckworth, 2005, p. 17.
39. C. Freeland, *Sale of the Century*, Abacus, 2005, p. 180.
40. S. F. Cohen, *Failed Crusade*, Norton, 2000, p. 122.
41. 'Why I Became a Russian Oligarch', *Financial Times*, 29 June 2000.
42. Quoted in *Observer*, 30 August 1998.

Chapter 3: Putin's Purge

1. A. Goldfarb with M. Litvinenko, *Death of a Dissident*, Simon & Schuster, 2007, p. 206.
2. Vladimir Voinovich, 'Russia's Blank Slate', *New York Times*, 30 March 2000.
3. D. Midgley and C. Hutchins, *Abramovich: The Billionaire from Nowhere*, HarperCollins, 2004, p. 114.
4. *East Constitutional Review*, vol. 19, no. 4, Fall 2000.
5. *Moscow Times*, 7 October 2003.

6. Goldfarb with Litvinenko, op. cit., p. 183.

7. Adi Ignattius, 'A Tsar is Born', *Time*, vol. 170, no. 27, 31 December 2007.

8. J. Laughland, 'Putin Has Been Vilified by the West – but He is Still a Great Leader', *Daily Mail*, 22 September 2007.

9. Vladimir Isachenkov, 'New Putin Biography on Shelves', *Associated Press*, 17 January 2002.

10. R. Polonsky, 'The Spy Who Came in from the Cold', *New Statesman*, 15 March 2004.

11. Speaking to the Frontline Club, 6 June 2007.

12. Ignattius, op. cit.

13. Goldfarb with Litvinenko, op. cit., p. 135.

14. 'Leaders: Putin's People, Russia's Government', *The Economist*, 25 August 2007.

15. Labour Minister Sergey Kalashnikov, news conference, 27 October 1999.

16. Interview with Anatoly Chubais, *Der Spiegel*, 25 September 2007.

17. Speaking on 'Rich in Russia', *Frontline*, PBS, October 2003.

18. 'Aeroflot, an Oligarch and a Complex Business Deal', *Financial Times*, 28 July 2000.

19. P. Klebnikov, *Godfather of the Kremlin*, Harcourt, 2000, pp. 286–7.

20. Goldfarb with Litvinenko, op. cit., p. 181.

21. Ibid., p. 182.

22. David E. Hoffman, *The Oligarchs*, Public Affairs, 2002, p. 487.

23. Goldfarb with Litvinenko, op. cit., p. 206.

24. Klebnikov, op. cit., p. 16.

25. Simon Bell, 'Russian Billionaires Beware', *Daily Telegraph*, 27 July 2003.

26. 'Particulars of Claim: Boris Berezovsky v Roman Abramovich', Commercial Court, High Court, 8 January 2008.

27. G. York, 'Kremlin Tightens Muzzle on Media', *Toronto Globe & Mail*, 21 November 2000.
28. *Vanity Fair*, July 2000.

Chapter 4: Hiding the Money

1. Jamestown news service, *Eurasian Monitor*, vol. 6, issue 214, 15 November 2000.
2. A. Goldfarb with M. Litvinenko, *Death of a Dissident*, Simon & Schuster, 2007, p. 237.
3. R. Kay, *Daily Mail*, 4 September 2008.
4. Patrick E. Tyler, 'Russian Says Kremlin Faked "Terror Attacks"', *New York Times*, 1 February 2002.
5. Ibid.

Chapter 5: The Russians Have Landed

1. Keith Dovkants, *Evening Standard*, 3 March 2008.
2. G. Tett, 'Russian Money Aids a Bear Market', *Financial Times*, 7 February 1994.
3. C. Freeland, *Sale of the Century*, Abacus, 2005, p. 158.
4. Quoted in P. Lashmar, et al., 'Russians in London', *Independent on Sunday*, 12 September 1999.
5. *Evening Standard*, 11 March 2002.
6. Blavatnik was born in Russia but is now an American citizen.
7. Knight Frank and Citi Bank, Annual Wealth Report, 2007; the rise in the relative prices in London compared to New York partly reflects the heavy depreciation in the dollar in the last three years. Had the dollar remained stable, New York would now be worth around a quarter more in pounds per square foot.
8. Knight Frank, Country Review, 2007.

Chapter 6: Boys with Toys

1. Quoted in *Sun*, 6 August 2007.
2. Quoted in *Financial Times*, 27 November 2004.

3. D. Midgley and C. Hutchins, *Abramovich: The Billionaire from Nowhere*, HarperCollins, 2004, p. 13.

4. Quoted in G. Rayner and O. Koster, 'Putin "Told Roman to Clean Up His Act"', *Daily Mail*, 15 March 2007.

5. Dominic Midgley, *Spectator*, 8 October 2005.

6. *Observer*, 24 December 2006.

7. T. Walker and R. Eden, 'Roman's Candle', *Sunday Telegraph*, 29 October 2006.

8. Quoted in A. Blundy, 'Cash and Caviar', *Guardian*, 8 September 1994.

9. Quoted in L. Thomas, 'Rich Russians Go on London Spending Spree', *Sunday Times*, 13 February 1994.

10. Quoted in C. Toomey, 'The Tsars Come Out to Play', *Sunday Times*, 23 April 2006.

11. Quoted in Stefanie Marsh, *The Times*, 13 July 2006.

12. Quoted in K. Murphy, 'Ruble Rousers', *New Republic*, 4 February 2007.

13. A. Akbar and A. Osborne, 'Harvey Nichols Goes East, *Independent*, 16 April 2005.

14. Quoted in Thomas, op. cit.

15. Ibid.

16. Quoted in V. Groskop, 'Tsar Attractions', *Guardian*, 19 August 2005.

17. *Vogue*, November 2006.

18. *Financial Times*, 8 October 2005.

Chapter 7: The Big Game Hunters

1. *International Herald Tribune*, 10 March 2007.

2. Quoted in M. Taylor, 'Salesroom Records Tumbled in a Frenetic Week', *Guardian*, 23 June 2007.

3. G. Barker, 'Party Could Run and Run', *Evening Standard*, 9 February 2007.

4. Abigail Asher, *Spear's Wealth Management Survey, Art and Collecting Special*, Spring 2007.

5. *The Times*, 22 August 2006.
6. Asher, op. cit.
7. *Express on Sunday*, 24 June 2007.
8. Quoted in *The Times*, 9 June 2007.
9. Ibid.
10. William Hazlitt, *Political Essays*, 1819.
11. Mike Von Joel, 'After the Second Home, Mistress and Boat – an Art Collection, That's the Thing', *State of Art*, Spring 2007.
12. Ibid.
13. 'The Great Russian Art Boom', Channel 4, 28 September 2008.
14. Ibid.
15. *The Times*, 22 August 2006.
16. Ian Cobain, 'Usmanov's responses to *Guardian* questions', www.guardian.co.uk, 19 November 2007.
17. See note 1.
18. Andrew Osborn, *Independent on Sunday*, 11 June 2006.
19. *Vogue*, November 2006.
20. Stefanie Marsh, *The Times*, 13 July 2006.
21. *Mail on Sunday*, 18 March 2007.
22. Quoted in *Sunday Times*, 13 July 2008.
23. Anna Politkovskaya, *A Russian Diary*, Harvill Secker, 2007, p. 43.
24. *Guardian*, 27 February 2003.
25. *Mineweb*, 15 January 2007.

Chapter 8: The Curse of Yukos

1. Michael Gillard, 'From the Kremlin to Knightsbridge', BBC Radio 4, November 2006.
2. Alan Cowell, *The Terminal Spy*, Doubleday, 2008, p. 174.
3. Russian money-laundering: hearings before the Committee on Banking and Financial Services, US House of Representatives, 21–22 September 1999, p. 191.

4. Khodorkovsky owned 28 per cent of Menatep, which, in turn, owned most of Yukos.

5. Thomas Catan, *Financial Times*, 16 May 2004.

6. Lucy Komisar, 'Yukos Kingpin on Trial', *CorpWatch*, 10 May 2005.

7. Gillard, op. cit.

8. Quoted in *Mail on Sunday*, 23 November 2003.

9. Gillard, op. cit.

10. Trade was another widely used means of siphoning off large volumes of money and defrauding Russia. Exporters would report selling at a price well below the actual price received and the difference would be stashed away in foreign bank accounts. Maria E. de Boyrie, Simon J. Pak and John S. Zdanowicz, 'Estimating the Magnitude of Capital Flight due to Abnormal Pricing in International Trade: the Russia–USA Case', Center for International Business and Educational Research Working Paper, Florida University, 2004.

11. Lucy Komisar, 'While Washington Denies Any Problem, Swiss Probe "Missing" $4.8 Billion Loan to Russia', *Pacific News Service*, 16 October 2000.

12. Simon Pirani, 'Oligarch? No, I'm Just an Oil Magnate', *Observer*, 4 June 2000.

13. *Guardian*, 15 December 2001.

14. 'The Tycoon and the President', *The Economist*, 21 May 2005.

15. Valentine Low, 'Russian Oil Baron Builds £10m Bridge with West', *Evening Standard*, 11 December 2001.

16. *Guardian*, 15 December 2001.

17. Lucy Komisar, 'Yukos Kingpin on Trial', *CorpWatch*, 10 May 2005.

18. Rachel Campbell-Johnston, 'Walpole's Coming Home', *The Times*, 2 October 2002.

19. Rob Blackhurst, *New Statesman*, 31 January 2005.

20. Andrew Jack, *Inside Putin's Russia*, Granta, 2005, p. 213.

21. Jack, op. cit., p. 310.
22. Quoted in *Financial Times*, 13 November 2003.
23. Quoted in Marshall Goldman, 'The Rule of Outlaws Is Over', *Transition Newsletter*, Vol. 14/15, 2004.
24. Kim Sengupta, *Independent*, 20 July 2004.
25. *Spectator*, 8 October 2005.
26. Sengupta, op. cit.
27. Quoted in A. Higgins and S. Liesman, 'Markets Under Siege', *Wall Street Journal Europe*, 24 September 1998.
28. Quoted in Nick Kochan, 'Mammon: Russia's Unorthodox Exile', *Observer*, 26 March 2006.
29. Standard Schaefer, 'Russia: Reforming the Reformers,' *Counterpunch*, 27 February 2004..
30. Pirani, op. cit.
31. Schaefer, op. cit.
32. Paul Starobin, 'A Russian's Plea to Back America', *BusinessWeek*, 14 March 2003.
33. Quoted in *Independent*, 12 January 2007.
34. Paul Klebnikov, *Wall Street Journal*, 17 November 2003.
35. See note 1.
36. Quoted in Peter Baker and Susan Glasser, 'How Democracy Was Rolled Back in Russia', *Wall Street Journal*, 8 June 2005.
37. 'Key Shareholder in YUKOS Granted Israeli Citizenship', *Haaretz*, 5 November 2003.

Chapter 9: Plotting Revolution

1. Strobe Talbott, *The Russia Hand*, Random House, 2003, p. 207.
2. Quoted in 'Worldbeaters', *New Internationalist*, December 2003.
3. *The Russian Godfathers: The Fugitive*, Oxford Productions, BBC2, 8 December 2005.
4. David Charter and Philip Webster, 'Groucho Trips up the G8 Spin Doctors', *The Times*, 13 July 2006.

5. New Perspective Quarterly, September 2004.

6. *Russian Godfathers*, op. cit.

7. Dow Jones International News, 17 November 2003.

8. Tony Halpin, 'Putin Critic Charged with Stealing $13 million from Bank', *The Times*, 31 July 2003.

9. 'There Is Nothing to Take Away from There', *Kommersant*, 13 May 2005.

10. Quoted in Mark Franchetti, 'Russian Threat to Reveal Putin's Corrupt Aides', *Sunday Times*, 24 April 2005.

11. Nick Paton Walsh, 'Moscow Diary: Crime Pays', *Guardian*, 2 April 2005.

12. Gordon Hahn, 'Managed Democracy? Building Stealth Authoritarianism in St Petersburg', *Demoktratizatsiya*, 12, no. 2, Spring 2004, pp. 195–231.

13. Paul Klebnikov, *Godfather of the Kremlin*, Harcourt, 2000.

14. Russia's GDP in 2004 was $458 billion.

15. Y. Osetinskaya, 'Thirty-Six Billionaires', *Vedomosti*, 13 May 2004.

16. Ibid.

17. Olga Kryshtanovskaya and Stephen White, 'Putin's Militocracy', *Post-Soviet Affairs*, 19, no. 4, (October–December 2003), pp. 289–306.

18. A. Cowell, *The Terminal Spy*, Doubleday, 2008, p. 48.

19. *New York Review of Books*, 13 April 2000.

20. *Sunday Times*, 23 December 2007.

21. *Guardian*, 13 April 2007.

22. Russian Interior Ministry News Bulletin, 11 December 2001.

23. 'Worldbeaters', op. cit.

24. Quoted in Michael Freedman. 'Dark Force', *Forbes*, 21 May 2007.

25. Minutes of Evidence Before the Foreign Affairs Committee, HC 495-iii, 18 July 2007.

Chapter 10: Murder Inc.

1. According to some accounts, there were more than three Russians at the meeting, at least initially. See Alan Cowell, *The Terminal Spy*, Doubleday, 2008, p. 8.
2. Ibid., p. 22.
3. Viv Groskop, interview with Marina Litvinenko, *Observer*, 3 June 2007.
4. Ibid.
5. *Sunday AM*, BBC1, 10 December 2006.
6. Thomas de Waal, 'Murder Most Foul', *Washington Post*, 27 July 2008.
7. Gary Busch, a London-based transportation consultant, quoted in Bryan Burroughs, 'The Kremlin's Long Shadow', *Vanity Fair*, 1 April 2007.
8. Martin Sixsmith, *The Litvinenko File*, Macmillan, 2007, p. 168.
9. Tom Mangold, 'The Litvinenko Mystery', BBC Radio 4, 16 December 2006.
10. Ibid.
11. Sixsmith, op. cit., p. 305.
12. Ibid., pp. 244–5.
13. *Moscow Times*, 24 April 2007.
14. Luke Harding, 'Putin Hits Back at UK by Expelling Diplomats', *Guardian*, 20 July 2007.
15. *Newsnight*, BBC2, 7 July 2008.
16. The group of three was joined by another man, but only as Litvinenko was leaving. The man's role remains unclear but he was not contaminated with polonium and is not believed to be a suspect.
17. A. Goldfarb with M. Litvinenko, *Death of a Dissident*, Simon & Schuster, 2007, Part V: The Return of the KGB.
18. Bryan Burroughs, 'The Kremlin's Long Shadow', *Vanity Fair*, 1 April 2007.
19. Quoted in C. Shulgan, 'I, Spy – Russia's Most Wanted', *Toronto Globe & Mail*, 31 March 2007.

20. 'Litvinenko Poisoning: An Interview with Yevgeny Limarov', *Kommersant-Vlast*, 25 June 2007.
21. Sixsmith, op. cit., p. 281.
22. Olga Kryshtanovskaya and Stephen White, 'Putin's Militocracy', *Post-Soviet Affairs*, vol. 19, no. 4, 2003.
23. Sharon Werning Rivera and David Rivera, 'The Russian Elite Under Putin: Militocratic or Bourgeois?', *Post-Soviet Affairs*, vol. 22, no. 2, 2006, pp. 125–44.
24. Arkady Ostrovsky, 'Yukos Crisis: Putin Oversees Big Rise in Influence of Security Apparatus', *Financial Times*, 1 November 2003.
25. Ibid.

Chapter 11: Showdown

1. Quoted in Catherine Belton, *Financial Times*, 13 July 2007.
2. Keith Dovkants, 'Abramovich Accused of £5 bn Shares Blackmail', *Evening Standard*, 11 October 2007.
3. This account is as reported by Berezovsky. Abramovich and his representatives refused to comment.
4. Kevin Dowling, *Sunday Times*, 7 October 2007.
5. 'Berezovsky v Abramovich', [2008] EWHC 1138 (Comm) (22 May 2008) paras 4(e) and 2; 'Particulars of Claim', Berezovsky v Abramovich, High Court, 8 January, 2008, p. 17.
6. Dominic Midgley and Chris Hutchins, *Abramovich: The Billionaire from Nowhere*, HarperCollins, 2004, p. 239.
7. Eric Reguly, *Toronto Globe & Mail*, 12 November 2007.
8. Luke Harding, *Guardian*, 24 July 2007.
9. Belton, op. cit.
10. Ibid.
11. Andrew Kramer, *New York Times*, 20 August 2006.
12. Ruling by Justice Clarke, 'Cherney v Deripaska' – 2008 EWHC 1530 (Comm), Queen's Bench Division, High Court, 3 July 2008, para. 58.

13. Belton, op. cit.

14. Quoted in ruling by Justice Clarke, para. 9.

15. Ibid., para. 9.

16. Ibid., para. 166.

17. Sabrina Tavernise, 'Handful of Corporate Raiders Transform Russia's Economy', *New York Times*, 13 August 2002.

18. Rusal always claimed that the dispute between Cherney and Deripaska was a matter for them and not the company, making the company's main owner the sole defendant.

19. Ruling by Justice Langley, 'Cherney v Deripaska' – 2007 EWHC 965 (Comm) – Case No. 2006 Folio 1218, Queen's Bench High Court, 3 May 2007, para. 39.

20. Ibid., para. 45.

21. Ruling by Justice Clarke, op. cit., para. 264.

22. Ibid., para. 47.

23. Ibid., para. 10.

24. Benjamin Wegg-Prosser, Guardian Blog, *Guardian*, 23 October 2008.

25. Jon Ungoed-Thomas and Nicola Smith, 'The Secret World of Lord Freebie', *Sunday Times*, 10 October 2008.

26. *Washington Post*, 25 January 2008.

27. John Helmer, 'Deripaska Settles Big London Claim to Speed Aluminium IPO', www.johnhelmer.net, May 2007.

28. Quoted in *Toronto Star*, 13 November 2007.

29. 'Jim Pettit: Immigration from Russia to the US Seems to Have Peaked and Is Now Falling', *Interfax*, 2007.

30. Martin Sixsmith, *The Litvinenko File*, Macmillan, 2007, p. 135.

31. Belton, op. cit., 13 July 2007.

32. Nicolas van Praet, 'Magna's Man in Moscow Remains a Mystery', *Financial Post*, 25 August 2007.

33. *Financial Times*, 19 July 2005.

34. *Mail on Sunday*, 30 April 2006.

35. *St Petersburg Times*, 2 May 2006.
36. Terry Macalister. 'City Are Worried by the Rush to Float', *Guardian*, 1 November 2006.
37. *Independent*, 27 June 2006.
38. Edward Lucas, 'We Must Be Tough with the Despot', *Daily Mail*, 13 July 2007.
39. John Helmer, 'Cherney and Putin to the Rescue of Russian Aluminium', Standart News Agency, 4 September 2007.
40. Belton, op. cit.

Chapter 12: Paint the Town Red

1. David Robertson, *The Times*, 11 October 2008.
2. Geordie Greig, 'Capital Gains', *Tatler*, June 2007.
3. *Independent*, 17 December 2006.
4. Chris Blackhurst, *Evening Standard*, 30 April 2007.
5. *Daily Mail*, 1 May 2007.
6. Quoted in J. Sherman, 'Super-Rich Barred as Kensington Keeps it in Family', *The Times*, 14 November 2005.
7. Helen Davies, *Sunday Times*, 12 November 2006.
8. *Sunday Times*, 4 July 2004.
9. Quoted in K. Sekules, 'The Best Town to Make an Upper Lip Stiff', *New York Times*, 7 February 2007.
10. Editorial, *Spear's Wealth Management Survey*, Winter 2006/7.
11. Rosie Cox, *The Servant Problem*, Tauris, 2006.
12. *Financial Times*, 27 October 2007.
13. See, for example, Doreen Massey, *World City*, Polity, 2007, chapter 2; Chris Hamnett, *Unequal City: London in the Global Arena*, Routledge, 2003; Greater London Authority, *London Divided: Income Inequality and Poverty in the Capital*, London, 2003.
14. *Evening Standard*, 6 July 2007.
15. Simon Parker and David Goodhart, 'A City of Capital', *Prospect*, April 2007.

16. Ajay Kapur et al., 'The Global Investigator. Plutonomy: Buying Luxury, Explaining Global Imbalances', *Citigroup Equity Research*, 14 October 2005.
17. Luke Harding, *Guardian*, 14 October 2008.
18. See note 1.
19. *Guardian*, 25 October 2008.
20. Andrew E. Kramer, *New York Times*, 18 October 2008.
21. Luke Harding, *Guardian*, 15 February 2010.

INDEX

Index

Index

Waddesdon Manor, Buckinghamshire 223
Wadley, Veronica 365
Wall Street financial scandals 17
Wall Street Journal 47
Wallis, Richard 127–8
Walpole, Sir Robert 225
Walpole Collection 225
Walsh, Nick Paton 268
Warren Mere House, Thursley, near Guildford, Surrey 110
Waterside Point, Battersea, London 2, 7
Watford, Mikhail 'Micha' 144
Webster, Assia 169
Webster, Stephen 169
Wechsler, William 64
Wentworth Park, Surrey 20, 144
West Bromwich Albion FC 319
Westbury Hotel, Mayfair 178
West LB 218
Westminster, Duke of 128, 157
Westminster Policy Partnership (later Public Policy Partnership) 226
Weybridge, Surrey 143
White, Marco Pierre 104, 162
White Russians 22
Whitechapel, London 21
Wigan, James 356, 357
Wildcat Ridge, near Aspen, Colorado 129
Willis, Bruce 205
Wilson, Governor Pete 50
Winchester College 165
Windsor, Berkshire 143
Windsor, Duke and Duchess of 129
Windsor, Lord Freddie 181
Windsor, Lady Gabriella 171
Windsor Great Park 170–71
Winehouse, Amy 202
Winslet, Kate 144
Witanhurst, Highgate 358
Wolfe, Tom 173
Wolfensohn, James 223
Wood, John D 141
Workers' Revolutionary Party 269
Workman, Robert 251
Workman, Chief Magistrate Timothy 250–51, 262, 269
World Bank 32, 223, 273
report (2004) 18–19

World Chechen Congress 269
World Economic Forum 49, 275, 330, 336
World Health Organization 208
World Trade Organization 330
www.Spletnik.ru (gossip website) 320
Wyndham, Henry 187

Yabloko 244
Yacht City 170
Yandarbiyev, Zelimkhan 268, 311
Yanukovich, Viktor 276
Yarichevsky, Boris 21
Yeltsin, Boris 46, 60, 165, 199, 337
1996 election campaign 49–51
bargain with the oligarchs 49–51, 66
and Berezovsky 40, 115
and the Chechnya conflict 53
economic reforms 23, 119
ends the Central Bank's monopoly 47
the 'family' 52, 56
funeral 319
ill, often drunk and rarely in control 34–5
indecisive and capricious 34
introduction of free-market economy 32
mass voucher scheme 33
mentally and physically in decline 71
and ORT 40
potential successor to 64
and Putin 70–71, 72, 73, 289
re-election (1996) 83, 274
resignation of 73
Notes of a President 40
Yeltsin family 71, 123
York, Duke and Duchess of 142
York, Peter: *The Official Sloane Ranger Handbook* 346
York House, Kensington 199
Young, Charles 227
Young, Scott 110
Yukos oil company 46, 59, 350, 361, 362
assets frozen 233

asylum in Britain for executives 282
and Curtis's funeral 11
enforced renationalization 233, 342
executives flee to UK 210–13, 305
and ExxonMobil 230
investigated by the state 239, 357
and ISC Global 237–8
and Khodorkovsky 48, 59, 209, 215, 218, 220, 221, 243
and Lord Gillford 227
and Lord Owen 226
market capitalization 48
and Menatep 5, 48, 215, 218
minority investors 6
Moscow headquarters 209
offices of Swiss company offices 5
offshore accounts 216
philanthropy 222–3
plans for 244–5
proposed huge dividend 245–6
raids of 210
restructuring 215
revenue from oil exports 217
and Rosneft 341
share offloading 218–19
share price 217–18, 222, 234
sued by companies 239–40
and Temerko 248, 249, 250
the Yukos curse 246–7, 251
Yumashev, Polina 56
Yumashev, Valentin 40, 52
Yushchenko, Viktor 276, 308
Yushenkov, Sergei 274

Zakaryan, Gagik 350
Zakayev, Akhmed 268–9, 282
Zampa Holdings Ltd 237
Zayed Al-Nahyan, Sheikh Sultan bin Khalifa bin 98, 99, 100, 102
Zhukov, Alexander 199
Zhukova, Daria ('Dasha') 159, 163, 180, 181, 189, 199–203, 320
Zilli menswear shop, New Bond Street 368
Zolotoi restaurant, Moscow 366
Zveri 205
Zyuganov, Gennady 49, 50, 274